FROMM

EasyGuide

TO

MIAMI &
THE KEYS

By
David Paul Appell

Easy Guides are ✦ Quick To Read ✦ Light To Carry
✦ For Expert Advice ✦ In All Price Ranges

FrommerMedia LLC

Published by
FROMMER MEDIA LLC

Copyright © 2015 by FrommerMedia LLC. All rights reserved. No part of this publication may be reproduced, stored in a retrieval system, or transmitted in any form or by any means, electronic, mechanical, photocopying, recording, scanning or otherwise, except as permitted under Sections 107 or 108 of the 1976 United States Copyright Act, without the prior written permission of the Publisher. Requests to the Publisher for permission should be addressed to support@frommermedia.com.

Frommer's is a registered trademark of Arthur Frommer. FrommerMedia LLC is not associated with any product or vendor mentioned in this book.

ISBN 978-1-62887-088-6 (paper), 978-1-62887-089-3 (ebk)

Editorial Director: Pauline Frommer
Editor: Pauline Frommer
Production Editor: Erin Geile
Cartographer: Andrew Dolan
Cover Design: Howard Grossman

For information on our other products or services, see www.frommers.com.

FrommerMedia LLC also publishes its books in a variety of electronic formats. Some content that appears in print may not be available in electronic formats.

Manufactured in the United States of America

5 4 3 2 1

A foreword TO THIS
EASY GUIDE TO MIAMI & THE KEYS
BY
ARTHUR FROMMER

Friends:

If your own most recent visit to Miami and Miami Beach was as far back as 5 years, then you haven't really seen either city.

Both have undergone a metamorphosis. What was once a place that critics called a Southern backwater has become an intensely colorful and dynamic metropolis of multiple cultures, the most "foreign" city in America, whose population is now one third Cuban and another third of other ethnic backgrounds, of which Latin America is the chief source. There's even a Russian community here, in the adjacent town of Aventura.

That massive immigration has brought energy, optimism, and development on a massive scale—and personal experiences for the tourist that make the visit both instructive and fun. You walk into a Cuban restaurant and the waitresses are only five months "off the boat" from Cuba. You wander a downtown street, and lo and behold there's a large museum of erotica that wouldn't be permitted in any other U.S. city (except perhaps Las Vegas). You go into a shop and its proprietor is from Colombia, having fled to Miami from the drug warfare in his own country. You pick up various newspapers and see ads for Spanish performers and theatrical events. The net effect is like vacationing in Central or South America.

And the food! Miami and Miami Beach have become capitals of cuisine, especially at their many Peruvian restaurants found in every neighborhood. I've had recent meals at places with names like "Mixtura" or "Aromas del Peru" that rival the gourmet levels found in a Paris or Hong Kong.

An explosion of attractions and events

Add a rich array of cultural opportunities—the nation's second largest performing arts center, a dozen large museums, scores of theaters and nightclubs, festivals and special events throughout the year, and you know why David Appell, author of our *Easy Guide to Miami and the Keys,* decided to move here some twelve years ago. After more than a decade of personal contact with (and inspection of) the lodgings, meals, and attractions of Miami and Miami Beach, he has written what I regard as the definitive guide to both. He has also, and quite naturally given his residential location, traveled extensively, and for long periods, in the Keys (now experiencing an economic boom, following its strong recovery from the economic crisis of 2008–10).

Our author is a long-experienced judge of travel values

David is a distinguished travel writer, a graduate of the prestigious Columbia University School of Journalism (and earlier of the Georgetown University School of Foreign Service), author of countless articles relating to travel, and Executive Editor of *Budget Travel Magazine* during the years when I was publishing it (in addition, by the way, to being totally fluent in Spanish!). Just as important, his writing style is one of the most powerful in travel journalism—as I think you'll agree after reading a few pages of his book.

When I come across such lines from his book as his description of a spiced sausages plate as "an artery clogging cholesterol bomb, for sure, but oh, so *delicioso*," I feel like shouting my pride that David Appell is an author of a Frommer travel guide. Try out his prose, and then tell me whether my reaction is just a publisher's enthusiasm—or well grounded!

Many thanks for your purchase of this Easy Guide. And a hearty Bon Voyage!

Arthur Frommer

CONTENTS

LIST OF MAPS

ABOUT THE AUTHOR

Longtime Miami resident **David Paul Appell,** a Columbia Graduate School of Journalism alumnus, is the former executive editor of *Arthur Frommer's Budget Travel* and **Caribbean Travel+Life.** In addition to freelance writing, he co-directs the travel social network Tripatini. com as well as EnLinea Media, a provider of online content and social-media-management services. Appell lives outside downtown Coral Gables with his Cuban-American husband and five dogs; speaks Spanish and six other languages; and is a fan of Peruvian food, parasailing, and preservation.

ABOUT THE FROMMER TRAVEL GUIDES

For most of the past 50 years, Frommer's has been the leading series of travel guides in North America, accounting for as many as 24% of all guidebooks sold. I think I know why.

Though we hope our books are entertaining, we nevertheless deal with travel in a serious fashion. Our guidebooks have never looked on such journeys as a mere recreation, but as a far more important human function, a time of learning and introspection, an essential part of a civilized life. We stress the culture, lifestyle, history, and beliefs of the destinations we cover, and urge our readers to seek out people and new ideas as the chief rewards of travel.

We have never shied from controversy. We have, from the beginning, encouraged our authors to be intensely judgmental, critical—both pro and con—in their comments, and wholly independent. Our only clients are our readers, and we have triggered the ire of countless prominent sorts, from a tourist newspaper we called "practically worthless" (it unsuccessfully sued us) to the many rip-offs we've condemned.

And because we believe that travel should be available to everyone regardless of their incomes, we have always been cost-conscious at every level of expenditure. Though we have broadened our recommendations beyond the budget category, we insist that every lodging we include be sensibly priced. We use every form of media to assist our readers, and are particularly proud of our feisty daily website, the award-winning Frommers.com.

I have high hopes for the future of Frommer's. May these guidebooks, in all the years ahead, continue to reflect the joy of travel and the freedom that travel represents. May they always pursue a cost-conscious path, so that people of all incomes can enjoy the rewards of travel. And may they create, for both the traveler and the persons among whom we travel, a community of friends, where all human beings live in harmony and peace.

Arthur Frommer

THE BEST OF MIAMI & THE KEYS

The bright lights and thumping clubs of Miami Beach; the vast, unspoiled expanse of Everglades National Park; and the "back country" of the Keys—South Florida has a little something for everyone. And don't be fooled by the glammer-than-thou celebrity playground known as South Beach. Although the chic elite do, indeed, flock to (and occasionally, ha-ha, get into trouble in) Miami's coolest enclave, it's surprisingly accessible to the average Joe. For every Philippe Starck–designed, bank account–busting boutique hotel on South Beach, there are Deco digs that are much less taxing on the pockets. For each pan-Mediterranean-Asian-fusion haute cuisine restaurant, there's a down-home, no-nonsense Latin bodega serving up hearty fare at surprisingly cheap prices.

Beyond all the glitzy, *Us Weekly*–meets–beach blanket bacchanalia, Miami offers an endless number of sporting, cultural, and recreational activities to keep you entertained. Its variety of beaches includes some of America's best. Plus, it has an array of shopping and nightlife activities including ballet, theater, and opera (as well as all the celebrity-saturated hotels, restaurants, bars, and clubs that have helped make Miami so famous).

Leave Miami for the Keys or the Everglades, and you're in for another one-of-a-kind experience, amid landscapes like no other in America. You walk (and drink) in the footsteps of Hemingway, get up-close and personal with the area's sea life, soak up the serenity of unspoiled landscapes, and much more.

THE best MIAMI/KEYS EXPERIENCES

o **Relishing the View from Bill Baggs Cape Florida State Park:** You haven't truly seen South Florida until you've checked out the view from the southern point of Key Biscayne. Whether it's the turquoise water or the sight of Stiltsville—seven still-inhabited aquatic cabins dating back to the 1930s, perched smack in the middle of the Biscayne Channel—it may take a little coercing to get you to leave. See p. 98.

- **Channeling Andy Warhol in Miami's Wynwood Arts District:** After waiting for years for this arty, funky area to come into its own, Miami's hipsters and artists have finally been rewarded with a neighborhood—still on the raw, edgy side—of galleries, studios, and even a few cool bars, tes, and restaurants that exude New York City's SoHo vibe. See chapters 4 and 8.
- **Communing With Flipper at the Dolphin Research Center:** Touch, swim, play, and even communicate with these engaging marine mammals at the nonprofit Dolphin Research Center in Marathon Key, home to a school of some 15 dolphins. See p. 175.
- **Canoeing the Everglades:** The Everglades are Florida's outback, resplendent in their swampy nature. The Everglades are best explored by slow-moving canoes, which offer an up-close and personal view of the area's inhabitants, from alligators and manatees to raccoons and Florida panthers. See chapter 10.

THE best FOOD & DRINK EXPERIENCES

- **Unleashing Your Inner Gourmand in Miami's Design District:** The home of high-end furniture showrooms and interior design firms is also home to some of Florida's most lauded eateries, such as **Michael's Genuine Food & Drink** (p. 72). Michael's Genuine is one of the hottest reservations in town, thanks to its locally sourced, organic seasonal cuisine, out-of-control desserts, buzzy bar scene, and colorful crowd.
- **Slowing Down on the Miami River:** Some consider dining on the Miami River to be industrial chic, while others call it seedy in a *Miami Vice* sort of way. Either way, dining here will offer a soothing escape from the city's hectic pace. **Garcia's Seafood Grille & Fish** (p. 68) is an urban oasis of fresh seafood with lots of local flavor.
- **Noshing in Miami's Little Havana:** For an iconic Miami Cuban experience, head to **Versailles** (p. 77), a garish Cuban diner filled with mirrors in which you can observe the colorful clientele who gather for home-style cooking and animated conversation. Or sample some of the delicacies of the city's growing Central American community at **Guayacán** Nicaraguan restaurant (p. 75).
- **Experiencing Joe's Stone Crab Restaurant:** You *will* wait in line at Miami Beach's landmark spot for crab, but it's never dull, and the hubbub of mostly northeastern U.S. accents and the occasional celebrity sighting will keep you entertained until you're seated for your crustacean feast. Dip medium, large, or jumbo crab into a tasty mustard-mayo sauce or just mustard, and save room for Key lime pie. See p. 62.
- **Spending a Sunday at Alabama Jack's:** There is nothing like hanging out, chugging cheap beer, chowing down on conch fritters, and watching a bunch of sauced septuagenarians dressed like *Hee Haw* extras line-dancing to great live country music, all on a Sunday afternoon. Even better is the spectacular waterfront setting that makes you truly appreciate why you're in Florida in the first place. See p. 165.

THE best WAYS TO SEE MIAMI & THE KEYS LIKE A LOCAL

- **Rummaging Through Other Peoples' Treasures:** A collector's dream come true, Miami's **Wolfsonian** is a treasure trove of sometimes quirky, often striking miscellany (for example, a matchbook that once belonged to the king of Egypt) and artifacts hailing from the propaganda age of World War II. See p. 87.

- **Strolling Through Little Havana:** A walk through **Little Havana** is a fascinating study in the juxtaposition and fusion of two very vibrant cultures in which pre-Castro Cuba is as alive and well as the McDonald's right next door. See p. 106.

- **Snorkeling in Looe Key National Marine Sanctuary, Bahia Honda State Park:** With 5⅓ square miles of gorgeous coral reef, rock ledges up to 35 feet tall, and a colorful and motley marine community, you may never want to come up for air. See p. 186.

- **Foreplay at Miami's Biltmore Golf Course, Biltmore Hotel:** If it's good enough for President Clinton, it's good enough for those of you who don't travel with a bevy of Secret Service agents. But the real question is: Are *you* good enough for the course? The 6th hole is notoriously tough, with distracting water hazards among other gotchas. Nonetheless, it's an excellent course with a picture-postcard setting. See p. 103.

- **Getting on the "List" at a Hot Miami Club:** Boy do I hate velvet ropes and "lists," but hey, it's what makes Miami's nightlife what it is. And to experience it like a local, you need to be on a list. Ask your concierge, ask a friend, ask a stranger, but whatever you do, do not pay to get on these lists. It's not worth it. For details, see chapter 9.

- **Hitting the Water:** What freeways are to Los Angeles, the water is to South Florida. Getting out on the wet stuff—by boat, Jet Ski, kayak, or canoe—will offer a unique perspective on the Florida landscape—not to mention a tan.

- **Schmoozing with the Locals on Islamorada:** Located right on the water alongside a bridge, **Island Grill** (p. 173) is *the* place locals go for fresh fish, views, and live music on any given day or night. Locals also gather at the **Islamorada Fish Company** (p. 174) for politics and gossip while enjoying stellar seafood and views.

- **Wearing Sunscreen:** You can see Florida however you choose, but whatever you do, don't forget the sunscreen. Bad sunburns are a dead giveaway that you're a tourist. Even in nasty weather, the sun's rays are still there.

THE best FAMILY EXPERIENCES

- **Airboating Through the Everglades:** Kids who can't slow down may do just that after they speed through the saw grass on an Everglades airboat. But it's more than just speed, it's an educational thrill ride, to say the least. See p. 156.

- **Flitting Around in Butterfly World:** Kids will be enchanted by the Key West Butterfly & Nature Conservancy, a magical place where live, exotic, rainbow-hued butterflies dwell in acres of waterfalls, orchids, roses, tropical gardens, and more. See p. 204.

o **Riding the Carousel at Crandon Park's Family Amusement Center:** Catch a ride on the restored carousel, the centerpiece of the park's new **Family Amusement Center** that includes an old-fashioned outdoor roller rink, dolphin-shaped splash fountain, and a host of marine play sculptures at the beachfront playground. See p. 90.

o **Exploring Jungle Island:** Watch your head! Because hundreds of parrots, macaws, peacocks, cockatoos, and flamingos are flying above. Tortoises, iguanas, and a rare albino alligator are also on exhibit. A bit cheesy, but the kids love it. See p. 85.

o **Discovering Miami's Museums:** Aspiring rock stars can lay down tracks and play instruments at the working music studio, while future news anchors will love the re-creation of the TV studio at the **Miami Children's Museum** (p. 86). The Patricia and Phillip Frost Museum of Science (p. 94) explores the mysteries of the universe with hands-on exhibits, engaging demonstrations, and a planetarium.

o **Learning about Nature at Sea Grass Adventures:** With **Sea Grass Adventures,** you can wade in the water on Key Biscayne with your guide and catch an assortment of sea life in the provided nets. At the end of the program, participants gather on the beach while the guide explains what everyone has just caught, passing the critters around in miniature viewing tanks. See p. 90.

> ### Impressions
>
> *What could be better than to sit on the beach playing cards in my shirt sleeves in January?*
> —Anonymous Miami Beach resident

o **Playing Marco Polo in 820,000 Gallons of Water:** The massive, spring-fed **Venetian Pool** is unlike any other pool out there, not only cinematically picturesque but with its 820,000 gallons of water replaced every single night. For some parents, that's enough said. See p. 93.

THE best OFFBEAT TRAVEL EXPERIENCES

o **Plunging Down to a "Dive" Bar:** In May 2000, the tequila company Cuervo celebrated Cinco de Mayo by submerging an actual full-size bar and six stools about 600 feet off South Beach's First Street beach. For divers, **Jose Cuervo Underwater Bar** is more than your average watering hole. See p. 104.

o **Satisfying Your Morbid Curiosity on the Ghostly, Ghastly Vice & Crime Coach Tour.** Perhaps you've heard the expression "a sunny place for shady people"? That's Florida, but especially Miami, a haven for the likes of Al Capone to O. J. Simpson and a place where dubious characters have come to reinvent themselves. However, at times, they also tend to re-incriminate themselves. See the spots where some of these crooks fell off the wagon—it's morbidly delicious. See p. 105.

o **Admiring the Coral Castle:** A batty 26-year-old Latvian, suffering from the unrequited love of a 16-year-old who left him at the altar, moved to South Miami and spent the next 25 years of his life carving huge boulders into a prehistoric-looking roofless "castle." See p. 95.

o **Experiencing Miami Duck Tours:** Sure it's touristy, but there's something kinda fun about cruising around (on both land and water) in a Hydra Terra Amphibious Vehicle—and just wait 'til you're cruising down Ocean Drive and your guide asks everyone to quack. See p. 106.

- **Exploring the Key West Cemetery:** This funky cemetery is the epitome of quirky Key West: irreverent and humorous. Many tombs are stacked several high, condo-style, because the rocky soil made digging 6 feet under nearly impossible for early settlers. Epitaphs reflect residents' lighthearted attitudes toward life and death. "I TOLD YOU I WAS SICK" is one of the more famous, as is the tongue-in-cheek widow's inscription "AT LEAST I KNOW WHERE HE'S SLEEPING TONIGHT." See p. 205.

- **Sleeping Under the Sea at Jules' Undersea Lodge:** Originally built as a research lab, this small underwater compartment, which rests on pillars on the ocean floor, now operates as a two-room hotel. To get inside, guests dive under the structure, 30 feet down, and pop up into the unit through a 4×6-foot "moon pool" that gurgles soothingly all night long. The underwater suite consists of two separate bedrooms that share a common living area. See p. 168.

THE best HISTORIC EXPERIENCES

- **Remembering the Civil Rights Era: Virginia Key Beach Park** is the former "col-ored only" beach that opened in 1945 and closed in 1982 because of high upkeep costs. After an $11-million renovation, the 83-acre historic site features picnic tables and grills, a new playground for children with special needs, and a miniature rail-road. The beach eventually plans to open a civil rights museum as well. See p. 81.

- **Exploring the Art Deco District:** A lot more than just pastel-colored buildings and neon, the Art Deco District is a Miami Beach landmark, and its preservation has been the passion of many. Although a historic building may today house a Johnny Rockets, it's what's on the outside that really counts. See chapter 7.

- **Barnacle State Historic Site:** Long before the condos invaded, "Cracker"-style houses were all the rage—well, pretty much the only game in town, actually. At the Barnacle sits Miami's oldest house, complete with period furnishings that some would say are back in again. See p. 93.

- **Nike Hercules Missile Base HM-69:** A product of decisions by President John F. Kennedy and his advisors that arose out of very real Cold War fears, this base was turned over to Everglades National Park in 1979 but not open to the public until 2004. From January to March, free ranger-led tours take visitors on a 90-minute driving and walking tour of the missile assembly building, barns where 12 missiles were stored, the guardhouse, and the underground control room. See p. 154.

- **Crane Point Hammock:** This privately owned, 64-acre nature area is considered one of the Keys' most important historic and natural sites, with what's probably the last virgin thatch-palm hammock in North America, as well as a rainforest exhibit and an archaeological site with prehistoric Indian and Bahamian artifacts. See p. 174.

- **Ernest Hemingway Home & Museum:** The writer's handsome stone house, built in 1851 and designated a literary landmark by the American Library Association in 2010, was one of the island's first to be fitted with indoor plumbing, a built-in fire-place, and sports its first swimming pool (look for the penny that Papa pressed into the cement). He owned the home from 1931 until his death in 1961. See p. 204.

- **Harry S. Truman Little White House:** On vacation from the Big House, Truman discovered the serenity of Key West and made his escape to what became known as the Little White House, which is open to the public for touring. The house is fully restored and the exhibits document Truman's time in the Keys. See p. 204.

THE best FREE EXPERIENCES

o **Taking in a Concert at the New World Center:** This stunning, sonically stellar, $154-million Frank Gehry–designed training facility, performance space, and outdoor park is said by the *New York Times* to have "the potential to be a game changer in classical music." A significant number of the events are free to the public, including its innovative outdoor "wallcasts." See p. 126.

o **Exploring Artists' Studios:** Right on South Beach's Lincoln Road, **ArtCenter South Florida** is free and open to the public, featuring dozens of resident artists doing their arty thing. See p. 84.

o **Taking In the Holocaust Memorial:** This heart-wrenching memorial is hard to miss and would be a shame to overlook. The powerful centerpiece, Kenneth Treister's *A Sculpture of Love and Anguish,* depicts victims of the concentration camps crawling up a giant yearning hand stretching up to the sky, marked with an Auschwitz number tattoo. Along the reflecting pool is the story of the Holocaust, told in cut marble slabs. Inside the center of the memorial is a tableau that's solemn and truly moving tribute to the millions of Jews who lost their lives. See p. 84.

o **Discovering the Frost Art Museum:** Among the permanent collection is a strong representation of American printmaking from the 1960s and '70s, photography, pre-Columbian objects from A.D. 200 to 500, and a growing number of works by contemporary Caribbean and Latin-American artists. A Smithsonian affiliate, it's South Florida's only museum to offer free admission daily. See p. 95.

o **Learning at the Florida Keys Eco-Discovery Center:** Some 6,000 square feet of interactive exhibits depict Florida Keys underwater and upland habitats—with emphasis on the ecosystem of North America's only living contiguous barrier coral reef, which parallels the Keys. Kids dig the interactive yellow submarine, while adults seem to get into the cinematic depiction of an underwater abyss. See p. 202.

o **Being a Ranger for a Day with the Everglades Ranger Programs:** More than two dozen ranger programs, free with entry, are offered each month during high season and give visitors an opportunity to gain an expert's perspective. They range from canoe and walking tours to birding and biking. See p. 150.

THE best BEACHES

o **For Nature and Tranquility:** The beach at **Bahia Honda State Park** in Bahia Honda Key is one of the loveliest and most peaceful in Florida, located amid 635 acres of nature trails and even a portion of Henry Flagler's railroad. See p. 184.

o **For Watersports: Hobie Beach,** located on the south side of Key Biscayne's Rickenbacker Causeway, is one of South Florida's most popular beaches for watersports lovers, featuring Jet Ski, sailboat, windsurfing, and sailboard rentals; shade, if necessary, from the Australian pines; and an inspiring view of the downtown Miami skyline. See p. 81.

o **For People-Watching: Lummus Park Beach** is world renowned, not necessarily for its sands, but for its location in Miami Beach's **South Beach** neighborhood. Here, seeing and being seen (and, occasionally, the obscene) go hand in hand with sunscreen and beach towels. See p. 80.

o **For Nude Sunbathing:** For that all-over tan, head to the north end of **Haulover Beach,** north of Miami Beach between Bal Harbour and Sunny Isles, nestled between the Intracoastal Waterway and the ocean. There's also a gay nude section, as well as an area for volleyball in the buff. See p. 101.

o **For Seclusion:** The producers of *Survivor* could convincingly shoot their show on the ultra-secluded, picturesque, and deserted **Virginia Key,** on Miami's Key Biscayne, where people go purposely not to be found. See p. 81.

o **For Gay Beachgoers:** In Miami, South Beach's **12th Street Beach** is the beach of choice for gay residents and travelers who come to show off just how much time they've spent in the gym and share news of upcoming parties and events. This beach is often the venue for some of the liveliest parties South Beach ever sees. See p. 80.

o **For Kids:** Miami's **Crandon Park Beach** is extremely popular among families with kids because of the shallow water created by a neighboring sandbar. Features include good parking, picnic areas, a winding boardwalk, eco-adventure tours, and a multiethnic mix of families grilling, dancing, and relaxing.

MIAMI & THE KEYS IN CONTEXT

Since the roaring '20s, Miami and the Keys, along with the rest of South Florida, have been a playground for the rich, famous, and freezing. It took a handful of wealthy folks to begin the region's transition from swamp to vacation destination. Tycoons Carl Fisher, Henry Flagler, and George Merrick get the credit for that, kick-starting SoFlo's fondness for development back in the '20s. The land boom eventually busted, a hurricane destroyed what was started, then came the Great Depression, and they were back at square one. But not for long. As the economy rebounded, roadways improved, and frosty winter weather continued to weigh upon northerners, the bottom tip of Florida was once again on the radar of everyone from entrepreneurs and vacationers to those looking for a permanent vacation in warmer climates. Enter the age of the condo canyons. But condos and go-go development are far from the area's only history, which stretches back to the Spanish colonial era and into pre-Columbian antiquity, making for an intoxicating blend of past and present.

MIAMI & THE KEYS TODAY

You could say South Florida has mostly moved beyond the economic doldrums, even if, of course, far more so for the affluent (many lower and middle income locals still remain underwater and struggling). Real estate and tourism/hospitality—two of the region's main drivers—are humming along again, even if not quite at the turbo-charged levels of the go-go years, with its hyper-luxury condo/hotel craze. And it does seem as if some giant "pause" button has been released, and new projects—hotels, restaurants, nightclubs, retails, and especially condos, more than 200 projects at last count—are chugging along or in the works from the Miami-Dade County line clear down to Key West.

The new boom vacuuming up the recession's leftover surplus has largely been fueled by cash-flinging richies from Russia, Brazil, and Latin America, for whom $5 million for an oceanfront penthouse is a downright deal. Bolstering South Florida's reputation as "a sunny place for shady people," one newspaper article reported that personal income here jumped 4.2% in recent years despite the fact that no one down there seems to actually work.

But hey, according to *Forbes,* a recent university study put Florida at only the 10th most corrupt state in the U.S., so it's all relative, I guess.

The latest big deal in Miami Beach is an $11-million renovation of the city's supremely uninspiring convention center, slated for December 2017. On the other side of the MacArthur Causeway, a fancy new home for the Miami Science Museum was set to open in 2015, while Miami voters were in summer 2014 being asked to approve a nearby proposal for SkyRise, a privately-financed 1,000-foot observation tower project built on the property of Bayside Mall, which would also involve a much-needed mall revamp and could provide a structure that could potentially become a Miami symbol a la the Empire State Building or Eiffel Tower.

Meanwhile, just north of here, the former *Miami Herald* property across from the Arsht Center for the Performing Arts, bought in 2011 by Asian gambling giant Genting, has remained a question mark. The original plan for a Las Vegas in miniature ignited a firestorm of opposition and was scaled back to a mixed-use development including a resort, hotel, condos, shops, restaurants, and park—and most likely a casino, if finally approved by the Florida legislature. Whatever it ends up being will still be big and glitzy, that's for sure.

At press time, the latest high-profile controversy of sorts was the quest by an investment group headed by soccer god David Beckham to build a stadium that would be home to a major-league soccer team, after sites on Watson Island and in Museum Park were rejected.

Elsewhere downtown, as well as in areas like Wynwood, Midtown Miami, the Design District, Coral Gables, and Biscayne Boulevard's "Upper East Side" have continued to see strengthening and new establishments opening (in newly arty but still largely gritty Wynwood, now they're even talking, yes, condos). An exception remains Coconut Grove, a once thriving bohemian nucleus, which continues to struggle.

And even the very different Florida Keys are in the middle of their own building boom, with several hotels being renovated in Key West and two new ones being built in Marathon—the first in 20 years.

And so it goes—the eternal dance of tourism, money, and politics. One thing seems amply clear though: The engine of Miami and the Keys that is the tourism industry may have been temporarily slowed by the downturn, but such is the drawing power of this region that it is now largely booming again. Our visitors and what we can offer them will continue to be a huge and probably decisive part of this region's future—at least until climate change puts us all under water.

THE MAKING OF MIAMI & THE KEYS

South Florida's Swampy Beginnings

Speaking of under water, Florida never did have dinosaurs, because back in dino days, that's where this peninsula was: totally submerged. It first came into existence as a land mass around 30 million years ago as sand and seashell sediments created marshland that gradually solidified into (mostly) dry land. Then during the later ice ages, local fauna came to include mammoths, mastodons, saber-toothed cats, Pleistocene horses, bison, and giant ground sloths. People came later still, of course—some 14,000 to 15,000 years ago. Here in South Florida, in 1998, archaeologists discovered a slew of artifacts on a riverside/bayside site in downtown Miami now known as the Miami Circle, determining that they dated back at least 2,000 years, from the Calusa or Tequesta tribes.

The post-Archaic cultures of eastern and southern Florida developed in relative isolation, and it's likely that the peoples living in those areas at the time of first European contact were direct descendants of the inhabitants of the areas in late Archaic times.

Spanish Rule & Native-American Culture

Spanish explorers of the early 16th century were likely the first Europeans to interact with the native population of Florida. The first documented encounter came with the first expedition of Juan Ponce de León to Florida in 1513, although they came across at least one native who spoke Spanish. In 1521, they encountered the Calusa Indians, who established 30 villages in the Everglades and successfully resisted European conquest—for a while, at least.

The Spaniards recorded nearly 100 names of groups they encountered. Tribes in South Florida at the time of first contact included the Tequesta, who lived on the southeast coast of the Everglades. Not surprisingly, all of these tribes ended up dwindling in numbers during the period of Spanish control of Florida.

The Seminoles, originally an offshoot of the Creek people who absorbed other groups, developed as a distinct tribe in Florida during the 18th century, and are now represented in the Seminole Nation of Oklahoma, the Seminole Tribe of Florida, and the Miccosukee Tribe of Indians of Florida, whose presences are alive and well today.

And Then There Was Miami

It wasn't long after Florida became the 27th state in the union in 1845 that Miami began to emerge as a city—kind of. During the war, the U.S. created Fort Dallas on the north bank of a river that flowed through southern Florida. When the soldiers left, the fort became the base for a small village established by William H. English, who dubbed it Miami, from the Indian word *Mayami,* meaning "big water."

DATELINE

1980 Race riots tear apart Miami. The Mariel boatlift brings 140,000 Cubans to Florida. The Miami Seaquarium celebrates its 25th anniversary.

1983 Thirty-eight overseas highway bridges from Key Largo to Key West are completed under the Florida Keys Bridge Replacement Program.

1984 Miami Metro Rail, Florida's only downtown elevated rail system, begins service.

1986 Treasure hunter Mel Fisher continues to salvage vast amounts of gold and silver from his discovery of the Spanish galleon *Nuestra Señora de Atocha,* which sank in 1622 during a hurricane off Key West. The TV series *Miami Vice* captures the nation's imagination, revitalizing interest in and tourism for South Florida.

1987 U.S. Census Bureau estimates indicate that Florida has surpassed Pennsylvania to become America's fourth most

In 1822, the Homestead Act offered 160 acres of free land to anyone who would stay on it for at least 5 years. Edmund Beasley bit, and in 1868 moved into what is now Coconut Grove. Two years later, William Brickell bought land on the south bank of the Miami River and Ephraim Sturtevant took over the area called Biscayne. In 1875, his daughter Julia Tuttle visited him and fell in love with the area, although not returning for another 16 years, when she would further transform the city.

In the meantime, Henry Flagler, who made a $50-million fortune working with John Rockefeller in the Standard Oil Company, came to Florida in the late 1800s because he thought the warm weather would help his wife's frail health. After moving down, Flagler built a railroad all the way down the east coast of Florida, stopping in each major town to build a hotel. Another railway honcho, Henry Plant, laid his tracks from Jacksonville to Tampa.

When her husband died in 1886, Julia Tuttle decided to leave Cleveland for Florida and asked Plant to extend his railroad to Miami. Plant declined, so Tuttle went to Flagler, whose own railroad stopped 66 miles away in what's now Palm Beach. Flagler laughed at Tuttle's request, saying he didn't see what Miami had to offer in terms of tourism.

After a devastating winter that killed all crops north of the state, Tuttle sent Flagler a bounty of orange blossoms to prove that Miami did indeed have something to offer. After Tuttle agreed to give Flagler some of her land along with William Brickell's, Flagler agreed to extend the railway. When the first train arrived in Miami on April 15, 1896, all 300 residents showed up to see it. Miami had arrived, and the tourist bureau began touting the city as "the sun porch of America, where winter is turned to summer."

Unlocking the Keys

No one knows exactly when the first European set foot on one of the Florida Keys, but as exploration and shipping increased, the islands became prominent on nautical maps. The nearby treacherous coral reefs claimed many lives. The chain was eventually called "keys," from the Spanish *cayos,* meaning "small islands." In 1763, when the

populous state. It's predicted that Florida will be the third most populous state by 2000.

1990 Panama's dictator Manuel Noriega is brought to Miami in January for trial on drug charges. Miami Dolphins founder Joe Robbie dies that same month.

1991 Queen Elizabeth II visits Miami. Five Navy bombers found by treasure salvagers are determined not to be the "Lost Squadron" of Bermuda Triangle fame that went down in 1945 off the coast of Florida. Miami and Denver are awarded new national Major

League Baseball franchises. The 1990 federal census puts Florida's population at 12,937,926, a 34% increase from 1980.

1992 Homestead and adjacent South Florida are devastated on August 24th by the then-costliest natural disaster in American history, Hurricane Andrew, with 58 direct or indirect deaths, 25,000 homes destroyed, and 10,000 others damaged. Twenty-two thousand federal troops were deployed, and shelters housed 80,000 residents.

continues

Spaniards ceded Florida to Britain in a trade for the port of Havana, an agent of the king of Spain claimed that the islands, rich in fish, turtles, and mahogany for shipbuilding, were part of Cuba, fearing that the English might build fortresses and dominate the shipping lanes.

The British realized the treaty was ambiguous, but declared that the Keys should be occupied and defended as part of Florida. The British claim was never officially contested. Ironically, Britain gave the islands back to Spain in 1783 to keep them out of the hands of the United States, but in 1821 all of Florida, including the necklace of islands, officially became American territory.

Many of Key West's early residents were immigrants from the Bahamas, known as Conchs (pronounced "Conks"), who arrived in growing numbers after 1830; many were descendants of Loyalists who'd fled the American Revolution.

In the 20th century, quite a few Key West residents started referring to themselves as "Conchs," and the term is now used for everyone who lives on the island. In 1982, Key West and the rest of the Florida Keys briefly declared their "independence" as the "Conch Republic" in a protest over a U.S. Border Patrol roadblock. Set up to search for illegal immigrants and drugs on U.S. 1 where the northern end of the Overseas Highway meets the mainland at Florida City, it caused traffic backups for 17 miles and essentially paralyzed the Keys. The "Conch Republic Independence Celebration" has been marked with parties, parades, and of course copious drinking every April 23rd since.

Recognizing the River of Grass

Thanks to the obsessive campaign of the Everglades's foremost advocate, landscape architect Ernest F. Coe, Congress passed a park bill in 1934. Ridiculed by opponents as the "alligator and snake swamp bill," the legislation stalled during the Great Depression and World War II. Finally, on December 6, 1947, President Harry Truman dedicated the Everglades National Park. In that same year, writer and activist Marjory Stoneman Douglas published *The Everglades: River of Grass*. She understood its importance as the major watershed for South Florida and as a unique ecosystem.

Among African Americans elected to Congress was Carrie Meek of Miami. Sixty-six in 1993, her political career saw her elected first to the Florida House of Representatives, next the Florida Senate, and then the U.S. House of Representatives.

1993 Janet Reno, state attorney for Dade County (Miami) for 15 years, is named attorney general of the U.S. by President Bill Clinton; Reno is the first woman to serve in this post in U.S. history. Although a pro-choice Democrat, she managed to win reelection four times in a conservative stronghold, the last time without opposition.

1996 Miami turns 100.

2000 Florida becomes the battleground of the controversial 2000 U.S. presidential election between Al Gore and George W. Bush (whose brother Jeb was Florida's governor). A count of the popular vote held on Election Day was extremely close (in favor of Bush) and mired in accusations of fraud and manipulation. Subsequent recount efforts degenerated into

THE LAY OF THE LAND

Because the population of South Florida is largely confined to a strip of land between the Atlantic Ocean and the Everglades, the Miami Urbanized Area (that is, zone of contiguous urban development) is about 110 miles long north to south but never more than 20 miles wide, and in some areas just 5 miles wide. South Florida is longer than any other urbanized area in the United States except for New York, and was America's eighth most densely populated urban area in the 2010 census. As of then, that area was 1,239 square miles, with a population of 5.5 million and a density of 4,442 per square mile (Miami and Hialeah, the area's second-largest city, recorded population densities rising to more than 10,000). By 2010 the Miami Urbanized Area had become the fourth-largest in the United States (this particular area, by the way, officially includes Miami-Dade County up to the Palm Beaches but excludes the Keys).

Statistics show that the state, once the fifth cheapest to live in, is now around the middle of the pack among U.S. states. But South Florida is both pricier than the state as a whole, and an area where the economy is strengthening; unemployment by mid-2014 had dropped to its lowest rate since 2008, and housing values were also recovering, though naturally far more at the luxury end of the market than the middle and low end.

Economics aside, it's also finally starting to sink in that there are other pressing issues to be dealt with. Though our current Republican-controlled legislature and governor Rick Scott deny it, scientists have observed changes in Florida consistent with the early effects of global warming: retreating and eroding shorelines, dying coral reefs, saltwater intrusion into inland freshwater aquifers, an upswing in forest fires, and warmer air and sea-surface temperatures. As glaciers melt and warming waters expand, sea levels will rise anywhere from 8 inches to 2½ feet over the next century. In Florida, seawater will advance inland as much as 400 feet in low-lying areas, flooding shoreline homes and hotels, limiting future development, and eroding the state's beloved beaches. People aren't kidding when they say that one day, Florida will be under water again.

Even now, some South Beach streets flood drastically during rainfalls; I once had to wade through knee-deep water there. And scientists say that in the nearer term, the

arguments over mispunched ballots, "hanging chads," and controversial decisions by Florida Secretary of State Katherine Harris and the Florida Supreme Court. Ultimately, the United States Supreme Court ended all recounts and let stand the official count by Harris, which was accepted by Congress.

2003 The Florida Marlins win the World Series.

2004 George W. Bush wins the presidential election again. His brother, Florida Gov. Jeb Bush, celebrates in the state capital, Tallahassee.

2006 The Miami Heat win the NBA championship.

2007 Jeb Bush vacates the governor's office, which is taken over by Charlie Crist, another Republican.

2008 Florida continues to be one of the fastest-growing states in the country. The economy still depends greatly on tourism, but expanding industries in business and manufacturing are strengthening its growth

continues

intensity of hurricanes is likely to increase, with a trend toward more severe storms. Miami Beach's mayor is pushing a $400 million project to shore up the city's drainage system, but until more support comes on the state and national level, such measures may be like sticking a finger in the dike. Well, fingers crossed . . .

2 SOUTH FLORIDA IN POP CULTURE

South Florida—and Florida in general—is a creative's dream come true. In this very diverse state, inspiration is practically hanging from the palm trees. In this context, Key West's well-deserved, ongoing status as a literary enclave is no surprise.

Fiction

o *The Perez Family* (W. W. Norton) by Christine Bell: Cuban immigrants from the Mariel boatlift exchange their talents for an immigration deal in Miami (also a 1995 movie by Mira Nair).

o *Miami, It's Murder* (Avon) by Edna Buchanan: Miami's Agatha Christie keeps you in suspense with her reporter protagonist and her life as an investigative crime solver in Miami.

o *To Have and Have Not* (Scribner) by Ernest Hemingway: One of the many must-reads by Key West's most famous resident.

o *In Cuba I Was a German Shepherd* (Grove Press) by Ana Menendez: Stories of people who gather in Little Havana to lament the loss of the good old days.

o *Naked Came the Manatee* (Ballantine Books) by Carl Hiaasen: Thirteen *Miami Herald* writers contributed to this hilarious story about the discovery of Castro's head.

o *Killing Mister Watson* (Vintage Books USA) by Peter Matthiessen: A fascinating story about the settlement of the Everglades and the problems that ensued.

o *The Yearling* (Collier MacMillan Publishers) by Marjorie Kinnan Rawlings: A classic about life in the Florida backwoods.

potential. State leaders face problems created due to huge population increases and environmental concerns.

2009 In October 2009, Florida, along with California and Nevada, posted America's highest foreclosure rates. To make matters worse, state unemployment rates skyrocketed to more than 11%. For the first time in more than 60 years, Florida experiences a population decline.

2010 South Florida starts warily emerging from its economic doldrums. If Travel Promotions Act funds aren't enough to boost tourism, LeBron James's move to the Miami Heat is seen in some circles as a huge shot in the arm. But a massive oil spill from a BP rig in the Gulf raises fears of sullied coastlines (one Keys charter boat company sues BP for even creating the "perception" of oil from the spill), though no such effects are evident.

2011 Tea Party–aligned Republican businessman Rick Scott narrowly becomes governor.

- *Seraph on the Suwanee* (Harper Perennial) by Zora Neale Hurston: A novel about turn-of-the-century Florida "white crackers."
- *Nine Florida Stories* (University Press of Florida) by Marjory Stoneman Douglas: The beloved Florida naturalist's fictional take on Florida, set in a scattering of settings—Miami, Fort Lauderdale, the Tamiami Trail, the Keys, and the Everglades—and revealing the drama of hurricanes and plane crashes, kidnappers, escaped convicts, and smugglers.
- *Tourist Season* (Warner Books) by Carl Hiaasen: Hiaasen is at his darkest, funniest, and finest in this book about a newspaper columnist who kills off tourists on a quest to return Florida to its long-gone, pristine state.

Nonfiction

- *Fool's Paradise: Players, Poseurs, and the Culture of Excess in South Beach* (Crown) by Steven Gaines: A New Yorker's love/hate take on America's alleged Riviera.
- *Miami Babylon: Crime, Wealth, and Power—A Dispatch from the Beach* (Simon & Schuster) by Gerald Posner: The name says it all about this investigative look at the sybaritic playground side of Miami.
- *Miami* (Vintage) by Joan Didion: An intriguing compilation of impressions of the Magic City.
- *Miami, the Magic City* (Centennial Press) by Arva Moore Parks: An authoritative history.
- *The Everglades: River of Grass* (Pineapple Press) by Marjory Stoneman Douglas: Eco-maniacs will love this personal account of the treasures of Florida's most famous natural resource.

Movies Filmed in Florida

- Clarence Brown's *The Yearling* (1946), based on novel by M. K. Rawlings.
- John Huston's *Key Largo* (1948), based on novel by Hemingway (gangsters, hurricanes, and Bogey and Bacall).

Cautiously optimistic and on the rebound from the burst bubble, South Florida starts stabilizing again thanks to an influx of cash-heavy foreigners from across the world, especially South America, Russia, and Malaysia.

2012 The Miami Heat win their second NBA championship.

2013 South Florida goes wild as the Heat win their third NBA championship, becoming the best shooting team in NBA history.

Mayors of Greater Miami cities of Miami Lakes, Homestead, and Sweetwater embroiled in corruption scandals.

2014 The real estate market enters full froth again, especially residential condominiums, with some 200 projects in varying stages of development.

- Guy Hamilton's *Goldfinger* (1964), the third James Bond film, which opens in Miami Beach, including settings at the Fontainebleau Hotel (p. 48).
- John Schlesinger's *Midnight Cowboy* (1969), based on novel by James Leo Herlihy.
- Ernest Lehman's *Portnoy's Complaint* (1972), based on novel by Philip Roth (Jewish culture).
- Lawrence Kasdan's *Body Heat* (1981), a crime thriller.
- Brian De Palma's *Scarface* (1983), in which Al Pacino plays a Miami gangster who arrived in the Mariel boatlift.
- Phillip Borsos's *The Mean Season* (1985), a Miami-set thriller about a serial killer.
- Ron Howard's *Cocoon* (1985), based on a science fiction novel by David Saperstein involving retirees.
- Jonathan Demme's *Married to the Mob* (1988), a comedy with Alec Baldwin and Michelle Pfeiffer that reaches its climax in Miami.
- Tim Burton's *Edward Scissorhands* (1990), a modern fairy tale filmed in Dade City and Lakeland.
- Chris Menges's *CrissCross* (1992) with Goldie Hawn, filmed at Key West's Eden House (p. 194) and other island locations.
- Mike Nichols's *The Birdcage* (1996), a South Beach drag comedy based on *La Cage aux Folles*.
- Andrew Bergman's *Striptease* (1996), based on novel by Carl Hiassen.
- John Singleton's *Rosewood* (1997), based on historic Rosewood massacre (African-American culture).
- Bobby and Peter Farrelly's *There's Something About Mary* (1998), a gross-out comedy with various South Beach locations.
- Spike Jonze's *Adaptation* (2002), loosely based on Susan Orleans's *The Orchid Thief.*
- Patty Jenkins's *Monster* (2003), biopic of serial killer Aileen Wournos.
- Taylor Hackford's *Ray* (2004), a biopic about musician Ray Charles, born in Florida.
- Michael Mann's *Miami Vice* (2006), based on the 1980s TV series.
- David Frankel's *Marley & Me* (2008), based on the best-selling novel of the same name by a former Fort Lauderdale *Sun Sentinel* reporter.
- Jason Reitman's *Up in the Air* (2009), starring George Clooney as a frequent flyer who comes through MIA and the Miami Airport Hilton.
- Michael Bay's *Pain and Gain* (2013), an action comedy with Mark Wahlberg and Dwayne "The Rock" Johnson, based on a true story about bodybuilding crooks (two still on death row) and a Romanian stripper in 1990s Miami.

Miami Sound

The Miami recording industry did not begin in the 1980s with Gloria Estefan's Miami Sound Machine. In fact, some major rock albums were recorded in Miami's Criteria Studios, among them *Rumours* by Fleetwood Mac and *Hotel California* by the Eagles. Long-time local music entrepreneur Henry Stone and his label, TK Records, created the local indie scene in the 1970s. TK Records produced the R&B group KC and the Sunshine Band along with soul singers Betty Wright, George McCrae, and Jimmy "Bo" Horne, as well as a number of minor soul and disco hits, many influenced by Caribbean music. In the 2000s, Miami has seen an enormous hip-hop boom featuring the likes of Daddy Yankee, Pitbull, Rick Ross, and more.

South Florida's Fab Fare

Before Florida started evolving into a bona fide gastronomic destination, one respected by eaters and chefs alike, two things about Floridian fare may have come to mind—oranges and early bird. And while both still play an important role in the state's rep, pop culturally or otherwise, there's now way more to South Florida food than just citrus and $3.99 prime rib; as the locavore movement rolls on, in which people prefer to eat or cook with only local ingredients, foods indigenous to the state include avocado, hearts of palm, star fruit, key lime, spiny lobster, and stone crabs, whether in some five-star fusion restaurant or a hole-in-the-wall beach shack with ice-cold beer, paper napkins, and plastic cutlery.

If there's any such thing as "South Florida cuisine," it would be "Floribbean," the fusion of Caribbean and Latin flavors with the aforementioned local Florida elements. Some food snobs shudder at the term and prefer the phrase "New World cuisine," pioneered by Miami-based chef Norman Van Aken. But it's all semantics. In any case, think crack conch chowder with orange, saffron, and coconut; or spiny lobster salad with mango.

The following is a good, but by no means comprehensive, list of typical (or atypical, rather) South Florida cuisine:

o **Cuban sandwiches:** Some say they originated in Miami, others say Tampa; wherever it was, it's a savory combo of ham, roast pork, Swiss cheese, pickles, and mustard, on crispy, crusty, toasted "Cuban bread," whose origin is still open to question.

o **Grouper sandwiches:** Or pretty much any fish (snapper, mahi-mahi, pompano, and so on) sandwich, though grouper pops up on many menus in many incarnations, from grilled and fried to blackened and jerked.

o **Mango salsa:** A widely used condiment. The Floribbean version of ketchup.

o **Conch fritters:** Fried balls of dough and chewy conch with a dash of cayenne pepper, Bahamian in origin but common throughout South Florida and the Keys.

o **Key lime pie:** Made from those luscious limes found, yes, in the Keys, these sweet/tart pies are everywhere throughout the region, and everywhere claims to have the best. You be the judge.

o **Hearts of palm salad:** Often found in old-school $6.99 prime rib, steak, and lobster houses, though often found in chichi eateries as well.

WHEN TO GO

To a large extent, the timing of your visit will determine how much you'll spend—and how much company you'll have—once you get to Miami and the Keys. That's because room rates can more than double during so-called high seasons, when countless visitors flock to the Sunshine State.

The weather determines the high seasons (see "Climate," below). In subtropical South Florida, high season is in the winter, from mid-December to mid-April, although if you ask tourism execs, the high season is now creeping longer into spring and even, in some parts, summer. On the other hand, you'll be rewarded with incredible bargains if you can stand the heat, humidity, and daily rain storms of a South Florida summer between June and early September.

Hurricane season runs from June to November, and—as seen in 2005, the most active hurricane season on record, and 2009, the quietest—you never know what can happen. Pay close attention to weather forecasts during this season and always be prepared. See "Climate," below.

Presidents' Day weekend in February, Easter week, Memorial Day weekend, the Fourth of July, Labor Day weekend, Thanksgiving, Christmas, and New Year's are busy throughout the state.

South Florida's so-called shoulder season is April through May and September through November, when the weather is pleasant throughout Florida and the hotel rates are considerably lower than during the high season. If price is a consideration, these months of moderate temperatures and fewer tourists are the best times to visit.

See the accommodations sections in the chapters that follow for specifics on the local high, shoulder, and off seasons.

CLIMATE   Contrary to popular belief, South Florida's climate is subtropical, not tropical. So we see more variations in temperature here than, say, the Caribbean islands.

Spring, which runs from late March to May, sees warm temperatures throughout Florida, but it also brings tropical showers.

Summer in Florida extends from May to September, when it's hot and quite humid throughout the state. You may not want to do anything too taxing when the sun is at its peak (though at least in coastal areas you'll have the benefit of sea breezes). Severe afternoon thunderstorms are common during the summer, so schedule activities for earlier in the day, and take precautions to avoid being hit by lightning during the storms. Those storms, by the way, often start out fierce and end with a rainbow and sunshine, so don't worry; just don't stand under a tree or on a golf course during the main act.

Autumn, roughly September through November, is a great time to visit, as the hottest days are gone and the crowds have thinned out. Unless a hurricane blows through, November is usually Florida's driest month. In these climate-changing times, though, one can never predict 100% sunshine. June through November is hurricane season here, but even if one threatens, the National Weather Service closely tracks the storms and gives ample warning if there's need to evacuate coastal areas.

Winter is usually a lovely time of year, but can get a bit nippy at times even in South Florida (northerners are often amused to see some Miamians whipping vests, scarves, hats, and gloves when the temperature drops below, oh, 70°F or so). At any rate, "cold snaps" usually last only several days down here, and daytime temperatures should quickly return to the low to mid 70s. Still, visiting in winter merits packing at least a light jacket.

For up-to-the-minute weather info, tune into cable TV's Weather Channel, or check out its website at www.Weather.com.

Miami's Average Monthly High/Low Temperatures & Rainfall

	JAN	FEB	MAR	APR	MAY	JUNE	JULY	AUG	SEPT	OCT	NOV	DEC
HIGH (°F)	76	77	80	83	86	88	89	90	88	85	80	77
HIGH (°C)	24	25	27	28	30	31	32	32	31	29	27	25
LOW (°F)	60	61	64	68	72	75	76	76	76	72	66	61
LOW (°C)	16	16	18	20	22	24	24	24	24	22	19	16
RAIN (INCHES)	2.0	2.1	2.4	3.0	5.9	8.8	6.0	7.8	8.5	7.0	3.1	1.8

Miami & the Keys Calendar of Events

JANUARY

Orange Bowl (www.OrangeBowl.org; ☎ **305/341-4771**), Miami. Football fanatics flock to the big Orange Bowl game (now held at Sun Life Stadium) on New Year's Day, featuring what seems to be a different corporate sponsor every year and two of the year's best college football teams. Call early if you want tickets; they sell out quickly. First week of January.

Key West Literary Seminar (www.KWLS.org; ☎ **888/293-9291**), Key West. Literary types have a good reason to put down their books and head to Key West. This 3-day event features a different theme every year, along with a roster of incredible authors, writers, and other literary types. The event is so popular it sells out well in advance, so call early for tickets. Second week of January.

FEBRUARY

Everglades City Seafood Festival (www.EvergladesSeafoodFestival.com; ☎ **239/695-2277**), Everglades City. What seems like schools of fish-loving folks flock down to Everglades City for a 2-day feeding frenzy, in which Florida delicacies from stone crab to gator tails are served from shacks and booths on the outskirts of this quaint Old Florida town. Admission is free; you pay for the food you eat at each booth. First full weekend in February.

Miami International Boat Show (www.MiamiBoatShow.com; ☎ **954/441-3231**), Miami Beach. If you don't like crowds, beware, as this show draws a quarter of a million boat enthusiasts to the Miami Beach Convention Center. Some of the world's priciest megayachts, speedboats, sailboats, and schooners are displayed for purchase or for gawking. Mid-February.

South Beach Wine & Food Festival (www.SoBeWineandFoodFest.com; ☎ **877/762-3933**), South Beach/throughout Miami. A 3-day celebration featuring some of the Food Network's best (or at least best-known) chefs, who do their thing in the kitchens of various restaurants and at events around town. In addition, there are tastings, lectures, seminars, and parties that are all open to the public—for a price, of course. Last weekend in February.

MARCH

Winter Party (www.WinterParty.com; ☎ **305/576-7300**), Miami Beach. Gays and lesbians from around the world book trips to Miami far in advance to attend this weekend-long series of parties and events benefiting the National Gay & Lesbian Task Force as well as local LGBT nonprofits. Early March.

Spring Break, Miami Beach, Key West, and other beaches. College students from all over the United States and Canada flock to Florida for endless partying, wet-T-shirt and bikini contests, free concerts, volleyball tournaments, and more. Three weeks in March.

Calle Ocho Festival (www.CarnavalMiami.com; ☎ **305/644-8888**), Little Havana. What Carnaval is to Rio, this 10-day extravaganza is to Miami. Also called Carnaval Miami, it features a street party spanning 23 blocks, with live salsa music, parades, and, of course, tons of savory Cuban delicacies. Those afraid of mob scenes should avoid this party at all costs. Mid-March.

Winter Music Conference (www.WMCon.com; ☎ **954/563-4444**), Miami/Miami Beach. For a week or more, electronica and dance music fans knock themselves out to the world's hottest sounds and DJs in various clubs and festivals. Mid- to late March.

APRIL

Conch Republic Independence Celebration (www.ConchRepublic.com; ☎ **305/296-0213**), Key West. A 10-day party celebrating the day the Keys "seceded" from the union. Events include a kooky bed race and drag queen race, mini-golf tournaments, cruiser car shows, and booze—lots of it. Mid-April.

JULY

Lower Keys Underwater Music Fest (www.LowerKeysChamber.com/Festival.cfm; ☎ **800/872-3722**), Looe Key. When you hear the phrase "the music and the madness," you may think of this amusing aural aquatic event in which boaters head out to the reef at the Looe Key Marine Sanctuary, drop speakers into the water, and pipe in all sorts of music, creating a disco-diving spectacular. Considering the heat at this time of year, underwater is probably the coolest place for a concert. Early/mid-July.

OCTOBER

Fantasy Fest (www.FantasyFest.net; ℂ **305/296-1817**), Key West. Halloween meets Mardi Gras as the streets of Old Town are overrun by costumed revelers who have no shame and no adult supervision. Oh, wait, this weeklong, sometimes R- to X-rated party *is* for adults, not for ages 17 and under. Anyway, make hotel reservations as early as possible, as they tend to fill up quickly for this week. Late October.

NOVEMBER

Miami Book Fair International (www.Miami BookFair.com; ℂ **305/237-3258**), Miami. Bibliophiles, literati, and some of the world's most prestigious authors descend upon Miami for a weeklong homage to the written word, which also happens to be the largest book fair in the United States. The weekend street fair is the best attended event of the entire affair, in which regular folks mix with wordsmiths such as Tom Wolfe, Salman Rushdie, Dan Brown, and Jane Smiley while indulging in snacks, antiquarian books, and literary gossip. All lectures are free but fill up quickly, so get there early. Mid-November.

White Party Week (www.WhiteParty.com; ℂ **305/576-1234**), Miami/South Beach. One of the premier stops on America's gay party circuit is a weeklong series of bashes and events. Last week of November to first week of December.

DECEMBER

Art Basel Miami Beach (www.ArtBaselMiami Beach.com), Miami Beach/Design District. Switzerland's most exclusive art fair and the world's most prominent collectors fly south for the winter and set up shop on South Beach and in the Design District with thousands of exhibitions, not to mention cocktail parties, concerts, and containers—as in shipping—that are set up on the beach and transformed into makeshift galleries. First or second weekend in December.

King Mango Strut (www.KingMangoStrut. org; ℂ 305/582-0955), Coconut Grove. The Grove gets its freak on in this longtime annual satirical parade in which "strutters" send up the issues and personalities of the day. Where else would you see the real mayor of Miami giving the key to the city to a drunken Rob Ford impersonator? Last Sunday of December.

RESPONSIBLE TRAVEL

Florida's biggest attraction isn't a theme park, but rather its natural resources. Thanks to some of the state's initiatives, keeping Florida green is becoming second nature. The **Florida Green Lodging** program, for instance, is a voluntary initiative of the Florida Department of Environmental Protection that designates and recognizes lodging facilities making a commitment to conserving and protecting Florida's natural resources. As of 2013, there were 695 designated Florida Green Lodging properties. In order to be considered for membership in this very exclusive group, motels, hotels, and resorts must educate customers, employees, and the public on conservation; participate in waste reduction, reusing, recycling, water conservation, and energy efficiency; and provide eco-friendly transportation. The designation is valid for 3 years from the date of issue, and all properties are required to submit environmental performance data every year as well as implement at least two new environmental practices from any of the six areas of sustainable operations. A list of properties can be found at www.Dep. State.FL.us/GreenLodging/Lodges.htm.

Eco-tourism isn't just a trendy catchphrase when it comes to tourism in Florida. The Florida Fish and Wildlife Conservation Commission estimates that outdoor activities have almost a $10-billion impact on the state's economy. The Everglades is an eco-tourism hot spot where responsible tourism isn't an option but a requirement for anyone visiting or working there. In fact, in 2010, the **Comprehensive Everglades Restoration Plan** began a process that will return some lands previously squandered for development to their formerly pristine, natural conditions. It's a multi-tiered, $13.5-billion restoration plan covering 16 counties over an 18,000-square-mile area that will take more than 30 years to complete.

OUTDOOR ACTIVITIES

Diving, boating and sailing, camping, canoeing and kayaking, fishing, golfing, tennis—you name it, you can find it in Miami and the Keys. These and other activities are described in the outdoor-activities sections of the following chapters, but here's a brief overview of some of the best places to move your muscles, with tips on how to get more detailed information.

The **Florida Sports Foundation** (www.FlaSports.com; ✆ 850/488-8347), publishes free brochures, calendars, schedules, and guides to outdoor pursuits and spectator sports throughout Florida. I've noted some of its specific publications in the sections below.

For excellent color maps of state parks, campgrounds, canoe trails, aquatic preserves, caverns, and more, contact the **Florida Department of Environmental Protection,** Office of Communications (www.Dep.State.FL.us; ✆ 850/245-2118). Some of the department's publications are mentioned below.

BIKING & IN-LINE SKATING   Florida's relatively flat terrain makes it ideal for bicycling and in-line skating. You can bike right into **Everglades National Park** along the 38-mile-long Main Park Road. Many towns and cities have designated routes for cyclists, skaters, joggers, and walkers, such as the paved pathways along Fort Lauderdale Beach and **Ocean Drive** on South Beach.

BOATING & SAILING   With some 1,350 miles of shoreline, it's not surprising that Florida is a boating and sailing mecca. In fact, you won't be any place near the water very long before you see flyers and other advertisements for rental boats and sailboat cruises. Many of them are mentioned in the chapters that follow.

Key West keeps gaining prominence as a world sailing capital. *Yachting* magazine sponsors the largest winter regatta in America here each January, and smaller events take place regularly.

Florida Fishing & Boating, available for free from the Florida Sports Foundation (see above), is a treasure trove of tips on safe boating; state regulations; locations of marinas, hotels, and resorts; marine products and services; and more.

CAMPING   Florida is literally dotted with RV parks. But for the best tent camping, look to Florida's national preserves and 160 state parks and recreation areas. Options range from luxury sites with hot-water showers and cable TV hookups to primitive island and beach camping with no facilities whatsoever.

Top spots include **Bill Baggs Cape Florida State Park** on Key Biscayne in Miami. In the Keys, the oceanside sites in **Long Key State Park** are about as nice as it gets.

In each of these popular campgrounds, reservations are essential, especially during high season. Each of Florida's state parks takes bookings up to 11 months in advance.

The **Florida Department of Environmental Protection,** Division of Recreation and Parks, (www.Dep.State.FL.us; ✆ 850/245-2118), publishes an annual guide of tent and RV sites in Florida's state parks and recreation areas.

Pet owners note: Pets are permitted at some—but not all—state park beaches, campgrounds, and food service areas. Before bringing your animal, check with the department or the individual park to see if your pet will be allowed. And bring your pet's rabies certificate, which is required.

For private campgrounds, the **Florida Association of RV Parks & Campgrounds** (www.CampFlorida.com; ✆ **850/562-7151**), issues an annual *Camp Florida* directory with locator maps and details about its member establishments.

CANOEING & KAYAKING   Canoers and kayakers have almost limitless options for discovery on picturesque rivers, sandy coastlines, quiet canals, marshes, and mangroves. Exceptional trails run through several parks and wildlife preserves, including **Everglades National Park** and **Briggs Nature Center,** on the edge of the Everglades near Marco Island.

Based during the winter at Everglades City, on the park's western border, **North American Canoe Tours, Inc.** (www.EvergladesAdventures.com; ✆ **239/695-3299**), offers daily guided canoe expeditions through the Everglades.

Forty creek and river trails covering 950 miles are itemized in the excellent free *Florida Paddling Trails* booklet and PDF published by the Florida Department of Environmental Protection, Office of Communications (www.Dep.State.FL.us; ✆ **850/245-2118**).

Specialized guidebooks include *A Canoeing and Kayaking Guide to the Streams of Florida: Volume 1, North Central Florida and Panhandle,* by Elizabeth F. Carter and John L. Pearce; and *Volume 2, Central and Southern Peninsula,* by Lou Glaros and Doug Sphar. Both are published by Menasha Ridge Press (www.MenashaRidge.com).

ECO-ADVENTURES   If you don't want to do it yourself, you can discover Florida's flora and fauna on guided field expeditions—and contribute to conservation efforts while you're at it.

The **Sierra Club,** the oldest and largest grass-roots environmental organization in the U.S., offers eco-adventures through its Florida chapters. Recent outings have included canoeing or kayaking through the Everglades, hiking the Florida Trail in America's southernmost national forest, and camping on a barrier island. You do have to be a Sierra Club member, but you can join at the time of the trip. Contact the club's national outings office (www.SierraClub.org; ✆ **415/977-5500**).

The Florida chapter of the **Nature Conservancy** has protected 578,000 acres of natural lands in Florida and presently owns and manages 4 preserves—open to the public for free or a small fee—and offers volunteer opportunities to help in the preservation these ecosystems. For details, visit www.Nature.org/Florida or call ✆ **407/682-3664.**

FISHING   In addition to the amberjack, bonito, grouper, mackerel, mahi-mahi, marlin, pompano, redfish, sailfish, snapper, snook, tarpon, tuna, and wahoo running offshore and in inlets, Florida has countless miles of rivers and streams, plus about 30,000 lakes and springs harboring more than 100 species of freshwater fish. Indeed, Floridians seem to fish everywhere: off canal banks and old bridges, from fishing piers and fishing fleets. You'll even see them standing alongside the Tamiami Trail (U.S. 41) that cuts across the Everglades—one eye on their line, the other watching for alligators.

Anglers 16 and older need a license for any kind of saltwater or freshwater fishing, including lobstering and spearfishing. Licenses are sold at bait-and-tackle shops around the state and online at MyFWC.com/license.

The **Florida Department of Environmental Protection** (www.Dep.State.FL.us; ✆ **850/245-2118**) publishes the annual *Fishing Lines,* a free magazine with a wealth of information about fishing in Florida, including regulations and licensing requirements. It also distributes free brochures with annual freshwater and saltwater limits. And the Florida Sports Foundation (www.FlaSports.com; © **850/488-8347**) publishes *Florida Boating & Fishing,* another treasure trove of information.

GOLF Florida is the unofficial golf capital of the United States. One thing's for sure: it can boast more golf courses than any other state—more than 1,250 at last count, and growing. Suffice it to say that you can tee off almost anywhere, anytime there's daylight. It's a rare city down here that doesn't have a municipal golf course—even Key West has 18 great holes.

Greens fees are usually much lower at the municipal courses than at privately owned clubs. Whether public or private, greens fees can vary greatly depending on the time of year. You could pay $150 or more at a private course during the high season, but less than half that when the tourists are gone. The fee structures vary so much that it's best to call ahead and ask, and always reserve a tee time as far in advance as possible.

You can learn the game or hone your strokes at one of several excellent golf schools in South Florida, including **Jimmy Ballard's** school at the Ocean Reef Club on Key Largo (www.JimmyBallardGolf.com).

You can get information about most South Florida courses, including current greens fees, and reserve tee times through **Tee Times USA** (www.TeeTimesUSA.com; © **800/374-8633** or 386/439-0001), which publishes a vacation guide with many stay-and-play golf packages.

Play FLA Golf, published by the Florida Sports Foundation (see above), lists every course in Florida. It's the state's official golf guide and is available from Visit Florida (www.VisitFlorida.com).

Golfer's Guide magazine publishes monthly editions covering most of Florida. It's available free at local visitor centers and hotel lobbies, or you can contact the magazine at www.GolfersGuide.com or © **843/842-7878**).

You can also get info from the **Professional Golfers' Association** (**PGA;** www. PGA.com; © **561/624-8400**); or the **Ladies Professional Golf Association** (**LPGA;** www.LPGA.com; © **386/274-6200**).

SCUBA DIVING & SNORKELING Divers love the Keys, where you can see magnificent formations of tree-size elk-horn coral and giant brain coral, as well as colorful sea fans and dozens of other varieties, sharing the waters with 300 or more species of rainbow-hued fish. Reef diving is good all the way from Key Largo to Key West, with plenty of tour operators, outfitters, and dive shops along the way. Particularly worthy are **John Pennekamp Coral Reef State Park** in Key Largo and **Looe Key National Marine Sanctuary** off Big Pine Key. *Skin Diver* magazine picked Looe Key as the number-one dive spot in North America. Also, the clearest waters in which to view some of the 4,000 sunken ships along Florida's coast are in the Middle Keys and the waters between Key West and the Dry Tortugas. Snorkeling in the Keys is particularly fine between Islamorada and Marathon. You might want to pick up a specialized guidebook. Some good ones include *Coral Reefs of Florida,* by Gilbert L. Voss (Pineapple Press) and *The Diver's Guide to Florida and the Florida Keys,* by Jim Stachowicz (Windward Publishing).

TENNIS Year-round sunshine makes Florida great for tennis. There are some 7,700 places to play throughout the state, from municipal courts to exclusive resorts. Some municipal facilities are equal in quality to expensive resorts—except they're free, or close to it. Some retired professionals even have their own tennis centers, including Chris Evert in Boca Raton.

Locally, the 26 courts at the **Crandon Park Tennis Center,** 7300 Crandon Blvd. (www.MiamiDade.gov/Parks/Crandon-Tennis.asp; © **305/365-2300**), get crowded on weekends because they're some of Miami's most beautiful. You'll play on the same courts as Lendl, Graf, Evert, McEnroe, Federer, the Williams sisters, and other greats; this is also the venue for one of the world's biggest annual tennis events, the Sony Ericsson Open. There's a pleasant, if limited, pro shop, plus many good pros. Thirteen courts are lit at night, and if you reserve at least 24 hours in advance, you can usually take your pick. Hard courts cost $4 person per hour during the day, $6 per person per hour at night. Clay courts cost $7 per person per hour daytimes, $9 at night. Grass courts are $11 per person per hour (daytime only). The courts are open weekdays from 8am to 10pm, weekends until 7pm.

SOUTH FLORIDA WILDLIFE

In addition to the usual suspects—alligators and crocodiles—the Sunshine State is home to a growing list of **endangered species,** including wild panthers, bobcats, and black bears. In fact, a total of 98 species of mammals call Florida home, among them armadillos, hogs, shrews, rabbits, possums, coyote, fox, lemurs, monkeys, deer, apes, and bats. Yes, bats. In fact, the Mexican free-tailed bat, the evening bat, and the big brown bat are common sightings everywhere in the state except the Keys and major metropolitan areas. Much cuter than bats are deer, the only native in the state being the **white-tailed deer,** which happens to be the major prey of the Florida panther. A smaller subspecies of these are **Key deer,** which live only in the Keys and are few and far between—only around 800 or so are in existence.

And contrary to popular belief, the "snowbird" is not the official fowl of Florida, a state with hundreds of species of land birds and water birds from vultures, eagles, and ospreys to owls, woodpeckers, pelicans, herons, ducks, loons, and anhingas.

Marine mammals, however, are the true stars of the state, with the **manatee** at the top of the endangered list. According to experts, the highest count of manatee in the state at one time was in 2001 with 3,276. As for Flipper, the most common dolphin in the state is the bottlenose dolphin, while the most frequent orca known to the state is the Atlantic northern white whale. Bottlenose dolphins are not endangered and have a stable future thanks to their adaptability. Climate change, however, is an inevitable factor many species are facing rapidly with little time to adapt. And although some animal activists protest that keeping dolphins in captivity for tourism is cruel, in some cases, the dolphin swims are performed in the ocean with wild dolphins, while other programs are conducted in aquarium environments. Those programs which are neither are what come under fire from the activists.

But back to that alligator. No thanks to global climate change, the American alligators are most affected by damage to their habitats. But that's not the only reason the gator's endangered: Increased levels of dioxins found in the bodies of water are also a key ingredient. Some would also say the alligator is also newly threatened by the recent Burmese python invasion that's straight out of a horror flick. Although the python situation is out of control due to irresponsible pet owners who discard them in the Everglades when they become unmanageable, it's not a major factor in the alligator's status as an endangered species.

In December 2009, Congress allotted an additional $15 million to the federal State and Tribal Wildlife Grant program to help bring wildlife action plans into alignment with climate change. For a list of opportunities, sites, outfitters, and guides for wildlife viewing throughout the state, visit www.MyFWC.com/Viewing.

SUGGESTED MIAMI & THE KEYS ITINERARIES

Miami and the Keys, along with the Everglades, serves up an impressive variety with all the go-go activities of a world-class city but also beautiful beaches, natural wonders, and quiet corners. Whether your interests lean toward the active or chill-out, plugged in or unplugged, culture or turn-'n'-burn, or a mix of all, you'll leave South Florida with a smile on your face.

The range of possible itineraries is endless; what I've suggested below is a very full program covering Miami and the Keys over a **weeklong period.** If possible, I'd recommend you extend your time—a week isn't enough for in-depth exploration—but I realize most of you are hardly awash in vacation time. So for those who want to taste a little of everything, I've laid out the highlights, keeping it all geographically viable and logical.

Important: Should limited time force you to include only the most obvious stops in your itinerary, you'll invariably come across only those who depend on you to make a living, which could leave you with the sense that South Florida is one big tourist trap. That's why it's so important to *get off the tourist track*—to experience the wacky, the kitschy, the stunning, the baffling, the moving, and the fascinating people, places, and things that make this one of America's most remarkable destinations.

MIAMI & THE KEYS HIGHLIGHTS

Whether you're a beach bum, a club hopper, a nature lover, or a people-watcher—there's something for everyone in this neck of South Florida. This tour provides you with a local's-eye view of some of the best diversions So Flo is known for. Feel free to mix and match stops from this itinerary to create your own perfect experience.

Day 1: South Beach ★★★

Arrive at Miami International Airport (or Amtrak station, Greyhound bus station, or by car) and check into your hotel (or at least drop your bags). Spend the rest of the morning on the beach, then hit **Lincoln Road** for lunch, grabbing a meal-sized salad or other tasty options from the large menu at **Nexxt Café** (p. 64), while taking in the colorful parade of locals and tourists. Spend some afternoon time shopping along Lincoln Road, then head over to the **Delano Hotel** for a cocktail at the **Rose Bar** (p. 130), followed by a late-afternoon amble on the paved path along the beach out back. If you're not staying here, head back to your own hotel for a disco nap. For dinner, make the obligatory pilgrimage to **Joe's Stone Crab** (p. 62) for the eponymous crabs or other seafood; if it's closed for the season, Chef Luciano's organic Italian/sushi at **The Delano**'s **Bianca** (p. 46) and the creative fusion of José Andrés' **Bazaar** at the **SLS** (p. 49) make scrumptious consolation prizes. Then hit the clubs: **WALL** (p. 135), **Mansion** (p. 135), **Cameo** (p. 134), **SET** (p. 135), or **Story** (p. 135). If you're still up for the boogie, hop in a cab and head to **LIV** (p. 134) at the **Fontainebleau.** Grab a late-night snack at **La Sandwicherie** (p. 132), then crash.

Day 2: More South Beach

Wake up early (yes, I know you were out late, but you can always catch a nap later) and enjoy sunrise on the beach. After breakfast at the **News Café** (p. 132), check out the original Miami supermodel, the Art Deco District, via a midmorning walking tour from the **Miami Design Preservation League** (see box on p. 81). Keep the cultural ball rolling with a museum visit depending on your interests: decorative arts/cultural history at the **Wolfsonian** (p. 87), Miami Jewish history at the **Jewish Museum of Florida** (p. 85), or fine art at the **Bass** (p. 84). Go ethnic Caribbean for lunch with Cuban at **Puerto Sagua** (p. 65) or Haitian at **Tap Tap** (p. 64), then hit that famous beach. Try not to spend too long out here, especially if it's been a while since you've been in the sun for any length of time. You'll definitely want a nap afterward, too. For dinner, check out the classy Mediterranean menu and the sexy SoBe scene at **Bâoli** (p. 61). You can hang out here to party the night away with all the pretty people, or you could round off the night with funky live music at the likes of **Jazid** (p. 136) or **The Cabaret** (p. 136).

Day 3: Miami–Coral Gables, Little Havana, Coconut Grove

Today you'll explore the other side of the causeway, where you can spend the night in Coral Gables out at the splendid, historic **Biltmore Hotel** (p. 56) or the downtown Gables' also charming, more moderately priced **Hotel St. Michel** (p. 57). If you don't check into the Biltmore, at least drop by for an eyeful of its magnificent public areas and pool, followed by a drive through the Gables' residential streets with their tropical foliage and fancy residences, with a stop along the way for a dip in the cinematic **Venetian Pool** (p. 93). Head a few blocks northeast to Little Havana for lunch and an eyeful of the local scene at **Versailles** (p. 77), followed by an exploration of the several-block stretch at the neighborhood's heart on SW Eighth Street (p. 39), otherwise known as **Calle Ocho,** whether on your own or with an organized walking tour. Then drop down to Coconut Grove to cruise its tropical byways and visit the magnificent **Vizcaya** mansion (p 94). Enjoy an exquisite nouvelle Caribbean dinner at **Ortanique** on the Gables' Miracle Mile (p. 67) or Latin fusion a few blocks east at **Casabe**

Miami & the Keys Highlights

Days 1–2	South Beach
Day 3	Coral Gables, Little Havana, Coconut Grove
Day 4	The Everglades
Day 5	Upper/Middle Keys
Days 6–7	Key West

(p. 65). Finally, before heading back to your hotel, catch a Latin performance or dance party at the Little Havana club **Hoy Como Ayer** (p. 138).

Day 4: The Everglades ★★★, Upper/Middle Keys ★★★

After breakfast, drive an hour-and-a-half southwest to explore one of America's most awesome ecosystems, the 40-mile-wide "River of Grass" (for full details, see chapter 10). Head for **Everglades National Park**'s southern entrance at the **Ernest F. Coe Visitor Center** (p. 149), get yourself oriented and educated, then push on into the park. You'll spend all day out here, with options—depending on your interests and level of fitness—including various walking trails, plus canoeing, kayaking, and motorboat tours (and for a fascinating spot of history amid all of that, there's a tour of the Cold-War era **Nike Hercules Missile Base,** p. 154). I highly recommend taking one of the ranger tours, which will highlight various fauna and flora you probably wouldn't otherwise notice. For lunch, you can pack a picnic or chow down in nearby Homestead at **El Toro Taco, Capri,** or the **White Lion** (p. 152). Once you've had your fill at afternoon's end, head back out to U.S. 1 and southward onto Key Largo for a down-home dinner overlooking the mangroves at **Alabama Jack's** (p. 165). Then make your way to your night's lodging in the **Upper or Middle Keys** (p. 166) and rest up for another busy day tomorrow.

Day 5: Upper/Middle Keys ★★★, Key West ★★★

After breakfast, hit the Overseas Highway to **John Pennekamp Coral Reef State Park** (p. 171) for several hours of snorkeling and canoeing amid breathtaking corals and tropical fish, capped off with a 2½-hour glass-bottom-boat tour. Continue south, grabbing lunch along the way at another waterside local icon, **Island Grill** (p. 173), until you reach Grassy Key. Here, spend the rest of the afternoon at the **Dolphin Research Center** (p. 175) with its "family" of bottlenose dolphins, sea lions, and exotic birds, including educational programs, dolphin encounters, and swimming with dolphins. Push on southward another hour and a half to Key West, and take a well-earned rest at your hotel or guesthouse. For dinner you could splurge at **Café Marquesa, Azur,** or **Square One** (p. 199 and 200) or economize tastily with some Caribbean goodies at **Paseo** or **El Siboney** (p. 201 and 202). If after this long day you're not too beat, stroll Duval Street and take in—well, the craziness around you, for starters—organized entertainment such as the live bands at classics such as **Sloppy Joe's** (p. 212), Jimmy Buffet's **Margaritaville** (p. 200), and the **Green Parrot** (p. 212).

Day 6: Key West ★★★

After breakfast at your hotel or guesthouse and the busy days you've had recently, how about a laid-back morning lazing around the pool? That, too, is part of the charm of Key West. Around noonish, rouse yourself and head to lunch under a spreading mahogany tree at the island's oldest and quaintest eatery, **Pepe's** (p. 201). Suitably fortified, set out for some sightseeing, wandering the leafy lanes to take in the many gorgeous restored Victorian-era homes; you can tour the splendid interior of one, the **Curry Mansion Inn** (p. 191), for free. Also be sure not to miss the **Ernest Hemingway Home** (p. 204), the **Oldest House** (p. 206), and the quirky **cemetery** (p. 205); get a great 360-degree view from atop the old **Key West Lighthouse** (p. 205). At the end of the afternoon, head over to Mallory Square where crowds, buskers, and street vendors have assembled for the daily sunset "watch party" (think you'll spot the elusive "green flash"?). For dinner, splurge on a romantic Key West classic at the Atlantic's edge, **Louie's Backyard** (p. 199), then hit Duval Street again (hey, it's what you do around here) for more shopping, drinking, and live music. This time, consider adding to the mix one of the drag shows at **La Te Da** (p. 195) or **Aqua** (p. 212); they're a hoot, a longstanding part of the local culture, and a hit with audiences of all persuasions.

Day 7: Key West ★★★

Pass on your lodging's breakfast this morning in favor of banana pancakes surrounded by roosters at hippie-chic **Blue Heaven** (p. 198) in Bahama Village. Before leaving the island you need to experience its watery side, either at picturesque **Fort Zachary Taylor State Park Beach** (p. 207) or on a **cruise** out to the reef (p. 207). When it's time to go, drop your wheels at the airport, then hop a flight back to Miami and homeward.

BEACHY KEEN SOUTH FLORIDA

South Florida's beaches have been more photographed—well, possibly—than Kimye. In addition to the sand and sparkling waters of the Atlantic, they have various personalities, from laid-back and remote to year-round partying. It may be fun to get a taste of all of these, if only for an hour or two at a time.

Day 1: Arrive in the Keys ★★★

Driving down from Miami airport, train station, or points north, check into the **Hawks Cay Resort** (p. 168) and take in the ocean views. Park yourself on a chaise-longue and enjoy one of the Florida Keys' best private beaches (one of its very few, by the way), perhaps mixed with some parasailing or swimming with dolphins. Make a dinner reservation for an outside table on the verandah at Latin-flavored **Alma,** where I recommend Florida mahi with crispy fried plantain, black beans and rice, and avocado truffle purée (carnivores will love the *churrasco* skirt steak with *boniato* mash and cilantro aioli). After dinner, listen to some live music while schmoozing or just chilling out around the fire pit.

Day 2: Bahia Honda State Park ★★★

Just a half-hour south of Hawks Cay is one of South Florida's most resplendent beaches. Spend the day in 524-acre **Bahia Honda** (p. 184) and lose yourself in the mangroves, beach dunes, and tropical hammocks. Not in the mood to spend all day in the park? Check out the **National Key Deer Refuge** (p. 184), where you'll catch a glimpse of the most famous residents of the Lower Keys, or go snorkeling at the **Looe Key National Marine Sanctuary** (p. 186), where you'll see more than 150 varieties of coral and magnificent tropical fish. Head back to Hawks Cay for a dinner of fresh seafood such as pan-seared local snapper (for non-pescavores, maybe Florida citrus-roasted chicken or veggie pappardelle).

Day 3: Downtown Miami/Key Biscayne ★★

Hit the scenic, sleepy, and often slow-moving Overseas Highway north, stopping for breakfast at the landmark **Green Turtle** (coconut French toast!; p. 172) or waterside at **Island Grill** (p. 173). Continue north on U.S. 1 to the Brickell Avenue corridor of lower downtown Miami, then hop over the bridge to Brickell Key to check in at the **Mandarin Oriental, Miami** (p. 56). Spend a little while on its cute artificial beach with a nice view of the skyline and the chance to spot dolphins. Then head back down Brickell Avenue and over the Rickenbacker Causeway to Key Biscayne. On this, the southernmost barrier island on the Atlantic coast, you'll able to beach hop until the sun goes down. For the party people, **Crandon Park Beach** is the place to be, with 2 miles of beach and lots of salsa emanating from various sunbathers' boom boxes. To counter that bass, check out the park's family amusement center, where a 1940s carousel spins to the tune of old-school organ music. Grab some much-needed peace and quiet at **Bill Baggs Cape Florida State Park** (p. 98), where you'll forget you're in Miami, thanks to the miles of nature trails and charmingly natural beach. Do lunch here at the **Lighthouse Cafe** (p. 98) before heading over to Virginia Key, the place where *Flipper* was filmed and Old Florida cracker-style houses serve as a backdrop to a funky beachfront party scene.

Beachy Keen South Florida

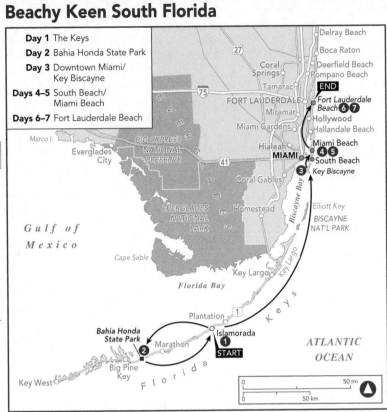

Day 1 The Keys
Day 2 Bahia Honda State Park
Day 3 Downtown Miami/
Key Biscayne
Days 4–5 South Beach/
Miami Beach
Days 6–7 Fort Lauderdale Beach

Days 4 & 5: South Beach/Miami Beach ★★★

Going to "the beach" takes on a totally different meaning when you're in SoBe. Not only does it mean sunbathing on **Lummus Park Beach** (p. 80), also known as South Beach, with a cornucopia of half-naked beautiful people, but also enjoying the surrounding sights, sounds, and tastes of the area's bars, restaurants, shops, hotels, and Art Deco architecture. There's a plethora of places to stay, whether you're on a budget or are willing to splurge; best of all, the beach (as in stretch of sand) is free and a great place to crash and watch the sun rise after spending a night out in the clubs. Farther up this barrier island, Miami Beach becomes Surfside, then swank Bal Harbour, then Sunny Isles Beach, all the while offering wide, glorious swaths of sand, along with wave action that usually doesn't win much in the way of accolades from serious surfers but does add a nice bit of froth to your frolics.

Days 6 & 7: Swanky & Annette—also known as Fort Lauderdale Beach ★★★

For another take on South Florida beach scene, cross the county line into Broward. Your dad may have spent spring break in Fort Lauderdale with his frat buds when the Beatles were just a random group of lads from Liverpool, but if he saw it now, he'd be floored. Sure, the beach is beautiful, clean, and visible from A1A, but the surrounding area—the once infamous Fort Lauderdale strip—has matured into a more sophisticated cafe scene with outdoor eateries, a mostly better class of bars (even though the legendary **Elbo Room** is still going strong), and more. If you must enter a beer-drinking contest, though, I'm sure you'll find one nearby. Don't miss a cruise through the Venice of America, a scenic, informative, and convenient way to make your way from one end of the strip to another. (See chapter 12 for details.)

SOUTH FLORIDA, FAMILY STYLE

Despite a thriving nightlife and sometimes R-rated (or worse) sensibility—and dress code (or lack thereof)—Miami, the Keys, and the rest of South Florida are definitely a kid-friendly destination. Although South Beach is probably not the best place overall for little ones, there are tons of other spots that are plenty family-friendly and won't have the kids whining that they wish they were at Disney World.

Day 1: South Beach ★★★

Start out your day with the wackiest (certainly the quackiest) tour in town, the 90-minute **Duck Tours** (p. 106). Alternatively, **Bike and Roll**'s Segway tour (p. 105) is also fun, just a bit closer to the ground. For lunch, grab a triple-decker burger or "TV Dinner" at **Big Pink,** 157 Collins Ave. (© **305/532-4700**), then zip halfway across the MacArthur Causeway to the **Miami Children's Museum** (p. 86), where the kids can spend a few hours channeling their inner grown-up in a bona fide TV and recording studio, among other cool stuff. Pop right across the street for more animal antics at **Jungle Island** (p. 85). After working up an appetite, take the crew to dinner at **Nexxt Café** (p. 64), with a pretty rockin' kids' menu and a front-row seat to not only the ever-entertaining Lincoln Road parade but right across from an astro-turfed little "island" that kids love racing around. Afterward, if you're OK with a little sugar, pop into the colorful, Willy Wonka–esque **Dylan's Candy Bar,** 801 Lincoln Rd. (www.DylansCandyBar.com; © **305/531-1988**). Cap off the evening by hitting the pins at the nearby **Lucky Strike** bowling alley (p. 139).

Day 2: Key Biscayne ★★★

Head to the **Miami Seaquarium** (p. 88), where the kids can swim with the dolphins, and then spend the rest of the day at the **Marjory Stoneman Douglas Biscayne Nature Center** (p. 90), where the entire family can explore an ancient fossil tidal pool. If there's time left, check out the **Bill Baggs Cape Florida State Park** (p. 98) and rent a hydrobike, or check out the brand-new **Crandon Park Family Amusement Center** (p. 90).

Day 3: South Beach ★★, Coral Gables ★★★, Coconut Grove ★★, Little Havana ★★

Get an early start and drive south to Homestead's legendary **Coral Castle** (p. 95). This wacky attraction won't take that long, so you'll want to follow that up with a stop at **Zoo Miami** (p. 96) or **Monkey Jungle** (p. 96), depending on your

South Florida, Family Style

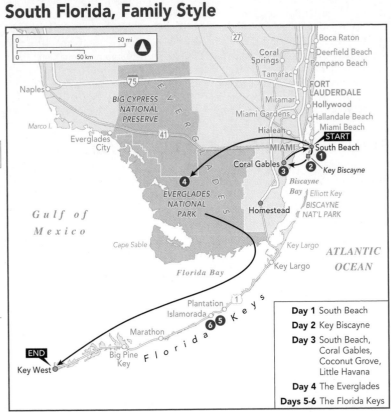

Day 1 South Beach
Day 2 Key Biscayne
Day 3 South Beach,
     Coral Gables,
     Coconut Grove,
     Little Havana
Day 4 The Everglades
Days 5-6 The Florida Keys

preference in critters. You're headed to Coral Gables next, so on the way up U.S. 1, stop at kid-friendly **Shorty's Bar-B-Q** (p. 76) for some sweet, Southern-style protein. Wash off that barbecue sauce and zoo-animal scent with a dip in the Gables' resplendent, refreshing **Venetian Pool** (p. 93). Cap off the afternoon with some planetarium and other hands-on action at nearby Coconut Grove's **Patricia and Phillip Frost Museum of Science** (p. 94). And for dinner, how about introducing the kids to the Cuban-style burgers, known as *fritas,* at Little Havana's **El Rey de las Fritas** (p. 74)?

Day 4: The Everglades ★★★

Head out west again today, into one of the eco-wonders of America, the **Everglades** (p. 145). In addition to budgeting a couple of hours for the round-trip drive, there's enough out here to keep you and the gang busy all day, from canoeing, kayaking, hiking, and motor boating to alligator shows where your kids can watch gator wrestling and even touch baby gators. Then of course there's what you might call the original thrill ride: the airboat (p. 156), offered at several spots. Out here you'll also find several restaurants to take the squirts to so they can tell their friends (and frankly, you can tell yours) that they tried alligator (p. 152).

Days 5 & 6: The Florida Keys ★★★

Outdoorsy and especially waterborne activities are what the Florida Keys excel in, and highlights along this 150-mile string of islands include snorkeling in **Looe Key National Marine Sanctuary** (p. 186); swimming with dolphins at Marathon's **Dolphin Research Center** (p. 175), **Hawks Cay resort** (p. 168), or **Theater of the Sea** (p. 176); the dolphin, sea lion, and parrot shows at the Theater of the Sea; a glass-bottom boat ride in **John Pennekamp Coral Reef State Park** (p. 171); cooing over adorable miniature deer at the **National Key Deer Refuge** (p. 184); feeding the tarpon at **Robbie's Pier** (p. 176); Jet Skiing at **Jerry's Watersports** in Marathon (p. 180); and parasailing at Hawks Cay. Down in Key West, kids will especially enjoy the touch tanks and shark shows at the old-fashioned **Key West Aquarium** (p. 204); walking amid free-flying butterflies at the **Key West Butterfly & Nature Conservatory** (p. 204); climbing the **Key West Lighthouse** (p. 205); history given the slightly Disneyfied, multimedia treatment at **Key West's Shipwreck Treasure Museum** (p. 205); and a biplane flight at **Conch Republic Air Force** (p. 209).

GETTING TO KNOW MIAMI

4

A week in Miami is not unlike watching some over-the-top "reality" show, only it's all real. Miami: the city where Jay-Z tipped a Miami Beach nightclub waitress 50 grand; where Justin Bieber was busted for drunk drag racing; where basketball superstar LeBron James's mom was hauled in after a spat with a Fontainebleau parking attendant; and where the paparazzi camps out for days, hoping to catch a glimpse of something or someone outrageous. But that's just a small sample of the surreal, Fellini-esque world that exists down here at the bottom of the U.S. map. Nothing in Miami is ever what it seems.

THINGS TO DO   Miami has endless sporting, cultural, and recreational activities to keep you entertained. From watersports and sunbathing on **Miami Beach** to alligators in the **Everglades,** Miami lives outdoors. Play golf at **Crandon Park,** watch manatees on **Coconut Grove**'s waterfront, or simply soak up the sun. On rainy days you can school yourself in Dutch and Italian tapestries at the outstanding **Bass Museum of Art,** or learn about the city's humble beginnings with a walking tour led by historian **Paul George.** For details, see chapter 7.

SHOPPING   Miami provides an eclectic shopping experience, from designer boutiques at **Bal Harbour** and the **Village of Merrick Park** to mainstream chains at **Bayside Marketplace.** Miami likes its megamalls, and one of the best is **Aventura Mall,** though the **Dolphin Mall** and **Dadeland Mall** also have their good points. Browse for new art and furniture in the **Design District,** or take home a little bit of Cuba with a hand-stitched *guayabera* shirt from **Little Havana.** Pick up incense and Indian imports from **Española Way**'s Mediterranean storefronts. For details, see chapter 8.

RESTAURANTS & DINING   High-end spots such as **The Forge** (p. 61) and **Bâoli** (p. 61) are booming, but budget options also abound. Especially sample Cuban along **Calle Ocho,** locally sourced foodie fare in the **Design District,** and casual comfort food in the Grove. Dine at an open-air cafe in **Coral Gables** while enjoying stone crab claws and a mojito, the city's signature cocktail. For details, see chapter 6.

NIGHTLIFE & ENTERTAINMENT   South Beach is Miami's uncontested nocturnal nucleus, but **Midtown/Wynwood, Brickell, South Miami,** and **Little Havana** are increasingly providing fun alternatives without the ludicrous cover charges and "fashionably late" hours (SoBe action starts after 11pm). Try some creative cocktails on **Lincoln Road** and sip martinis in the **Design District**'s swank lounges. Watch live jazz and flamenco at the **Fillmore Miami Beach at the Jackie Gleason Theater,** or listen to a star DJ spin at the **New World Center's Soundscape.** For details, see chapter 9.

THE best MIAMI EXPERIENCES

o **Picking Strawberries in Homestead:** Long before Miami became all about local, sustainable, and organic, Homestead was rocking all three categories, and still is thanks to its roadside farm stands and fields aplenty of strawberries, tomatoes, and all sorts of exotic fruit. There's nothing like going down there and picking your own.

o **Picnicking at the New World Center:** There's something singularly sensational about picnicking at Miami Beach's sonically stunning, visually arresting, culturally unparalleled **New World Center** (p. 126)—especially when, like most of the time, the entertainment is free.

o **Jet-Skiing Among the Rich and Famous:** Yachts are a dime a dozen in Miami and they sure are pretty, but when it comes to being one with the water, the preferred transportation of choice for the biggest players in town—such as Enrique Iglesias, Rosie O'Donnell, or Justin Bieber—is the Jet Ski. It's easy, it's zippy, and you never know who you may be cruising past.

o **Quaffing Cuban Coffee in Little Havana:** Little Havana is Miami's most culturally rich neighborhood, where pre-Castro Cubans and more recent Central American immigrants mix with everyone else in a frenzied fusion set to a Latin beat. You needn't speak the language to appreciate the energy.

o **Learning to Salsa:** If the only salsa you're familiar with is the kind you put on your tacos, get over to **Bongo's Cuban Café** (p. 137), the hottest salsa club north of Havana, where Miami's most talented salsa dancers will teach you how to move your two left feet in the right direction.

ORIENTATION

Miami is a fascinating city to explore, be it by foot, bike, scooter, boat, or car. And because of its larger-than-life persona, it comes across as a lot bigger than it really is; though the city comprises many different neighborhoods, it's difficult to learn the lay of the land. The "Magic City" is a package of a little less than 2,000 square miles.

Arriving

Carved out of scrubland in 1928 by Pan American Airlines, **Miami International Airport (MIA)** has become second in the United States for international passenger traffic and 10th in the world for total passengers. It's also had a (sometimes deserved) rep as a pain in the . . . but anyway, ongoing renovations are remedying some of its shortcomings. You can change money or use your ATM card at a Bank of America located near the exit. Visitor information is available daily from 6am to 10pm at the **Miami International Airport Visitor Counter,** Terminal E, second level (✆ **305/876-7000**); you can also find info at **www.Miami-Airport.com**. Because MIA is South Florida's busiest airport, you may want to consider flying into less congested **Fort Lauderdale Hollywood International Airport (FLL;** ✆ **954/359-1200**), closer to north Miami than MIA, about a 45-minute drive (depending on traffic!) to areas like South Beach, downtown, Coral Gables, and Coconut Grove. FLL also has more low-cost airlines.

Words to Live By

I figure marriage is kind of like Miami; it's hot and stormy, and occasionally a little dangerous . . . but if it's really so awful, why is there still so much traffic?
—Sarah Jessica Parker's character, Gwen Marcus, in *Miami Rhapsody*

GETTING INTO TOWN

Miami International Airport is about 6 miles west of downtown and about 10 miles from the beaches, so it's likely you can get from the plane to your hotel room in less than half an hour. Of course, if you're arriving from an international destination, it will take more time to go through Customs and Immigration.

BY CAR   Major auto-rental firms are consolidated in the 6,500-vehicle **MIA Rental Car Center** (www.Miami-Airport.com/cip_rcc.asp), reachable via train from airline terminals, and 10 smaller firms have locations nearby. See the "Rentals" section, under "Getting Around," on p. 41, for a list of major rental companies in Miami. Signs at the airport's exit clearly point the way to various parts of the region, but your rental outfit should also provide directions to your destination. If you're arriving late at night, you might want to take a taxi to your lodging and have the car delivered to you the next day.

BY TAXI   Taxis line up in front of a dispatcher's desk outside MIA's arrivals terminals. Most cabs are metered, though some have flat rates to popular destinations. The fare should be about $20 to Coral Gables, $25 to downtown, and $35 to South Beach, plus tip, which should be about 15% (a bit more for each bag the driver handles). Depending on traffic, the ride to Coral Gables or downtown takes about 15 to 20 minutes, 20 to 25 minutes to South Beach.

BY VAN OR LIMO   Group limousines (multi-passenger vans) circle the arrivals area looking for fares. Destinations are posted on the front of each van, and a flat rate is charged for door-to-door service to the area marked.

   SuperShuttle (www.SuperShuttle.com; ✆ **305/871-2000**) is one of the largest airport operators, charging generally $15 to $40 per person for a ride within Miami-Dade county. Its vans operate 24 hours a day and accept American Express, MasterCard, and Visa. This is a cheaper alternative to a cab (if you're traveling alone or with one other person), but be prepared to be in the van for quite some time, as you may have to make several stops to drop passengers off before you reach your own destination.

   Rather pricier, one-way private car service will run $110 to $130. Companies include **Aventura Worldwide Transportation** (www.aventuralimo.com; ✆ **800/944-9886**) and **Limo Miami** (www.limomiami.us; ✆ **305/742-5900**).

BY PUBLIC TRANSIT   A major hassle in South Florida. Slow and unreliable, buses to downtown leave the airport only once per hour (from the arrivals level), and connections are spotty at best. It could take about 1½ hours to get to South Beach this way. Trips to downtown and Coral Gables are more direct. The fare is $2.25, plus an additional 50¢ for a transfer. For those heading to South Beach from the airport, the Airport-Beach Flyer provides direct express service from MIA to Miami Beach and costs $2.65. With only one minor stop en route, the trip to the beach takes about a half hour—not too bad. There's now also a Metrorail line which can get you to areas including Coconut Grove and downtown for $2.25 (details at www.MiamiDade.gov/Transit/Miami-International-Airport-Station.asp).

Visitor Information

The most up-to-date information is provided by the **Greater Miami Convention and Visitor's Bureau** (www.MiamiandBeaches.com; ✆ **800/933-8448** or 305/539-3000). Several chambers of commerce in greater Miami will send out information on their particular areas.

If you arrive at Miami International Airport, you can pick up visitor information at the main visitor counter on the second floor of Terminal E. It's open daily 6am to 10pm.

Always check local newspapers for special events during your visit. The city's only daily, the *Miami Herald,* is a good source for current listings, particularly the "Weekend" section on Fridays. Even better is the free weekly alternative paper *Miami New Times,* available in bright red boxes throughout the city. Other sources for dining, entertainment, culture, and more include www.MiamiHerald.com, www.Miami.City search.com, www.Miami.com, and www.MiamiNewTimes.com.

City Layout

Miami seems confusing at first, but quickly becomes easy to navigate. The cluster of buildings that make up the downtown area is at the geographic heart of the city. In relation to downtown, the airport is northwest, the beaches are east, Coconut Grove is south, Key Biscayne is southeast, Coral Gables is west, and the rest of the city is north.

FINDING AN ADDRESS Metro Miami is divided into dozens of areas with official and unofficial boundaries. Street numbering in the city of Miami is fairly straightforward, but you must first be familiar with the numbering system. The mainland is divided into four sections (NE, NW, SE, and SW) by the intersection of Flagler Street and Miami Avenue. Flagler divides Miami from north to south, and Miami Avenue divides the city from east to west. It's helpful to remember that avenues generally run north-south, while streets go east-west. Street numbers (1st St., 2nd St., and so forth) start from here and increase as you go farther out from this intersection, as do numbers of avenues, places, courts, terraces, and lanes. Streets in Hialeah are the exceptions to this pattern; they are listed separately in map indexes.

Getting around the barrier islands that make up Miami Beach is easier than moving around the mainland. Street numbering starts with First Street, near Miami Beach's southern tip, and goes up to 192nd Street, in the northern part of Sunny Isles. As in the city of Miami, some streets in Miami Beach have numbers as well as names. When listed in this book, both name and number are given.

The numbered streets in Miami Beach are not the geographical equivalents of those on the mainland, but they are close. For example, the 79th Street Causeway runs into 71st Street on Miami Beach.

STREET MAPS It's easy to get lost in sprawling Miami, so a reliable map is essential. The **Trakker Map of Miami,** available at most bookstores, is a four-color accordion map that encompasses all of Miami-Dade County. Some maps list streets according to area, so you'll have to know which part of the city you're looking for before the street can be found.

The Neighborhoods in Brief

South Beach—The Art Deco District
South Beach's 10 miles of beach are alive with a circuslike, sometimes frenetic atmosphere and are center stage for a motley crew of characters, from eccentric locals, seniors, snowbirds, and college students to gender-benders, celebrities, club kids, and curiosity seekers.

Bolstered by a Caribbean-chic cafe society and a sexually charged, tragically hip nightlife, people-watching on South Beach (1st St.–23rd St.) is almost as good as a front-row seat at a Milan fashion show. But although the beautiful people do flock here, models aren't the only sights worth drooling over. The thriving Art Deco District within South Beach has the largest concentration of Art Deco architecture in the world (in 1979, much of the area was listed in the National Register of Historic Places). The pastel-hued structures are supermodels in their own right—except *these* improve with age.

Miami Beach   In the fabulous '50s, Miami Beach was America's Riviera. The stomping ground for the Rat Pack and mobsters like Meyer Lansky (and Al Capone before him), its huge, self-contained resorts became vacations unto themselves, complete with activities and entertainment. Then in the 1960s and '70s, people who fell in love with Miami began to buy apartments rather than rent hotel rooms. Tourism declined and many hotels fell into disrepair.

But since the late 1980s and South Beach renaissance, the Miami Beach revitalization wave has kept rolling. Huge beach resorts like the renovated, Vegas-y Fontainebleau (p. 48) have been finding their niche with new international tourist markets and attracting large convention crowds. New generations of Americans are quickly rediscovering the qualities that originally made Miami Beach so popular, and finding out that the sand and surf now come with a thriving international city—a technologically savvy city complete with free Wi-Fi with 95% coverage outside, which means on the sand, and 70% indoors up to the second floor of any building.

Before Miami Beach gives way to the city of Surfside comes North Beach, with uncrowded beaches, some restaurants, and examples of Miami modern architecture. For more on North Beach and its gradual renaissance, check www.gonorthbeach.com.

Surfside, Bal Harbour, and **Sunny Isles** make up the top of the barrier island of which Miami Beach is the bottom. Hotels, motels, restaurants, and beaches line Collins Avenue and, with some key exceptions, the farther north one goes, the more common cheaper lodging becomes. Excellent prices, location, and facilities make Surfside and Sunny Isles attractive places to stay, although, despite a slow-going renaissance, they can still be a little rough around the edges. Revitalization is in the works for these areas, and while it's unlikely they'll ever become as chic as South Beach, they do have that potential. Keep in mind that beachfront properties are at a premium, so many of the area's moderately priced hotels have been converted to condominiums, leaving fewer affordable options than in the past.

In exclusive and ritzy Bal Harbour, few hotels besides the swank One Bal Harbour and St. Regis remain amid the many beachfront condo towers. Instead, fancy homes, tucked away on the bay, hide behind gated communities, and the Rodeo Drive of Miami (known as the Bal Harbour Shops) attracts shoppers who don't bat an eye at four-, five-, and even six-figure price tags.

Note that **North Miami Beach,** a residential area near the Miami-Dade/Broward County line (north of 163rd St.; part of north Miami-Dade County), is a misnomer. It is actually northwest of Miami Beach, on the mainland, and has no beaches, though it does have some of Miami's better restaurants and shops. Located within North Miami Beach is the posh residential community of **Aventura,** best known for its high-priced high-rise condos, the Turnberry Isle Resort, and Aventura Mall.

Note: South Beach, the historic Art Deco District, is treated as a separate neighborhood from Miami Beach.

Key Biscayne   Forested and secluded, this is not part of the Florida Keys, but rather a barrier island south of Miami Beach, off the shores of Coconut Grove. It's connected to the mainland by the long Rickenbacker Causeway (with a $1.75 toll).

Largely an exclusive residential community with million-dollar homes and sweeping water views, Key Biscayne also offers visitors great public beaches, a top (read: pricey) resort hotel, world-class tennis facilities, and a few decent restaurants. Hobie Beach, adjacent to the causeway, is the city's premier spot for windsurfing, sailboarding, and jet-skiing (see "Outdoor Activities," p. 100). On the island's southern tip, **Bill Baggs State Park** has great beaches, bike paths, and dense forests for picnicking and partying.

Downtown   Miami's downtown boasts one of the world's coolest cityscapes. Unfortunately, that's about all it offers—for now. But while by day a vibrant community of students, businesspeople, and merchants make their way through bustling streets, where vendors sell fresh-cut pineapples and mangoes while young consumers on shopping sprees lug bags and boxes, at night, downtown is mostly desolate (except for NE 11th St., where there's a developing nightlife scene) and not a place where you'd want to get lost. Downtown does have a mall (Bayside Marketplace, where many cruise passengers come to browse), some culture (Metro-Dade Cultural Center), and a few decent restaurants, as well as the sprawling American Airlines Arena (home to the NBA's Miami Heat). A slow-going project to revitalize downtown promises a cultural arts center, urban-chic dwellings and lofts, and an assortment of hip boutiques, eateries, and bars, all to bring downtown back to a life it never really had. The city has even rebranded the downtown area with a new ad campaign, intentionally misspelling it as DWNTN in a bid to appeal to hipsters (yeah, I don't get it either). For details, check www.DowntownMiami.com.

Midtown/Wynwood What used to be called El Barrio is now one of Miami's hippest, still burgeoning areas. Just north of downtown and divided roughly by I-395 to the south, I-195 to the north, I-95 to the west, and Biscayne Boulevard on the east, Wynwood actually includes the Miami Design District, but has developed an identity of its own thanks to an exploding, albeit still gritty, arts scene made popular by a mix of cheap rents and corporate promotion including major exposure during Art Basel. Although there are still only a very small handful of bars and restaurants, Wynwood is an edgy area for creative types with loft and gallery spaces affordable (for now) and aplenty. Also within Wynwood is Midtown Miami, a mall-like town-center complex of apartment buildings surrounded by retailers—most notably Target—and restaurants. Like neighboring Wynwood, it's gritty and a work in progress favored by young hipster types who aren't averse to living in "transitional" areas.

Design District With restaurants springing up between galleries and furniture stores galore, the Design District is for some the new South Beach, adding a touch of New York's SoHo to an area formerly known as downtown Miami's "No Go." That's stretching it (no beach, usually not much sidewalk

traffic), but there's no question that the district, a hotbed for furniture-import companies, interior designers, architects, and more, has also become a player in Miami's ever-changing nightlife. Its bars, lounges, clubs, and restaurants—including one of Miami's best, **Michael's Genuine Food & Drink** (p. 72)—ranging from überchic and retro to progressive and indie, have helped the area become hipster central for SoBe refugees and artsy bohemian types. The district is loosely bounded by NE 2nd Avenue, NE 5th Avenue East and West, and NW 36th Street to the south. Details: www.MiamiDesignDistrict.net.

Biscayne Corridor From downtown, near Bayside, northward to the 70s (affectionately dubbed by some the Upper East Side), where trendy curio shops and upscale eateries keep opening, Biscayne Boulevard back in the day was Miami's main drag, but like South Beach fell on hard times, and its 1950s- and 1960s-era hotels (in that doo-wop style here dubbed "MiMo" for Miami Modern) turned dodgy and dilapidated. In recent years the area's been rehabbing itself as a safe and hip neighborhood where visitors and locals alike can wine, dine, and shop—with a big assist from Miamians fleeing the high rents of the beaches. They're renovating Biscayne block by block, trying to make this famous boulevard worthy of a weekend outing. Get lodging, dining, and other information at **www. MiMoBoulevard.org**.

Little Havana In this small section of Miami you will indeed get a taste of the sounds, tastes, and rhythms (if not so much the look) of Cuba's capital city, and you don't have to speak a word of English to live a full life here—everything is bilingual, and sometimes in Spanish only.

Cuban and other Latin coffee shops, tailor and furniture stores, and inexpensive eateries line Little Havana's main thoroughfare, SW 8th Street, better known as Calle Ocho (pronounced *Ka-yey O-choh*). Salsa and merengue throb from old record stores while elderly gents in *guayaberas* (loose-fitting button-down shirts) smoke cigars over games of dominoes. There's also something of a gallery and shopping scene. In fact, I highly recommend trying to make it here the last Friday of the month for the fun gallery night Viernes Cultural (Cultural Friday).

Coral Gables "The City Beautiful," designed by George Merrick in the early 1920s, was Miami's first planned development. Houses here were built in a Mediterranean style along lush, tree-lined streets named after places in Spain and Italy, opening onto beautifully carved plazas, many with centerpiece fountains. The best architectural examples of the era have Spanish-style tiled roofs and are built from Miami oolite, native limestone commonly called "coral rock." The Gables' European-flavored shopping and business district is home to quite a few international corporations, and throughout the city you'll find landmark hotels, great golfing, upscale shopping to rival Bal Harbour, and some of Greater Miami's best restaurants, helmed by renowned chefs. More details: www.CoralGablesChamber.org/Visit.

Coconut Grove An artsy, hippie hangout in the psychedelic '60s, Coconut Grove once was awash in locals in tie-dyed duds. Nowadays they seem to be more into the Gap. Chain stores, theme restaurants, a multiplex, and plenty of bars make the Grove a commercial success, but at the expense of more alternative types. Ritzier folks have taken their place, thanks in part to several luxury resorts. The neighborhood's heart is the intersection of Grand Avenue, Main Highway, and McFarlane Road, and the center of it all is CocoWalk, filled with boutiques, eateries, and bars. Sidewalks can get busy, especially at night when University of Miami students come out to play. The Grove is also notable for some of Miami's most fascinating tourist attractions, led by Vizcaya Mansion (p. 94). More details: www.CoconutGrove. com.

Southern Miami-Dade County To locals, South Miami is both a specific area, southwest of Coral Gables, and a general region that encompasses all of the county's southern reaches, including Kendall, Perrine, Cutler Ridge, the Redlands, and Homestead. For the purposes of clarity, this book has grouped all these southern suburbs under the rubric "southern Miami-Dade County." This heavily residential area is a mix of ugly strip malls with pockets of graciously upscale neighborhoods and some farmland. Tourists don't usually stay in these parts unless they're on their way to or from the Everglades or the Keys. However, southern Miami-Dade County contains some of the city's top attractions, meaning that you're likely to spend at least some time here.

GETTING AROUND

Officially, Miami-Dade County has opted for a "unified, multimodal transportation network" (translation into real-people-speak: you can get around the city by train, bus, and taxi). However, in practice, this would-be network doesn't work very well. Things have improved a bit thanks to the $17-billion "Peoples' Transportation Plan," which has offered a full range of transport services at several community-based centers throughout the county, but unless you are going from downtown Miami to a not-too-distant spot, you're mostly better off in a rental car or a cab.

Furthermore, with the exceptions of South Beach and the downtowns of Coconut Grove and Coral Gables, Miami is not really a walker's city. Because it's so spread out, most attractions are too far apart to make walking between them possible. In fact, most Miamians are so used to driving they'll hop in a car just to go several blocks.

By Public Transit

BY RAIL Two rail lines, operated by the **Metro-Dade Transit Agency** (www. co.Miami-Dade.FL.us/transit; ⓒ **305/770-3131**), run in concert.

Metrorail, the city's modern train system, is a 25-mile, 23-station elevated line that runs mostly between downtown Miami and the southern suburbs. Some locals have referred to this semi-useless network as Metro*fail*. If you're staying in Coral Gables or Coconut Grove, you can park your car at a nearby station and ride the rails downtown. Utility has improved a bit with the extension of a line to Miami International Airport, but trains still don't go most places tourists go, except for Vizcaya (p. 94) in the Grove. Metrorail operates daily from about 5am to midnight. The fare is $2.25.

Metromover, a 4½-mile elevated line, circles the downtown area and connects with Metrorail at the Government Center stop. Riding on rubber tires, the single- or double-car train winds past many of the area's major attractions and its shopping and business districts, running 5am to midnight. You may not go very far on the Metromover, but you will get cool views from the towering height of the suspended rails. System hours are daily from 5am to midnight, and the ride is free.

BY BUS   Miami has various bus routes, but its sprawling layout just isn't very conducive to getting around this way; instead of getting to know Miami, you'll find that relying on public buses will acquaint you only with how it feels to wait at bus stops. In short, it's a grueling experience. Maps are available by mail, either from the Greater Miami Convention and Visitor's Bureau (see "Visitor Information," p. 36) or by emailing Miami-Dade Transit via the website above. Locally, call ☎ **305/770-3131** for public-transit information. In South Beach, the **South Beach Local** is more doable, running every 12 to 20 minutes from South Pointe to Collins Park at 21st Street and Park Avenue (as well as across to Belle Isle and Alton Road) from 8:40am to 12:30am Monday through Saturday and 11am to 12:30am on Sunday. Regular bus fare is $2.25.

By Car

Unless you're staying exclusively in South Beach or are headed directly to the port for a cruise, anyone counting on exploring Miami to even a modest degree needs a car. Many restaurants, hotels, and attractions are far from one another, so any other form of transportation is pretty much impractical.

When driving across a causeway or through downtown, allow extra time to reach your destination because of frequent drawbridge openings. Some bridges open about every half-hour for large sailing vessels to make their way through the wide bays and canals that crisscross the city, stalling traffic for several minutes.

RENTALS   It seems as though every car-rental company, big and small, has at least one office in Miami, making it one of the cheaper places in the world to rent wheels. Many firms regularly advertise rates in the neighborhood of $150 per week for their economy cars. You should also check with your airline: There might be special discounts when you book a flight and reserve your rental car simultaneously. A minimum age, generally 25, is usually required of renters (some agencies have also set maximum ages).

Locally present national car-rental companies include **Alamo** (www.Alamo.com; ☎ **877/222-9075**), **Avis** (www.Avis.com; ☎ **800/331-1212**), **Budget** (www.Budget.com; ☎ **800/527-0700**), **Dollar** (www.Dollar.com; ☎ **800/800-4000**), **Hertz** (www.Hertz.com; ☎ **800/654-3131**), **National** (www.NationalCar.com; ☎ **877/222-9058**), and **Thrifty** (www.Thrifty.com; ☎ **800/847-4389**). One excellent company that has offices in every conceivable part of town and offers extremely competitive rates is **Enterprise** (www.Enterprise.com; ☎ **800/261-7331**).

Comparison shop before you make any decisions—car-rental prices can fluctuate more than airfares. Many companies also offer GPS rentals.

Finally, think about splurging on a convertible, which offers one of the best ways to enjoy the beautiful surroundings (while getting a tan).

PARKING   Keep quarters on hand to feed meters, but many have already been replaced by payment stations that you feed cash or credit card and get a printed receipt to display on your dash. Street parking is increasingly tricky in South Beach, downtown, and the centers of Coconut Grove and Coral Gables, and fines for illegal parking can be stiff, starting at $18 for an expired meter and going way up from there.

In addition to parking garages, valet services are commonplace. Because parking is such a premium in South Beach as well as in Coconut Grove, rates tend to be jacked up—especially when there are special events. You can expect to pay $10 to $20 for valeting in these areas (as well as SoBe garages, especially on weekends in season).

LOCAL DRIVING RULES   Florida law allows drivers to make a right turn on a red light after a complete stop, unless otherwise indicated. In addition, all passengers are required to wear seat belts, and children 3 and under must be securely fastened in government-approved car seats.

By Taxi

If you're not planning on moving around much within Miami (and especially if you plan to hang out pretty much just in South Beach), an occasional taxi is a good alternative to renting a car and dealing with the parking hassles that come with that. Meters start at about $2.50 for the first ⅙ of a mile and cost around $2.40 for each additional mile. There are standard flat-rate charges for popular routes—for example, Miami Beach's Convention Center to Coconut Grove will cost about $26. Many cabs have a fuel surcharge of $1 per person. For specifics on rates, check www.TaxiFareFinder.com.

Major cab companies include **Yellow Cab** (✆ 305/444-4444) and, on Miami Beach, **Central Cab** (✆ 305/532-5555).

By Bike

For reasons of traffic and sprawl, getting around longer distances in Greater Miami is a challenge. But some smaller areas can be a biker's paradise, such as Key Biscayne and especially Miami Beach, where the hard-packed sand and boardwalks make for easy and scenic routes, and the city's compact size makes it easy to get around.

Miami Beach and Surfside are now also among the growing number of European and U.S. cities with bike-share programs. The local version is **Deco Bike** (✆ 305/532-9494), with more than 100 solar-powered stations that let you use a credit card to rent bikes at one and drop off at another; rates range from $4 for a half hour to $24 for a full day. For more info and a map of stations, log on to www.DecoBike.com. Other parts of Miami are expected to add their own versions by 2015.

[FastFACTS] MIAMI

Area Code   The original area code for Miami and all of Miami-Dade County is 305; it has since been joined by area code 786. All local calls, even just across the street, require dialing the area code (305 or 786) first.

Business Hours   Banking hours vary, but most banks are open weekdays from 9am to 3pm. Several stay open until 5pm or so at least 1 day during the week, and most banks feature automated teller machines (ATMs) for 24-hour banking.

Most stores are open daily from 10am to 6pm; however, there are many exceptions (noted in "Practical Matters: The Shopping Scene," in chapter 8, p. 108). As for business offices, Miami is generally a 9-to-5 town.

Dentists If you're in absolute need of a dentist, go to www.1800dentist. com. Or contact Dr. Jean Jacques Edderai, who specializes in emergency dental work and features a 24/7 dental service (www.North MiamiBeachDentist.com; ☎ **305/947-7999**).

Doctors/Hospitals In an emergency, call an ambulance by dialing ☎ **911** (a free call) from any phone. The Dade County Medical Association sponsors a physician referral service (☎ **305/324-8717**), available weekdays from 9am to 4:30pm.

The better local hospitals include **Aventura Hospital** in Aventura (2845 Aventura Blvd., www.AventuraHospital. com; ☎ **305/682-7000**); **Baptist Hospital** in west Miami (8900 N. Kendall Dr., www.BaptistHealth.net; ☎ **786/596-1960**); **Doctors Hospital** in Coral Gables (5000 University Dr., www. BaptistHealth.net; ☎ **786/ 308-3000**); **Jackson Memorial/University of Miami** (1611 NW 12th Ave.; www.JacksonHealth.org; ☎ **305/585-1111**); and **Mount Sinai** in Miami Beach (4300 Alton Rd.); www.MSMC.com; ☎ **305/ 674-2121**). Avoid **Mercy Hospital.**

Emergencies To reach the police, an ambulance, or the fire department, dial ☎ **911** from any phone; no coins are needed. Emergency hot lines include **Switchboard of Miami** for crisis intervention (☎ **305/ 358-4357**) and the **Poison**

Information Center (☎ **800/222-1222**).

Internet Access Free public Wi-Fi is available in parts of Miami, including downtown and Miami Beach (though honestly, I find the signal often iffy), as well as at Starbucks and in South Beach at **Caffè di Mauro,** 1464 Washington Ave. (☎ **305/673-5774**), open daily from 8am 'til midnight, and **Cybr Caffe**, 1574 Washington Ave. (☎ **305/ 534-0057**), open daily from 9am to 11pm.

Liquor Laws Only adults 21 or older may legally purchase or consume alcohol in the state of Florida. Minors are usually permitted in bars, as long as the bars also serve food. Liquor laws are strictly enforced; if you look young, carry identification. Beer and wine are sold in most supermarkets and convenience stores. Most of the city of Miami's liquor stores are closed on Sunday. Liquor stores in the city of Miami Beach are open daily.

Lost Property If you lost something at the airport, call the **Airport Lost and Found** office (☎ **305/ 876-7377**). If you lost it on the bus, Metrorail, or Metromover, call **Metro-Dade Transit Agency** (☎ **305/ 770-3131**).

Newspapers & Magazines The *Miami Herald* is the county's only English-language daily. Not surprisingly, it's especially known for its extensive Latin America/Caribbean coverage. It also has a decent Friday

"Weekend" entertainment guide. The most respected alternative weekly is the giveaway tabloid *New Times,* which contains up-to-date listings and reviews of food, films, theater, music, and whatever else is happening in town. Also free, if you can find it, is *Ocean Drive,* an oversize glossy magazine that's limited on text (no literary value) and heavy on ads and society photos. It's what you should read if you want to know who's who and where to go for fun; it's available at a number of chic South Beach boutiques and restaurants, as well as on some newsstands. In the same vein and also free, *Miami Magazine* has slightly more literary value in addition to the gloss, and it's also a bit more widely available.

For a large selection of newspapers and magazines in both English and other languages, try **News Café,** 800 Ocean Dr., South Beach (☎ **305/538-6397**), as well as branches of **Books and Books** in South Beach (927 Lincoln Rd.; ☎ **305/532-3222**) and Coral Gables (265 Aragon Ave.; ☎ **305/ 442-4408**).

Pharmacies **Walgreens Pharmacy** has countless locations all over the county, including in South Beach on Collins Ave. at Fifth St., 23rd St., and Lincoln Rd., as well as one at 1845 Alton Rd. Then there's **CVS,** which is usually located wherever there's a Walgreens. **Navarro** is a local Latin pharmacy chain you'll see in mainland Miami.

Police   For emergencies, dial 𝄟 **911** from any phone. No coins are needed for this call. For other police matters, call 𝄟 **305/595-6263.**

Post Office   Conveniently located post offices include 1300 Washington Ave. in South Beach, 251 Valencia Ave. in Coral Gables, and 3191 Grand Ave. in Coconut Grove. There's one central number for all: 𝄟 **800/275-8777.**

Restrooms   Stores rarely knowingly let customers use their bathrooms, and as a rule restaurants reserve theirs for patrons. However, most malls have restrooms, as do fast-food restaurants. Public beaches and large parks often provide toilets, though in some places you may have to pay or tip an attendant. Most large hotels have clean restrooms in their lobbies.

Safety   As always, use your common sense and be aware of your surroundings at all times. Don't walk alone at night, and be extra wary when walking or driving through downtown Miami and especially its surrounding areas. Certain residential streets west of Coconut Grove's commercial center also merit caution when on foot.

Reacting to several highly publicized crimes against tourists several years ago, local and state governments alike have taken additional steps to help protect visitors. These measures include special highly visible police units patrolling the airport and surrounding neighborhoods, and better signs on the state's most tourist-traveled routes.

Taxes   A 6% state sales tax (plus 1% local tax, for a total of 7% in Miami-Dade County [from Homestead to North Miami Beach]) is added on at the register for all goods and services purchased in Florida. In addition, most municipalities levy special taxes on restaurants and hotels. In Surfside, hotel taxes total 12%; in Bal Harbour, 11; in Miami Beach (including South Beach) and the rest of Miami-Dade County, 13%. Food and beverage tax in Miami Beach, Bal Harbour, and Surfside is 9%; in Miami-Dade restaurants not located inside hotels, it's 8%, and in restaurants located in hotels 9%.

Time Zone   Miami, like New York, is in the Eastern Standard Time (EST) zone. Between the second Sunday of March and the first Sunday of November, daylight saving time is adopted, and clocks are set 1 hour ahead. America's eastern seaboard is 5 hours behind Greenwich Mean Time.

Transit Information   For Metrorail or Metromover schedule information, transit over to www.MiamiDade.gov/Transit or call 𝄟 **305/891-3131.**

Weather   Hurricane season in Miami runs June through November. For an up-to-date recording of current weather conditions and forecast reports, call 𝄟 **305/229-4522.** Also see the "When to Go" section in chapter 2 for more information on the weather.

WHERE TO STAY IN MIAMI

Hotels and resorts have been part of the mix in Miami ever since magnate Henry Flagler's railroad opened South Florida up to well-heeled tourism from chillier climes. The boom has gone on steroids in recent years, mostly in Miami Beach, whose renaissance from the late 1980s onward turned what used to be a beachfront retirement community dubbed "God's waiting room" into a hot spot for an eclectic mix of both jetsetters and regular folks from across the planet. And while the fanciest/priciest spots get much of the attention, there are also affordable options that can put you right in the thick of the action.

Particularly in South Miami Beach, many of the old hotels from the 1930s through the '50s have been transformed into chic new boutique hotels, and more come online each year (in fact, when booking you may want to ask if any construction or renovation will be going on during your stay). Also keep in mind when choosing a hotel that particularly in South Beach, the scene on streets like Ocean Drive or Collins and Washington avenues is all about the party, not getting a good night's sleep (it may help a bit to ask for a room at the rear of the property).

Furthermore, farther north in Miami Beach you'll find a slew of affordably priced options an easy cab or bus ride away—more than a few of them directly on the sand, even. And of course across the causeways on mainland Miami are yet more, especially in areas such as downtown, Coral Gables, and Coconut Grove—closer to the many other attractions and landmarks that make Miami unique, while still within easy driving distances of South Beach.

The aim here is to highlight the most affordable hotels and resorts, but also those in all price ranges that in some way best reflect the character and history of Miami.

PRACTICAL MATTERS: THE MIAMI HOTEL SCENE

SEASONS & RATES   South Florida's tourist season begins in mid-November and lasts until Easter, though if you ask the city's most ardent spin doctors, the season now lasts year-round. It all depends on where and when you're here and what's going on at the time. Hotel prices escalate until about March, after which they begin to decline. During the off-season, hotel rates are typically 30% to 50% lower than their winter highs. But timing isn't everything. Rates also depend on your hotel's proximity to the

PRICE categories

Expensive	Above $250
Moderate	$150–$250
Inexpensive	Under $150

beach and how much ocean you can see from your window. Small motels a block or two from the water can be up to 40% cheaper than similar properties right on the sand.

Rates are broken down into two broad categories: winter (generally, Thanksgiving through Easter) and off-season (about mid-May through Aug). The months in between, the shoulder season, should fall somewhere in between the highs and lows, while rates always go up on holidays. Remember, too, that state and city taxes can add as much as 12.5% to your bill in some parts of Miami. Some hotels, especially those in South Beach, also tack on additional service charges, and don't forget that parking is a pricey endeavor.

LONG-TERM STAYS If you plan to visit for a month, a season, or more, think about renting a condominium, apartment, or a room in a long-term hotel. Long-term lodgings exist in every price category and in general are extremely reasonable, especially during the off-season. Check with the reservation services below, or write a short note to the chamber of commerce in the area where you plan to stay. In addition, many local real estate agents handle short-term rentals (meaning less than a year).

RESERVATION SERVICES Central Reservation Service (www.Reservation-Services.com; ☏ **800/950-0232**) works with many of Miami's hotels and can often secure discounts of up to 40%. It also gives advice on specific locales, especially in Miami Beach and downtown. During holiday time, there may be a 3- to 5-day minimum stay required to use its services. Call or log on for details.

For bed-and-breakfast information across the state, check **Florida Bed and Breakfast Inns** (www.Florida-Inns.com; ☏ **561/223-9550**). For details on the boutique hotels ubiquitous in Miami Beach and scattered across the county, check the **Greater Miami Convention and Visitor's Bureau**'s site, **www.MiamiBoutiqueHotels.com**.

MIAMI BEACH
Expensive

Delano South Beach ★★★ The dean of SoBe boutique hoteldom is still very much holding its own 2 decades after Ian Schrager and Philippe Starck remade Robert Swartburg's 1947 classic, launching an international trend of white-on-white decor, tall billowy curtains, poolside beds, and hipper/than-thou vibe (in fact, it jacked up rates quite a bit in 2014). Much of it is still in place, though the sterility of all the white in the rooms is now relieved by touches of color, especially green, and the attitude dialed back slightly. The Delano very much remains a player, with the Vegas outfit now managing the restaurant and bars—the Rose Bar (p. 130), FDR (p. 129), and Delano Beach Club—deploying a nighttime doorman to keep the riffraff out. The Umi sushi/sake bar serves some superlative stuff (love the "big eye tuna pizza"), and under Neapolitan chef Luciano Sautto, the organic Italian menu at Bianca is a revelation. Offerings are rounded out by a sweet little spa upstairs and a state-of-the-art basement gym.

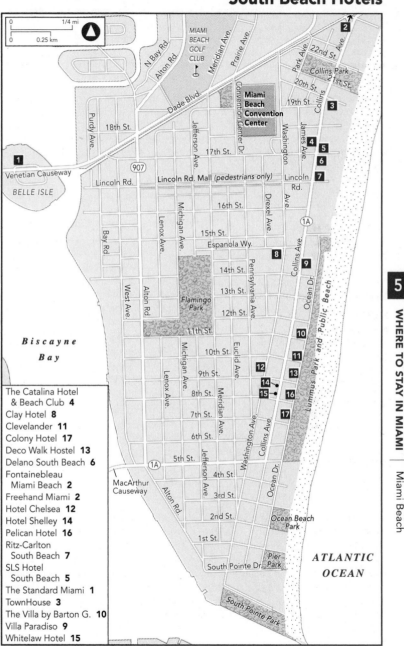

The Catalina Hotel
  & Beach Club **4**
Clay Hotel **8**
Clevelander **11**
Colony Hotel **17**
Deco Walk Hostel **13**
Delano South Beach **6**
Fontainebleau
  Miami Beach **2**
Freehand Miami **2**
Hotel Chelsea **12**
Hotel Shelley **14**
Pelican Hotel **16**
Ritz-Carlton
  South Beach **7**
SLS Hotel
  South Beach **5**
The Standard Miami **1**
TownHouse **3**
The Villa by Barton G. **10**
Villa Paradiso **9**
Whitelaw Hotel **15**

And if you're wondering what that aroma is in the public areas, it's green tea and lemongrass.

1685 Collins Ave. (at 17th St.), South Beach. www.Delano-Hotel.com. (✆ **800/555-5001** or 305/672-2000. 194 units, including 1 penthouse. Winter from $795 city view, $1,550 suite, $2,500 bungalow, $4,300 penthouse; off-season from $645 city view, $1,250 suite, $1,300 bungalow, $3,400 penthouse. Extra person $50. Valet parking $37 overnight. Pets accepted up to 20 lbs. ($100 per stay). **Amenities:** 3 restaurants; 3 bars; children's program (seasonal); concierge; gym; outdoor pool; room service; spa; Wi-Fi is $15 per day for up to 3 devices.

Fontainebleau Miami Beach ★★★ Ring-a-ding-ding is back in the swing at a longtime classic designed by Morris Lapidus in the 1950s a couple of dozen blocks above South Beach—with today's glam supplied not by Elvis, Marlene Dietrich, and the Rat Pack but the likes of Lady Gaga, Katy Perry, and Pitbull. Renovated and expanded to the tune of a cool billion dollars in 2008, this three-tower behemoth sprawling over 20 acres provides enough amenities and variety to please a wide spectrum, from party-hearty types and urban sophisticates to families and conventioneers (those seeking a quiet hideaway, not so much). A dozen bars, lounges, and eateries include three top destination restaurants: Scarpetta (Italian), Hakkasan (Chinese; my favorite for atmospherics), and Gotham Steak. The main lobby Bleau Bar, meanwhile, is quite the nighttime vision in glowing pink and blue. Out back is an impressive network of pools large and small, loud and laid-back. The 40,000-square-foot Lapis Spa lays on water circuits, rain rooms, the works. Guest rooms, both comfortable and functional, are contemporary with a touch of retro (just watch that minibar; lift it for more than 20 seconds, you've bought it).

> ## Checking into Hotel Bars
>
> While South Beach is known for its trendy club scene, hotel bars all over Miami are also very much a part of the nightlife—and may affect your choice of digs. Among the choice watering holes in the properties listed here are the **Rose Bar** and **FDR** at the Delano, **Hyde Beach** at the SLS, the **Broken Shaker** at the Freehand, and **MO Bar** at the Mandarin Oriental. For others, see "Swankest Hotel Bars," p. 131.

4441 Collins Ave. (north of W. 44th St.), mid-Miami Beach. www.Fontainebleau.com. (✆ **800/548-8886** or 305/538-2000. 1,504 units. Winter from $429 double, from $509 suite; off-season from $259 double, from $299 suite. Valet $38 overnight, $25 day visitor, $20/day resort fee (includes Wi-Fi). Pets welcome (one-time fee $100). **Amenities:** 12 restaurants/lounges; concierge; fitness center; 11 pools with cabanas; spa; 6 shops; nightclub; beach access/service; room service; kitchenette in suites; iMacs with high-speed Internet.

Pelican Hotel ★★ The Delano often gets the credit for launching the South Beach boutique hotel boom, but this bird actually took wing a bit earlier, launched in 1994 by Italian clothing/accessories brand Diesel. With a company whose motto is "Only stupid can be truly brilliant," you wouldn't expect conventionality. Each of this green triple-decker Deco landmark's 25 themed rooms is a cheeky original, often with names to match ("Me Tarzan, You Vain," "Bang a Boomerang," and of course "Best Whorehouse"). No pool, but hey, the Atlantic is a boomerang's toss away. The main amenity of note is a 30-seat sidewalk restaurant specializing in Italian seafood (try the salmon with porcini mushrooms).

826 Ocean Dr. (btw. 8th and 9th sts.), South Beach. www.PelicanHotel.com. (✆ **800/773-5422** or 305/673-3373. 25 units. Winter $359–$399 double; off-season $165–$220 double. Valet parking $25.

Pets welcome up to 30 lbs. ($100 plus $25/day). **Amenities:** Restaurant; bar; concierge; passes to area fitness centers; room service; free Wi-Fi.

Ritz-Carlton South Beach ★★★   This isn't your usual Ritz-Carlton, full of formal frippery. This one's gone native, a more laid-back 2004 reincarnation of the midcentury MiMo ("Miami Modern") Hotel Di Lido designed in the early 1950s by the iconic Morris Lapidus. It's since become one of my favorite SoBe luxe mixes of pedigree, location, family-friendliness, and services, situated both on the beach and literally at the crossroads of South Beach, Lincoln Road, and Collins Avenue, an easy walk to most everything. The interior has preserved much of the MiMo flavor while sprinkling contemporary touches—not to mention $2 million worth of world-class art, such as the striking pieces in the lobby from Catalan modern masters Joan Miró and Antoni Tàpies. The pool is still pretty buzzy much of the time—and especially during Sunday champagne brunch, which you'll want to reserve when you book your room. Restaurantwise, the One LR Bistro does a lovely contemporary American/Spanish menu, but for livin' *la vida* SoBe, the DiLido Beach Club out back is hard to beat.

1 Lincoln Rd. (Collins Ave.), South Beach. www.RitzCarlton.com. ✆ **800/241-3333** or 786/276-4000. 375 units. Winter from $499 double, suites from $749; off-season from $299 double, suites from $359. Valet parking $38 overnight, $27 day visit. Pets 25 lbs. or less welcome ($250 one-time charge). **Amenities:** 2 restaurants; 2 bars; various shops; babysitting; beach access/service; children's program; fitness center; outdoor heated pool; 24/7 room service; spa; watersports equipment/rentals; Wi-Fi $10/day.

SLS Hotel South Beach ★★★   This reincarnation of yet another Art Deco beachfront hotel by maestro Morris Lapidus, the 1939 Ritz Plaza was reborn to much celebrity-studded fanfare in 2012. The stylish decor by Philippe Starck (who helped launch the local boutique-hotel trend in 1995 with his work at the Delano next door) mixes elegance with playfulness and a touch of sexy; walls of the white rooms, for example, sport canvas printed with squiggles winking at Louis XV villa paneling (other touches: one of the best rainfall showers I've experienced, and an, ahem, artfully placed mirror over the bed). The other big influence is Spanish celebrity chef José Andrés—as in the front-lobby bar accented in red, black, and shots of vintage Spanish divas; and especially in the main Bazaar restaurant, with a masterful menu of Spain-meets-Florida-meets-Latin-America-meets-Singapore. Katsuya delivers sleek Japanese, and out back the social scene snaps, crackles, and pops at a bar, two pool decks, and Hyde Beach, which serves lunch but turns into a nightlife must when the sun goes down. The location is super convenient for various highlights such as Lincoln Road, Ocean Drive, and even the Bass Art Museum.

1701 Collins Ave. (at 17th St.), South Beach. SLSHotels.com/SouthBeach. ✆ **800/548-8886** or 305/674-1701. 140 rooms, including 10 villas. Winter from $415 double; off-season $285 double. Resort fee of $30/day includes Wi-Fi. Valet parking ($44 overnight, $30 day visit; municipal parking nearby). Pets up to 25 lbs. welcome ($150 one-time fee). **Amenities:** 2 pools; beach services; 3 restaurants; bar/lounge; fitness room; spa/beauty services; iPad in rooms.

The Standard Miami ★★★   Slightly off the beaten track on a small, condo-crammed island linked to South Beach by the Venetian Causeway, hotshot hotelier André Balazs rescued the decrepit 1950s Lido Spa and in 2005 transformed it into an adults-only boutique oasis whose spa facilities and services are very much the star of the show, with the longest list in town of wellness treatments and dozens of sundry activities and classes focusing on fitness, meditation, and beyond—some of which I'd never even heard of. Despite the cool factor, the vibe is mellow and non-"scene-y," with rocking chairs in the lobby and guests padding around in white waffle robes (though I've also been to promoter events here that import a touch of more stereotypical SoBe glitz). Decor blends Scandinavian-mod with leftover 50s notes (like the lobby's terrazzo floor and the entire facade); rooms are organized around landscaped central gardens crowned by a huge infinity pool right on Biscayne Bay (a pool, by the way, with soothing music piped underwater); and on-premises dining focuses on organic Mediterranean fare, with plenty to keep vegetarians happy, too. A way different way to do South Beach, for sure.

40 Island Ave., Belle Isle, Miami Beach. www.StandardHotels.com. ✆ **305/673-1717.** 100 units. $349–$1,249; off-season $199–$749. Day pass $75 Mon–Thurs; $125 Fri–Sun. Additional daily $20 resort fee. Valet parking $37 overnight, day visit from $10. Pets up to 25 lbs. permitted (one-time fee $150). **Amenities:** Restaurant; bar; concierge; fitness center including Pilates and yoga; pool; sauna; spa; mani-pedi salon; shops; lounge with ping-pong/foosball; acupuncturist and holistic MD; 24-hour room service; free Wi-Fi.

The Villa by Barton G. ★★★   It's fair to say this Ocean Drive hotel is unique not just in Miami but probably the world. For 'tis the former Versace Mansion, the 1930 Mediterranean manse transformed into an over-the-top party palace by the eponymous flamboyant Italian designer murdered on its front steps in 1997. After many ups and downs, the newest owners reopened it in 2014, under the management of local restaurateur/impresario Barton G. Weiss, to one-percenters itching to indulge in the sybaritic likes of enormous themed suites worthy of a Renaissance prince (with frescoed walls and ceilings, original paintings, the works); a pool inlaid with a thousand mosaic tiles (including 24-karat gold); a cozy watering hole with an onyx bar; rooftop sundeck; and an indoor/outdoor Mediterranean restaurant with $58 entrees.

1116 Ocean Dr. (at 11th St.). www.TheVillabyBartonG.com. ✆ **305/573-8003.** 10 suites. Winter $1,050–$5,000, low season $695–$1,950. **Amenities:** Restaurant; bar; 2 lounges; pool; spa services; free Wi-Fi.

Moderate

The Catalina Hotel & Beach Club ★★   Ready for the over-the-top, booze-and-bikinis side of South Beach? If you caught a show on the CW in 2012 called *The Catalina,* you pretty much know what's coming. This centrally located property dates from 1952, and whether or not it is, as it claims, SoBe's "coolest hotel," young owner Nathan Lieberman is certainly trying his darnedest (for example, free happy-hour cocktails followed by two hours of all you can drink for $25). It's actually three hotels combined into one, with the "rock star" rooms in the middle building more bare-bones and designed for partying, the rest more stylish and a bit quieter. Similarly, the "bamboo pool" out back is mellow while the rooftop pool is meant for loud music, going topless, and general carryings on. One of the in-house restaurants, Maxine's Bistro, is

Hotel Dining	
Few would choose a hotel by its dining options, but some of Miami's best restaurants can be found inside hotels, with top tables besides the ones mentioned in this chapter including the W's **The Dutch** and **Mr Chow,** the Setai's **The Restaurant,** Casa Tua's eponymous	eatery, the Betsy Hotel's **BLT Steak,** the Sanctuary's **Ola,** JW Marriott Marquis' **db Bistro Moderne,** EPIC's **Area 31,** Fairmont Turnberry's **Bourbon Steak, Traymore** in Metropolitan by Como, and **Nobu** at the Shore Club.

open 24/7, and the other, Kung Fu Sushi, stays open after midnight. It's not everybody's cup of hooch, but if Snooki and The Situation are your role models, hey, knock yourself out.

1732 Collins Ave. (btw. 17th and 18th sts.), South Beach. www.CatalinaHotel.com. © **877/762-3477** or 305/674-1160. 190 units. Winter $225–$300 double; off-season $125–$250 double. Rates include continental breakfast bar and unlimited happy-hour cocktails daily from 7–8pm. Valet parking $32 overnight, $20 day visit. Pets accepted (up to 20 lbs.) at no charge. **Amenities:** 2 restaurants; 3 bars; 2 outdoor pools; complimentary airport shuttle; beach-club access; spa services, nightclub & gym passes; free bikes; high-speed Wi-Fi ($15/day).

Clevelander ★★   This 1938 Art Deco classic is an Ocean Drive standout because its entire "front yard" is one big watering hole, hopping and bopping day and night. Staff is usually great, and the 60 rooms are comfortable (if on the small side) and pretty stylish in a deco-meets-mod kind of way since its $50-million refurb in 2009. But really, it's all about the partying, above all on the aforementioned "pool patio" (yes, there is a pool in there somewhere), attended by hot girls in Hooters-like getups. And should you desire to catch "da game" while partying, there's a wall of TV screens in the sports bar at the back. Two more opportunities a little higher up come in the form of roof spaces equipped with what I can only describe as tiled wading pools, as well as (of course) bars. As for getting any sleep—well, you didn't come here to sleep, did you?

1020 Ocean Dr. (at 10th St.), South Beach. www.Clevelander.com. © **877/532-4006** or 305/532-4006. 60 units. Doubles $212–$309 in winter; $178–$296 off-season. Valet parking $34 overnight (municipal lots nearby). **Amenities:** Cafe; 5 bars; concierge; outdoor pool; rooftop deck; room service; free Wi-Fi.

Hotel Chelsea ★★   Another Deco building (1936) turned hotel, the Chelsea is intimate and nicely renovated, from the terrazzo-floored lobby to smallish but soothing rooms in beige and dark wood (designed, the owners say, according to feng-shui principles). But probably the main thing is its central location—not on Ocean Drive or even Collins Avenue, but one more block in, on Washington, lined with oodles of restaurants and nightspots (so no on-premises restaurant is no biggie). And although it's not party central as, say, the Catalina or Clevelander are, the target audience here is similar, so the lobby bar does its best to kick things up a notch at night with the help of a DJ. Before heading out for the evening, some guests grab a cocktail from said bar and hang at one of the tables or orange sofas on the marble-tiled patio out front to scope out the action on the avenue. If this matters to you, by the way: the Wi-Fi's better the closer you are to the lobby, but the music of course is louder.

944 Washington Ave. (btw. 9th and 10th sts.), South Beach. www.TheHotelChelsea.com. © **305/534-4069.** 42 units. Winter $195–$350 double, $165–$295 king, $200–$450 mini-suite; off-season $176–$295 double, $125–$195 king, $115–$165 mini-suite. Valet parking ($32 overnight, day visit $20; municipal parking nearby). Pets accepted (up to 40 lbs.) at no charge. **Amenities:** Bar; free shuttle to/from MIA; concierge; ATM; guest passes to local clubs; complimentary happy hour 7–8pm daily; free Wi-Fi.

Townhouse ★★   If you're into chic SoBe boutique hotels with attitude, usually you need to brace yourself for chic boutique rates, which is why the five-story Townhouse, built in 1939 and given its current incarnation by New York restaurateur Jonathan Morr and Paris designer India Mahdavi, could be a value worth bookmarking. A half-block in from the beach, its vibe is minimalist and white, from the lobby to the 69 rooms. Notable features include a bougainvillea-accented roof deck where I've attended my share of parties, and at press time the basement restaurant was closed to

Miami Beach

THE best HOTEL SPAS

o **Club Essentia at the Delano,** 1685 Collins Ave., South Beach (☎ **305/673-6100**), overlooks the Atlantic from the top of SoBe's original boutique hotel (p. 46) and features the stellar likes of a milk-and-honey massage that make it popular with celebs and laywomen alike. Lose yourself in a revitalizing tub of fragrant oils, algae, or minerals, or try the collagen, mud, and hydrating masks.

o **Bliss Spa at the W South Beach,** 2201 Collins Ave., South Beach (☎ **305/938-3123**), probably the hippest spa in town, offers rad treatments including the Ginger Rub, Hangover Herbie, Betweeny Wax, and Triple Oxygen Treatment.

o **The Ritz-Carlton Key Biscayne Spa,** 415 Grand Bay Dr., Key Biscayne (☎ **786/365-4197**), is a sublime, 20,000-square-foot West Indies–colonial style Eden with dozens of treatments such as a Piña Cola Body Polisher and a "Signature Tropical Paradise Hydrating Wrap" with a choice of mandarin orange or papaya pineapple.

o **The Standard,** 40 Island Ave., Belle Isle (☎ **305/704-3945**), is a 21st-century version of an old-school, Borscht Belt–style Miami Beach *schvitz,* but with plenty of New Age touches and treatments added. It features an authentic Turkish hammam and cedar sauna room, plus outside there's a splendid pool right on the bay.

o **Turnberry Isle Miami,** 19999 W. Country Club Dr., Aventura (☎ **305/933-6930**), offers 25,000 sprawling square feet with a voluminous array of treatments, Finnish saunas, Turkish steam rooms, turbulent whirlpools, and bracing cold-plunge tubs that are sure to give you a lift—gentle or bracing, as you wish.

o **The Spa at Mandarin Oriental,** 500 Brickell Key Dr., downtown (☎ **305/913-8332**), is a luxe, tri-level spa in an island hotel (p. 56) that attracts the likes of Jennifers Aniston and Lopez. It's known for innovative, restorative treatments inspired by the traditions of Chinese, Ayurvedic, European, Balinese, and Thai cultures. The 17 treatment rooms are done up in bamboo, rice paper, glass, and natural linens, and two split-level suites include multi-jet tubs and views over Biscayne Bay.

o **Canyon Ranch Hotel & Spa Miami Beach,** 6801 Collins Ave., Miami Beach

transition to an "upscale European pub." Noise an issue? Ask for a room away from Collins Avenue.

150 20th St. (at Collins Ave.), South Beach. www.TownhouseHotel.com. ☎ **877/534-3800** or 305/534-3800. 69 units. Winter $175–$275 double; off-season $108–$165 double. Rates include Continental breakfast. **Amenities:** Restaurant; bar; roof deck; bike rental; beach service; concierge; workout stations; washing machines; valet parking ($34 overnight, $20 visitors); room service; free Wi-Fi.

Villa Paradiso ★★   One of the various low-slung converted Art Deco apartment buildings up and down this stretch of Collins Avenue, this one, currently run by Frenchman Pascal Nicolle, houses 17 studios and one-bedroom suites that are pretty

(📞 **305/514-7000**), is a spa's spa. The largest in Miami (70,000 square feet), its pampering is also among the most comprehensive, from traditional massages, scrubs, and treatments to ultimate health and wellness programs regulated by medical pros.

o **Lapis at the Fontainebleau Miami Beach,** 4441 Collins Ave., Miami Beach (📞 **305/674-4772**), may be located in Miami's hugest hotel (p. 48), but once inside, you'll feel like you're the only one in the universe, with highlights including a mineral water-jet pool with red-seaweed extract and heated hammam benches, and a massage combined with a series of electric currents that's like a nip/tuck without the nipping.

o **Acqualina Spa by ESPA,** 17875 Collins Ave., Sunny Isles Beach (📞 **305/918-6844**). The first of this elegant European brand in the United States, Acqualina is a luxurious two-story, 20,000-square-foot affair overlooking the Atlantic in a high-rise beach-resort city north of Miami Beach. It has 16 treatment rooms and the latest facials, advanced massages, and Ayurvedic experiences.

o **Exhale Spa at EPIC Hotel,** 270 Biscayne Blvd. Way, downtown (📞 **305/423-3900**), has 12,000 square feet on the 16th floor devoted to "lifestyle, mind and body," with treatments like a Japanese mushroom facial mask and a massage based on Chinese martial arts, plus programs such as "core fusion mind and body classes."

o **The Spa at Viceroy Miami,** 475 Brickell Ave., downtown (📞 **305/503-0369**). Designed by minimalism maestro Philippe Starck, this stunning 28,000 square feet on the 15th-floor looks like a funky-mod take on a library, what with the bookshelves and all. But most libraries don't sport sofas, fireplaces, dramatic downtown and river views, and most especially hot and cold sunken marble baths as well as treatment rooms featuring billowing white curtains.

o **The Spa at the Setai,** 2001 Collins Ave., South Beach (📞 **305/520-6900**), a stellar, Asian-style spa (in keeping with the rest of the property) that purports to derive its philosophy of relaxation from ancient Sanskrit legend, natural elixirs, eternal youth, and Asian treatments and ingredients such as green tea.

sweet. They don't have much in the way of views, looking out as they do over a lushly landscaped but narrow courtyard, yet by virtue of their wood floors and yellow walls they exude appealing warmth and coziness. Furniture's an eclectic mix—a spot of wicker here, midcentury chic there, Asian mod over there. If you're looking to spread out, maybe cook for yourself a bit, and enjoy some peace and quiet after a day at the beach or a night out on the town, this could be your hideaway right in the thick of things.

1415 Collins Ave. (btw. 14th and 15th sts.), South Beach. www.VillaParadisoHotel.com. 📞 **305/532-0616**. 17 units. Winter $165–$325; off-season $99–$185. Additional person $15. **Amenities:** Garden; free Wi-Fi.

Whitelaw Hotel ★★ Inside and out, white is indeed the law at this SoBe party-scene stalwart, another converted Deco building. The Whitelaw likes to tout its playfulness and hipness, starting with the motto, "clean sheets, hot water, stiff drinks" and moving right along to its whimsical decor—think Victorian-meets-*Barbarella*. Although stylish, fun, clean, and reasonably comfortable, rooms are smallish (as in most other local prewar building conversions), but the joint is definitely geared toward the more festive set who aren't going to be spending all that much time in them. Some of that partying is right on-site, meaning *mucho* boom-boom for chunks of each day and night in its bar and white-leather-padded lobby, spilling onto the terrace; the owners themselves allow that families and folks looking for peace and quiet should probably bark up a different tree. By the way, the bar here does a pretty good job with breakfast, lunch, and light dinner fare.

808 Collins Ave. (at 8th St.), South Beach. www.WhitelawHotel.com. ✆ **877/762-3477** or 305/398-7000. 49 units. Winter $165–$350 double/king; off-season $125–$295 double/king (may spike during special events). Valet parking ($32 overnight, $20 day visit; municipal lot nearby). Pets accepted (up to 40 lbs.) at no charge. **Amenities:** Bar/lounge/cafe; rooftop sundeck; free MIA airport shuttle; concierge; free nightclub passes; free Wi-Fi.

Inexpensive

Clay Hotel ★★ A real South Beach original with its pink stucco facade and striped awnings, the Clay has had a colorful history since the 1930s: Al Capone ran gambling out of here; Desi Arnaz launched the rumba craze; and showbiz has found it a tasty backdrop for TV shows and music videos, from *Miami Vice* onward. Its location is especially appealing for the little pedestrian lane alongside, Española Way, possibly Florida's most charming, European-feeling stretch, lined with fetching restaurants and boutiques (meanwhile, on Washington Avenue, a cafe called Delicious serves meal specials for Clay guests). For years this seven-building complex was a mix of hotel and hostel, and although the dorms are now reserved for language-school students, the private rooms are still among the best deals in town, starting at $100 per night. For its mix of comfort, ambience, location, and affordability, this is a primo SoBe bet. *Tips:* To cut down on dining bills, efficiencies are also available, and to cut down on noise at bedtime, request a room away from Española and Washington.

1438 Washington Ave. (at Española Wy.), South Beach. www.ClayHotel.com. ✆ **800/379-2529** or 305/534-2988. 137 units. Winter $120–$3000 double; off-season $100–$200 double. Specials available offering one night free or half-off. Valet parking $20 (municipal parking nearby). **Amenities:** Cafe; lounge; concierge; free Wi-Fi.

Colony Hotel ★★ It's nice to see that not all those restored Deco darlings along Ocean Drive are destined to become absurdly pricey. Built in the late 1930s as one of the first hotels designed by Miami Deco doyen Henry Hohauser, this is now an attractive deal both physically (conserving yet updating its distinctive period look in recent renovations) and fiscally (starting at less than $100 a night). Behind the famous blue-neon Colony sign, you'll find 4-dozen spiffy little rooms with all the necessary mod cons (including nice big flatscreen TVs), a front-lobby bar, and the Columbus restaurant specializing in Italian. All in all, eminently worth colonizing. ✆ **305/673-0088.** 48 units. Doubles $85–$160. Discounts for 5/7-night stays. Valet parking $24 overnight (municipal parking nearby). **Amenities:** Restaurant; bar; discounted club passes; iPhone dock; free Wi-Fi.

736 Ocean Dr. (btw. 7th and 8th sts.), South Beach. www.ColonyMiami.com.

Deco Walk Hostel ★★ Here's something you don't see every day: a spiffy Ocean Drive spot to crash for $30 a night. On a second floor above a couple of shops and an ice cream counter (and right next door to well-known club Fat Tuesday), Michael Ohana recently gave his 132-bed hostel a zippy overhaul, providing the young and the restless a kick-butt front-row seat to all the action. Most equipped with triple bunk beds, rooms are all white, warmed up with spots of colorful art here and there, and blond wood furnishings a bit reminiscent of IKEA; you can choose either single-sex or co-ed quarters, and to ramp up the social factor even more, two-into-one dorms. Public spaces are appealing, including a bright, high-ceilinged lobby, a bar/lounge area on a 3,500-square-foot rooftop deck (along with Jacuzzi, pool table, ping pong, and big-screen TV), and a communal kitchen with brushed stainless steel appliances.

928 Ocean Dr. (btw. 8th and 9th sts.), South Beach. www.DecoWalkHostel.com.© **305/531-5511.** 10 rooms/120 beds. Dorm beds $30; includes continental breakfast. Valet parking ($25). **Amenities:** Bar; roof lounge; Jacuzzi; pool table; ping-pong; kitchen; laundry facilities; ATM; free Internet terminals; free Wi-Fi.

Freehand Miami ★★   In a cream-and-yellow 1936 Deco building a 15-minute-stroll north of the main South Beach action, the Indian Creek Hotel re-emerged from an $8-million 2012 overhaul as a hip, retro-flavored "hostel-plus." Public spaces have a comfy, vintage vibe (staffers tell us the elevator is Miami Beach's oldest), while rooms are on the IKEA side, with blond wood furnishings and cool colors accented by mod art from local artists (except for the bathrooms, still in funky, old-fashioned Deco tile); one drawback is that most lack closets. The premises are scattered with pastimes, from board games and bocce to ping-pong and an upright piano, but out back the centerpiece is the pool, surrounded by lush local vegetation and right across the brick terrace from a gourmet cocktail bar, the Broken Shaker (p. 128), with light bites and tipples so terrific they made James Beard Award finalist. At press time, an adjoining building was slated to add a restaurant with market-fresh cuisine by early 2015.

2727 Indian Creek Dr. (at 28th St.), Miami Beach. www.TheFreehand.com.© **305/531-2727.** 81 rooms/suites, 278 dorm beds. Doubles from $149, efficiency bungalows sleeping four from $199, dorm beds from $30. Street parking passes ($11/day). **Amenities:** Restaurant (imminent); bar; outdoor pool; bike rentals ($16/day); continental breakfast included; Saturday afternoon barbecue; free Wi-Fi.

Hotel Shelley ★★   Like sister property the Chelsea over on Washington Avenue, the purple-trimmed Shelley is a refurbished Deco darling (1936) with a middle-of-it-all SoBe location—mixing hints of Deco with some of the now expected accoutrements of today's boutiques, such as gauzy curtains, liberal use of white, and marble baths. Service is good, but rooms are smallish (admittedly par for the course in these old buildings); there's no elevator (it's just 3 stories) and if you care about Wi-Fi, it's in the lobby only. Finally, another little cool trendy extra: The destination bar/lounge (pouring noon–5am) is not just the usual booze-o-rama but also a hookah bar, with 150 flavors of tobacco.

844 Collins Ave. (btw. 8th and 9th sts.), South Beach. www.HotelShelley.com.© **877/762-3477** or 305/531-3341. 49 units. Winter $145–$225 double, $165–$245 king, $165–$300 mini-suite; off-season $75–$125 double, $95–$145 king, $115–$165 mini-suite. Valet parking ($32 overnight, $20 day visit). Pets accepted (up to 20 lbs.) at no charge. **Amenities:** Bar/lounge; free MIA airport shuttle; concierge; free nightclub passes; daily happy hour; weekly karaoke night; use of rooftop terrace and hot tub at nearby Hotel Chesterfield; free Wi-Fi in lobby.

> ### Impressions
>
> *I think South Beach targets vacationers who, if not affluent, would like to feel that way for a little while.*
> —Rachel Ponce on PBS's *Going Places*

ELSEWHERE IN MIAMI

Lodgings away from Miami Beach are a more mixed bag, consisting largely of a few prominent luxury resorts, a good number of more business-oriented properties (especially downtown and along Brickell Avenue), and most local outposts of familiar national and international chains of varying price points. Following is a carefully curated selection of lodgings with the most local spirit and feel.

For maps of hotels in this section, see p. 66 and 69.

Expensive

Biltmore Hotel ★★★   The phrase "historic grande dame" can be overused, but this elegant señora, with a tower modeled after Seville's famous Giralda, fits it to a T. The imposing neo-Spanish-colonial pile, rising regally over a 150-acre Coral Gables spread and dating back to city founder George Merrick's original plan in 1926, has seen a lot of history (glamorous and otherwise) since, to this day regularly hosting heads of states, CEOs, and celebrities. Backdrops include the huge, statue-lined pool and atmospheric period lobby with columns, bird cages, and ceilings part coffered, part star-spangled (you might well stumble across a boldface name, or at least a semi-celeb; on my last visit it was a pair of cable news talking heads, lunching poolside). Room decor is classic, in keeping with the vintage feel of the place, but amenities are certainly up to date. The serpentine basement gym in particular boasts the latest equipment and one of the buzzier hotel gym scenes I've seen, thanks to local members. The courtyard restaurant is a charmer, with a Sunday brunch known as one of South Florida's best. The classy Palme d'Or, meanwhile, does a creative job with *la cuisine française* under chef Gregory Pugin, a veteran of Joël Robuchon and Le Cirque, whose signature concoctions—such as a sea urchin, fennel, ginger, and lemongrass gelée—are a revelation.

1200 Anastasia Ave. (at DeSoto and Columbus Blvds.), Coral Gables. www.BiltmoreHotel.com. (C) **855/311-6903.** 273 units, including 130 suites. Winter $395–$895 double; off-season $229–$499 double; year-round $659–$6,500 specialty suites. Resort fee $20/day. Valet ($25 overnight, $12 day visitors; free self-parking). Pets welcome (free with $500 deposit). **Amenities:** 4 restaurants; 4 bars; concierge; gym; spa; outdoor pool; 18-hole golf course; 10 lighted tennis courts; room service; Wi-Fi included.

Mandarin Oriental, Miami ★★★   There are by now an awful lot of pretty great—even splendid—luxury hotels throughout Miami's Brickell Avenue/financial/ office district just south of downtown. But the one I still find among the most "contemporary Miami" in spirit (despite its Asian origins) is the cool wedge-shaped property a quick pop over the bridge on Brickell Key. This island locale allows the Mandarin to be the only downtown hotel to offer something resembling a sandy beach—and a thrilling urban view of the skyscrapers (not to mention occasional dolphin sightings, like I had on my last visit). Luxury, serenity, discretion (a plus for the celebs that pass through) pretty much sum it up here, whether in the wood-and-stone lobby, superb two-story spa, pair of restaurants (one the nouvel Peruvian **La Mar,** the other the contemporary fusion **Azul,** both among Miami's top destination dining spots), or elegant, pale-yellow rooms—all not just with water/skyline views but also balconies. If you're a spa fan, by the way, this one's worth a special visit (see box p. 52), even if you don't stay here.

500 Brickell Key Dr., Brickell Key, downtown. www.MandarinOriental.com/Miami. (C) **866/888-6780** or 305/913-8288. 326 units. Double $459–$900; suite $1,300–$6,500. Valet parking ($36 overnight, $21 day visitor). Pets welcome ($100 one-time fee). **Amenities:** 3 restaurants; 4 bars;

beach club; 2 shops; children's activities; concierge; fitness center; outdoor Jacuzzi; outdoor jogging trail; infinity pool; full-service holistic spa; nearby golf; 24-hour room service; Wi-Fi (additional charge).

Moderate

Hotel St. Michel ★★   Like the Biltmore, this vintage Coral Gables charmer is a perfect example of the romance and Mediterranean flavor the city's creators were aiming for back in the 1920s—except on a more intimate scale, at a fraction of the rates, and with the advantage of a location right in the downtown Gables, thus an easy stroll to a slew of dining, shopping, and cultural options. Built in 1926 as the Hotel Sevilla, later deteriorated into a flophouse, and restored by new owner Stuart Bornstein in the early '80s, the vine-covered St. Michel proudly displays lovely original details including tile work, wood floors, ceiling fans in the hallways, and a vintage elevator (you have to ring the front-desk person to operate it for you). The individually appointed rooms have a gracious mix of early-20th-century antique and early-21st-century amenities. The in-house restaurant, Segundo Muelle, is Peruvian.

> ### Wanna Be Signin' Something
>
> Celebrity tidbit: When Michael Jackson stayed at the **Mandarin Oriental, Miami,** he felt the urge to sign his name to a painting in his suite—despite the fact that he didn't paint it. Amused, the hotel decided to keep it. Imagine what it's worth now?

162 Alcazar Ave. (at Ponce de Leon Blvd.), Coral Gables. www.HotelStMichel.com. *©***800/848-4683** or 305/444-1666. 28 units. Winter $189 double, $239 suite; off-season $119 double, $149 suite. Extra person $10. Parking $14. **Amenities:** Restaurant; concierge; free Wi-Fi.

Hotel Urbano ★★   A fresh, fetching, even somewhat arty boutique property built in 2010, it's perhaps one of the area's more unexpectedly located: below the high-rise canyon of the Brickell Avenue business district, where both Brickell and Interstate 95 feed into Highway U.S. 1 as well as the Rickenbacker Causeway over to Key Biscayne. But this puts visitors in easy range of a fair number of offerings in Coconut Grove, Coral Gables, and elsewhere, with South Beach just a short drive away. On two floors, rooms (most with balconies) are crisp, contemporary, and done up in warm tones with original art—plus there's more of said art all throughout the public areas, all of it for sale by Art Fusion Galleries in the Design District (in fact, a daily happy hour with complimentary nibbles and two-for-one tipples is designed to play off this art collection). A modest but quite charming pool area provides a cozy oasis including cabanas and a fire pit, overlooked by a 24/7 fitness room on the second floor that's small but does the job quite well. The bistro, meanwhile, serves tasty sandwiches, salads, and small plates.

2500 Brickell Ave. (at SE 25th Rd.), downtown. www.HotelUrbanoMiami.com. *©***877/499-5265** or 305/854-2070. 65 units. Winter $159–$289 double; off-season $109–$169 double. Valet parking ($24 overnight, $20 day visit). Pets welcome at no charge. **Amenities:** Restaurant; bar; fitness room; outdoor pool; room service; child care; free Wi-Fi.

Inexpensive

B2 Miami Downtown ★★   Bursting in 2013 onto a local hotel scene not known for stylish, upscale-feeling, centrally located bargains, the B2 is a snazzy revelation, and not just because of the colored-light show playing across its facade nightly. It's got the chic boutique-hotel thing down pat, with white and pearl-gray tones throughout, plus all the cushiness and mod cons you'd expect in the rooms (phones with MP3 capability, even). Add several compact but top-notch on-premises amenities such as a spa treatment room; fitness room; and **Biscayne Tavern,** run by restaurateur Jeffrey Chodorow of China Grill fame, serving artery-busting but delish updated comfort food; only a pool is lacking. Crown it with a primo location: front and center on downtown's waterfront, across from Bayfront Park and Bayside mall, around the corner from the cruise port, and down the street from the fancy new art and science museums and the arena where the Miami Heat play and world-class entertainment acts do their thing. South Beach is over the causeway, and everything else in Miami is pretty easily accessible from here, too.

146 Biscayne Blvd. (at NE 1st St.), downtown. www.b2MiamiDowntown.com. ℭ **866/884-2592** or 305/358-4555. 243 units. $129–$169 double; $200–$220 junior suites sleeping up to 4. Valet parking ($25 overnight, $5–$22 day visitors; lots/metered parking nearby). **Amenities:** Restaurant; bar; spa; fitness room; complimentary morning coffee/tea in lobby; iPad upon request; room service; free Wi-Fi.

Historic Miami River Hotel ★★

Miami's really not a "quaint inn/bed-and-breakfast" kind of town, nor does it have practically anything left dating as far back as 1906. So that makes this little oasis of olde South Florida, on the National Register of Historic Places, a rara avis indeed (and if you've seen *Marley & Me,* you've already had a glimpse). The former Miami River Inn is a cluster of wood-clapboard buildings amid palms and lignum vitae trees with 38 rooms and 14 apartments. Rooms are classic B&B—pastel colors, striped wallpaper, wainscoting, hardwood floors, floral prints, white wicker, and stuffed 19th-century-style furniture—while apartments are sleek and modern. Out back off a grassy, lantern-encircled oval (croquet, anyone?) are a pool and a Jacuzzi. The other quirky thing is its location, west of downtown's Brickell area in a working-class section of East Little Havana. There's little of interest within walking distance, but no biggie, because it's fairly central to quite a bit of the Miami that is, from Coral Gables out west to South Beach east, over the causeway.

437 SW 2nd St. (at S. River Dr.), Miami. www.HistoricRiverHotel.com. ℭ **800/468-3589** or 305/325-0045. 52 units. Winter $87–137 double; $127–187 apartment; off-season $67–$107 double; $107–$157 apartment. Rates include continental breakfast. Free onsite parking. **Amenities:** Pool; Jacuzzi; free Wi-Fi.

Zen Village ★

If Miami can be said to still have a "crunchy" side left, it would have to be in the community of Coconut Grove, where consumerism hasn't entirely crowded out pockets of a once-thriving counterculture such as this Buddhist center run by Taiwan-born Master Chufei Tsai, an easy stroll from all the Grove's downtown. Seekers of spiritual enlightenment and/or a lodging steal with some singular personality will find the tiny bed-and-breakfast here a jewel in the lotus. Amid a secluded, tranquil setting accented by classic Eastern touches such as a stupa, Tibetan prayer wheel, and koi pond are four simple but elegant rooms with private baths and one shared studio space with a soaring ceiling and lots of natural light. It may not literally be nirvana, but it is pretty nifty.

3750 Main Hwy. (btw. Franklin Ave. and Royal Rd.), Coconut Grove. ZenVillage.org. ℭ **305/567-0165.** 5 units. Communal room $55 per person. Doubles $85–$125. Rates include breakfast. **Amenities:** Tea room.

WHERE TO EAT IN MIAMI

Not all that long ago, Miami was nothing to write home about, culinarily speaking, Today it's a smorgasbord of both the sophisticated and the down home, spread over more than 6,000 restaurants, cafes, and assorted eateries. Tropical fusion cuisine—sometimes dubbed Floribbean—is a specialty, melding Californian-Asian with Caribbean and Latin elements to create world-class flavors all its own (think mango chutney splashed over fresh swordfish or a spicy sushi sauce served alongside Peruvian ceviche).

And yet, for all the foodie fanfare and celebrity chefs, there's no shortage of spots to score a quality meal at moderate or even cheap prices, and often in the process explore a new cuisine—particularly with a Latin accent. From the beaches to Kendall out west and Homestead down south, immigrants especially from the Caribbean and Latin America have brought their skills and flavors to the Miami area for your delectation (one good option is to seek out foodie and ethnic food shops that have tables). And if you like seafood, you'll be pleased to hear that due to its abundance hereabouts, it doesn't have to sink your budget.

As for ambience, if you're craving a "scene" with your steak, then South Beach is it. As in many cities in Europe and Latin America, it's fashionable to dine late in SoBe, preferably after 9pm, sometimes as late as midnight. And service is notoriously slow and snooty, but it comes with the (surf 'n') turf. Of course, it's also possible to find restaurants that buck the trend and actually pride themselves on good, even friendly service, especially on the mainland in places such as Coral Gables, Coconut Grove, downtown, and Midtown.

Many restaurants keep extended hours in high season (roughly Dec–Apr) and may close for lunch and/or dinner on Monday, when the traffic is slower. Always call ahead, as schedules do change. During the months of August and September, many Miami restaurants participate in Miami Spice (**www.MiamiRestaurantMonth.com**), in which three-course lunches and dinners are served at affordable prices. Also, always look carefully at your bill—a growing number of restaurants, especially in South Beach, are adding a gratuity of 15 to 18% to your total due to the enormous influx of European tourists who aren't accustomed to tipping because at home the service charge is included. Keep in mind that this is the *suggested* amount and can be adjusted, either higher or lower, depending on your assessment of the service provided. In part because of this tipping-included policy, South Beach wait staff are increasingly known for their lackadaisical or inattentive service. Feel completely free to adjust the tip if you feel your server deserves more or less.

What I've striven for in the highly curated listings in this chapter is to provide restaurants that best capture the essence of Miami past and present—its history, its settings, its cultures, and its sensibilities. It's far from comprehensive, but I hope it's incisive.

best MIAMI RESTAURANT BETS

o **Best splurges:** In this book, a Miami Beach trio takes the cake for different reasons: there's **YUCA** (p. 62), a nouvel-Latino pioneer with a ringside seat right on the Lincoln Road runway; South Beach's somewhat more secluded **Bâoli** (p. 61), an import from the French Riviera that's become beautiful-people central; and **The Forge** (p. 61), an extravagant steakhouse classic that has managed to keep reinventing itself as an A-list perennial.

o **Best Value:** Some of the best, heartiest meal deals can be found right on the street corner, in bodegas and modest Latino eateries such as **Versailles** (p. 77) and **Antigua Guatemala** (p. 73) in Little Havana and **Puerto Sagua** (p. 65) on South Beach, where everything from *arroz con pollo* and Cuban sandwiches to simple eggs and toast won't set you back your next vacation.

o **Best Service:** Service in South Florida is typically less than stellar, but at the Biltmore's **Palme d'Or** (p. 56) it's impeccable (as it should be at those prices). And at **Joe's Stone Crab** (p. 62), career servers are throwbacks to the day and age when service was as paramount as food to the fine dining experience.

o **Best Waterfront Dining:** Believe it or not, the choices right on the water in Miami are few and far between. One funky (and, as it happens, exceptionally good-value) exception is **Garcia's Seafood Grille** (p. 68) which perches over the Miami River west of downtown. (And parenthetically, over on Biscayne Bay, the Mandarin Oriental Hotel's global fusion restaurant, **Azul** and Peruvian **La Mar** (p. 56), also serve up swell views of the Miami skyline.)

o **Best Cuban Restaurant:** There's always a debate on who has the best, most authentic Cuban cuisine, with all the choices around here, it's probably an unwinnable one. But for those who have never been to Havana, Miami's **Versailles,** in Little Havana (p. 77), is a must-visit for tasty fare in generous portions at paltry prices amid a, well, *unique* atmosphere.

o **Best Seafood:** Two of your best catches are South Beach's classic **Joe's Stone Crab** (p. 62) and the slightly out-of-the-way **Garcia's Seafood Grille** (p. 68) west of downtown's Brickell area.

o **Best Sunday Brunch: Michael's Genuine Food & Drink** (p. 72) in the Design District could win every "best of" categories thanks to its locally sourced, organic, seasonal cuisine; out-of-control desserts; buzzy bar scene; and colorful crowd of foodies, hipsters, celebrities, and assorted culinary dignitaries. And the brunch is truly in a category of its own (exhibits A and B: kimchi Benedict and strawberry and yuzu Pop-Tarts). Brunch at the **Biltmore Hotel** (p. 56), meanwhile, is deservedly a classic.

o **Best People-Watching:** The **News Café,** in South Beach (p. 132), practically invented the sport of people-watching, encouraging its customers to sit at an outdoor table all day if they want, taking in the passing parade of people while sipping a cappuccino. Lincoln Road's Euro-fabulous **Segafredo Espresso** café (p. 130) and **Nexxt Cafe** (p. 64) provide a front-row seat to the hordes who amble along the pedestrian mall. And as noted below, French Riviera import **Bâoli** (p. 61) is one of the current "it" spots for "beautiful people."

MIAMI BEACH

The renaissance of South Beach started in the late '80s and early '90s and still continues as classic cuisine fuses with more chic, nouveau developments. The ultimate result has spawned dozens of first-rate dining spots. In fact, big-name restaurants from across the country have capitalized on South Beach's international appeal and have continued to open branches here with great success. A few old standbys remain from the *Miami Vice* days, but the flock of newcomers dominates the scene, with places going in and out of style as quickly as the tides.

In South Beach, upscale restaurants open and close at a dizzying pace, and here you'd never guess the economy was still sluggish; at least when it comes to restaurants, things always seem to be popping. According to one poll, Miamians dine out more than anyone else in the USA. And since it's impossible to list them all, I say just stroll and browse. Most post their menus outside. With few exceptions, places on Ocean Drive are crowded with tourists and priced accordingly, so for value you'll do better to venture over to the avenues and side streets west of Ocean. More economical local eats are scattered among the pricier restaurants along Lincoln Road, and much more common up and down the stretch of Alton Road that runs south of Lincoln Road's western end.

Expensive

Bâoli Miami ★★★ MEDITERRANEAN/FRENCH   Cannes and South Beach are birds of a chichi feather, so when Le Bâoli made the *grand jeté* from Boulevard de la Croisette to Collins Avenue in 2010, it struck a chord with elite local partyati, celebs included (the publicists aren't shy about name-dropping Beyoncé, Clooney, DiCaprio, Dolce/Gabbana), and remains a hot resto-nightspot. Behind a blank streetside facade you'll find an indoor-outdoor space whose movie-set-like interplay of retro-chic, verdant foliage, sultry soundtrack, and sexy lighting could make almost anyone look hot (good thing, too, because when I've been in, a high percentage of both crowd and servers has been model-level gorgeous). I especially love the romantic courtyard. The menu? Classy, top-quality Euro surf 'n' turf. Chef Gustavo Vertone may be Argentine, but there's much homage to Bâoli's Côte d'Azur roots and its Mediterranean neighbors—terrine de foie gras, bouillabaisse, gazpacho, branzino, risotto—sprinkled with Asian-influenced likes of robata grilled salmon fillet and miso-broiled Chilean sea bass. Weekly highlights include Wednesday night's "My Boyfriend Is Out of Town"; on that and some other nights, the postprandial partying can carry on until 4am.

1906 Collins Ave. (at 20th St.). www.BaoliMiami.com. ✆ **305/674-8822.** Reservations recommended. Appetizers $14–$29; main dishes $19–$95. Daily 7pm–4am.

The Forge ★★★ STEAKHOUSE/ECLECTIC   Like the Fontainebleau Hotel, this is a Miami Beach classic dating back to the 30s, a hangout for both celebrities and wiseguys. Under the well-connected longtime owner Shareef Malnik, it has managed to adapt to the times nicely, refurbing in 2010 and in 2014 introducing a menu under new chef Christopher Lee that's brought the cuisine to a whole new level. The core of that menu, of course, remains steak, but Lee's other creations are just as tasty, from "Jamaican jerk bacon" to miso-marinated Chilean sea bass to a droll "pastrami duck breast" with rye gnocchi (pastrami on rye, get it?). The decor, meanwhile, is eclectically charismatic (from oak paneling and exposed brick to stained glass to Jetsons mod); the wine cellar still legendary; and the bar a veritable oenological amusement park thanks to an automat dispensing 80 top-notch wines.

432 41st St./Arthur Godfrey Rd. (btw. Sheridan and Royal Palm Aves.). www.TheForge.com. ✆ **305/538-8533.** Reservations recommended. Appetizers $10–$19; main dishes $30–$58. Sun–Thurs 6pm–midnight, Fri–Sat 6pm–1am.

Joe's Stone Crab ★★ SEAFOOD   From humble origins in Joe Weiss' lunch counter in 1913, this now enormous, retro-feeling classic in southernmost South Beach, run by his descendants like a well-oiled machine, may no longer be the last word in seafood hereabouts. But attention must be paid, as Mrs. Loman would say. And Joe's does deliver, for the most part. The storied stone-crab claws, served with a mustard-based dipping sauce, may or may not be your cup of brine (they're served cold, and last time I was in I detected a whiff of the ammoniac; in any case, some folks actually prefer the king crab), but on the menu there are plenty of other marine critters, along with land-based meat and fowl. Highlights to look out for include the seafood bisque; the lobster mac and cheese; the sides of creamed spinach, slaw, and hash browns; and for dessert, one of South Florida's better key lime pies. The vibe and certainly the decor are a mite old-school and the service usually pretty good; just keep in mind that you'll want to budget for time as well as a hefty check, because no reservations are taken. You put your name on the list and settle in for a bit of a wait (usually shorter at lunch than dinner).

11 Washington Ave. (btw. Commerce St. and S. Pointe Dr.). www.JoesStoneCrab.com. ✆ **305/673-0365** or 673/4611 for takeout. Reservations not accepted. Appetizers $14–$18; main dishes $17–$60. Sun 11:30am–2pm and 4–10pm; Mon–Thurs 11:30am–2pm and 5–10pm; Fri–Sat 11:30am–2pm and 5–11pm. Summer open Wed–Sun for dinner only; closed August to mid-Oct.

YUCA ★★ NOUVEL CUBAN   To happen across it today, you'd think this is just another fancy Lincoln Road Latin restaurant-cum-nightspot. It's got that whole Deco-meets-sleek-white-chic thing going on; floor-to-ceiling windows; live *música cubana* every Thursday and Saturday evening, plus a Friday salsa night upstairs from 11pm to 3am. But YUCA (Spanish for cassava root as well as an English acronym for "Young Urban Cuban-American") is also a key part of local history—it pioneered both Nuevo Latino cuisine and the rebirth of Lincoln Road, opening here back in 1989, when I can tell you from personal experience this now buzzing street was dead, dead, dead. The place has had its ups and downs over the years, but has hung on and today is a strong performer again under Chef Francisco Javier Rodríguez, with the tasty likes of goat-cheese croquettes, guava barbecue ribs, and plantain-coated mahi-mahi. A dandy spot for a mojito, too!

501 Lincoln Rd. (at Drexel Ave.). www.Yuca.com. ✆ **305/532-9822.** Reservations advised for weekend dinner. Tapas/small dishes $6–$12, main courses $24–$48. Daily noon–11:30pm.

Moderate

Chalán on the Beach ★★ PERUVIAN   I'm finding the cuisine of Peru seems to be the flavor of the decade in Miami, which has of course spawned lots of overpriced nouvel treatment. But this beige-tiled longtime stalwart (founded by Mario Abanto in 1997) is the real, honest Inca deal, with its classic takes on ceviche, *papa a la huancaína* (potatoes in creamy, cheesy sauce with a touch of zing), *ají de gallina* (chicken in the same sauce) and a long menu of savory beef, chicken, and especially seafood dishes that'll leave you wanting more. The original, by the way, El Chalán, is out west near Tropical Park and the Palmetto Expressway at 7971 Bird Rd., ✆ **305/266-0212.**

1580 Washington Ave. (at 16th St.). ✆ **305/532-8880.** Reservations advised for weekend dinner. Main courses $12–$20. Sun 11am–midnight; Sun–Thurs 11am–10pm; Fri–Sat 11am–11pm.

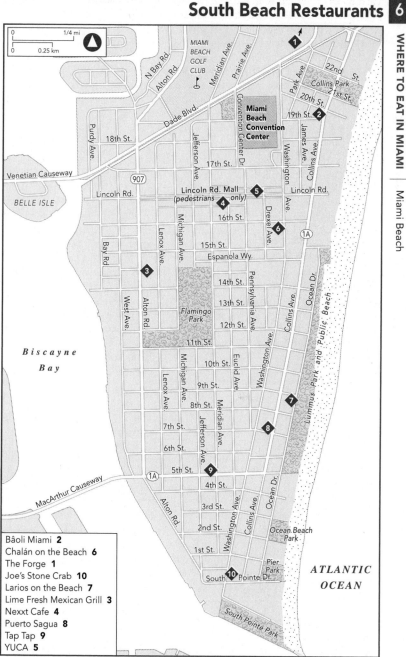

Bâoli Miami **2**
Chalán on the Beach **6**
The Forge **1**
Joe's Stone Crab **10**
Larios on the Beach **7**
Lime Fresh Mexican Grill **3**
Nexxt Cafe **4**
Puerto Sagua **8**
Tap Tap **9**
YUCA **5**

Larios on the Beach ★★ CUBAN   Come on, shake your taste buds, baby, at singer/music mogul Gloria Estefan's South Beach eatery, serving up solid Cuban classics since 1992. Dishes such as *mojo*-marinated roast pork, shrimp in creole sauce, and fried sweet plantains by and large hit the right notes amid a recently renovated all-white decor; plus there are now menu items like a low-cal "Cuban wrap" and a "vegetarian platter." But my favorite perk is the prime location in the middle of the Ocean Drive *vida loca;* the outdoor tables boast some of this sidewalk runway's best ringside seating, while a roving *bolero* band (think Buena Vista Social Club) serve up swell menus of *bésame mucho* chestnuts Wednesday through Sunday.

820 Ocean Dr. (btw. 8th and 9th sts.). www.BongosCubanCafe.com. ℂ **305/532-9577.** Reservations recommended. Main courses $17–$49; sandwiches $12–$14. Sun 11am–midnight; Mon–Thurs 11am–midnight; Fri–Sat 11am–2am.

Nexxt Cafe ★★ AMERICAN/ECLECTIC   Close to midway along South Beach's premier dining/shopping runway, Nexxt has become a Lincoln Road mainstay thanks to its prime perch, with a bevy of outdoor tables right alongside the endless parade; a menu long and varied enough to please almost anyone, from picky kids to pick-at-their-arugula models; and fare that's usually pretty tasty, occasionally imaginative, and served in satisfying portions. I especially like meal-size salads such as the Thai cilantro cashew chicken, but the fare runs the gamut from plain to fancy, including a variety of burgers (but a mac-and-cheese burger, really?) and sandwiches, pizzas, pastas, big honkin' Angus steaks, tapas, and more. There's an early-bird happy hour 4 to 6pm daily, with $5 appetizers and half-off drinks. For Sunday brunch and most evenings for dinner you'll find most outdoor tables full, but there are enough of them that wait times are usually no biggie. Service can be slow and occasionally less than service-oriented, but this, too, makes it a SoBe classic. What's yer rush, anyway?

700 Lincoln Rd. (at Euclid Ave.). www.NexxtCafe.com. ℂ **305/532-6643.** Burgers/sandwiches $11–$16; meal-size salads $15–$19; main courses $15–$24. Mon–Thurs 11:30am–11pm; Fri 11:30am–midnight; Sat 10am–midnight; Sun 10am–11pm.

Tap Tap ★★ HAITIAN   In case you hadn't already heard, Haiti supplies one of the Caribbean's more distinctive dollops to Miami's cultural stew, and yet good Haitian restaurants are not exactly thick on the ground. This SoBe mainstay named after that country's colorful buses is a big exception, and one of the better, more colorful, and accessible spots locally to sample the country's *kwizin kreyol* (Creole cuisine). What's that mean? For starters, Caribbean staples such as rice and red beans, coconut, cassava, plantains, okra, conch, tropical fruits—and rum, of course (Haiti's fine Barbancourt brand is featured). Here's your chance to try some slightly exotic goodies you may not find back home, such as conch ceviche, stewed or grilled goat, and soursop; there's also enough here to keep vegetarians reasonably happy. Menu aside, Haiti's best-known cultural calling card, painting, is a star attraction here; not only is almost every available patch of wall filled with colorful, compelling island imagery, but so are the tabletops and even some of the chairs. Get even more of the cultural flavor Thursdays and Saturdays, when a house band does its thing.

819 5th St. (btw. Jefferson and Meridian Aves.). www.TapTapMiamiBeach.com. ℂ **305/672-2898.** Reservations accepted but not necessary. Appetizers $6–$10; main courses $8–$22. Daily noon–11pm.

Inexpensive

Lime Fresh Mexican Grill ★★ TEX MEX   We are admittedly not blessed when it comes to good *comida mexicana* in Miami, but I do love me the food (especially its "surfer-style" fish tacos with spicy ranch dressing), the breezy vibe, and the prices at this "healthy burrito shop," founded by local entrepreneur John Kunkel in 2004 ("healthy" being relative, of course, fresh, low-carb ingredients notwithstanding). You can go classic or get fancy with the likes of an avocado bacon quesadilla. And they'll do veg versions of everything on the menu. You eat to a club-like soundtrack in a covered outdoor patio, and you never know who might show up—Madonna and Miami Heat guard Dwayne Wade have done so in the past. There are no longer lines out the door, but the formula here has become such a hit that that locations have opened not only downtown, in Midtown, Dadeland, and North Miami Beach (see the website below for addresses), but also as far afield as Alabama, Ohio, and—I kid you not—Santiago, Chile.

1439 Alton Rd. (btw. 14th and 15th sts.). www.LimeFreshMexicanGrill.com. © **305/532-5463.** Burritos $6.50–$7.25. Tacos $2.75–$3.25. Daily 11am–11pm.

Puerto Sagua ★★ CUBAN   Surrounded these days by chichi shops, this blast-from-the-past Latin dive—with wood paneling, fluorescent lighting, a drop ceiling, and stick-to-your-ribs Cuban fare—has been and remains popular with generations of old-timers, late-night clubbers, and a motley mélange of locals and in-the-know visitors who appreciate a good feed at good prices. Classics include the *sandwich cubano* (ham, roast pork, Swiss cheese, mustard, and pickles on pressed Cuban-style baguette), as well as a similar sandwich called a *medianoche; picadillo,* a ground-beef hash a bit like sloppy joe filling but with loaded with garlic, onions, olives, and raisins; and shrimp *enchiladas* in a tangy, tomato-based sauce.

700 Collins Ave. (at 7th St.). © **305/673-1115.** Appetizers $2–$20; sandwiches/salads $5–$9; main courses $7–$39. Daily 7:30am–2am.

ELSEWHERE IN MIAMI

Expensive

Bread and Butter ★★★ NOUVEL CUBAN   Albert Cabrera's cozy nook on a downtown Coral Gables side street may have a white-bread anglo moniker, but what comes out of the kitchen is a scrumptious marriage of Cuban comfort food and creative fusion reflecting his pedigree with South Florida culinary luminaries such as Norman Van Aken of La Broche and Robin Haas of Baleen. Here a hearty, just-like-abuela-used-to-make, meat-and-potatoes dish like carne con papa gets transmogrified into short ribs with green-olive piccata, potato gratin, and red-wine sauce. Or my favorite, the classic Cuban-style frita (hamburger with savory sausage mixed in), gussied up with kimchi, cilantro, onion, and sriracha ketchup. For dessert, classic flan gets the goat-cheese treatment and a lovely version of torrejas (French toast) come with guava maple syrup. There's a nice little wine list, but what matches the Brooklyn gastropub feel—complete with white subway tiles and hanging bulbs—especially well is the list of interesting bottled and draft brews and ciders.

2330 Salzedo St. (btw. Miracle Mile and Giralda St.), Coral Gables. www.BreadandButterCounter. com. © **305/442-9622.** Reservations recommended for weekend dinner. Small dishes $7–$15, main dishes $26–$32. Mon–Fri 11:30am–4pm, 5:30pm–11pm; Sat 5:30pm–midnight, Sun 11:30am–4pm, 5:30pm–11pm.

Casabe 305 Bistro ★★★ NOUVEL LATIN   Pioneered in Miami beginning in the 1980s, contemporary Latin and fusion cuisine are still very much a mainstay of the South Florida dining scene. But what I find especially appealing and intriguing about Diego Texera's little jewel of a spot between downtown and Coral Gables is its provenance (there are lots of Venezuelans in Miami, but darn few spots to sample their cuisine, let alone nouvelle versions thereof) and its setting (a charming, homespun-feeling

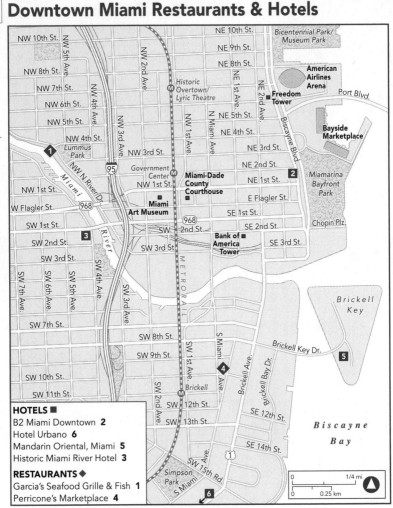

HOTELS ■
B2 Miami Downtown **2**
Hotel Urbano **6**
Mandarin Oriental, Miami **5**
Historic Miami River Hotel **3**

RESTAURANTS ◆
Garcia's Seafood Grille & Fish **1**
Perricone's Marketplace **4**

bungalow from the 1930s tucked into an otherwise blah stretch of Coral Way). Much of the menu changes regularly, but standouts I've had recently include a silky, soulful corn chowder; *tostones* (flattened fried plantains) topped with ceviche; duck with tamarind coulis; a bready Venezuelan specialty called *tequeños,* stuffed with cheese and served with a guava sauce zinged with chipotle; and custard made from the tropical fruit *guanábana* (much tastier than its pucker-up name in English, soursop). Regular tasting menus are available. And heads up, vegetarians: Texera has a macrobiotic background, so there's usually something nice here for you, too. If you're up for venturing a bit off the beaten path, you'll be glad you did.

1762 Coral Way (btw. SW 17th and 18th Aves.), Miami. www.facebook.com/Casabe305Bistro. ⓒ **786/310-7510.** Reservations recommended on weekends/for brunch. Appetizers $7–$11; main dishes $19–$29; brunch items $6–$13. Tues–Sat 5–11pm; Sun 11am–5pm.

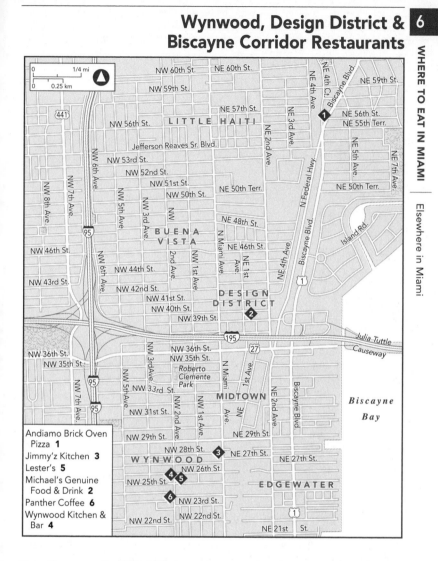

Andiamo Brick Oven Pizza **1**
Jimmy'z Kitchen **3**
Lester's **5**
Michael's Genuine Food & Drink **2**
Panther Coffee **6**
Wynwood Kitchen & Bar **4**

Ortanique on the Mile ★★★ CARIBBEAN   Sometimes drowned out by all the Latino noise is the fact that Miami is also a top U.S. city for folks from the English-speaking Caribbean. Since 1999, Delius Shirley and Chef Cindy Hutson's little gem in downtown Coral Gables has been the star among the strangely few local restaurants focusing more on the West Indies end of the pond, with a little of the French Antilles thrown in—much less an upscale, nouvelle version thereof. How about jerk-rubbed foie gras over a warm salad of mache lettuce, crisp potatoes, and duck confit drizzled with a sauce of burnt orange marmalade and Grand Marnier? Or a "West Indian–style" bouillabaisse (in coconut curry broth)? Decor is warm and soothing, with details suggesting the islands, such as mahogany wainscoting and gingerbread trim. Shirley and

Hutson also run acclaimed restaurants in Grand Cayman and the Bahamas, where the locals know from fancy Caribbean eats.

278 Miracle Mile (btw. Ponce de Leon Blvd. and Salzedo St.), Coral Gables. www.Ortanique Restaurants.com/Miami. ℂ **305/446-7710.** Reservations requested. Appetizers/salads $12–$28; main courses $22–$55; 3-course prix fixe $36. Lunch Mon–Fri 11:30am–2:30pm; dinner Mon–Tues 6–10pm, Wed–Sat 6–11pm, Sun 5:30–9:30pm.

Rusty Pelican ★★★ INTERNATIONAL   After a multi-million-dollar refurb in 2011, this Key Biscayne landmark dating back to 1972 is more sleek nouvelle phoenix than ungainly oxidized waterfowl, with a very contemporary feel and sophisticated surf-and-turf menu from new chef Jim Pastor, a veteran of the W Hotel in South Beach. But one thing that hasn't changed, which makes dining here a surefire memory-maker: the million-dollar view over Biscayne Bay. Birds (pelicans included) swoop by, local scullers and kayakers slice through the water just feet away, and behind it all in the distance is downtown Miami's high-rise skyline. Creative entrees include local black sea bass in cinnamon broth and Barolo-braised lamb shanks, but my favorite part of the menu is the diverse "small plates," such as grouper sliders (also great beef sliders), a tasty pork-belly skewer that isn't slimy or fatty as pork belly tends to be, wild-mushroom cappuccino, ceviche, sushi, and more. The happy-hour and bar scene, meanwhile, makes it easy to strike up conversations with locals, if you're so inclined.

3201 Rickenbacker Causeway (at Rickenbacker Marina), Key Biscayne. www.TheRustyPelican.com. ℂ **305/361-3818.** Reservations recommended. Small plates $12–$16; main dishes $17–$53. Sun–Thurs 11am–11pm; Fri–Sat 11am–midnight.

Moderate

Garcia's Seafood Grille & Fish ★★ SEAFOOD   In 1976, the Cuban refugee García brothers added a restaurant side to the seafood market and wholesaler they'd founded a decade earlier, and today it's a cherished institution for locals with a hankering for edibles from the ocean. Its location very much off the beaten path—along the Miami River west of downtown's Brickell area—lends even more authenticity, not to mention some great atmosphere as you take in the river and distant high-rise skyline from the outdoor decks both upstairs and downstairs. The menu's fishy indeed—the only non-pescavore concession being a chicken breast entree—and despite having gotten a touch fancier of late with additions such as salmon in tamarind mustard sauce, it remains largely about fresh seafood simply prepared (grilled, blackened, or fried). I

CARIBBEAN CAFFEINE: CUBAN coffee

Café cubano is a longstanding tradition in Miami, and despite the more than a dozen Starbucks that dot the Miami landscape, many locals still rely on the Cuban joints for their daily caffeine fix.

You'll find it served from the takeout windows of hundreds of *cafeterías* or *loncherías* around town, especially in Little Havana, downtown, Hialeah, and the beaches. Depending on where you are and what you want, you'll drop between 40¢ and $1.50 per cup.

The best *café cubano* has a thin but rich layer of foam on top formed when the hot espresso shoots from the machine into the sugar below. The result is the caramely, sweet, potent concoction that's a favorite of locals of all nationalities.

And try asking for it *en español*: "Un cafecito, por favor!"

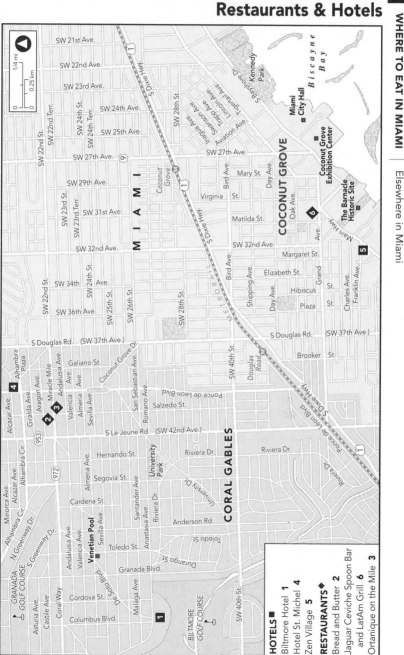

HOTELS ■
Biltmore Hotel **1**
Hotel St. Michel **4**
Zen Village **5**
RESTAURANTS ◆
Bread and Butter **2**
Jaguar Ceviche Spoon Bar
and LatAm Grill **6**
Ortanique on the Mile **3**

especially like the grouper—whether in the form of fried "fingers," chowder, sandwich, or filet—and the conch fritters are some of the moistest and most flavorful I've had anywhere (speaking of conch, here you can order it as a steak—one of the only times I've ever seen it offered without breading involved). Other specialties include oysters on the half shell and stone crabs in season.

398 NW N. River Dr. (at NW 4th St.), Miami. www.GarciasMiami.com. ℂ **305/375-0765.** Reservations usually not necessary. Appetizers $6–$14; sandwiches $9–$10, main dishes $13–$17. Daily 11am–10pm.

Jaguar Ceviche Spoon Bar & LatAm Grill ★★ PAN-LATIN   Way too wordily named, but never mind. To me, Jaguar presents the perfect Miami mix of contemporary Latino feel, flavor, and accessible prices. This colorful, cheerful dining room with sidewalk seating right in downtown Coconut Grove obviously gives pride of place to its tangy ceviches, and the six-spoon sampler is highly recommendable. But I'm still enjoying working my way through the rest of the menu, a tasty trip through Mexico, Peru, Brazil, Argentina, Chile, and Uruguay, with vegetarian options thrown in. If you're a seafood fan, try the house special chupe de camarón, a Peruvian-style shrimp chowder with rice, egg, and *ají* (a very slightly spicy yellow chili).

3067 Grand Ave. (btw. Main Hwy, and Matilda St.), Coconut Grove. www.JaguarHG.com/Jaguar Spot. ℂ **305/444-0216.** Reservations recommended for weekend dinner. Sandwiches $14–$17, main dishes $14–$33. Mon–Thurs 11:30am–11pm; Fri 11:30am–11:30pm, Sat 11am–11pm, Sun 11am–10pm.

Perricone's Marketplace ★★ ITALIAN/AMERICAN   Onetime New Yorker Steven Perricone has been running this Miami fixture several short blocks west of downtown's Brickell Avenue high-rise corridor since 1996, and even though the area has lately become chockablock with fancy-schmancy eateries, Perricone's has remained a beloved destination for locals (especially as a weekend brunch spot). Why? For starters, good service and reliably tasty food with a bit of an Italian bent—if you're a seafoodie, don't pass up the house version of *cioppino* (shrimp, mussels, scallops, fresh ahi tuna, and salmon medallions over linguine all swimming in a rich briny broth). The pasta list in particular is long and creative, as are those for entree salads (heads up, vegetarians) and desserts. But what kicks it all up to the next level is the gracious, lovely indoor-outdoor oasis feel, filled with lush greenery that does a fine job of whisking you away from the surrounding big city. Before leaving, stop in the gourmet market up front for a gelato that's among the most authentic we've come

---

Roasting to the Occasion

If you find yourself in Wynwood jonesing for java, don't miss **Panther Coffee,** 2390 NW 2nd Ave. (www. PantherCoffee.com; ℂ **305/677-3952;** daily 'til 8pm), a boho beanery where the beans are roasted right on site, focusing on small-batch coffees and specialty drinks; there's also a branch in South Beach west of Lincoln Road, at

1875 Purdy Ave., open daily 'til 9pm. Back in Wynwood right near Panther is **Lester's,** 2519 NW 2nd Ave. (www. LestersMiami.com; ℂ **305/456-1784**), a jolty coffee and wine bar that's reminiscent of an artist's living room; it's open until 10pm weekdays and on Friday and Saturday until midnight.

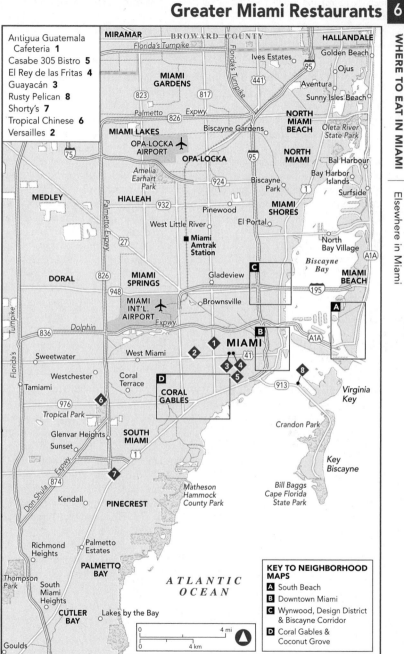

Antigua Guatemala Cafeteria **1**
Casabe 305 Bistro **5**
El Rey de las Fritas **4**
Guayacán **3**
Rusty Pelican **8**
Shorty's **7**
Tropical Chinese **6**
Versailles **2**

KEY TO NEIGHBORHOOD MAPS

A South Beach
B Downtown Miami
C Wynwood, Design District & Biscayne Corridor
D Coral Gables & Coconut Grove

across in Miami, amid an array of cheeses, cold cuts, wines, and other Italian goodies.

15 SE 10th St. (at S. Miami Ave.), Miami. www.Perricones.com. © **305/374-9449.** Sandwiches $10–$14; pastas $15–$22; main dishes $21–$38. Mon–Thurs 11am–11pm; Fri 4–11:30pm; Sat 8am–11:30pm; Sun 9am–11pm. Marketplace open from 7am daily. Valet parking $5.

Michael's Genuine Food & Drink ★★★ NEW AMERICAN Since it opened in 2007, local foodies (and a few savvy visitors) have embraced this little Design District bistro wedged into a breezeway amid chichi showrooms and art galleries, because of its unassuming owner-chef Michael Schwartz and its mission to be Miami's locavore ground zero (though given the vagaries of Florida agriculture, Swartz sometimes has to go farther afield—but always keeping it organic). One thing I especially like is the variety of plate sizes for every budget and appetite. In the past, my faves on the constantly changing menu have included chargrilled octopus with gigante bean salad, roast peppers, tomato harissa, and green olives; wood oven-roasted yellowjack with kalamata olive tapenade, and creative wood-oven pizzas like the one with Fontina, slow-roasted pork, shaved onions, and—wait for it—peaches. The wine list is modest but well curated, but they do hope you'll try their home-brewed ale, light and slightly citrusy. By the way, if you're out in Miami Beach but too chilled out to schlep across the causeway, Schwartz finally opened an outpost in SoBe's Raleigh Hotel in 2013.

130 NE 40th St. (btw. NE 1st and 2nd Aves.), Design District. www.MichaelsGenuine.com. © **305/573-5550.** Reservations recommended. Dishes $14–$46. Mon–Fri 11:30am–3pm; Mon–Thurs 5:30–11pm; Fri–Sat 5:30pm–midnight; Sun 11am–2:30pm and 5:30–10pm.

Tropical Chinese ★★ CHINESE What's particularly "Miami" about a Chinese restaurant, you might wonder? Ordinarily not much, but over the years this attractively decorated space tucked into the unprepossessing Tropical Park Plaza strip mall west of Coral Gables has become a beloved institution for residents of a region with a dearth of decent Chinese dining. In addition to a tasty regular menu, Tropical happens to serve a wide array of some of the most delicious dim sum this side of Hong Kong, 7 days a week—siu mai, steamed pork buns, leek and scallion dumplings, stuffed bean curd skin, and of course those queasily photogenic chicken feet. Favorites on the menu include the roast duck, sizzling black pepper beef (with green peppers and red onions), pepper-salt tofu squares, and a nice version of Singapore rice noodles; I haven't yet gotten to the abalone and the jellyfish salad. The space offers a wide view into the kitchen (always comforting, no?) as well as a touch of elegance—one most notably festooned with a bevy of round red paper lanterns—and the crowd and vibe are usually lively without ever getting overwhelming. I'd say this one's worth the drive even all the way from Miami Beach—and being right off one of the expressways, not even much of a schlep.

7991 Bird Rd. (btw. SW 78th and 79th sts.), Westchester. www.TropicalChineseMiami.com. © **305/262-7576.** Reservations recommended on weekends. Dim sum $3–$7; main courses $13–$36. Dim sum Mon–Fri 11:30am–3:30pm; Sat 11am–3:30pm, Sun 10:30am–3:30pm; dinner Mon–Thurs 3:30–10:30pm, Fri–Sat 3:30–11pm; Sun 3:30–10pm.

Wynwood Kitchen & Bar ★★ LATIN/WORLD FUSION Art has of course been a part of Miami culture in one form or another all along. But in the past decade

Miami has developed one of America's coolest modern-art scenes, partly spurred by the annual extravaganza Art Basel. This refurbed warehouse in the middle of that scene's ground zero, the Wynwood neighborhood north of downtown, serves up Venezuela-born Miguel Aguilar's creative Latin-inspired fusion in the form of small plates such as, say, Mexican corn anointed with cheese and chipotle aioli, or a delicate chicken empanada reincarnation of the classic tomato-based Cuban beef dish *ropa vieja.* The surroundings are even more striking—huge, dramatic paintings and sculptures inside, wall murals out on the patio that make it feel like dining in an art gallery, and a cool soundtrack ranging from progressive jazz to Colombian *cumbia* to Coldplay. Before or after your repast, take a meander through the attached art park, called Wynwood Walls, filled with striking murals done by well-known street and graffiti artists. Thursday through Saturday evenings, live music is added to the mix.

2550 NW 2nd Ave. (at NW 26th St.), Wynwood. www.WynwoodKitchenandBar.com.℃ **305/722-8959.** Dishes $7–$16. Reservations recommended for dinner in winter, during Art Basel, and Wynwood gallery nights (the second Sat of each month). Mon–Thurs 11:30am–3:30pm, 5:30pm–11pm; Fri–Sat 11:30am–3:30pm, 5:30pm–midnight; bar open Mon–Sat until 1am.

Inexpensive

Andiamo Brick Oven Pizza ★★ PIZZERIA One of Miami's best pizza joints is a tire shop. Well, was. This stretch of Biscayne Boulevard is known for its MiMo (Miami Modern, from the 1950s and early '60s) architecture, and visionary Mark Soyka (also owner of South Beach's **News Café,** p. 132, pioneered local gentrification by creating the stylish nearby restaurant **Soyka** and, in 2001, taking a 1954 tire dealership and transmogrifying it into an equally stylish indoor-outdoor (mostly outdoor) pizzeria. A large variety of pies ranges from basic mozzarella and basil to the fully loaded "Godfather," including Italian sausage, pepperoni, meatballs, onions, peppers, mushrooms, and olives. Nice service, fun atmosphere (including projection screens showing movies, videos, and sundry sports and other events), kick-butt pies, and tasty panini and salads—so yeah, *andiamo* (let's go)!

5600 Biscayne Blvd. (at NE 4th Ct.), Upper East Side. www.AndiamoPizzaMiami.com.℃ **305/762-5751.** Pizzas $9–$19, sandwiches $8.25–$8.75. Sun–Thurs 11am–11pm; Fri–Sat 11am–midnight.

Antigua Guatemala Cafetería ★★ GUATEMALAN Most people still think of Little Havana as Cuban, but these days they're actually outnumbered by Central Americans, and of this region's cuisine, I've found Guatemalan the tastiest. Appointed in yellow adobe inside and out, this cozy, family-oriented spot in Little Havana is Miami's premier Guatemalan restaurant as well as a tasty bargain. What's the grub like? In addition to some items in common with Guatemala's neighbor Mexico—fajitas, refried beans, corn tortillas, the rice-based drink *horchata*—this cuisine stars some fascinatingly unique dishes and produce. Order one of the *antojito* (appetizer) platters, then a main dish such as *puerco adobado* (marinated pork) and *chilaquiles* (a

---

Impressions

Miami is the same place that New Orleans was a hundred years ago in the emergence of different cultures. It's fascinating because in the same way North Americans have come to understand the difference between Northern Italian and Southern Italian, we're coming to understand the difference between Peruvian, Venezuelan, and Brazilian cuisine.
—Chef Norman Van Aken

AREPA TO YUCA: MIAMI latin cuisine AT A GLANCE

Miami dining serves up a tasty culinary tour of Latin America—especially countries such as Cuba, Argentina, Peru, Colombia, Nicaragua, and Brazil. Although many restaurants have menus in English for the benefit of *norteamericano* diners, here are translations and suggestions for filling and delicious meals in case they don't:

Arepa: A corn flatbread common in Venezuela and Colombia, eaten with cheese and other accompaniments.

Arroz con pollo: Roast chicken served with saffron-seasoned yellow rice and diced vegetables.

Camarones enchilados: Shrimp in a slightly tangy-sweet, tomato-based sauce.

Ceviche: Raw seafood seasoned with spice and vegetables and marinated in vinegar and citrus to "cook" it; originally Peruvian but present in various Latin cuisines.

Chimichurri: A savory Argentine dressing based on parsley, garlic, and olive oil, paired with steak and sometimes chicken.

Croquetas: Golden-fried croquettes of ham, chicken, or codfish.

Empanada: A pastry with various fillings such as beef, chicken, tuna, or spinach, particularly a specialty of Argentina.

Feijoada: Brazil's national dish, a black-bean stew with beef, pork, and other items.

Flan: Bequeathed to all Latin countries by Spain, it's egg custard in liquid caramel, and is also made in variations including cheese and coconut.

Frijoles negros: Black beans, served in soup or over white rice.

Frita: A Cuban-style hamburger with beef, pork, *chorizo* sausage, garlic, and spices, served with potato sticks.

concoction of tortillas, egg, and cheese). They don't serve some of the specialties I most love from this country, but I still make sure to get over here every once in a while.

2741 W. Flagler St. (btw. NW 27th and 28th Aves.), Little Havana. ✆ **305/643-0304.** Appetizers $1–$9; main dishes $6–$20. Sun–Thurs 8am–11pm; Fri–Sat 8am–midnight.

El Rey de las Fritas ★ CUBAN   One of the town's best fritas, the tasty Cuban take on the hamburger, is given extra zing by pork, savory chorizo sausage, spices such as paprika, a secret-ingredient dressing, and a serving of fried julienned potatoes. This brightly-lit, diner-ish-feeling Little Havana joint on Calle Ocho (the local moniker for Southwest Eighth Street) is great for locals-watching, too. *Fritas* here also come with cheese, fried egg, even sweet fried plantains, and the menu includes various other Cuban sandwiches and dishes. Whatever you order, wash it down with guarapo (fresh-squeezed sugarcane juice) or a tropical shake in flavors such as mango, guava, and trigo (wheat). Some say that rival El Mago de las Fritas, 5828 SW 8th St. (www.elmagodelasfritas.com; ✆ **305/266-8486**), does fritas better, but that of course is a matter of taste; if you want to compare, feel free to drive 40 blocks west.

1821 SW 8th St. (btw. SW 18th and SW 19th Aves.), Little Havana. www.ElReydelasFritas.com. ✆ **305/644-6054.** *Fritas*/sandwiches $4–$8; main dishes $6–$10. Mon–Sat 8am–10:30pm; Sun 8am–10pm.

Mofongo: Popular especially in Puerto Rico and the Dominican Republic, a dish of mashed fried green plantains served in a broth with beef, shrimp, or chicken.

Palomilla: Thinly sliced beef, similar to American minute steak, usually served with onions, parsley, and a mountain of French fries.

Pan Cubano: Long, white, crusty Cuban bread. Ask for it *tostado* ¾ toasted and flattened on a grill with lots of butter.

Papa a la huancaína: Peruvian sliced potatoes with very slightly spicy cheese sauce.

Picadillo: From the Caribbean, a ground-beef hash mixed with (depending on the island) peppers, onions, pimientos, raisins, and olives.

Plátanos (or maduros): Soft, mildly sweet bananas, fried and caramelized.

Pollo asado: Roasted chicken with onions and a crispy skin.

Pupusa: Originating in El Salvador and now part of other Central American cuisines, it's a thick, soft corn tortilla stuffed with cheese and served with various fillings.

Ropa vieja: A tomatoey shredded beef stew whose name literally means "old clothes."

Tostones: Green, unsweet plantains, flattened and fried.

Tres leches: Of Nicaraguan origin but now pan-Latin, "three milks" is a white cake drenched in a blend of milk, evaporated milk, and condensed milk, with a whipped-cream topping

Vaca frita: Cuban-style shredded beef, fried with onions and lemon juice.

Yuca con mojo: The tuber cassava boiled and served in a savory sauce of onions, garlic, and olive oil.

Guayacán ★★ NICARAGUAN   A Little Havana stalwart since 1987, this restaurant, named for the ironwood tree, showcases the tasty specialties of the single-largest nationality of Little Havana's now majority Central American population in the kind of cozy, woody setting I recall from small towns in Nicaragua. I recommend one of the sampler platters with goodies such as fried cheese, cheese-stuffed soft corn tortillas, and my favorite: exquisitely spiced sausages and fried, marinated pork chunks (an artery-clogging cholesterol bomb, for sure, but oh, so delicioso for an occasional treat). Wash it down with the rice-pineapple drink *arroz con piña,* and cap it off with tres leches ("three milks"), a cream-drenched white cake so tasty it's been adopted by various other Latin cuisines.

1933 SW 8th St. (btw. SW 19th and 20th Aves.), Little Havana. www.GuayacanRestaurantMiami. webs.com. ☏ **305/649-2015.** Main dishes $10–$19. Sun–Thurs 11am–10pm; Fri–Sat 11am–11pm.

Jimmy'z Kitchen ★★ CARIBBEAN/AMERICAN   A recentish addition to the artsy Wynwood neighborhood north of downtown, this offshoot of a tiny South Beach original is hip, airy, usually fairly buzzy, and serves some of the tastiest grub I've ever enjoyed in an eatery this affordable. Veteran chef Jimmy Carey may be as gringo as it gets, but passion for the Latin and Caribbean flavors shines in menu items like his version of Cuba's classic *sandwich cubano* (roast pork, black forest ham, Swiss

Yes, Miami is now firmly part of Food Truck Nation. Top trucks include **gastroPod Mobile Gourmet** (www.GastropodMiami.com), a vintage Airstream operated by a veteran of the likes of New York City's Aquavit and Spice Market, as well as Ferrán Adrià's legendary El Bullí, and serving up some serious street food—triple-decker sliders stuffed with shaved pork belly on a potato bun, short-rib hot dogs. Joining this retro-fab, nomadic kitchen-on-wheels on the streets of Miami are at least 100 food trucks, including a few of the original pioneers: **Latin Burger and Taco** (www.LatinBurger.com); "Asian funk fusion" from **Sakaya Kitchen's Dim Ssam a gogo** (www.SakayaKitchen.com); a grilled-cheese purveyor cheekily called **Ms. Cheezious** (www.MsCheezious.com); the **Purple People Eatery** (www.PurplePplEatery.com) dishing out foodie faves such as a truffle-oil-infused bison burger with goat cheese and fried quail egg; and more. Also deserving honorary mention, though it rolls on carts instead of trucks, **Feverish Ice Cream** (www.FeverishIceCream.com) serves gourmet (and vegan-friendly) frozen treats in flavors including chocolate salted coconut and mango bourbon. Truck meetups happen weekly in places such as downtown and Wynwood; for schedules and the overall definitive guide to Miami trucks and where to find them, check out **www.MiamiFoodTrucks.com**

cheese, pickles, and yellow mustard on pressed Cuban bread), jerk chicken breast salad, guava or mango cheesecake, and above all his absolutely to-die-for *mofongo* (popular in Puerto Rico, the Dominican Republic, and Cuba, it's fried mashed plantains bathed in a tomatoey broth with shrimp, pork, steak, chicken, or fish). Pretty cool international beer list, too. And by the way, if you'd like to pop into the tiny original, you'll find it at 1542 Alton Rd. (© **305/534-8216**), and there's now a third location out west near Dadeland mall (9050 South Dixie Hwy., © **305/670-1503**).

2700 N. Miami Ave. (at NE 27th St.), Wynwood. www.JimmyzKitchen.com. © **305/573-1505.** Sandwiches $8–$12, salads $7–$15, main dishes $11–$22. Sun–Thurs 11am–10pm, Fri–Sat 11am–11pm.

Shorty's ★★ BARBECUE   If you're a BBQ fan, it may well be worth the drive out to the Dadeland area of Kendall (and a hop and a skip from Dadeland Mall, p. 111) to sample the finger-lickin' goodies at this landmark vestige of Miami's pre-Latin Southern heritage, a roadhouse founded by late Georgia native E. L. "Shorty" Allen in 1951 (who wafted off to that great smokehouse in the sky in 2013 at age 104). All the classics are here in heaping platters—smoky, tender ribs; pulled pork; brisket and chicken, all accompanied by sides such as fried green tomatoes, fried okra, coleslaw, sweet potatoes, and corn on the cob (for dessert, the key lime pie is unusually tart and tasty). The woody, down-home, honky-tonk atmosphere—picnic tables, exposed beams, hanging railroad lanterns, paper towels on spindles for napkins—is of course part of the mystique. Shorty's has since spawned four other South Florida locations, but naturally, locals swear by the original.

9200 S. Dixie Hwy./U.S. 1 (at Dadeland Blvd.), Kendall. www.Shortys.com. © **305/670-7732.** Sandwiches/burgers $8–$9.50; platters $9–$14. Sun–Thurs 11am–10pm; Fri–Sat 11am–11pm.

Versailles ★★ CUBAN   Calle Ocho's most famous mainstay as well as Miami's best known Cuban icon, Versailles (pronounced "ver-*SIGH*-yes") is something of a marvel not just for longevity (est. 1971) but also its prices and look. We don't know if its kitschy mirrors and chandeliers were meant to evoke the Sun King's palace for real or with tongue in cheek, but they sure make an unforgettable backdrop to a parade of local characters, from blue-haired *abuelitas* to late-night club kids. Versailles still delivers the goods menu-wise, with fare that's tasty, authentic, and still quite affordable. Plantain soup, roast pork with onions, *vaca frita* (shredded grilled beef), guava pastries, Cuban-style coffee that's as sweet as it is strong—all the classics are here, and then some. On the lighter side, you can't go wrong with a pressed *sandwich cubano.*

3555 SW 8th St. (at SW 36th Ave.), Little Havana. www.VersaillesRestaurant.com. © **305/444-0240.** Main courses $5–$20. Mon–Thurs 8am–2am; Fri 8am–3am; Sat 8am–4:30am; Sun 9am–1am.

EXPLORING MIAMI

7

I f there's one thing Miami doesn't have, it's an identity crisis. Multiple personalities, certainly—in fact, it's just this region's vibrant, multifaceted image and offerings that attract millions each year from all over the world. South Beach may be on the top of many local to-do lists, but the rest of Miami-Dade—a fascinating assemblage of multicultural neighborhoods, some on the verge of a popularity explosion—shouldn't be overlooked. The 21st-century "Magic City" now pulls an eclectic mix of old and young, celebs and plebes, American and international, and geek and chic with an equally varied menu of activities.

For starters, Greater Miami boasts some of the world's best natural beauty, with dazzling blue waters, fine sandy beaches, and lush tropical parks. Man-made brilliance, in the form of crayon-colored architecture, never seems to fade in Miami's unique Art Deco district. For cultural variation, you can experience the tastes, sounds, and rhythms of Cuba in Little Havana.

As in any metropolis, though, some areas aren't as great as others. Downtown Miami, for instance, is still in the throes of a major but slow renaissance in which sketchy warehouse areas are being gradually turned hip. In contrast to this development, however, are stubbornly poverty-stricken areas of downtown such as Overtown, Liberty City, and Little Haiti (though Overtown has made stabs at reinventing part of itself as the "Overtown Historic Village," showcasing landmarks such as the famous Lyric Theater and the home of D. A. Dorsey, Miami's first African-American millionaire). While I obviously advise you to exercise caution when exploring the less traveled parts of the city, I'd also be remiss if I were to tell you to bypass them completely.

Lose yourself in Miami's nature, its neighborhoods, and, best of all, its people—a sassy collection of artists and intellectuals, beach bums and international transplants, dolled-up drag queens, and bodies beautiful.

SIGHTS BY THEME

HISTORIC HOME
Barnacle State Historic Site ★★, p. 93
Vizcaya Museum and Gardens ★★★, p. 94

HISTORIC SITE
Ancient Spanish Monastery ★★★, p. 88
Coral Castle ★★, p. 95
Venetian Pool ★★★, p. 93

MONUMENT/MEMORIAL
Holocaust Memorial ★★★, p. 84

MUSEUM
Coral Gables Museum ★★, p. 92
Jewish Museum of Florida ★★, p. 85

Miami Children's Museum ★★, p. 86
Patricia and Phillip Frost Museum of Science ★★, p. 94
Wolfsonian ★★★, p. 87
World Erotic Art Museum ★★, p. 87

NATURE RESERVE
Marjory Stoneman Douglas Biscayne Nature Center ★★, p. 90

PLANETARIUM
Patricia and Phillip Frost Museum of Science ★★, p. 94

ZOO
Jungle Island ★★, p. 85
Monkey Jungle ★, p. 96
Zoo Miami ★★★, p. 96

MIAMI'S BEACHES

Perhaps Miami's most popular attraction is its incredible 35-mile stretch of beachfront, from the tip of South Beach north to Sunny Isles, then circling Key Biscayne and numerous other islands dotting the Atlantic. The characters of Miami's many beaches are as varied as the city's population: There are beaches for swimming, socializing, or serenity; for families, seniors, or gay singles; some to make you forget you're in the city, others loomed over by huge condominiums. Whatever type of beach vacation you're looking for, you'll find it in one of Miami's two distinct beach areas: Miami Beach and Key Biscayne. And in keeping with today's technology, Miami Beach is now officially a hot spot—as in a wireless hot spot, offering free Wi-Fi with 95% coverage outdoors (70% indoors) throughout the entire city and, yes, even on the sand.

MIAMI BEACH'S BEACHES   Collins Avenue fronts more than a dozen miles of white-sand beach and blue-green waters from 1st to 192nd streets. Although most of this stretch is lined with a solid wall of hotels and condos, beach access is plentiful. There are lots of public beaches here, wide and well maintained, complete with lifeguards, restroom facilities, concession stands, and metered parking (bring lots of quarters). Except for a thin strip close to the water, most of the sand is hard packed—the result of a $10-million Army Corps of Engineers Beach Rebuilding Project meant to protect buildings from the effects of eroding sand.

From Desert Island to Fantasy Island

Miami Beach wasn't always a beachfront playground. In fact, it was a deserted island until the late 1800s, when a developer started a coconut farm there. That sparked interest from many other developers, including John Collins (for whom Collins Avenue is named), who began growing avocados. Other visionaries admired Collins's success and eventually joined him, establishing a ferry service and dredging parts of the bay to make the island more accessible. In 1921, Collins built a 2½-mile bridge linking downtown Miami to Miami Beach; today Miami Beach has six links to the mainland.

Miami's Best Beaches & Natural Areas

12th Street Beach **4**
Bill Baggs Cape Florida
    State Park **10**
Crandon Park Beach **9**
Fairchild Topical Botanic
    Garden **11**
Hialeah Park **2**
Hobie Beach **6**
Lummus Park Beach **3**
Marjory Stoneman
    Douglas Biscayne
    Nature Center **8**
Oleta River State
    Recreation Area **1**
Preston B. Bird and
    Mary Heinlein Fruit
    and Spice Park **12**
South Pointe Park **5**
Virginia Key
    Beach Park **7**

Lummus Park Beach (www.MiamiBeachFL.gov/ParksandRecreation; ☎ **305/673-7730**), also known simply as South Beach, runs along Ocean Drive from about 6th to 14th streets in South Beach. It's the best place to go if you're seeking entertainment as well as a great tan. On any day of the week, you might spy models primping for a photo shoot, scantily clad sun-worshippers avoiding tan lines (going topless is legal here, but not bottomless), and an assembly line of washboard abs off of which you could (but shouldn't) bounce your bottle of sunscreen. Bathrooms and changing facilities are available on the beach, but don't expect to have a Gisele Bündchen encounter in one of these. Most people tend to prefer using the somewhat drier, cleaner bathrooms of the restaurants on Ocean Drive.

South Beach's **12th Street Beach** (☎ **305/673-7714**) is *the* place to be for Miami's gay beach scene. Here you'll observe the strutting, kibitzing, and gossiping of Miami's comely gay population. You might even find yourself lucky enough to happen upon a feisty South Beach party while you're soaking up some rays. If you can hold it, skip the public bathroom and head over to The Palace on Ocean Drive to use its bathroom.

In general, the beaches on this barrier island (all on the eastern, ocean side of the island) become less crowded the farther north you go. A wooden boardwalk runs along the hotel side of the beach from 21st to 46th streets—about 1½ miles—offering a terrific sun-and-surf experience without getting sand in your shoes. Miami's lifeguard-protected public beaches include 21st Street, at the beginning of the boardwalk; 35th Street, popular with an older crowd; 46th Street, next to the Fontainebleau Hotel; 53rd Street, a narrower, more sedate beach; 64th Street, one of the quietest strips around; and 72nd Street, a local old-timers' spot.

KEY BISCAYNE'S BEACHES   If Miami Beach doesn't provide the privacy you're looking for, try Virginia Key and Key Biscayne. The tollbooths to the Rickenbacker Causeway ($1.75) can get backed up on weekends, when beach bums and tan-o-rexics flock here, but the 5 miles of public beach are blessed with softer sand and are less developed and more laid-back than the hotel-laden strips to the north. In 2008, Key Biscayne reopened the historic **Virginia Key Beach Park,** 4020 Virginia Beach Dr. (www.VirginiaKeyBeachPark.net; *C* **305/960-4600**), the former "colored only" beach that opened in 1945 and closed in 1982 due to high upkeep costs. After an $11-million renovation, the 83-acre historic site features picnic tables and grills, shoreline shore-up, a playground for children with special needs, a vintage carousel, and a miniature train ride. It's open from 7am to sunset daily, with free admission.

On the south side of Key Biscayne's Rickenbacker Causeway, **Hobie Beach** (*C* **305/361-2833**) is one of South Florida's most popular beaches for watersport fans, featuring Jet Ski, sailboat, windsurfing, and sailboard rentals; shade, if necessary, from the Australian pine; and a sublime view of the downtown Miami skyline.

SOUTH BEACH & THE ART DECO DISTRICT

South Beach's 10 miles of beach are alive with a frenetic, circus-like atmosphere and are center stage for a motley crew of characters, from eccentric locals, seniors, snow-birds, and college students to gender-benders, celebrities, club kids, and curiosity seekers. Individuality is as widely accepted on South Beach as Visa and MasterCard.

Although the beautiful people do flock to South Beach, the models aren't the only sights worth drooling over. The thriving Art Deco District within South Beach has the largest concentration of Deco architecture in the world (in 1979, much of South Beach was listed in the National Register of Historic Places). The district is roughly bounded by the Atlantic Ocean on the east, Alton Road on the west, 6th Street to the south, and Dade Boulevard (along the Collins Canal) to the north. Most of the finest examples of the whimsical Art Deco style are concentrated along three parallel streets—Ocean Drive, Collins Avenue, and Washington Avenue—from about 6th to 23rd streets.

---

walking BY DESIGN

The Miami Design Preservation League offers several tours of Miami Beach's historic architecture, all of which leave from the Art Deco Welcome Center at 1001 Ocean Dr., in Miami Beach ($22 per person). A self-guided audio tour ($17; available in several languages) turns the streets into a virtual outdoor museum, taking you through Miami Beach's Art Deco district at your own pace. Guided tours conducted by local historians and architects offer an in-depth look at the structures and their history. They'll often add specialty tours covering everything from architecture to food; call for details. For reservations or more info, visit www.MDPL.org or call *C* **305/672-2014.**

Miami or Madrid?

On a tiny street in South Beach, there's a piece of Spain that's so vibrant, you almost feel as if you're in Madonna's "La Isla Bonita" video. In 1925, Miami Beach developer NBT Roney hired architect Robert Taylor to design a Spanish village on the property he just purchased on a street called **Española Way.** Today, the historic Mediterranean-Revival-style Spanish Village—or Plaza De España—envisioned by Roney and complete with fountain, stretches from Washington Avenue to Drexel Avenue and features charming boutiques, cafes, and a weekend market.

Simply put, Art Deco is a style of architecture that, in its heyday of the 1920s and 1930s, used to be considered ultramodern. Today, fans of the style consider it retro fabulous. According to the experts, Art Deco made its debut in 1925 at an exposition in Paris in which it set a stylistic tone, with buildings based on early neoclassical styles with the application of exotic motifs such as flora, fauna, and fountains based on geometric patterns. In Miami, Art Deco is marked by the carefully restored, pastel-hued buildings that line South Beach and Miami Beach, but it's a lot more than just color. If you look carefully, you will see the intricacies and impressive craftsmanship that went into each building in Miami back in the '20s, '30s, and '40s.

After years of neglect and calls for the wholesale demolition of its buildings, South Beach got a new lease on life in 1979. Under the leadership of Barbara Baer Capitman, a dedicated crusader for the Art Deco zone, and the Miami Design Preservation League, founded by Baer Capitman and five friends, an area made up of an estimated 800 buildings was granted a listing on the National Register of Historic Places. Designers then began highlighting long-lost architectural details with soft sherbet shades of peach, periwinkle, turquoise, and purple. Developers soon moved in, and the full-scale refurbishment of the area's hotels was underway.

Not everyone was pleased, though. Former Miami Beach commissioner Abe Resnick said, "I love old buildings. But these Art Deco buildings are 40, 50 years old. They aren't historic. They aren't special. We shouldn't be forced to keep them." But Miami Beach kept those buildings, and Resnick lost his seat on the board.

Today hundreds of new establishments—hotels, restaurants, and nightclubs—have renovated these older, historic buildings, putting South Beach on the cutting edge of Miami's cultural and nightlife scene.

Exploring the Area

If you're touring this unique neighborhood on your own, start at the **Art Deco Welcome Center,** 1001 Ocean Dr. (www.MDPL.org; ℭ **305/763-8026**), run by the Miami Design Preservation League. The only beachside building across from the Clevelander Hotel and bar, the center gives away lots of informational material, including maps and pamphlets, and runs guided tours around the neighborhood. Art Deco books (including *The Art Deco Guide,* an informative compendium of all the buildings here), T-shirts, postcards, mugs, and other paraphernalia are for sale. It's open daily 10am to 7:30pm.

Take a stroll along **Ocean Drive** for the best view of sidewalk cafes, bars, colorful hotels, and even more colorful people. Another great place for a walk is **Lincoln Road,** lined with boutiques, large chain stores, cafes, and funky art and antiques stores. The Community Church, at the corner of Lincoln Road and Drexel Avenue, was the

South Beach Attractions

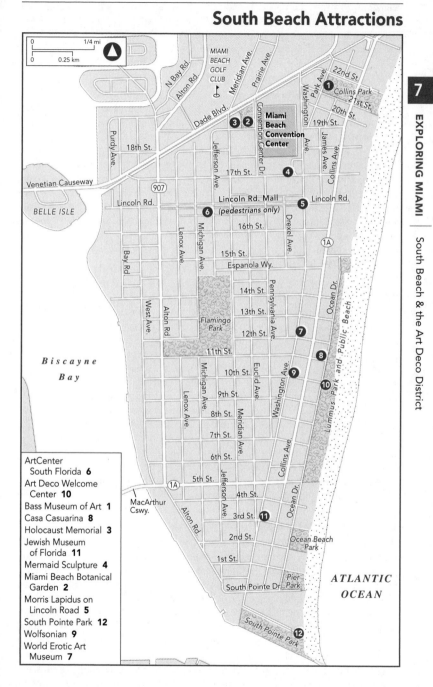

ArtCenter
  South Florida **6**
Art Deco Welcome
  Center **10**
Bass Museum of Art **1**
Casa Casuarina **8**
Holocaust Memorial **3**
Jewish Museum
  of Florida **11**
Mermaid Sculpture **4**
Miami Beach Botanical
  Garden **2**
Morris Lapidus on
  Lincoln Road **5**
South Pointe Park **12**
Wolfsonian **9**
World Erotic Art
  Museum **7**

neighborhood's first church and is one of its oldest surviving buildings, dating from 1921. Then there's the Herzog & de Meuron–designed parking garage at 1111 Lincoln Rd., which is, oddly enough, not only a place to park cars, but a stylish eye-catcher that's also the hub of several trendy new shops and restaurants (including **Nespresso Café,** an ultramodern European-style spot serving light fare and coffee). Architecture buffs will love the building; shopaholics and foodies will love what's in it.

ArtCenter South Florida ★★ ART GALLERY   With a prime spot near the midpoint of Lincoln Road, this 30-year-old gallery complex became a groundbreaking redevelopment pioneer at a time when this pedestrian mall was still a pathetically dilapidated shadow of its original self. There are 45 studio spaces rented at deeply subsidized rates to artists in every medium from all over the world, and part of the deal is that they open their spaces and make themselves available to the public. It's a great opportunity to get an eyeful of some stimulating, sometimes provocative sights and sounds, and what's cutting-edge and upcoming in the art world. Things perk up especially on the first Saturday evening (7–10pm) of each month, when a "studio crawl" has all the artists out in force. Also open to the public is a second space, called Project 924, just down Lincoln Road at—you guessed it—number 924.

800 Lincoln Rd. (at Meridian Ave.). www.ArtCenterSF.org. ✆**305/674-8278.** Admission free. Mon–Thurs noon–9pm; Fri–Sat 11am–10pm; Sun 11am–9pm.

Bass Museum of Art ★★★ ART MUSEUM   Fine art may not be the first thing that leaps to mind when you think South Beach, but if you have any cultural leanings (or are simply looking for something to do on a rainy or otherwise non-beach day), you might be pleasantly surprised by the riches harbored here. Its white coral-stone facade fronts a more recently added annex designed by Arata Isozaki, marking its half-century anniversary this year. The permanent collection includes some 3,000 works or objects stretching back to ancient Greece and Egypt (mummy anyone?), including European and American masters such as Rubens, Botticelli, and Benjamin West. Much of the focus, though, is on temporary shows such as one themed on gold (boy, do they know their audience) and a multimedia installation including a mesmerizing live-action recreation of the famous Velázquez painting *The Maids of Honor* (OMG, was that Peter Dinklage in a dress?). Families who happen to be here on the last Sunday of each month can enjoy IDEA@thebass, a family day that includes children's art activities, scavenger hunts, yoga, performances, and prizes.

2121 Park Ave. (2100 Collins Ave., at 21st St.). www.BassMuseum.org. ✆**305/673-7530.** Admission $8 adults, $6 students and seniors, free ages 6 and under, free last Sun of the month. Wed–Sun noon–5pm.

Holocaust Memorial ★★★ MONUMENT/MEMORIAL   This heart-wrenching memorial is hard to miss and would be a shame to overlook. The powerful centerpiece, Kenneth Treister's *A Sculpture of Love and Anguish,* depicts victims of the concentration camps crawling up a giant yearning hand stretching up to the sky, marked with an Auschwitz number tattoo. Along the reflecting pool is the story of the Holocaust, told in cut marble slabs. Inside the center of the memorial is a tableau that is one of the most solemn and moving tributes I've seen to the millions of Jews who lost their lives to the Nazis. You can walk through an open hallway lined with photographs and the names of camps and their victims. From the street, you'll see the outstretched arm, but do stop and tour the sculpture at ground level.

1933 Meridian Ave. (at Dade Blvd.). www.HolocaustMMB.org. ✆**305/538-1663.** Free admission. Daily 10am–10pm.

Jewish Museum of Florida ★★ MUSEUM   Why, in a way, is this one of South Beach's most relevant museums? Many people don't realize that the today world-celebrated Deco District was built back in the 1920s and 30s essentially as a Jewish ghetto. Since developers—in what were then more desirable nabes—refused to sell to the sons and daughters of Abraham (illustrated here by a sign quoting a charming local hospitality industry boasting, "Always a View, Never a Jew"). However, this pair of buildings, including a 1929 former synagogue, doesn't dwell on the negative but focuses more on the myriad, sometimes surprising, ways Jews have made their mark not just in Miami but throughout Florida all the way back to the *conversos* thought to have arrived with Ponce de León; groundbreakers also include mobster Meyer Lansky, whose name is even on a stained-glass window on the right-hand side of the main exhibition hall, and the first Jewish Miss America, Bess Myerson, who donated photos and memorabilia. It's a modest collection of pictures and text with a smattering of multimedia and original artifacts, but it's likely to be an eye-opener.

301 Washington Ave. www.JewishMuseum.com. ✆ **305/672-5044.** Admission $6 adults, $5 seniors and students, $12 families. Tues–Sun 10am–5pm. Closed Jewish holidays.

Jungle Island ★★ ZOO   Once upon a time, most people just zipped across tiny Watson Island on the causeway between downtown and Miami Beach. In the past decade, though, Watson has become one of Miami's top family draws, thanks to the Miami Children's Museum (below) and this pricey but excellent diversion for kids and animal lovers. The 19-acre park features an Everglades exhibit, a petting zoo, and several theaters, jungle trails, and aviaries. Living here are hundreds of parrots, macaws, peacocks, cockatoos, and flamingos. Continuous shows star bicycle-riding cockatoos, high-flying macaws, and numerous stunt-happy parrots. One of the most popular shows is "Tale of the Tiger," featuring awesome animals. Jungle Island also features the only African penguins in South Florida as well as a liger—part lion, part tiger—and endangered baby lemurs. There are also tortoises, iguanas, and a rare albino alligator on exhibit. *Tip:* The park's website sometimes offers downloadable discount coupons, so take a look before visiting, because you definitely don't want to pay full price for this park. To see all the shows and exhibits, expect to spend upwards of 4 hours. *Note:* The former South Miami site of (Parrot) Jungle Island is now known as **Pinecrest Gardens,** 11000 Red Rd. (www.Pinecrest-FL.gov; ✆ **305/669-6990),**

A Japanese Garden

If you ask someone what Japanese influences can be found in Miami, they'll likely point to Nobu, Sushi Siam, Sushi Rock Cafe, and even Benihana. But back in the '50s, well before sushi became a thing, Kiyoshi Ichimura became obsessed with Miami and started sending people and things from Tokyo, including carpenters, gardeners, and a landscape architect, to design and build the San-Ai-An Japanese Garden. Originally located in the Jungle Island space,

the garden was dismantled and re-created adjacent to the park, at 1101 MacArthur Causeway on Watson Island (www.FriendsofJapaneseGarden.com). The new 1-acre garden was renamed **Ichimura Miami–Japan Garden** in honor of its original benefactor, and its sculptures and Japanese artifacts are managed by a coalition of city organizations. Japanese holidays and festivals are celebrated here. It's open daily from 9am to 6pm, and admission is free.

roadside **ATTRACTIONS**

The following examples of public art and prized architecture are great photo opportunities and worth visiting if you're in the area.

o **Casa Casuarina, aka the Versace Mansion:** Morbid curiosity has led hordes of folks here, once the only private home on Ocean Drive. Built in the 1930s as a replica of Christopher Columbus's son's palace in Santo Domingo, the house was originally called *Casa Casuarina* (House of the Pine). Legendary Italian designer Gianni Versace bought it in 1992 and spent $33 million on bringing it up to his extravagant standards. Five years later, he was gunned down on its front steps by a deranged stalker. If you can get past that, you should definitely note the intricate Italianate architecture that makes this house stand out from its streamlined Deco neighbors. After years as a luxe restaurant and massively pricey hotel, it was put up for sale in 2012, for an astounding $125 million. After selling for just $41.3 million in 2014, it reopened as Villa by Barton G. (p. 50), usually accessible only to guests and restaurant diners. It's at the corner of Ocean Drive and 11th Street in South Beach.

o **Mermaid Sculpture:** A pop-art masterpiece designed by Roy Lichtenstein, this sculpture captures the buoyant spirit of Miami Beach and its environs. It's in front of the Jackie Gleason Theater of the Performing Arts at 1700 Washington Ave.

o **Morris Lapidus on Lincoln Road:** Famed designer/architect, Morris Lapidus—the "high priest of high kitsch"— best known for the Fontainebleau Hotel (p. 48), created a series of sculptures that are angular, whimsical, and quirky, competing with the equally amusing mix of pedestrians who flock to Lincoln Road. In addition to the sculptures on Lincoln Road (at Washington Ave.), which you can't miss, Lapidus also created the **Colony Theater,** 1040 Lincoln Rd., built by Paramount in 1943; the 1928 **Sterling Building,** 927 Lincoln Rd., whose glass blocks and blue neon are required evening viewing; and **H&M** department store (until 2012 the Lincoln Theater), 541 Lincoln Rd., which features a remarkable tropical bas-relief.

which features a petting zoo, mini waterpark, lake, natural hammocks, and banyan caves. It's open daily from 9am until 5pm; admission is $3 for adults, $2 for kids.

MacArthur Causeway/I-395, Watson Island (north side). www.JungleIsland.com. ⟨✆⟩ **305/400-7000.** Admission $35 adults, $33 age 62 and older, $27 ages 3–10, free for U.S. military personnel with valid ID/ages 2 and under. Parking $8 per vehicle. Mon–Fri 10am–5pm; Sat–Sun 10am–6pm.

Miami Children's Museum ★★★ MUSEUM   Kids really take to practically every corner of this multi-media, fairly high-tech, two-story museum, starting with the "pretend-professions" zone on the ground floor, where they can try out a police motorcycle, a mock fire truck, a model doctor's office and supermarket, and more. Upstairs highlights include an art and music space where it's all about touching and looking, and they can, for example, get hands gunked up with paint or record their own tunes. Keep in mind that weekday mornings are most crowded, being prime time for local school groups. There's usually one big temporary exhibit at any given time, such as the recent, very cool one about dinosaurs—including animatronics. Stop in the shop on your way out; it's one toy store parents will appreciate as much as the little squirts.

980 MacArthur Causeway, Watson Island. www.MiamiChildrensMuseum.org. © **305/373-5437.** Admission $18 ages 1 and over, $14 Florida residents. Daily 10am–6pm.

Wolfsonian ★★★ MUSEUM Its big, blocky white facade and fancy stonework are a one-of-a-kind presence amid the commercial/touristy scene on Washington Avenue. One of my favorite Greater Miami museums displays a one-of-a-kind permanent collection of mostly European and U.S. artifacts, artwork, artisanry, and design from the late 19th- to mid-20th centuries. The difference here is that this isn't purely art for art's sake, but a reflection of history, society, politics, and socio-economic issues. So yes, those 1926 stained-glass panels, for example, are luminous and lovely, but they also reflect themes and allegories relating to Ireland's independence. Fascinating political and World War II propaganda posters are part of the mix, as are vintage stoves, vacuum cleaners, Bauhaus furniture, and other items from a particular era of modernization. The fifth floor is the permanent collection, while other floors host rotating exhibitions such as 2014's "The Rebirth of Rome," focusing on art and architecture in fascist Italy. Also check out the funky museum store, with beautiful books, DVDs, retro objects both decorative and useful, and a cafe (also open to non-museum visitors) where you can eat/drink organic while watching black and white silent movies on a large flatscreen TV (last time I was in, it was Buster Keaton in *The General*).

1001 Washington Ave. (at 10th St.). www.Wolfsonian.org.© **305/531-1001.** Admission $7 adults; $5 seniors, students with ID, and ages 6–12; free after 6pm Fri. Sat–Tues noon–6pm; Fri noon–9pm.

World Erotic Art Museum ★★ MUSEUM Funny story. There was this Jewish lady of a certain age in New Jersey whose son asked her to find him some sexy art for his bachelor pad, and guess what? He nixed the painting because it was too tasteful! Meanwhile, mom had become intrigued by art dealing with human sexuality. Eventually Naomi Wilzig's collection grew to thousands, and she decided to share it with the world. As of 2005, Miami Beach has been the beneficiary. Spread over 12,000 square feet of a onetime office space is an impressive mix of museum-quality fine and folk art with pop-culture objects (such as the notorious white phallus sculpture from *A Clockwork Orange*) and, yes, the occasional comic relief (Mickey Mouse, is that you?).

Art-a-Palooza on the Beach

For a few days in December, Miami becomes a cultural mecca as art lovers from around the planet flock here for the very popular offshoot of Switzerland's **Art Basel** (www.ArtBasel.com/en/Miami-Beach). The focal points of Art Basel are the huge exhibition at the Miami Beach Convention Center and the installations and performances at **Collins Park Cultural Center** (www.CollinsPark.us), a trio of arts buildings on Collins Park and Park Avenue (off Collins Ave.), bounded by 21st to 23rd streets; these are the **Bass Museum of Art** (p. 84), the new Arquitectonica-designed home of the Miami City Ballet, and the Miami Beach Regional Library, an ultramodern building designed by architect Robert A. M. Stern. A few cultural institutions that are part of the emerging Collins Park neighborhood are local arts organization **SoBe Arts** at the Carl Fisher complex; the **Miami Beach Botanical Garden;** and the **Holocaust Memorial** (p. 84).

You'll spot names such as Picasso, Gauguin, Botero, Dalí, and Miró, along with exquisite artifacts from antiquity and special exhibitions from the likes of Helmut Newton and Tom of Finland. Best of all, Naomi is often on hand to give tours. As she told me, "When the mayor of Miami Beach comes here to award the key to the city to a Miami tourism bureau honcho, I guess you could say we've 'arrived.'"

1205 Washington Ave. (at 12th St.). www.WEAM.com. © **305/532-9336.** Admission $15 adults, $14 seniors and students. Minimum age 18. Mon–Thurs 11am–10pm; Fri–Sun 11am–midnight.

NORTH MIAMI BEACH

Ancient Spanish Monastery ★★★ HISTORIC SITE   Most of the "historic" buildings throughout Greater Miami are "neo" this and ersatz that, but this gorgeous cloister is the real deal: a Cistercian monastery built in Segovia, Spain in the 12th century, then dismantled and brought to the United States in 1925 by none other than *Citizen Kane* newspaper tycoon William Randolph Hearst. This isn't merely a tourist attraction, but also home to an Episcopal church, St. Bernard de Clairvaux. It's super-popular for weddings, photo shoots, and other special occasions, and thus can close without notice, so call ahead. There's also a small collection of historic artifacts in the lobby. Combine a visit with the nearby Museum of Contemporary Art, Oleta River Park, and/or Aventura/Bal Harbour malls.

16711 W. Dixie Hwy. (btw. NW167th and NW 170th sts.), North Miami Beach. www.Spanish Monastery.com. © **305/945-1461.** Admission $8 adults, $5 students/ages 62 and over/U.S. military. Mon–Sat 10am–4:30pm; Sun 11am–4:30pm.

NORTH MIAMI

Museum of Contemporary Art (MoCA) ★★ ART MUSEUM   Founded in 1996, the big kahuna in the city of North Miami anchors its main downtown drag, NE 125th Street, once tipped as South Florida's next hot urban center, complete with slick marketing moniker (NoMi, of course). Well, that never gelled, but if you happen to be in the area (for example at the ginormous **Aventura Mall,** p. 110), MoCA is worth a look. It's quite small for a major museum—some 12,000 square feet—but it does boast a well-curated collection of today's art scene, even if you'd need to be a real maven to recognize most of the names, besides maybe Louise Nevelson, Julian Schnabel, and Nam June Paik. It's one of the few U.S. contemporary art museums that collects, as opposed to mostly hosting rotating shows, and it also schedule parties, concerts, lectures, and other events. Check the website, though, because as of 2014 MoCa's finances and administration were in a rough patch, and there was even talk of merging with the Bass Museum. In any case, when you do visit, pop across the street afterward for a bite/cuppa/something stronger at hipster hangout Luna Star Cafe.

770 NE 125th St. (btw. NE 7th and 8th aves.), North Miami. www.MOCANoMi.org. © **305/893-6211.** Admission $5 adults, $3 seniors and students with ID, free for ages 12 and under/U.S. military/veterans. Tues–Sun 11am–5pm.

KEY BISCAYNE

Miami Seaquarium ★ AQUARIUM   If you've been to Orlando's SeaWorld, you'll find Miami's version something of a letdown—it's a lot smaller (35 acres) and less well maintained. Still, if you go you'll want to get here early, and allow at least 3 hours to tour grounds and take in all four of the daily shows (you can cut it to 2 hours

Miami Area Attractions

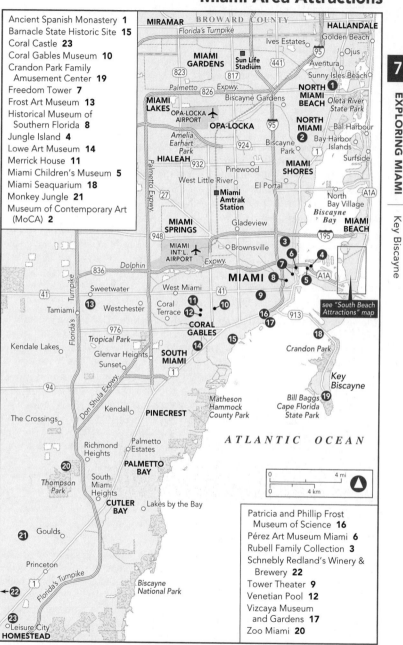

A Carousel by the Sea

At the **Crandon Park Family Amusement Center,** 4000 Crandon Blvd., Key Biscayne (© **305/361-5421**), there's an outdoor roller rink, a dolphin-shaped splash fountain and marine sculptures, and an old-fashioned carousel, crafted in 1949 by the Allan Herschell Company and restored to its former glory. Even the music—provided by an old-fashioned organ—is historic. The amusement area is open from 10:30am to 5pm on weekends, and three rides on the carousel cost $1.

if you limit yourself to the better, albeit corny, "Flipper" and "Killer Whale and Dolphin" shows). The Dolphin Encounter allows visitors to touch and swim with dolphins in the Flipper Lagoon. Offered daily at 12 and 2:30pm, this costs $139 per adult, $99 for ages 5 to 9, $45 per adult observer, and $36 per observer ages 3 to 9. Reservations are necessary for this program (call © **305/365-2501**). A sea lion show and a stingray touch pool have also recently been added. Like SeaWorld, the Seaquarium has been engendering controversy, especially recently, because of the campaign to return its killer whale Lolita to Puget Sound where she was originally captured. At press time it was possible the Seaquarium's new owners would take a new stance on the matter.

4400 Rickenbacker Causeway (south side), Virginia Key en route to Key Biscayne. www.Miami Seaquarium.com. © **305/361-5705.** Admission $40 adults, $30 ages 3–9, free for ages 2 and under. Parking $8. Daily 9:30am–6pm (ticket booth closes at 4:30pm).

Marjory Stoneman Douglas Biscayne Nature Center ★★ NATURE RESERVE   If you only have time for one activity on Key Biscayne, skip the Seaquarium and head here for **Sea Grass Adventures,** in which a naturalist from the center introduces kids and adults to an amazing variety of creatures that live in the sea-grass beds of the Bear Cut Nature Preserve near Crandon Beach on Key Biscayne. You will be able to wade in the water with your guide and catch an assortment of sea life in nets provided by the guides. At the end of the program, participants gather on the beach while the guide explains what everyone has just caught, passing the creatures around in miniature viewing tanks. Call for available dates, times, and reservations. The center and grounds themselves are worth a visit, even if you opt not to participate in one of the scheduled programs.

6767 Crandon Blvd. (Crandon Park North Beach entrance, just past Crandon Park Marina). www. BiscayneNatureCenter.org. © **305/361-6767.** Free admission to the center; $14 for Sea Grass Adventures and other tours/programs. Daily 10am–4pm.

DOWNTOWN

Historical Museum of Southern Florida ★★ MUSEUM   This Smithsonian Institution–affiliated institution has an impressive collection of stuff that has defined Florida since pre-history, including the Seminoles, early 20th-century Florida homes, aviation (especially big on Pan Am—anybody remember Pan Am?), and maritime history. Recent exhibitions, meanwhile, have included "Mission Artifacts of Spanish Florida" and another dedicated to reggae legend Bob Marley. The Miami-Dade Cultural Center, where it's housed, is an elevated, fortresslike complex designed by Philip Johnson, also home to the main branch of the Miami-Dade Public Library, which sometimes features art and cultural exhibits. Keep in mind that the plaza onto which

CUBAN-AMERICANS' ellis island

Driving north on Biscayne Boulevard in downtown Miami, some may be distracted by the traffic, the neon lights coming from the Bayside Marketplace, or the monstrous new high-rises. But even though it's now dwarfed by those surrounding towers, a still dramatic presence on this heavily trafficked stretch is the **Freedom Tower,** 600 Biscayne Blvd. at NE 6th St. (www.MDCMOAD.org; ✆ **305/237-7700**), built in 1925 and modeled after the Giralda Tower in Seville, Spain. Once home to the now-defunct *Miami Daily News* and *Metropolis* newspapers, the building was sold in 1957 to the U.S. General Services Administration, which used it to process more than 500,000 Cubans fleeing the island after Fidel Castro and his merry men took over.

Considered the Ellis Island of the Cuban exile community, the building today known as the Freedom Tower has remained largely vacant over the years (the Feds moved out in 1974), despite hopes and unfulfilled plans to turn it into a museum reflecting its historical significance. In 2004, developers donated the tower to Miami Dade College, which has since used the space for hosting various exhibitions and cultural programs. In 2008 the tower was designated a U.S. National Historic Landmark. Its art exhibitions are open to the public Wednesday through Sunday from noon to 5pm.

the complex opens is a bit of a hangout for downtown Miami's street people, which can make it slightly off-putting, though not dangerous; the adjacent parking garage (see below) has a skywalk directly into the museum plaza.

101 W. Flagler St. (at NW 2nd Ave.), downtown. www.HistoryMiami.org. ✆ **305/375-1492.** Admission $8 adults, $7 seniors and college students with ID, $5 ages 6–12, free ages 6 and under; free second Sat of the month. Mon–Sat 10am–5pm; Sun noon–5pm. Discounted parking at Miami-Dade Cultural Center Parking Garage, 50 NW 2nd Ave.

Pérez Art Museum Miami ★★★ ART MUSEUM   Opened in downtown's still unfinished "Museum Park" in December 2013, the new iteration of our publicly-owned Miami Art Museum (its name unfortunately hijacked by real estate developer Jorge Pérez), is an admittedly impressive bit of business indeed, which in addition to displaying collected artists such as Louise Nevelson, Wifredo Lam, Marcel Duchamp, and Roy Lichtenstein also stages exhibitions like that of Chinese dissident artist Ai Weiwei in 2014, and Canadian installation artist Geoffrey Farmer through February 2015. This being Miami, there's a particular emphasis on the Latin American and the Caribbean. There's also a nice restaurant called Verde, and a very browse-able shop.

1103 Biscayne Blvd. (at NW 11th St.). www.PAMM.org. ✆ **305/375-3000.** Admission $12 adults, $10 seniors, $6 ages 13–18, free for under age 13 and students with ID. Tues–Sun 10am–6pm; Thurs also 6–9pm.

THE DESIGN DISTRICT

Rubell Family Collection ★★★ ART MUSEUM   One of the world's great collections of cutting-edge contemporary art (including Jean-Michel Basquiat, Maurizio Cattelan, Keith Haring, Damien Hirst, Cady Noland, Charles Ray, Cindy Sherman, and Andy Warhol) is owned by the Rubell family, Miami hoteliers, and is housed in a 40,000-square-foot former Drug Enforcement Agency facility 10 minutes from South

digging MIAMI

Until the controversial discovery of the archaeological site known as the Miami River Circle, the oldest existing artifacts in the city were presumed to be hanging in the closets of Miami's retirement homes. In September 1998, during a routine archaeological dig at the mouth of the Miami River, several unusual features were discovered cut into the bedrock: a prehistoric circular structure, 37 feet in diameter, with intentional markings of the cardinal directions as well as a 5-foot-long shark and two stone axes, suggesting the circle had ceremonial significance to Miami's earliest inhabitants, the Tequesta Indians. Radiocarbon tests confirm that the circle is about 2,000 years old.

Although some have theorized that the circle is a calendar or Miami's own version of Stonehenge, most scholars believe that the discovery represents the foundation of a circular structure, perhaps a council house or a chief's house. Expert scientists, archaeologists, and scholars who have made visits to the site indicate that the circle is of local, regional, and national significance. Local preservationists formed an organization, Save the Miami Circle, to ensure that developers didn't raze the circle to make way for condominiums. As a result, the circle remains put, albeit surrounded by the EPIC and Viceroy/Icon hotels and condos, and the mystery continues. See www.Miami Circle.org for more information.

Beach. Rotating exhibitions include the well-known 30 Americans. Starting during December's Art Basel, there's a seasonal program of lectures, artist talks, and performances as well as a research library, bookshop, and sculpture garden. A complimentary guided tour is given at 3pm Wednesday and Friday, and a free audio tour is available for mobile gadgets.

95 NW 29th St. (at NW 1st Ave.). www.RubellFamilyCollection.com. ✆ **305/573-6090.** Admission $10 adults, $5 students and under age 18. Dec–May Tues–Sat 10am–6pm; June–Nov Wed and Fri 3pm for tours only.

CORAL GABLES

Coral Gables Museum ★★ MUSEUM   Since its founding in the 1920s by developer George Merrick, Coral Gables has become one of Florida's most beautiful, historic, cultural, and well-heeled cities—yet it wasn't until 2011 that local leaders finally achieved a city museum. The result occupies 24,000 square feet in downtown's original fire and police HQ, a creamy coral-stone Mediterranean-Revival affair adorned with carved heads of long-ago firemen. At the core of the nine light, airy galleries lies the story of how the Gables was carved out of orange groves and wilderness, including plenty of period documents, artifacts, and fascinating photos and artwork. Beyond that, rotating exhibitions focus on, for example, local artists, Coral Gables sister cities, and a variety of themes with less immediately obvious local connections (such as the recent *Photos of Pavia,* focusing on that Italian city in the 19th through 21st centuries). I'd recommend pairing this with a visit to the founding family's nearby homestead, **Merrick House,** 907 Coral Way (✆ **305/460-5361**), open for tours Sunday and Wednesday (call for details).

285 Aragon Ave. (btw. Ponce de Leon Blvd. and Salzedo St.), Coral Gables. www.CoralGables-Museum.org. ✆ **305/603-8067.** Admission $7 adults, $5 students and seniors, $3 ages 6-12, free for under age 6. Tues–Fri noon–6pm; Sat 11am–5pm; Sun noon–5pm.

Tower of Celluloid

A cultural gem in Little Havana, the **Tower Theater,** 1508 SW Eighth St. (www.TowerTheaterMiami.com; ✆ **305/643-8706**), is one of Miami's oldest cultural landmarks, opening in 1926 as the finest state-of-the-art theater in the South. After the Cuban influx in the 1960s, the theater started showing English-language programming with Spanish subtitles, eventually switching to all Spanish. After years of closings and changing hands, the theater was purchased by the City of Miami and in 1993 added to the National Register as a historic site. After a complete renovation in 1997, the Tower was back to its Deco glory, and these days it's managed by Miami Dade College, which continues the theater's history with multi-language cultural and arts programming, including art-house films and exhibitions of Cuban art by highly regarded artists such as Carlos Navarro.

Lowe Art Museum ★★★ ART MUSEUM   Miami's oldest art museum, the 61-year-old Lowe is an appealing, undersung mix of art, folk art, and objects that cross into the realm of archaeology and anthropology, including ancient Maya and Greek pottery, Tang dynasty ceramics, and some marvelous woodwork from Africa and Oceania. While most local art museums rely more heavily on rotating exhibitions, here more of the focus is on the impressive permanent collection, which includes a who's who of art history both classic and recent: El Greco, Monet, Gainsborough, Goya, Lichtenstein, Tintoretto, Pepper, and Stella. The newest addition (2008) is a gallery devoted to glass and ceramic art, including smaller works by Chihuly and Picasso. There are, of course, temporary exhibitions, too, and top-quality ones—for example, a fascinating recent survey of engravings of the voyages of Captain Cook.

1301 Stanford Dr. (entrance at Ponce de León Blvd.) at University of Miami, Coral Gables. www. LoweMuseum.org. ✆ **305/284-3535.** Admission $10 adults, $5 seniors and groups of more than 10, free for students with ID and under age 12. Tues–Sat 10am–4pm; Sun noon–4pm.

Venetian Pool ★★★ POOL/HISTORIC SITE   One of America's most beautiful and unusual swimming pools, built in 1923, is hidden behind pastel stucco walls and honored with a listing in the National Register of Historic Places. Two underground wells (meaning water's definitely on the nippy side) feed the free-form lagoon, which is shaded by three-story Spanish porticos and has both fountains and waterfalls. During summer, the pool's 820,000 gallons of water are drained and refilled nightly, thanks to an underground aquifer, ensuring a cool, *clean* swim. Visitors are free to swim and sunbathe here, just as Johnny Weissmuller and the late Esther Williams did decades ago. For a modest fee, your kids (or you) can learn to swim during special summer programs.

2701 DeSoto Blvd. (at Toledo St.), Coral Gables. www.VenetianPool.com. ✆ **305/460-5306.** Admission Apr–Oct $12 adults, $6.60 ages 3–12; Nov and Feb–Mar $7.70 adults, $4.15 for ages 3–12. Children must be at least 3 (proof of age required) or 38 in. tall. Hours subject to change but generally Mon–Fri 11am–5:30 or 6:30pm; Sat–Sun 10am–4:30pm. Closed on major holidays; call or log on for current hours.

COCONUT GROVE

Barnacle State Historic Site ★★ HISTORIC HOME   The former home of naval architect and early settler Ralph Middleton Munroe is now a museum in the heart of the Grove. It's the oldest house in Miami (1891), on 5 acres of natural hammock (hardwood forest) and landscaped lawns. The quiet surroundings, wide porches, and period furnishings illustrate how Miami's first snowbird lived in the days before condo-mania and luxury hotels. Enthusiastic and knowledgeable state park employees provide a wealth of historical information to those interested in quiet, low-tech attractions such as this one. On Wednesdays from 6:30 to 7:45pm, there's sunset yoga by the sea ($15). Call for details on the fabulous monthly moonlight concerts of folk, blues, or classical music, with picnicking encouraged ($7–$10; free under age 10).

3485 Main Hwy. (btw. Commodore Plaza and McFarlane Rd.). www.FloridaStateParks.org/TheBarnacle. © **305/442-6866.** Admission $2. Tours $3 adults, $1 ages 6–12. Fri–Mon 9am–5pm. Tours Fri–Mon at 10am, 11:30am, 1pm, and 2:30pm.

Patricia and Phillip Frost Museum of Science ★★ MUSEUM/PLANETARIUM

Nowadays it seems a key badge of world-class cities is a big, shiny, pricey science museum. Miami will join that club when MSM moves into splashy new downtown quarters in 2015 (and as part of the deal, this publicly owned museum had to take the name of a rich donor). In the meantime, kids still seem to get a kick out of what's in these modest current digs, including exhibits about topics such as hurricanes (*very* locally relevant), hydropower, kinetic energy (a dance floor where dance moves power the strobe lights), and live animals including snakes, tarantulas, and the birds and reptiles house in the outdoor annex connected to the wildlife rescue center (a star attraction is George the female North American bald eagle). Others relating to conservation and fitness are less "fun" but well presented for a young audience. The jewel in the crown is a planetarium with a half-dozen star and laser shows a day. Right across the road is Vizcaya (below), so if that manse is also on your agenda, you may want to plan accordingly.

3280 S. Miami Ave. (just south of the Rickenbacker Causeway). www.MiamiSci.org. © **305/646-4200.** Admission $15 adults; $11 seniors, students, and ages 3–12; free for ages 2 and under. Daily 10am–6pm; 1st Fri of every month 8:30am–10pm; call for show times (last show 4pm Mon–Fri and 5pm Sat–Sun).

Vizcaya Museum and Gardens ★★★ HISTORIC HOME

Astride Biscayne Bay, early-20th-century Midwestern farm equipment honcho James Deering

---

vintage MIAMI

Although it's hardly Napa Valley, Miami does have an actual winery: **Schnebly Redland's Winery & Brewery,** 30205 SW 217th Ave., Homestead (www.Schnebly Winery.com; © **888/717-9463** or 305/242-1224), in whose $1.5-million tasting room you can sample various vintages. I've tried some, and although they're a little fruity for my taste (specialties include mango, guava, avocado, carambola, and lychee), it's still worth a trip down just to see the press deck where fruit becomes juice and eventually wine.

More recently, Peter and Denisse Schnebly added a craft brewery with its own tours and tastings of products like Big Rod coconut ale, Shark Bait wheat ale, and Gator Tail brown ale. There are 30- to 40-minute tours on weekends for $7 per person and daily tastings for $7 to $10. On Friday and Saturday nights, there's live music starting at 6pm for $10 per person. It's open 10am to 5pm Monday to Thursday, 10am to 11pm Friday and Saturday, and noon.

bequeathed Miami one of America's most distinctive grand manses (built in 1916), where you could describe the vibe as "Renaissance Italianate meets the tropics." As that might suggest, the place is ridiculously photogenic, and in fact you're almost guaranteed to spot one or multiple photo shoots involving brides or *quinceañeras* (Cuban sweet 16s); as for the likes of you—snapshots outside only. Thirty-four rooms furnished in heavy Old-World style are arranged around a bright, airy courtyard that was once open to the elements and is now covered by a huge glass skylight. You can get a guided tour of the first floor, then check out the upper two floors yourself, or for $5 pick up a helpful audio guide. Do pop into the gift shop/cafe, whose wares are definitely a cut above the norm (and this has to be the first time I've ever seen a discount table in a shop like this). The gardens are also an integral part of the experience—formal in the European style closer in, then gradually growing wilder and more Floridian—meaning slash pines, live oaks with Spanish moss, even mangroves. Finally, a heads-up: the street entrance, on the south side of South Miami Avenue, is all too easy to sail right by.

3251 S. Miami Ave. (just south of Rickenbacker Causeway). www.VizcayaMuseum.org. ✆ **305/250-9133.** Admission $18 adults, $12 seniors, $6 ages 6–12, free for ages 5 and under. Wed–Mon 9:30am–4:30pm.

SOUTH MIAMI-DADE COUNTY

Coral Castle ★★ HISTORIC SITE   There's plenty of competition, but this may be Florida's strangest attraction. In 1923, the story goes, a 26-year-old Latvian crazed by being dumped at the altar by a 16-year-old (I *hate* when that happens), moved here, to what was then the boonies. He spent the next quarter century carving huge boulders into a Flintstones-like roofless "castle," now on the National Register of Historic Places. It seems impossible that one rather scrawny little dude could have done all this, but there are scores of affidavits on display from neighbors swearing to it. Experts have apparently studied Ed Leedskalnin's methods to help figure out how the great pyramids and Stonehenge were built. Rocker Billy Idol was said to have been inspired by this place when he wrote "Sweet 16." An interesting 25-minute audio tour guides you through. Although overpriced and under-maintained, Coral Castle's worth a visit if you're in the area (likely en route to or from the Keys), about 37 miles from Miami.

28655 S. Dixie Hwy. (btw. SW 157th Ave. and SW 284th St.), Homestead. www.CoralCastle.com. ✆ **305/248-6345.** Admission $15 adults, $12 ages 65 and up, $7 ages 7–12. Group rates available. Sun–Thurs 8am–6pm; Fri–Sat 8am–8pm

Frost Art Museum ★★ ART MUSEUM   You just may be surprised by this very underrated, Smithsonian-affiliated collection way out west on the Florida International University campus (but less of an odyssey than you might expect—just hop on the Dolphin Expressway). The permanent collection includes 20th-century American and Latin American art by the likes of Robert Motherwell, Rufino Tamayo, and Robert Rauschenberg, along with ancient pieces from Africa, Asia, and the pre-Columbian Americas. The rotating exhibitions are usually stimulating, such as 2013's "Concealed Spaces," which made me think anew about famous paintings such as Da Vinci's *Last Supper* and Botticelli's *Birth of Venus* by taking out all the people. Others have local and/or topical links, including *Bang!* by French-born Robert Einbeck, an exploration in painting of gun violence, and Eugene Savage's early-20th-century paintings of the Florida Everglades Seminoles. And parents, there's even something here that kids can relate to: Off the lobby is a small interactive center that teaches about art and how/why it's made (actually, pretty cool for grownups, too).

10975 SW 17th St. (entrances on SW 107th Ave. and SW 117th Ave.). http://TheFrost.FIU.edu. ☎ **305/348-2890.** Free admission. Tues–Sat 10am–5pm; Sun noon–5pm.

Monkey Jungle ★ ZOO   Honestly, I'm not a fan of this place. It's smelly, the monkeys are either sleeping or in heat, and it's really far from the city, even farther than the zoo. But if primates are your thing and you'd rather pass on the zoo, it could well be a good option. You'll see rare Brazilian golden lion tamarins and Asian macaques. There are no cages to restrain the antics of the monkeys as they swing, chatter, and play their way into your heart. Screened-in trails wind through acres of "jungle," and daily shows feature the talents of the park's most progressive pupils. People who come here aren't monkeying around—many of the park's frequent visitors are scientists and anthropologists. In fact, an interesting archaeological exhibition excavated from a Monkey Jungle sinkhole displays 10,000-year-old artifacts, including human teeth and animal bones. An attraction that's somewhat amusing, if you can call it that, is the Wild Monkey Swimming Pool, a show in which you get to watch monkeys diving for food. If you can stand the humidity, the smell, and the bugs (flies, mosquitoes, and so on), expect to spend about 2 hours here.

14805 SW 216th St. (btw. SW 147th and SW 149th aves.), South Miami. www.MonkeyJungle.com. ☎ **305/235-1611.** Admission $30 adults, $28 seniors and active-duty U.S. military, $24 ages 4–12; website discount of $2 for adults, $1 for children. Daily 9:30am–5pm (tickets sold until 4pm).

Zoo Miami ★★★ ZOO   This 330-acre complex is quite a distance from Miami proper and the beaches—about 45 minutes—but worth the trip. Isolated and never

---

A berry GOOD TIME

South Florida's farmland has been steadily shrinking in the face of industrial expansion, but you'll still find several spots where you can get back to nature while indulging in a local gastronomic delight—picking your own produce at the "U-Pic-'Em" farms that dot south Miami-Dade's landscape. Depending on what's in season, you can get everything from fresh herbs and vegetables to a mélange of citrus fruits and berries. During berry season—January through April—it's not uncommon to see hardy pickers leaving the groves with hands and faces that are stained a tale-telling crimson. On your way through south Dade, keep an eye out for the bright red U-PIC signs.

There are also a number of fantastic fruit stands in the region. **Burr's Berry Farm,** 12741 SW 216th St. (☎ **305/251-0145**), located in the township of Goulds, about an hour from downtown

Miami, has created a sensation with its fabulous strawberry milkshakes. To get there, go south on U.S. 1 and turn right on SW 216th Street; the stand is about 1 mile west. It's open daily 9am to 5:30pm.

For fresh fruit in a tasty pastry or tart, head over to **Knaus Berry Farm,** 15980 SW 248th St. (www.KnausBerryFarm. com, ☎ **305/247-0668**), in an area known as the Redlands. Some people call this an Amish farm, but it's actually run by a family from a sect of German Baptists. The stand sells items ranging from fresh flowers to homemade ice cream, but be sure to indulge in one of its famous homemade cinnamon buns. Be prepared to wait in a long line to stock up—people flock here from as far away as Palm Beach. Head south on U.S. 1 and turn right on 248th Street. The stand is 2½ miles farther on the left, and open Monday through Saturday from 8am to 5:30pm.

really crowded, it's also almost completely cageless (most animals are kept apart by cleverly designed moats). It's a fantastic spot to take younger kids; there are wonderful play areas, safari cycles for rent, and the zoo offers several daily programs designed to educate and entertain, such as the "Wildlife Show" and "Animal Tales." Residents include lions, chimpanzees, Komodo dragons, koalas, emus, and meerkats. The air-conditioned monorail and tram tours offer visitors a nice overview. The zoo is always upgrading its facilities, including the impressive aviary, Wings of Asia. Cool activities include the Samburu Giraffe Feeding Station, where for $3 you get to feed the giraffes veggies; the Kaziranga Camp Rhino Encounter, where you can feed an Indian rhino for $3; and Humpy's Camel Rides, where you can hop on a camel for $5. Amazon & Beyond features jaguars, anacondas, giant river otters, harpy eagles, a stingray touch tank, an interactive water-play area, the Flooded Forest building with a unique display of a forest before and during flood times, and an indoor Cloud Forest that houses reptiles. At 27 acres and a cost of $50 million, this exhibit is massive and makes Zoo Miami the third zoo in the country to have giant river otters, one of its key species. "Wings Down Under: A Parrot Feeding Adventure" is a fun, interactive experience where for $3 you can enter an aviary with approximately 400 free-flying budgies, cockatiels, and rosellas (all Australian parrots) and have them fly down to your hands to feast on seeds from a cup. There's a Dr. Seuss–inspired Wacky Barn in the children's zoo where they get to hand-feed and touch barn animals such as sheep, mini-horses, ponies, goats, pot-bellied pigs, and more. Private tours and overnights are available for those who really want to commune with nature. *Note:* The distance between animal habitats can be great, so you'll do *a lot* of walking. There are benches, shaded gazebos, cool misters, a water-shooting mushroom, and two water-play areas strategically positioned throughout the zoo so you can escape the heat; still, because it can get very hot during the summer months, get started in the early morning—also because you'll need a good chunk of the day here if you want to see it all.

12400 SW 152nd St. (at SW 124th Ave.), South Miami. www.ZooMiami.org. ✆ **305/251-0400.** Admission $16 adults, $12 ages 3–12; $1 discount on website. Daily 9:30am–5:30pm (ticket booth closes at 4pm).

NATURE PRESERVES, PARKS & GARDENS

Please note that the nature areas in this section are mapped earlier in the chapter, on p. 80.

The Miami area is a great place for outdoor types, with beaches, parks, nature preserves, and gardens galore. Although South Beach is more known for sand than greenery, **South Pointe Park ★★,** 1 Washington Ave. (www.MiamiBeachParks.com; ✆ 305/673-7006), reopened after a $22.4-million renovation that transformed the formerly shabby spot into 18 waterfront acres of green space, walkways, a playground, and an observation deck.

Although historic **Hialeah Park ★★** (2200 E. 4th Ave., btw. E. 21st and E. 32nd sts.; www.HialeahParkCasino.com; ✆ 305/885-8000), is primarily known for horse racing, it's also known for its legendary flock of neon-pink flamingos, which still roam the property and are definitely worth a photo op. After decades of decay, the park was renovated and reopened in 2009, although experts say the restoration of the National Historic Landmark to its full glory will take years and $100 million to complete. Admission is free.

At the historic **Bill Baggs Cape Florida State Park** ★★★, 1200 Crandon Blvd. (www.FloridaStateParks.org/CapeFlorida; ✆ **305/361-5811**), at the southern tip of Key Biscayne about 20 minutes from downtown Miami, you can explore the wilds and enjoy some of the most secluded beaches in Miami. South Florida's oldest lighthouse (1825) is also out here. Damaged during the Second Seminole War (1836) and again in 1861 during the Civil War, it was out of commission until being restored to working condition in 1978 by the U.S. Coast Guard. The park is also recognized as a site within the U.S. National Park Service's National Underground Railroad Network to Freedom, commemorating the trip to the British Bahamas by escaped slaves before the lighthouse was constructed. A rental shack leases bikes, hydrobikes, kayaks, and many more water toys. It's a great place to picnic, but there are also two restaurants on-site: the Lighthouse Cafe, which serves homey Latin food, including great fish soups and sandwiches, and the Boater's Grill, offering casual waterfront dining (just be careful that the raccoons don't get your lunch). Bill Baggs has been consistently rated as one of the top 10 beaches in the U.S. for its 1¼ miles of wide, sandy beaches and its secluded, serene atmosphere (though I must say that last time I was there, on a June late afternoon, I had never seen it so crowded!). Admission is $8 per vehicle with up to eight people (or $4 for a vehicle with only one person; $2 to enter by foot or bicycle). It's open daily from 8am to sunset. Lighthouse tours are available Thursday through Monday at 10am and 1pm. Arrive at least half an hour early to sign up—there is room for only 10 people on each tour. Take I-95 to the Rickenbacker Causeway and take that all the way to the end.

Fairchild Tropical Botanic Garden ★★★, 10901 Old Cutler Rd., in south Coral Gables (www.FTG.org; ✆ **305/667-1651**), is the largest of its kind in the continental United States. A veritable rainforest of both rare and exotic plants, as well as 11 lakes and countless meadows, are spread across 83 acres, with palmettos, vine pergola, palm glades, and other unique species creating a scenic, lush environment. More than 100 species of birds have been spotted at the garden (ask for a checklist at the ticket desk), and it's home to a variety of animals. In fact, bird lovers will go batty over the Keys Coastal Habitat, a 4-acre paradise featuring a densely planted collection of plants native to South Florida that was designed to attract migratory birds and other wildlife. Don't miss the 30-minute narrated tram tour (departures on the hour 10am–3pm Mon–Fri and 10am–4pm Sat–Sun) to learn about the various flowers and trees. There's also a museum, a cafe, a picnic area, and a gift shop including edible gifts and fantastic books on gardening and cooking. Fairchild often hosts major art exhibits by the likes of Dale Chihuly and Roy Lichtenstein. The 2-acre rainforest exhibit "Windows to the Tropics" will save you a trip to the Amazon. Most people visit the Jason Vollmer Butterfly Laboratory and the Clinton Family Conservatory, featuring an exhibit of rare butterflies, birds, hummingbirds, orchids, fish, and tropical plants. Expect to spend at least 2 hours here. Admission is $25 for adults, $18 for age 65-plus, $12 for ages 6 to 17, and free for ages 5 and under. It's open daily, except Christmas, from 7:30am to 4:30pm. Take I-95 south to U.S. 1, turn left onto Le Jeune Road, and follow it straight to the traffic circle; from there, take Old Cutler Road 2 miles to the park.

Named after the late champion of the Everglades, Key Biscayne's **Marjory Stoneman Douglas Biscayne Nature Center** ★★, 6767 Crandon Blvd. (www.Biscayne NatureCenter.org; ✆ **305/361-6767;** p. 90), is housed in a $4-million facility and offers hands-on marine exploration, hikes through coastal hammocks, bike trips, and walks along the local beaches and habitats led by environmentalists and historians. Call to reserve a spot on a regularly scheduled weekday or weekend program. Be sure to wear comfortable, closed-toe shoes for hikes through wet or rocky terrain. It's open daily 10am to 4pm. The park has a $6 per car parking fee; admission to the nature center is free. Special programs and tours cost $14 per person. Call for weekend programs. To get there, take I-95 to the Rickenbacker Causeway exit (no. 1) and take the causeway all the way until it becomes Crandon Boulevard. The center is on the east side of the street (the Atlantic Ocean side) and about 15 minutes from downtown Miami.

Because so many people are focused on the beach itself, the **Miami Beach Botanical Garden,** 2000 Convention Center Dr. (www.MBGarden.org; ℭ **305/673-7256**), remains a secret garden. The lush, tropical 4½-acre garden is a fabulous natural retreat from the hustle and bustle of the silicone-enhanced city. It's open Tuesday through Sunday from 9am to 5pm; admission is free.

The **Oleta River State Recreation Area** ★★, 3400 NE 163rd St., North Miami (www.FloridaStateParks.org/OletaRiver; ℭ **305/919-1846**), consists of 993 acres—the largest urban park in the state—on Biscayne Bay. The beauty of the Oleta River, combined with the fact that you're essentially in the middle of a city, makes this park especially worth visiting. With miles of bicycle and canoe trails, a sandy swimming beach, kayak- and mountain-bike-rental shop, Blue Marlin Fish House Restaurant, shaded picnic pavilions, and a fishing pier, Oleta River State Recreation Area allows for an outstanding outdoor recreational experience away from of the big city. There are 14 rustic cabins out here which sleep four people ($55 per night, and guests need to bring their own linens). Bathrooms and showers are outside, as is a fire circle with a grill for cooking. For reservations, call ℭ **800/326-3521.** It's open daily from 8am to sunset. Admission for pedestrians and cyclists is $2 per person. By car, the driver plus car costs $4; the driver plus one to seven passengers and car costs $6. Take I-95 to exit 17 (S.R. 826 E.) and go all the way east until just before the causeway. The park entrance is on your right. Driving time from downtown Miami is about a half-hour.

Down south in the town of Homestead, the **Preston B. Bird and Mary Heinlein Fruit and Spice Park** ★, 24801 SW 187th Ave. (www.FruitandSpicePark.org; ℭ **305/247-5727**), harbors rare fruit trees that can't survive elsewhere in the U.S. If a volunteer is available, you'll learn some fascinating things about this 30-acre living plant museum, where the most exotic varieties of fruits and spices—ackee, mango, Ugli fruits, carambola, and breadfruit—grow on strange-looking trees with unpronounceable names. There are also original coral rock buildings dating back to 1912. The Strawberry Folk Festival in February and an art festival here in January are among the park's most popular—and populated—events. The best part? You're free to take anything that has naturally fallen to the ground (no picking here). If the ground is bare, fret not. The Mango Café in the park's historic Bauer-Mitchell-Neill House features indoor and outdoor garden seating, is open for lunch and late-afternoon dining, and serves "Florida tropical" cuisine—fruit salads, lots of dishes with mango, smoothies, shakes, and, my fave, the Florida lobster roll. You'll also find samples of interesting fruits and jellies made from the park's bounty, as well as exotic ingredients and cookbooks in the gift store. Admission to the spice park is $8 for adults and $2 for ages 6 to 11. It's open daily from 9am to 5pm (closed on Christmas). Tours are included in the price of admission and are offered at 11am, 1:30pm, and 3pm. Take U.S. 1 south, turn right on SW 248th Street, and go straight for 5 miles to SW 187th Avenue. The drive from Miami should take 45 minutes to an hour.

ESPECIALLY FOR KIDS

Miami is a lot more kid-friendly than many people realize. Toss aside the images of scantily clad sunbathers, trashed reality stars, and nightlife in general, and you've got yourself the ideal place to bring children. Warm weather and tons of outdoor activities and restaurants make Miami one of the more child-friendly cities—as long as you know where to go. Because of Miami's mostly magnificent weather, there are ample strolling opportunities for the antsiest kids, from Lincoln Road Mall on South Beach to Aventura Mall in North Miami Beach. What's particularly distinctive about Miami is that parents tend to take their kids out with them everywhere—even at night. This is especially true on Lincoln Road. As touristy as it may be, Bayside Marketplace is another good kids' spot, but during the day only. Kids love the boats coming in and out of the marina there and in Coconut Grove. When all else fails, grab a pail, shovel, and umbrella and hit the beach. Sand and surf almost never ceases to amuse. Here are some of the most kid-friendly attractions in Miami:

Aventura Mall (p. 110)
Bayside Marketplace (p. 111)
Coral Castle (p. 95)
Fruit and Spice Park (p. 99)
Jungle Island (p. 85)
Lincoln Road (p. 82)
Miami Children's Museum (p. 86)
Miami Seaquarium (p. 88)
Monkey Jungle (p. 96)
Patricia and Phillip Frost Museum of Science (p. 94)
Sea Grass Adventures (p. 90)
Venetian Pool (p. 93)
Zoo Miami (p. 96)

OUTDOOR ACTIVITIES

BIKING The cement promenade on the southern tip of South Beach is a great place to ride. Biking up the beach (either on the sand or along the beach on a cement pathway, which is a lot easier) is great for surf, sun, sand, exercise, and people-watching—just be sure to keep your eyes on the road, as the scenery can be distracting. Most of the big beach hotels rent bicycles, as does SoBe's **Miami Beach Bicycle Center,** 601 5th St. (www.BikeMiamiBeach.com; ℭ **305/674-0150**), which charges $5 per hour, $18 for up to 24 hours, and $80 weekly. It's open Monday through Saturday from 10am to 7pm, Sunday from 10am to 5pm.

Miami Beach and Surfside also recently joined the growing number of European and U.S. cities installing bike share programs. The local version is **Deco Bike** (ℭ **305/532-9494**), with more than 100 solar-powered stations that let you use a credit card to rent bikes at one and drop off at another; rates range from $4 for a half-hour to $24 for a full day. For more information and a map of stations, log on to www.DecoBike.com. Other parts of Miami were expected to add their own versions by 2015.

For those looking to literally power-bike, **Electribike,** based at Haulover Beach (www.ElectribikeFL.com; ℭ **888/663-7717** or 786/387-1594), has just what you need and will even deliver to your hotel. A mix of pedaling and motor power known as "pedal-assist," it's especially easy on the knees, and rates are $45 per day. Simply order online or by phone the day before.

Bikers can also enjoy more than 130 miles of paved paths throughout Miami. The beautiful and tranquil streets of Coral Gables and Coconut Grove (several bike trails are spread throughout these neighborhoods) are great for cyclists, where old trees form canopies over wide, flat roads lined with grand homes and quaint street markers.

The terrain in Key Biscayne is perfect for biking, especially along the park and beach roads. If you don't mind the sound of cars whooshing by your bike lane, **Rickenbacker Causeway** is also fantastic, as it is one of the only bikeable inclines in Miami from which you get fantastic elevated views of the city and waterways. However, be warned that this is a tough ride, especially going up the incline. **Key Cycling,** 328 Crandon Blvd., Key Biscayne (www.KeyCycling.com; ✆ **305/361-0061**), rents bikes from $20 for 2 hours, $24 a day, or $100 a week. It's open weekdays 10am to 7pm, Saturday 10am to 6pm, and Sunday 10am to 3pm.

If you want to avoid the traffic altogether, head out to **Shark Valley** in the Everglades National Park (p. 145)—one of South Florida's most scenic bicycle trails and a favorite haunt of city-weary locals.

Biking note: Children 15 and under are required by Florida law to wear a helmet, which can be bought at any bike store or retail outlet selling biking supplies.

BOATING   Private rental outfits include **Beach Boats,** 2400 Collins Ave., Miami Beach (www.BoatRentMiami.com; ✆ **305/534-4307**), where powerboats rent for some of the best rates on the beach. At the low end, you can rent a 21-footer for $98 per hour not including tax or gas, with a 2-hour minimum; a 4-hour rental will get you a free hour. Cruising is permitted only in and around Biscayne Bay (ocean access is prohibited), and renters must be 21 or older to rent. The office is on the inland waterway and is open daily from 10am to sunset. If you want a specific type of boat, call ahead to reserve. Otherwise, show up and take what's available.

FISHING   Fishing licenses are required in Florida. If you go out with one of the fishing charter boats listed below, you're automatically accredited because the companies are. If you go out on your own, however, you must have a Florida fishing license, which costs a non-state resident $17 for 3 days and $30 for a week. Visit http://License.MyFWC.com or call ✆ **888/347-4356** for more information.

Some of the best surf-casting in the city can be had at **Haulover Beach Park** at Collins Avenue and 105th Street, where there's a bait-and-tackle shop right on the pier. **South Pointe Park,** at the southern tip of Miami Beach, is another popular fishing spot and features a long pier, comfortable benches, and a great view of the ships passing through Government Cut, the deep channel made when the port of Miami was dug.

You can also do some deep-sea fishing in the Miami area. One bargain outfitter, the **Kelley Fishing Fleet,** at North Miami's Haulover Marina, 10800 Collins Ave., at 108th St. (www.MiamiBeachFishing.com; ✆ **305/945-3801**), has half-day, full-day, and night

---

A Whole New World

Every Columbus Day, Biscayne Bay becomes a veritable mob scene of boaters celebrating the discovery of another day off of work. The unofficial Columbus Day Regatta has become a tradition in which people take to the water for a day of boating, sunning, drinking, and sometimes literally the bare necessities, as they often strip down to their birthday suits in an eye-opening display of their appreciation for Columbus's discovery of the nude, er, new world.

fishing aboard diesel-powered "party boats." The fleet's emphasis on drifting is geared toward trolling and bottom-fishing for snapper, sailfish, and mackerel. Half-day trips are $45 for adults and $35 for children up to 12 years old, and full-day trips are $68 for adults and $56 for children; a 10% discount coupon is available online. Daily departures are at 9am, 1:45pm, and 8pm, and there is a late-night trip departing Saturday at 1am that costs $50 for adults and $38 for children; reservations are recommended.

Also at the Haulover Marina, although there's no shortage of private charter boats, Captain Dawn Mergelsberg's **New Choice Charters** (www.FishMiamiBeach.com; ✆ 305/965-2079) is a good pick because she puts individuals together to get a full boat. The *Two Tales* is a 34-foot SeaVee powered by twin Mercury outboards equipped for light tackle or big-game fish such as marlin, tuna, mahi-mahi, shark, and sailfish. The cost is $160 per person. Private, full-day trips are available for groups of six people per vessel and cost $1,350; half-days are $600. Group rates and specials are also available. Morning and afternoon trips are available daily; call or email for details and reservations. Beginners and children are always welcome.

If you're all about big game—marlin, dolphin, tuna, wahoo, swordfish, and sailfish—Captain Charlie Hotchkiss's *Sea Dancer* (www.SeaDancerCharter.com; ✆ 305/775-5534) offers a first-class experience on a 38-foot Luhrs boat complete with tuna tower and air-conditioned cabin. Catch and release, or fillet your catch to take home. The *Sea Dancer* also offers two fun water adventures, including a 6-hour "Bar Cruz" to watering holes in Miami and Fort Lauderdale, or a "Sandbar Cruz," which drops anchor out by Biscayne Bay's historic Stiltsville, where you'll swim, play sports, and bounce on a water trampoline—all in the middle of the bay. Transport is available to wherever the boat may be docked. Rates are $700 for a half-day, $1,000 to $1,200 for a full day, and $500 for the specialty tours. Tours are also available to Bimini (call for pricing).

Key Biscayne offers deep-sea fishing to those willing to get their hands dirty and drop a bundle. The competition among the boats is fierce, but the prices are basically similar, whichever you choose: the going rate is about $400 to $500 for a half-day and $600 to $900 for a full day of fishing. These rates are usually for a party of up to six, and the boats supply you with rods and bait as well as instruction for first-timers. Some will also take you out to the Upper Keys if the fish aren't biting in Miami.

You might also consider the following, out of the Key Biscayne marina, in relatively good shape and nicer than most: *Sonny Boy* (www.SonnyBoySportFishing.com; ✆ 305/361-2217), and *L&H* (www.LandHSportFishing.com; ✆ 305/361-9318).

Bridge fishing in Biscayne Bay is also popular in Miami; you'll see people with poles over almost every waterway. But look carefully for signs telling you whether it's legal to do so wherever you are; some bridges forbid fishing.

GOLF   There are more than 50 private and public links in the Miami area. You can get information on many from the **Greater Miami Convention and Visitor's Bureau** (www.MiamiandBeaches.com/Things-to-Do/Golf; ✆ 800/933-8448).

The best hotel courses in Miami are found at the **Trump National Doral,** home of the legendary Blue Monster course, as well as the Gold Course, designed by Raymond Floyd, and the Great White Shark Course. The resort also manages one of the most popular local links among real enthusiasts. Formerly known as the Silver Course, the redesigned Jim McLean Signature Course has, according to experts, one of the toughest starting holes in Florida and, again, is very popular with locals, so book in advance. The semiprivate 18-holer is open from 7am to 6pm in winter and until 7pm during the summer. Cart and greens fees vary. Check www.DoralResort.com or call ✆ 305/592-5000 for information.

Other hotels with winsome links include the **Turnberry Isle Miami** (www.TurnberryIsleMiami.com), with two Robert Trent Jones, Sr.–designed courses for guests and members, and the **Biltmore Hotel** (p. 56), my pick for best public course because of its modest greens fees and an 18-hole, par-71 course on the hotel's spectacular grounds. It's so good that despite his penchant for privacy, Bill Clinton prefers teeing off at this course more than any other in Miami.

Otherwise, the following represent some of the area's best public courses. **Crandon Park Golf Course,** formerly known as the Links, 6700 Crandon Blvd., Key Biscayne (www.CrandonGolfClub.com; ✆ **305/361-9129**), is the number-one-ranked municipal course in the state and one of the top five in the country. The park is situated on 200 bayfront acres and offers a pro shop, rentals, lessons, carts, and a lighted driving range. The course is open daily from dawn to dusk; greens fees (including cart) range from $80 to $220, depending on the season, for nonresidents and include a cart. Special twilight rates are also available. Golf club rental is available for $55.

Known as one of the best in the city, the **Country Club of Miami,** 6801 NW 186th St., at NW 68th Ave., Hialeah (www.GolfCCMiami.com; ✆ **305/829-8456**), has three 18-hole courses of varying degrees of difficulty. You'll find lush fairways, rolling greens, and some history, to boot. The west course, designed in 1961 by Robert Trent Jones, Sr. and updated in the 1990s by the PGA, was where Jack Nicklaus played his first professional tournament and Lee Trevino won his first professional championship. The course is open daily from 6am to sunset. Cart and greens fees range from $22 to $60, depending on the season and tee times.

The recently renovated **Miami Beach Golf Club,** 2301 Alton Rd., South Beach (www.MiamiBeachGolfClub.com; ✆ **305/532-3350**), is a gorgeous, 80-year-old course that, par for the, er, course in Miami Beach, received a $10-million face-lift. Miami Heat players and Matt Damon have been known to tee off here. Greens fees range from $100 to $200, depending on the season.

JET SKIS/WAVERUNNERS Don't miss a chance to tour the islands on the back of your own spunky watercraft. Nerve, though, is a prerequisite, as Miami's waterways are full of speeding Jet Skiers and boaters who think they're in the F1 Powerboat finals. Many beachfront concessionaires rent a variety of these popular (and loud) water scooters. The latest models are fast and smooth. **American WaterSports,** at the Miami Beach Marina, 390 Alton Rd. (www.Jetskiz.com; ✆ **305/538-7549**), is the area's most popular spot for Jet-Ski rental. Rates begin at $74 for a half-hour and $109 for an hour, not including gas. It also runs fun Jet-Ski tours past celebrity homes beginning at $119 an hour.

KAYAKING The **Blue Moon Outdoor Center** rents kayaks at 3400 NE 163rd St., in Oleta River Park (www.BlueMoonOutdoor.com; ✆ **305/957-3040**). Kayak rentals for self-guided tours include single or tandem kayaks and canoes. All rates are for the first 1½ hours. Rates are $23 for a single kayak, $33 for a tandem kayak, $37 for a canoe. Paddle down several calm water routes and spot blue herons, bottlenose dolphin, and possibly manatees. Kayaking classes are offered by instructors certified by the ACA (American Canoe Association), and there's also stand-up paddleboarding. Rentals start at $37. The park has 16 miles of mountain-bike trails rated green for easy, blue for intermediate, and black for difficult. Rates for full-suspension mountain bikes begin at $25. Guided eco-tours are available by reservation. There are also some really cool monthly full-moon kayak and bike trips, including a bonfire on the beach. The center is open daily from 9am to 7:30pm (from 8am on weekends).

SAILING   You can rent sailboats and catamarans through the beachfront concessions desks of some resorts.

Aquatic Rental Center, on northern Biscayne Bay in Pelican Harbor Marina, 1275 NE 79th St. (www.ArcMiami.com; ✆ **305/751-7514**), can also get you out on the water. A 21-to-25-foot sailboat rents for $90 for 2 hours, $130 for 3 hours, $160 for a half-day, and $225 for a full day. A Sunfish sailboat for two rents at $35 per hour. If you've always dreamt of winning the America's Cup but can't sail, the able teachers here will get you started. A 10-hour course over 5 days costs $400 for one person, $500 for two.

SCUBA DIVING & SNORKELING   In 1981, the U.S. government began a wide-scale project designed to increase the number of habitats available to marine organisms. One of its major accomplishments has been the creation of nearby artificial reefs, which have attracted all kinds of tropical plants, fish, and animals. In addition, **Biscayne National Park** (p. 157) offers a protected marine environment less than an hour's drive south of downtown.

Several dive shops around the city offer organized weekend outings, either to the reefs or to one of more than a dozen old shipwrecks around Miami's shores. Check "Divers" in the Yellow Pages for rental equipment and a full list of tour operators.

Diver's Paradise of Key Biscayne, 4000 Crandon Blvd. (www.KeyDivers.com; ✆ **305/361-3483**), offers one dive expedition per day during the week and two per day on the weekends to the more than 30 wrecks and artificial reefs off the shores of Miami Beach and Key Biscayne. You can take a 3-day certification course for $499, which includes all dives and gear. If you already have your C-card, a dive trip costs about $110 if you need equipment, and $65 if you bring your own. It's open Tuesday through Friday from 10:30am to 5pm, and weekends from 8am to 2pm. Call ahead for dive times and locations. For snorkeling, they will set you up with equipment and maps on where to see the best underwater sights. Mask, fins, and snorkel rental is $65.

South Beach Diver and Surf Center, 850 Washington Ave., Miami Beach (www.SouthBeachDivers.com; ✆ **305/531-6110**), will also be happy to tell you where to go under the sea and will provide you with scuba rental equipment as well. You can rent snorkel gear for about $12. It also does dive trips to Key Largo three times a week and dives off Miami on Sunday at $125 for a two-tank dive or $90 if you have your own equipment. Night dives and trips to the USS *Spiegel Grove,* a dive site in Key Largo, are $10 extra.

The funniest and most apropos South Beach diving spot has to be the **José Cuervo Underwater Bar,** located 150 yards southeast of the 2nd Street lifeguard station—a 22-ton concrete margarita bar that was sunk on May 5, 2000. The "Sinko De Mayo" is designed with a dive flag roof, six bar stools, and a protective wall of tetrahedrons.

SWIMMING   There is of course no shortage of water in the Miami area! See the Venetian Pool listing (p. 93) and the "Miami's Beaches" section on p. 79 for descriptions of swell swimming options.

TENNIS   Hundreds of South Florida tennis courts are open to the public for a minimal fee. Most operate on a first-come, first-served basis and are open from sunrise to sunset. For details, check with the **City of Miami Beach Recreation, Culture, and Parks Department** (www.MiamiBeachParks.com) or the **Miami-Dade County Parks, Recreation and Open Spaces Department** (www.MiamiDade.gov/Parks). Of the nearly public tennis courts throughout Miami, the 26 hard clay and grass courts at the **Crandon Park Tennis Center,** 7300 Crandon Blvd. (www.MiamiDade.gov/Parks/

Crandon-Tennis.asp; ℂ **305/365-2300**), are the best and prettiest—and therefore can get crowded on weekends. You'll play on the same courts as Lendl, Graf, Evert, McEnroe, Federer, the Williams sisters, and other greats; this is also the venue for one of the world's biggest annual tennis events, the Sony Ericsson Open. There's a pleasant, if limited, pro shop, plus many good pros. Thirteen courts are lit at night, and if you reserve at least 24 hours in advance, you can usually take your pick. Hard courts cost $4 person per hour during the day, $6 per person per hour at night. Clay courts cost $7 per person per hour during the day, $9 at night. Grass courts are $11 per person per hour (there are no night hours). The courts are open weekdays from 8am to 10pm, weekends until 7pm.

Other courts are pretty run-of-the-mill and can be found in most neighborhoods. I do, however, recommend the **Miami Beach public courts at Flamingo Park,** 1001 12th St., in South Beach (ℂ **305/673-7761**), where there are 17 clay courts that cost $10 per person an hour for nonresidents (add $1.50 for night play). It's first-come, first-served, and is open 8am to 9pm weekdays, 8am to 8pm weekends.

WINDSURFING   Many hotels rent windsurfers to their guests, but if yours doesn't have a watersports concession stand, head for Key Biscayne. **Sailboards Miami,** Rickenbacker Causeway (www.SailboardsMiami.com; ℂ **305/892-8992**), operates out of two big yellow trucks on Windsurfer Beach, the most popular (though my pick for best is Hobie Beach) windsurfing spot in the city. For those who've never ridden a board but want to try it, it offers a 2-hour group lesson for $79 that's guaranteed to turn you into a wave warrior, or you get your money back (alternatively, private lessons go for $35 per half hour, $65 per hour). After that, you can rent a board for $25 to $30 an hour. If you want to make a day of it, a 10-hour prepaid card costs $240 (you can use the card multiple days until the time on it runs out). Kayaks can also be rented. Hours are Friday through Tuesday from 10am to 6pm. Make your first right after the tollbooth (7/10 of a mile after the tollbooth at the beginning of the causeway—you can't miss it) to find the outfitters.

ORGANIZED TOURS

In addition to the tours listed below, a great option for seeing the city is a tour led by **Dr. Paul George ★★★,** a history professor at Miami-Dade Community College and a historian at the Historical Museum of Southern Florida. There's a variety of tours on foot, bike, boat, and bus, some focusing on such neighborhoods as Little Havana, Brickell Avenue, Key Biscayne, and even Stiltsville, the "neighborhood" of houses on stilts in the middle of Biscayne Bay; others are designed around themes such as Miami cemeteries, the Miami River, eco-history, and "ghostly, ghastly vice and crime." The often long-winded explanation can be a bit much for those who just want a quick look around, but Dr. George sure knows his stuff. Tours leave from downtown's Historical Museum at 101 W. Flagler St. (p. 90); the cost is $25 to $49. For details and reservations, visit www.HistoryMiami.org/tours, or call ℂ **305/375-1621.**

Bike and Roll ★★   Tours by bicycle cover South Beach as well as areas of downtown and Key Biscayne, and there's also a bike/kayak combo. Also, you wouldn't know it from the name, but the company runs Segway tours both in South Beach and along downtown's Brickell Avenue.

www.BikeandRoll.com/miami. ℂ **305/365-3018.** Bike tours $40 adults, $30 kids; Segway tours $59 adults, $49 seniors/kids.

Eco-Adventure Tours ★★ For the eco-conscious traveler, the Miami-Dade Parks and Recreation Department offers guided nature, adventure, and historic tours involving biking, canoeing, snorkeling, hiking, and bird-watching all over the city. www.MiamiEcoAdventures.com. ✆ **305/365-3018.** Prices $25–$165.

Gray Line Miami ★★ Take a tour and get tan as the double-decker buses cruise you through Miami Beach, downtown Miami, Coconut Grove, Little Havana, and Coral Gables from 9am to 6pm daily. A 24-hour hop-on, hop-off pass for the Miami Beach or Grove/Gables loops costs $45 for adults and $30 for ages 4 to 11; a 48-hour hop-on, hop-off pass for all routes costs $50 for adults and $40 for ages 3 to 11. www.GraylineMiami.com. ✆ **877/643-1258.**

Little Havana Cuban Cuisine & Culture Walk ★★★ Historian Pepe Menéndez guides a savory swing through Little Havana, stopping for samples of local cuisine and strong, sweet coffee and even stopping to play dominoes with the locals. A tour also includes a visit to the Bay of Pigs Museum, area social clubs, and a *botánica,* one of the shops that cater to devotees of *Santería,* an Afro-Cuban religion akin to Haiti's *Voudon* (Voodoo). www.HistoryMiami.org/tours. ✆ **305/375-1621.** Tour $30.

Miami Culinary Tours ★★★ There once was a time when Miami was largely about either early-bird specials or models who didn't eat. Now you can graze your way through the city's tastiest neighborhoods, maybe leaving with a few extra pounds to prove it. Miami-as-melting-pot takes on a completely edible meaning thanks to these custom-crafted, specialized tours. And while Little Havana has always been a mouthwatering mecca of Cuban food, this tour operator is like having your own private Rosetta Stone without all the repetition. Choose from 2½-hour tours of South Beach's or Little Havana's best bites, or the "Miami Food Tasting Tour," a 3½-hour Cuban-inspired epicurean adventure throughout the city. www.MiamiCulinaryTours.com. ✆ **888/213-3761.** South Beach or Little Havana tours $59.

Miami Duck Tours ★★ This is the corniest, kookiest tour in the county, beaks down (or, as the company itself says, the "quackiest" way to visit Miami and the beaches). Whatever you call it, it's goofy. The *Watson Willy* is the first of several Miami Duck Tours "vesicles" (part vessel, part vehicle—technical name: Hydra Terra Amphibious Vehicle). Each seats 49 passengers, plus a captain and tour guide, and

---

Venice in Miami

Located just off Miami Beach, Florida's own Venetian Islands (NE 15th St. and Dade Blvd.) were joined in 1926 by a bascule bridge known as the **Venetian Causeway.** A series of 12 bridges stretching between Miami and Miami Beach link all the islands and features octagonal concrete entrance towers that give you a great view of the water. The oldest causeway in Greater Miami, the Venetian is rickety in a charming way, with fantastic views of the bay, city, and the mammoth docked cruise ships, not to mention glimpses of some of Miami's most beautiful waterfront homes. Bikers and joggers especially love the causeway thanks to its limited traffic (due in part to a $1.75 vehicle toll) and pretty scenery

leaves from South Beach's Lincoln Road and a second location at downtown's Bayside, traveling through downtown Miami and South Beach. Then after driving the streets in the duck, you'll plunge into Biscayne Bay for a cruise past all the swank houses. Hey, if it swims like a duck . . .

1661 James Ave., South Beach and at Bayside, 401 Biscayne Blvd., downtown. www.DuckToursMiami. com. ℭ **305/673-2217.** Tickets $32 adults, $26 ages 65 and up, $18 ages 4–12, $5 under age 4.

Redland Tropical Trail Tours ★★   Check out South Florida farmlands—yes, they do exist in an area near Homestead called the Redlands—on this circuit of stops, tastings, and sightseeing that will take you from gardens and jungles to an orchid farm, an actual working winery, a famous fruit stand, and more. There's no cost to follow the trail with a map (available on the website) on your own, but call for pricing information for certain attractions found on the trail.

www.RedlandTrail.com or www.TropicalEverglades.com. ℭ **305/245-9180.**

MIAMI SHOPPING

8

Miami is one of the world's premier shopping cities; more than 12 million visitors come every year and typically spend billions. People come from all over—especially from Latin America and Europe—in search of some products that are "all-American" (in other words, Levi's, Nike, Timberland, and such).

So if you're not into swimming, catching rays, and other outdoor activities; are looking for a break or rainy-day diversion; or are simply a retail-therapy enthusiast, you'll be in good company in one of Miami's many malls—and you are not likely to emerge empty-handed. In addition to the strip malls, Miami offers a choice of malls, from the upscale Village of Merrick Park and mammoth Aventura Mall to the hyper-ritzy Bal Harbour Shops and touristy yet scenic Bayside Marketplace (to name just a few).

Miami also offers more unique shopping spots, such as the up-and-coming area above downtown known as the Biscayne Corridor, where funky boutiques defy the Gap, and Little Havana, where you can buy hand-rolled cigars and *guayaberas* (loose-fitting cotton or gauzy shirts, traditionally for men but also now marketed to women).

You may want to order the Greater Miami Convention and Visitors Bureau's **"Shop Miami: A Guide to a Tropical Shopping Adventure."** Although it's limited to information about the bureau's paying members, it provides some good advice and otherwise unpublished discount offers. The glossy little pamphlet is printed in English, Spanish, and Portuguese, and provides details about transportation from hotels, translation services, and shipping. For a copy, call ℂ **888/766-4264.**

PRACTICAL MATTERS: THE SHOPPING SCENE

As a rule, shop hours are Monday through Saturday from 10am to 6pm and Sunday noon to 5pm. Many stores stay open late (until 9pm or so) one night of the week, usually Thursday. Shops in Coconut Grove are open until 9pm Sunday through Thursday, and even later on Friday and Saturday. South Beach's stores also stay open later—as late as midnight. Department stores and shopping malls keep longer hours as well, with most staying open from 10am to 9 or 10pm Monday through Saturday, noon to 6pm on Sunday. With all these variations, you may want to call specific stores to verify hours.

A state and local sales tax of 7% is added to the price of all nonfood purchases.

Most Miami stores can wrap your purchase and ship it anywhere in the world via United Parcel Service (UPS). If they can't, you can send it yourself, either through FedEx (© **800/463-3339**), UPS (© **800/742-5877**), DHL (© **800/225-5345**), or through the U.S. Mail (see "Fast Facts: Miami & the Keys" p. 232).

SHOPPING AREAS

Most of Miami's shopping happens at the many large malls scattered from one end of the county to the other. However, excellent boutique shopping and browsing can be found in the following areas (see "The Neighborhoods in Brief" on p. 37 for more information about these areas):

AVENTURA   On Biscayne Boulevard between Miami Gardens Drive and the county line at Hallandale Beach Boulevard is a 2-mile stretch of major retail stores including Target, Best Buy, DSW, Bed Bath & Beyond, Loehmann's, Old Navy, Sports Authority, and more. And right above them is the mammoth **Aventura Mall,** housing a fabulous collection of shops and restaurants. Nearby in Broward County's Hallandale Beach, the Village at Gulfstream Park is a new outdoor dining, shopping, and entertainment complex at the ever-expanding racetrack.

> **Impressions**
>
> Someday . . . Miami will become the great center of South American trade.
> —Julia Tuttle, Miami's founder, 1896

BISCAYNE CORRIDOR ★   Amid the gentrifying doo-wop motels of yesteryear, funky, kitschy, and arty boutiques have sprung up along the stretch of Biscayne Boulevard from 50th Street to about 79th Street. Everything from hand-painted tank tops to pricey Diane von Furstenberg dresses can be found here, but it's not just about fashion: Furniture stores selling antiques and modern pieces exist along here as well, so look carefully, because you may find something that would cause the appraisers on *Antiques Road Show* to flip their wigs.

COCONUT GROVE   Downtown Coconut Grove, centered on Main Highway and Grand Avenue and branching onto the adjoining streets, is one of Miami's most pedestrian-friendly zones. The Grove's wide sidewalks, lined with cafes, bars, and boutiques, can provide hours of browsing pleasure. It's a mix of chain stores (Gap, Victoria's Secret, and so on), many of them based at the **Coco Walk** complex, and funky holdovers from the days when the Grove was more bohemian.

CORAL GABLES   Actually only a half-mile long, the downtown shopping street known as **Miracle Mile** was an integral part of George Merrick's original city plan. Today the strip still enjoys popularity, especially for its gift shops, bridal shops, ladies' boutiques, and haberdashers. Several blocks south of here, the upscale **Village of Merrick Park,** an 850,000-square-foot outdoor shopping complex between Ponce de Leon Boulevard and Le Jeune Road, houses Nordstrom, Neiman Marcus, Gucci, and Jimmy Choo, to name just a few.

DESIGN DISTRICT   Though still primarily an interior design, art, and furniture hub, this district a few blocks northwest of downtown is slowly adding retail, with a few funky and fabulous boutiques catering to those who don't have to ask, "How much?"

DOWNTOWN MIAMI   If you're looking for discounts on all types of goods—especially watches, fabric, buttons, lace, shoes, luggage, and leather—Flagler Street, just west of Biscayne Boulevard, is the best place to start. I wouldn't necessarily recommend buying expensive items here, as many stores seem to be on the shady side and don't understand the word "warranty." But you can still have fun here as long as you're a savvy shopper and don't mind haggling. Most signs are printed in English, Spanish, and Portuguese; however, many shopkeepers may not be entirely fluent in English. Straddling South Miami Avenue between 9th and 10th streets downtown, the large **Mary Brickell Village** complex west of Brickell Avenue hasn't become so much a shopping destination as much as a dining and nightlife magnet, with a slew of trendy restaurants and bars. But there are a few interesting boutiques scattered among them.

LITTLE HAVANA   Take a stroll down Calle Ocho (aka SW 8th Street) between SW 27th Avenue and SW 12th Avenue, where you'll find some lively street life and various shops selling cigars, baked goods, shoes, *guayaberas* (distinctive Cuban shirts), furniture, and record stores specializing in Latin music. A Spanish dictionary or the Frommer's Translator app might not be *una mala idea.*

MIDTOWN   For more mainstream creature comforts—Target, PetSmart, Loehmann's, Homegoods, and West Elm—check out the **Shops at Midtown Miami** at N. Miami Avenue and NE 36th Street, a sprawling outdoor shopping and dining complex helping to develop a gritty neighborhood.

SOUTH BEACH ★   South Beach has definitely come into its own as far as trendy shopping is concerned. While chains such as the Gap and Banana Republic have dropped anchor here, several higher-end stores have also opened on a southern stretch of Collins Avenue, which has become sort of the Madison Avenue of Miami. For the hippest clothing boutiques (including Armani Exchange, Ralph Lauren, Intermix, Benetton, Levi's, Barneys Co-Op, Guess, Club Monaco, and Nicole Miller, among others), stroll along this fetching strip of the Art Deco District.

For those interested in a little more fun with their shopping, check out legendary Lincoln Road. This pedestrian mall, designed in 1960 by Morris Lapidus, is home to an array of shops hawking clothing, books, tchotchkes, and art, as well as a bevy of sidewalk restaurants, with a multiplex movie theater at one end and the Atlantic Ocean at the other.

MALLS

There are so many malls in Miami that it would be impossible to mention them all. What follows is a list of the biggest and most popular.

You can find any number of nationally known department stores, including Saks Fifth Avenue, Bloomingdale's, Sears, and JCPenney, in the malls listed below. And Miami's homegrown **Burdines** is now **Macy's,** located at 22 E. Flagler St., downtown; 1675 Meridian Ave. (just off Lincoln Rd.) in South Beach; and in Dadeland mall (below).

And truly hardcore shoppers (as well as bargain-hunters) might find it well worth the hour or so drive up to the western Broward County city of Sunrise, site of **Sawgrass Mills,** the largest darn outlet mall in the whole U.S. of A. (p. 228).

Aventura Mall ★★   A multimillion-dollar makeover has made this spot one of South Florida's premier shopping destinations. With more than 2.3 million square feet of space, this airy, Mediterranean-style mall has a 24-screen movie theater and more than 300 stores, anchored by the likes of Nordstrom, Macy's, JCPenney, and Sears. Specialty stores are impressive and high-end, including Calvin Klein, Missoni, Ted Baker, Hugo Boss, Coach, Diesel, Henri Bendel, Hervé Léger by Max Azria, True Religion, and more. A large indoor playground, Adventurer's Cove, is a great spot for kids, and the mall frequently offers activities and entertainment for children. The many restaurants include Cheesecake Factory, Grand Lux Cafe, the Grill on the Alley, and Sushi Siam, plus a food court mixing the usual suspects with local operations. 19501 Biscayne Blvd. (at 197th St.), Aventura. www.AventuraMall.com. ℭ **305/935-1110.**

Bal Harbour Shops ★★ This double-decker, indoor-outdoor mall, one of the country's most prestigious and pricey, hawks the fanciest stuff from the most chichi brands going: Giorgio Armani, Dolce & Gabbana, Fendi, Harry Winston, Gucci, Agent Carolina Herrera, Chanel, Chloé, Diane Von Furstenberg, Stella McCartney, Hublot, Tourneau, and many others, sandwiched between Neiman Marcus and Saks Fifth Avenue. Well-dressed shoppers stroll covered walkways amid lush greenery, and pause for coffee or a meal at several good cafes and topnotch restaurants such as Carpaccio and Makoto (with some of South Florida's most amazing sushi; the sampler is a true work of art). Parking costs $1.50 an hour with a validated ticket, $5 without (you can stamp your own at the Saks entrance even without making a purchase). 9700 Collins Ave. (at 97th St., opposite St. Regis Hotel), Bal Harbour. www.BalHarbourShops.com. ℭ **305/866-0311.**

Bayside Marketplace ★ Popular with cruise passengers, this waterfront marketplace in the heart of downtown is filled with the usual big-chain suspects (Gap, Guess, Victoria's Secret) as well as a slew of tacky gift shops and carts hawking assorted junk. The second-floor food court is stocked with dozens of fast-food choices and bars. Most of the eateries and bars stay open later than the stores. There's Bubba Gump Shrimp Co., Hooters, Hard Rock Cafe, Chili's, the Knife, and the best spot for drinks and snacks, Largo Seafood & Grill. Parking ranges from $3 to $10, depending on days and times. Although I wouldn't recommend you necessarily drop big bucks here, you should go by just for the view (of Biscayne Bay and the Miami skyline) alone; a flotilla of tour boats is also based here. The adjacent Bayfront Park amphitheater hosts large-scale concerts and festivals, which can cause major pedestrian and vehicle traffic jams. 401 Biscayne Blvd. (at NE 4th St.), downtown. www.BaysideMarketplace.com. ℭ **305/577-3344.**

CocoWalk ★ Despite the usual complement of Americana (Gap, Victoria's Secret, Cheesecake Factory, and so on), this pretty, Mediterranean-style outdoor mall, with its alfresco architecture, is inviting not only for shoppers but also friends or spouses who'd prefer to sit at an outdoor cafe while said shopper is busy in the fitting room. Fat Tuesday on the second floor attracts a happy-hour and late-weekend-night crowd, and on that same floor, one cool homegrown shop worth noting is Palm Produce (p 118). There's also a multiplex with cushy assigned seats and at-seat food-and-drink service, and Thursday through Sunday evenings you can also take in live music on the steps. 3015 Grand Ave. (at Main Hwy./McFarlane Rd.), Coconut Grove. www.CocoWalk.net. ℭ **305/444-0777.**

Dadeland Mall ★★ One of the United States' first malls, it's kept up with the times and features more than 185 specialty and chain shops, anchored by Macy's, JCPenney, Nordstrom, and Saks Fifth Avenue. It also boasts the country's largest Limited/Express store. More than 20 eateries serve from the adjacent food court. New retailers are constantly springing up around this centerpiece of South Miami suburbia. If you're not in the area, however, the mall probably isn't worth the trek. 7535 N. Kendall Dr. (U.S. 1 and SW 88th St.), Kendall. www.Simon.com/Mall/Dadeland-Mall. ℭ **305/665-6226.**

Dolphin Mall ★★ As if Miami needed another mall, this $250-million monster way out west is along the same lines as Broward County's monstrous Sawgrass Mills (p. 228). Its 1.4 million square feet crammed with outlets such as Last Call (Neiman Marcus), AIX Armani Exchange, and Bloomingdale's, plus several discount stores, a 19-screen movie theater, and a bowling alley. 11401 NW 12th St. (at NW 111th Ave.; near intersection of Florida Tpk. and S.R. 836), Sweetwater. www.ShopDolphinMall.com. ℂ **305/365-7446.**

The Falls ★★ Traffic on U.S. 1 to this outdoor shopping center can border on brutal, but once you get there, the vibe leans toward the serene, with landscaping involving water (and fountains but no actual falls) and tropical foliage. You'll find a multiplex and more than 100 stores both moderately priced and upscale-ish, including Ralph Lauren, Miami's first Bloomingdale's, Macy's, Crate & Barrel, Brooks Brothers, Abercrombie, and Swarovski. If you are planning to visit any of the nearby attractions, which include Zoo Miami (p. 96) and Monkey Jungle (p. 96), check with customer service for information on discount packages. 8888 SW 136th St. (at U.S. 1, about 3 miles south of Dadeland Mall), Kendall. www.ShoptheFalls.com. ℂ **305/255-4570** or 305/255-4571.

The Shops at Midtown Miami ★★ Located off Biscayne Boulevard in a transitional, still somewhat gritty, area north of the Design District and Wynwood, Miami's newest retail complex is more of a locals' spot, with Target, West Elm, Marshall's, and PetSmart. There are also great dining options around here, including Five Guys Burgers and Fries, the Cheese Course, Lime Fresh Mexican Grill, 100 Montaditos (featuring literally 100 varieties of little Spanish-style sandwiches), and Sugarcane Raw Bar. 3401 N. Miami Ave. (at NW 36th St.), Midtown Miami. www.ShopMidtownMiami.com. ℂ **305/573-3371.**

The Shops at Sunset Place ★★ Especially popular with teens and college kids, this indoor-outdoor complex has a 24-screen movie complex and an IMAX theater, a Splitsville bowling alley, a Disney store, LA Fitness, and a video arcade, as well as mall standards such as Victoria's Secret, Gap, Hollister, American Eagle Outfitters, Armani Exchange, and so on. Eateries include Panera Bread, Johnny Rockets, and Marhaba Arabian restaurant. The surrounding South Miami commercial area is an engaging and walkable neighborhood of restaurants and shops including a Whole Foods. 5701 Sunset Dr. (at 57th Ave. and U.S. 1), South Miami. www.Simon.com/Mall/The-Shops-at-Sunset-Place. ℂ **305/663-0482.**

The Village at Gulfstream Park ★★ For a mix of shopping and gambling, the Gulfstream horse track's new outdoor dining and entertainment venue, just over the Broward County line above Aventura, features an expanding list of businesses—Crate & Barrel, Pottery Barn, Williams-Sonoma, and West Elm, among clothing and accessories boutiques; bars; and restaurants including Yard House, BRIO Tuscan Grill, and American Pie Brick Oven Pizza. 501 S. Federal Hwy. (at SE 5th St.), Hallandale Beach. www.TheVillageatGulfstreamPark.com. ℂ **954/378-0900.**

Village of Merrick Park ★★ Giving Bal Harbour Shops a run for its money, this Mediterranean-style outdoor mall in Coral Gables consists of high-end stores such as Jimmy Choo, Diane von Furstenberg, Neiman Marcus, Miami's first Nordstrom, and upscale eateries such as Villaggio, SAWA, and Yard House. In fact, the owners of Bal Harbour Shops were so paranoid they'd lose business to Merrick Park that they shoveled a ton of cash into an ad campaign making sure people wouldn't forget that Bal Harbour was here first. Duly noted. 358 San Lorenzo Ave. (btw. Bird Rd., Ponce de Leon Blvd., and U.S. 1), Coral Gables. www.VillageofMerrickPark.com. ℂ **305/529-0200.**

SHOPPING A TO Z
Antiques & Collectibles

Miami's antiques shops are scattered in small pockets around the city. Many that feature lower-priced furniture can be found in North Miami, in the 1600 block of NE 123rd Street, near West Dixie Highway. About a dozen shops sell china, silver, glass, furniture, and paintings, but you'll find the bulk of the better antiques in Coral Gables and in Southwest Miami along Bird Road between 64th and 66th avenues and in the **Bird Road Art District** between 72nd and 74th avenues (p. 115). For international collections from Bali to France, check out the burgeoning scene in the Design District centered on NE 40th Street west of 1st Avenue. Miami also hosts several large antiques shows each year. The most prestigious, in its 53rd year, the **Original Miami Beach Antique Show** hits the Miami Beach Convention Center (www.OriginalMiami BeachAntiqueShow.com; ✆ **239/732-6642**) at the end of January or early February. Exhibitors from all over come to display their wares, with jewelry a particular specialty. Miami's concentration of Art Deco buildings from the '20s and '30s also means makes this is one of the best cities to find top selections of Deco furnishings and decor. A word to serious collectors: **Dania Beach** (www.VisitDaniaBeach.com/Antiques. asp), in Broward County about a half-hour from downtown Miami, is considered the antiques capital of South Florida, so you may want to consider browsing in Miami and shopping up there.

Alhambra (Antiques) ★★ This fabulous store specializes in 18th-, 19th-, and 20th-century French and other European antiques, furniture, accessories, lighting, and art. It also has a garden collection of antique jars and pots, as well as a cool collection of vintage birdcages. The store prides itself on the fact that it doesn't use outsourced buyers or wholesalers; every piece has been acquired by the owners on trips to Europe. 2850 Salzedo St. (at Palermo Ave.), Coral Gables. www.AlhambraAntiques.com. ✆ **866/446-1688.**

Miami Twice ★★ "Retro" means different things to different age groups, and so for 3 decades Miami's raddest retro retailer, a short drive west of Coral Gables, has an ever-changing collection of vintage clothing, designer purses, accessories, and jewelry. There's also an excellent selection of new lines of clothing, jewelry, costumes, and masquerade masks that have that retro feel, as well as antiques and collectables dating from 1850 to 1970. Throughout October it dresses itself up as a big Halloween costume shop. 6562 Bird Rd. (btw. SW 65th and 67th aves.), Miami. www.MiamiTwice.com. ✆ **305/666-0127.**

Modernism Gallery ★★ Specializing in 20th-century furnishings from the likes of Gilbert Rohde, Noguchi, and Heywood Wakefield, this Coral Gables-based outfit stocks some beauteous examples of Deco items from France and the United States. If it doesn't have what you're looking for, ask; the staff possesses an amazing knack for tracking down the rarest items. 770 Ponce de Leon Blvd. (at Bobadilla St.), Coral Gables. www. ModernismGallery.com. By appointment only. ✆ **305/442-8743.**

Stone Age Antiques ★★ Movie posters, military memorabilia, tribal masks, cowboy hats—you name it, this off-the-beaten-path shop, in business for nearly a half century on the river just east of the airport, probably has it. Its salty specialty, though, is nautical antiques. Looking for a certain ship's wheel or prow figurehead? Well, ahoy, matey, it could very well be here. 3236 NW S. River Dr. (off NW 33rd Ave.), Miami. www. StoneAge-Antiques.com. ✆ **305/633-5114.**

Worth Galleries ★★ A great place to browse—if you don't mind a little dust—this huge warehouse harbors an impressive stash of very large antique lighting and 20th-century chandeliers, as well as modern art and antique oil paintings. The furniture is hand selected in Europe. And for a different era, it offers a large selection of fine vintage contemporary furniture that includes midcentury modern and Art Deco periods. 2520 SW 28th La. (off SW 27th Ave. and U.S. 1), Miami. www.WorthGalleries.com. 𝒞 **305/285-1330.**

Art Galleries

Britto Central ★★ Although dismissed by serious collectors, flamboyant Brazilian pop artist Romero Britto is inescapable in Miami, his unmistakable, cartoonishly cheerful style splashed across buildings and public spaces all over the county (with the bill footed by we the taxpayers). Unsurprisingly, his Lincoln Road HQ is, like it or not, also Miami's most-high-profile gallery. 818 Lincoln Rd. (btw. Jefferson and Meridian aves.), South Beach. www.Britto.com. 𝒞 **305/531-8821.** Sun–Thurs 10am–11pm, Fri–Sat 10am–midnight.

CIFO ★★ An outstanding nonprofit gallery established by Cuban-American entrepreneur Ella Fontanals-Cisneros to foster cultural exchange among the visual arts, CIFO supports emerging and midcareer contemporary multidisciplinary artists from Latin America. 1018 N. Miami Ave. (at NW 10th St.), downtown. www.cifo.org. 𝒞 **305/445-3880.** Thurs–Fri noon–6pm, Sat–Sun 10am–4pm during exhibitions (call or check online for dates).

Diana Lowenstein Fine Arts ★★ One of Miami's pre-eminent modern art figures, Lowenstein has made her gallery in the burgeoning Wynwood area of downtown Miami a must-visit for serious collectors and admirers. 2043 N. Miami Ave. (at NW 21st St.), Wynwood. www.DLFineArts.com. 𝒞 **305/576-1804.** Tues–Fri 10am–5pm; Sat 10am–3pm.

Emerson Dorsch ★★ An expansive gallery known for hosting fabulous parties for the who's who in the art world, Dorsch carries some seriously funky exhibitions. 151 NW 24th St. (at N. Miami Ave.). www.DorschGallery.com. 𝒞 **305/576-1278.** Tues–Sat noon–5pm.

Fredric Snitzer Gallery ★★ The catalyst to the explosion of the Wynwood arts scene, this warehouse pays homage to works by local stars and New World School of the Arts grads, as well as artists from Cuba's legendary '80s generation. 2249 NW 1st Place (at N. Miami Ave.), Wynwood. www.Snitzer.com. 𝒞 **305/448-8976.** Tues–Sat 10am–5pm.

Gary Nader Fine Art ★★ If you're into Latin American art by the likes of Botero, Matta, and Lam, this is the place for you. In addition, there are monthly exhibits of emerging artists. 62 NE 27th St. (at N. Miami Ave.), Wynwood. www.GaryNader.com. 𝒞 **305/576-0256.** Mon–Sat 10am–6pm.

Margulies Collection ★ This 45,000-square-foot Wynwood warehouse is the city's crown jewel, showcasing contemporary and vintage photography, video, sculpture, and installations in various genres, including pop art, minimalism, and expressionism. 591 NW 27th St. (at NW 6th Ave.), Wynwood. www.MarguliesWarehouse.com. 𝒞 **305/576-1051.** Wed–Sat 11am–4pm; extended hours during Art Basel. Admission charge $10.

Books

You can find local branches of **Barnes & Noble** in Coral Gables at 152 Miracle Mile (𝒞 **305/446-4152**); South Miami at 5701 Sunset Dr. (𝒞 **305/662-4770**); and out west in Kendall at 12405 N. Kendall Dr. (𝒞 **305/598-7727**), with the same excellent selection,

AN ARTY bird OF A DIFFERENT FEATHER

Wynwood may have famously become ground-zero for Miami's increasingly impressive gallery scene, but an older (since the late 1980s), 24-block arts cluster out west near the Palmetto Expressway, now known as the **Bird Road Art District** (www.TheBirdRoadArtDistrict.com; ℰ **305/467-6819**), offers not only more accessible prices but the chance to interact with more than 40 local artists and artisans—some three quarters of them of Latin American origin—right in their studios. Spaces include Cuban-American artist MANO's Fine Art Project Space, glassblower Matthew Miller's Nickel Glass, Irma García's Arte Venezolano, and Federico Scipioni's Stained Glass of Miami. Several, such as Humberto Benitez, Néstor Arenas, Luis Fuentes, and Miguel Rodez also turn out Cuba-themed work miles above the schmaltz of the Calle Ocho galleries. There are wonderfully quirky shops here, too, such as fascinating international kitchen products from Ancient Cookware and a riot of high-quality antiques at León Antiques. Browse the website for details; also, at the number above, MANO's wife Cuqui Beguiristain can steer you to spots based on your interests and budget. There's an art walk on the third Saturday of each month, and a couple of live performance stages. Just south of Bird Road (aka SW 40th St.) between SW 72th and SW 75th avenues, the district's open year round, but the best months to visit are October through March.

appealing atmosphere, and popular cafes you find in this chain throughout the U.S. In addition, Miami is home to one of America's better independent booksellers:

Books & Books ★★★   A dedicated following turns out to browse at this warm, wonderful indie bookseller and courtyard bar/cafe in Coral Gables, founded in 1982. Besides the current bestsellers, you'll find some lovely art books and local literature. If that's not enough intellectual stimulation, there are free lectures almost every night by noted authors, experts, and personalities. At its South Beach location, 927 Lincoln Rd. (ℰ **305/532-3222**), you'll rub elbows with tanned and buff South Beach bibliophiles, and have the option of a full restaurant menu, too. And if you happen to be at the ritzy Bal Harbour Shops and looking for a break from Gucci, Prada, and Choo, there's another branch here (ℰ **305/864-4241**). Finally, on the way out, check out the one at Miami International Airport Concourse D, Gate D25 (ℰ **305/876-0468**). 265 Aragon Ave. (btw. Ponce de Leon Blvd. and Salzedo St.), Coral Gables. www.BooksandBooks.com. ℰ **305/442-4408.**

Cigars

Although it's still illegal to bring Cuban cigars into the United States, somehow, they show up at every dinner party and nightclub in town. Not that I condone it, but if you hang around cigar smokers here, no doubt one will be able to tell you where to score some of these highly prized smokes. Watch out for counterfeits, though—usually Dominican cigars rebanded as Cubans. Some aficionados say that Dominican sticks, made from tobacco grown from Cuban seeds, can be as good or better than Cubans anyway, and most of the better imports you'll find are from the DR, Nicaragua, or Honduras.

Cigar culture is booming in Miami, and nowhere more than in Little Havana, whose "downtown" is lined with shops, some of which employ *viejitos* (little old-timers) or younger immigrants who learned classic cigar rolling in Cuba and show you how it's done here—needless to say, great photo ops. Several shops have been shown to be a little shady, though (see above), so buyer beware. The businesses listed below sell high-quality hand-rolled cigars made with domestic- and foreign-grown tobacco.

Cuba Tobacco Cigar Co. ★★ Little Havana's second-oldest cigar shop was founded by Pedro Bello after he arrived from Cuba in 1970, and sells its own Bello brand, grown and rolled in the Dominican Republic and Honduras with shade-grown wrapper from Connecticut. Not only are a couple to a half-dozen rollers on hand every day at these cozy premises, but often so is the entire friendly Bello family: Pedro Jr. oversees the operation, Pedro Sr. greets visitors outside, and wives and kids help run things. 1528 SW 8th St. (btw. SW 15th and 16th aves.), Little Havana. www.CubaTobaccoCigarCo.com. ℰ**305/649-2717.**

El Crédito Cigar Factory ★★ Little Havana's oldest cigar emporium is the place to go not necessarily for low prices, but for a smokin' selection of torpedos, robustos, and panetelas from well-known Cuban brands re-established in the DR, such as Macanudo, Partagás, and Cohiba. It no longer has rollers in-house, but next to the shop is a nice, roomy lounge where you can unwrap your booty and sit for a leisurely smoke. 1106 SW 8th St. (at SW 11th Ave.), Little Havana. ℰ**305/858-4162.**

Mike's Cigars ★★ Mike's may have abandoned its old digs for a bigger, newer location, but since 1950 it's been one of the oldest and best smoke shops in the county, selling the best from Honduras, the Dominican Republic, and Jamaica, as well as the very hot local brand La Gloria Cubana. Many say it's got the best prices, too. Mike's boasts the biggest local selection of cigars, and the employees speak English. It also runs fun in-store events that dudes love, involving cigars, football, and booze. 1030 Kane Concourse (at 96th St.), Bay Harbor Island. www.MikesCigars.com. ℰ**305/866-2277.**

Beauty & Cosmetics

Brownes Merchants & Trading Co. ★★ This outfit is SoBe's go-to beauty destination, where the young and the young-at-heart peruse antique display cases filled with anti-aging serums, French soaps, lotions, and potions. The selection of makeup, haircare, skincare, and bath/body products includes Darphin, Skinceuticals, Molton Brown, Nars, and Diptyque. Feel free to browse and sample, as salespeople are not pushy. If you do need help, they're experts when it comes to all things pulchritude, especially in the salon/spa where you can get coiffed, colored, buffed, and waxed. Signature treatments include the Kneipp deluxe manicure/pedicure, Caudalie facial, and the Well-being massage. There's also an outpost in the Design District, 32 NE 39th St. 1688 Jefferson Ave. (btw. Lincoln La. and 17th St.), South Beach. www.BrownesBeauty.com. ℰ**305/538-7544.**

MAC South Beach ★★ Viva la glam! The innovative brand of makeup is all here, and if you're lucky you may get a free makeover. 673A Collins Ave. (at 7th St.), South Beach. www.MACCosmetics.com. ℰ**305/604-9040.**

Sephora ★★ The Disney World of makeup offers a dizzying array of cosmetics, perfumes, and styling products. Unlike Brownes & Co., though, personal service and attentiveness are at a minimum. Browsing can be a head-spinning experience (but at least it'll be a pretty head). Other locations include Aventura (p. 110) and Dadeland (p. 111) malls. 721 Collins Ave. (btw. 7th and 8th sts.), South Beach. www.Sephora.com. ℰ**305/532-0904.**

Clothing & Accessories

Miami didn't become a fashion capital, believe it or not, until the pastel-hued, Armani-clad cops on *Miami Vice* got their close-ups. Before that, it was all about old guys in white patent leather shoes and well-tanned babes in bikinis. These days it boasts some of the same high-end shopping you find on Rue de Faubourg St. Honoré in Paris or London's Bond Street. You'll find all the *haute couture* labels at the posh Bal Harbour Shops or at the Village of Merrick Park. For funkier frocks, South Beach is the spot, where designers like Nicole Miller, Ralph Lauren, and Giorgio Armani—well, Armani Exchange—compete for window shoppers with local up-and-coming designers, some of whom design for drag queens and club kids only. Miami's edgy Upper East Side and Design District neighborhoods are also slowly but surely coming along as hotspots for hip wear. Collins Avenue between 7th and 10th streets has become quite upscale, including the likes of Armani Exchange, True Religion, Ugg Australia, and Intermix, along with the inescapable Gap and Banana Republic. Then there's the Herzog & de Meuron–designed open-sided parking lot at Lincoln and Alton roads, the quintessence of multitasking, which also including shops and restaurants (it's so cool it also books events and photo shoots). Then of course, there's also more mainstream (and affordable) shopping in a plethora of malls and shopping/entertainment complexes (see "Malls," p. 110).

UNISEX

Atrium ★★ Young Hollywood always makes Atrium a stop on their South Beach shopping list. With highfalutin' designer brands at designer prices, don't be surprised if you see that $200 white T-shirt on an Olsen twin in the latest *Us Weekly*. 1931 Collins Ave. (btw, 18th and 19th sts.), South Beach. www.AtriumNYC.com. ✆ **305/695-0757.**

Barneys Co-Op ★★ An outpost of Barneys New York, only more "affordable." If you consider a T-shirt for $150 "affordable," then knock yourself out. Otherwise, Barneys Co-Op is still great for browsing and marveling over the fashion victims who do pay such idiotic prices. 832 Collins Ave. (btw. 8th and 9th sts.), South Beach. ✆ **305/421-2010.**

BASE ★★ A hipster hangout, featuring clothing that's fashionable, and, it goes without saying, pricey. BASE is also known for its cool and funky CD collection (all for sale, of course), coffee-table books, and nice-smelling candles. There are outlets in the Delano and Mondrian hotels, too. 927 Lincoln Rd. (btw. Michigan and Jefferson aves.), South Beach. www.BaseWorld.com. ✆ **305/531-4982.**

En Avance ★★ If you couldn't get into LIV or Story last night, consider plunking down a chunky chunk of change for the au courant labels that En Avance is known for. One outfit bought here, and the doormen have no ground to stand on when it comes to high-fashion dress codes. 53 NE 40th St. (btw. NE 1st and Miami aves.), Design District. www.EnAvance.net. ✆ **305/576-0056.**

> ### Impressions
>
> *We're the only city that has big-butt mannequins.*
> —Anna Maria Diaz-Balart, Miami-based fashion designer

H&M ★★ What makes the South Beach branch of the Swedish mega-retailer especially notable is not its bright, cheerful three-floor premises (including a gargantuan video screen with what a friend of mine called "epilepsy-inducing" footage) or its appealing, fairly trendy merch at appealing prices, but the venue: the Lincoln Theater, built in classic Deco style in 1936 and for 20 years home to the New World Symphony (p. 126). 551 Lincoln Rd. (at Pennsylvania Ave.), South Beach. www.HM.com. ✆ **855/466-7467.**

Palm Produce Resortwear ★★   A local retailer that has spread to Palm Beach and New York's Hamptons, it carries great swimwear and linen garb for men and women, and in 2013 its Coconut Grove's flagship launched First Flight Out, an accessories line themed after aviation (especially locally based airline icon Pan-American); there's also a fascinating display of Pan-Am stuff. At CocoWalk, level 2, 3015 Main Hwy. (at Grand Ave.). Coconut Grove. www.PalmProduce.com or www.TheFirstFlightOut.com. ✆ **305/774-7220.**

Urban Outfitters ★★   It took a while for this urban outpost to hit Miami, but once it did, it became a favorite for the young hipster set who favor T-shirts that read "Princess" instead of Prada. Cheapish, utilitarian, and funky, it's an excellent spot to pick up a pair of cool jeans or some funky tchotchkes for your pad. www.UrbanOutfitters. com. 653 Collins Ave. (btw. 6th and 7th sts.), South Beach (✆ **305/535-9726**). Also Dadeland Mall, 7535 N. Kendall Dr., Kendall (✆ **305/663-0619**), and Aventura Mall, 19575 Biscayne Blvd. (✆ **305/ 936-8358**).

The Webster ★★   A Parisian-style couture emporium straight out of *Women's Wear Daily,* Webster features runway-ready *prêt à porter* for men and women by all those boldface names you read in the fashion magazines. It's so swank that in high season there's often a bar serving champagne, caviar, and other high-ticket tummy ticklers. 1220 Collins Ave. (btw. 12th and 13th sts.), South Beach. Also in Bal Harbour Shops. www. TheWebsterMiami.com. ✆ **305/674-7899.**

WOMEN'S

Belinda's Designs ★★   This German designer makes some of the most beautiful and intricate teddies, nightgowns, and wedding dresses. Some might find the styles a little too Stevie Nicks, but the frocks are certainly impressive—and so are the prices. 917 Washington Ave. (btw. 9th and 10th sts.), South Beach. www.belindasdesigns.net. ✆ **305/532-0068.**

Kore Boutique ★★   A high-fashion boutique east of Wynwood, with dressy and chic-casual wear as well as shoes, jewelry, and bags, all at pretty affordable prices. 2925 Biscayne Blvd. (btw. NE 29th and 30th sts.), Miami. www.koreboutique.com. ✆ **305/573-8211.**

Silvia Tcherassi ★★   Ms. Tcherassi is a prominent fashion designer who in many ways embodies the new Miami. She hails from Barranquilla, Colombia, first of all, and draws inspiration from such south-of-the-border icons as Fernando Botero and Frida Kahlo (she also uses a lot of lace—a very Latin touch). Her Coral Gables atelier and Village of Merrick Park boutique carry both ready-to-wear and bridal lines. 4101 Ponce de Leon Blvd (btw. Bird R. and Altara Ave.) Coral Gables. www.SilviaTcherassi.com. ✆ **305/529-0004.** Also in the Village at Merrick Park (350 San Lorenzo Ave., Coral Gables; ✆ **305/461-0009**).

MEN'S

Cubavera ★★   A mostly menswear line launched by Cuban-Americans George and Isaac Feldenkreis in 2000, it sexes up the traditional *guayabera* with tropical colors and patterns, along with adding linen and cotton pants and blazers. The line has added some items for women, but those are available online only; here it's all about the dudes. This stuff is just great, and very Miami—I own several items myself. 934 Lincoln Rd. (btw. Michigan and Jefferson aves.), South Beach. www.Cubavera.com. ✆ **305/535-1331.**

La Casa de las Guayaberas ★★   Miami's top purveyor of the traditional yet retro-hip Cuban *guayabera*—a loose-fitting, pleated, button-down shirt—was founded by Ramon Puig, who emigrated to Miami in the 1960s and, until his death at the age of 90 in 2011, used the same scissors he did back then. Today there's a team of seamstresses who hand-sew 20 shirts a day in all colors and styles. Prices range from $15 to $375. 5840 SW 8th St. (btw. SW 58th and 59th aves.), Little Havana. www.RamonPuig.com. ✆ **305/266-9683.**

Pepi Bertini European Men's Clothing ★★   Coral Gables men's store features a complete selection of mostly Italian men's shirts, suits, ties, shoes, and accessories by Canali, Lanvin, and Bruno Magli, as well as master tailor Pepi's own custom-made shirts. 315 Miracle Mile, Coral Gables. www.PepiBertini.com. ✆ **305/461-3374.** Closed Sun/Mon.

ACCESSORIES

MIA Jewels ★★   Fun and funky necklaces, bracelets, rings, and accessories in all price ranges. At Aventura Mall, 19575 Biscayne Blvd. (at 197th St.), Aventura. www.MIAJewels. com. ✆ **305/931-2000.**

SEE ★★   This fantastic eyewear store features an enormous selection of stylish specs at decent prices. The staff is patient and knowledgeable. 921 Lincoln Rd. (btw. Michigan and Jefferson aves.), South Beach. www.SeeEyewear.com. ✆ **305/672-6622.**

HIGH-END JEWELRY

For name designers such as Gucci and Tiffany & Co., your best bet is **Bal Harbour Shops** (see "Malls," p. 110).

Santayana Jewelry ★★   If you like bling and want to take home uniquely local examples thereof, Miriam Santayana and company's creative offerings are baubles—from bracelet charms to full-blown necklaces—inspired by stained glass, tropicalia such as palm trees, and Cuban culture (some pieces incorporate Cuban coins, others are based on hometown symbols and even cuisine, such as a funky ring in the image of a traditional *café cubano* maker). www.Santayana.com. 4100 Salzedo St. (btw. Bird Rd. and Altara Ave.), Coral Gables, ✆ **305/361-2786.** Also 640 Crandon Blvd. (at E. Enid Dr.), Key Biscayne. ✆ **305/361-2786.**

Seybold Building ★★   Jewelers who specialize in an assortment of goods (diamonds, gems, watches, rings, and such) gather here daily to sell diamonds and gold. With 200 jewelry stores located inside this independently owned and operated multilevel treasure chest, the glare as you go in is blinding. You'll be sure to spot handsome and up-to-date designs, but not too many bargains. 36 NE 1st St. (btw. N. Miami Ave. and NE 1st Ave.), downtown. www.SeyboldJewelry.com. ✆ **305/374-7922.**

Turchin Love and Light Jewelry ★★   Apart from the fact that you might spot boldface names such as Jennifer Aniston shopping here, this tiny Design District jewel box is a standout for its collection designed using unique artifacts made in Tibet, Nepal, Africa, India, Bhutan, and Pakistan. And there are plenty of choices for less than $300. 130 NE 40th St. (btw. NE 1st and 2nd aves.), Design District. www.TurchinJewelry.com. ✆ **305/573-7117.**

Food & Drink

There are myriad ethnic markets in Miami, from Cuban *bodegas* (little grocery stores) to Jamaican import shops and Guyanese produce stands. I've listed a few of the biggest and best markets that sell prepared foods as well as staples. Also, on Saturday mornings, vendors set up stands on South Beach's Lincoln Road loaded with papayas, melons, tomatoes, and citrus, as well as cookies, ice cream, and sandwiches.

Epicure Gourmet Market ★★ Epicure carries not just fine wines, cheeses, meats, fish, and juices, but prime produce like Portobello mushrooms the size of a yarmulke (this neighborhood landmark is known for supplying the Jewish residents of the beach with ethnic favorites like matzo ball soup, gefilte fish, and deli items). Prices are steep but generally worth it. There's a larger, newer Epicure at 17190 Collins Ave. in Sunny Isles Beach (*(C)* 305/947-4581), with an expansive outdoor cafe and bar which hosts wine tastings, and another in Coral Gables, 4711 Le Jeune Rd. (*(C)* **305/503-8001**). 1656 Alton Rd. (btw. Lincoln Rd. and 17th St.), South Beach. www.EpicureMarket.com. *(C)* **305/672-1861.**

Gardner's Market ★★ Anything a gourmet or novice cook could want can be found here. One of the oldest (1912) and best grocery stores in Miami, this Coconut Grove institution offers great takeout and the freshest produce. 3117 Bird Ave. (btw. Matilda St. and Bridgeport Ave.), Coconut Grove. www.GardnersGrove.com. *(C)* **305/476-9900.**

Graziano's Market ★★ For the best of edible Argentina, tango your way into this well-stocked gourmet market/bakery/cafe in downtown Coral Gables (which also happens to be a brunch favorite of mine). The pastries and empanadas are luscious; there's more substantial grub available as well, along with a popular a happy-hour special involving Malbec. There are several Graziano's restaurants, as well, in the Gables, downtown, and elsewhere. 2301 Galiano St. (at Giralda Ave.), Coral Gables. www. GrazianosGroup.com. *(C)* **305/460-0001.**

Laurenzo's Italian Center ★★ An *abbondanza* of Italian food—homemade ravioli, hand-cut imported Romano cheese—plus fresh fish and meats, and one of Miami's most comprehensive wine selections. The neighboring store is full of just-picked herbs, salad greens, and vegetables from around the world, and a daily farmer's market runs from 7am to 6pm (8am–5pm on Sun), and daily specials lure bargain-seekers from all over. If you can't wait to eat when you get back to your hotel, there's a cafe here, too. 16385 W. Dixie Hwy. (at NE 164th St.), North Miami Beach. www.Laurenzos Market.com. *(C)* **305/945-6381**.

Marky's ★★ Do your tastes run toward caviar, foie gras, and truffles? Head up Biscayne Boulevard to this gourmet shop that originally specialized in delicacies of Mother Russia. These days you'll find all of the above (the caviar's Russian, Israeli, and domestic), plus fine cheeses, Scottish smoked salmon, and all sorts of kosher and international goodies. (And be sure to ask about the secret back room.) 687 NE 79th St. (btw. Biscayne Blvd. and NE 7th Ave.). www.Markys.com. *(C)* **305/758-9288.**

Paul Bakery ★★ Flaky, crusty, and generally *délicieux*—the Lincoln Road out-post of the well-known French chain turns out lovely versions of baked faves both savory and sweet, including croissants, brioches, baguettes, macarons, and fruit tarts. Can't wait to gobble the goodies? There are tables inside and outside (great for people-watching, of course). 450 Lincoln Rd. (at Drexel Ave.), South Beach. www.Paul-USA.com. *(C)* **305/531-1200.**

Gifts/Souvenirs

Sentir Cubano ★★ Unique to Miami is the chance to pick up nifty gifts or mementos relating to South Florida's Cuban culture. There are souvenir shops in Little Havana, but "Feeling Cuban," out on a non-touristy stretch of Calle Ocho (as SW 8th St is locally known), is oriented toward locals and so stocks a fairly good-quality selection of merch. Examples: paintings and photos with Cuban images and themes; kitch-enware; clothing (and not just T-shirts); music and movies; tiles and other decor; even some antiques. And if you're in the market for toilet paper with Fidel Castro's face on it, look no further. 3100 SW 8th St. (at SW 31st Ave.), Little Havana. www.SentirCubano.com. ✆ **877/999-9945.**

Music Stores

If you are one of the few who still buys music in stores, believe it or not there are not one but three that sell everything from vintage vinyl to soon-to-be-extinct CDs.

Casino Records Inc. ★★   At this compact shop in the heart of Little Havana's "downtown," with Miami's best selection of Latin music (both current and vintage), the young, hip salespeople speak English and know their tunes. There are also DVDs of concerts and foreign films. Casino's slogan translates to "If we don't have it, forget it." Believe us, they've got it. 2290 SW 8th St. (at SW 16th Ave.), Little Havana. www.Casino RecordsMiami.com. ✆ **786/394-8899.**

Sweat Records ★★   If Miami had cellars, this place would be like that basement where your coolest friends hang out, where indie music soon to hit the radio plays before anyone else hears it. Founded in 2005 by a DJ and a DJ-turned-criminal-defense-attorney (hey, it's a dodgy neighborhood), Sweat is also a vegan coffee and treats bar with free Wi-Fi. It also sells magazines, books, and gifts and hosts events and parties. Right next door is Churchill's Pub (p. 136), a great indie music venue. 5505 NE 2nd Ave. (at NE 55th St.), Little Haiti. http://SweatRecordsMiami.com. ✆ **786/693-9309.**

Yesterday and Today Records ★   For diehard collectors, Miami's best-stocked treasure trove of vinyl—yes, kids, it was once common on turntables as well as floors—may be worth the drive pretty far out west, stocking every genre of music imaginable in just about every format (bet you could even track down some 8-track tapes). 9274 Bird Rd./SW 40th St. (btw. SW 92nd and 93rd aves.), Olympia Heights. www. VintageRecords.com. ✆ **305/554-1020.**

Sporting Goods

People-watching seems to be the number-one sport in South Florida, but for more jockish pursuits, check out the following.

Bass Pro Shops Outdoor World ★★   It's a wee bit of a schlep out west to the Dolphin Mall (p. 112), but if you're a fishing, hunting, camping, boating, and/or sports enthusiast, you'll be in heaven at this superstore. Depending on where you're based, you might actually find the even larger Broward County standalone, 200 Gulf Stream Way (✆ **954/929-7710**), more convenient, plus it does in-house events such as fly-fishing and archery demonstrations, classes in marine safety, and so forth. At Dolphin Mall, 11401 NW 12th St. (at NW 111th Ave.), Sweetwater. www.BassPro.com. ✆ **305/341-4200**.

Edwin Watts Golf Shops ★★   Miami boasts two of the more than 90 Edwin Watts branches throughout the U.S. Southeast. One of these full-service golf retail shops is out west in Doral, the other up in North Miami Beach. You can find it all here, including clothing, pro-line equipment, gloves, bags, balls, videos, and books. Plus you can get coupons for discounted greens fees on many courses. 15100 N. Biscayne Blvd. (at NE 151st St.), North Miami Beach. www.EdwinWattsGolf.com. ✆ **305/944-2925**); 8484 NW 36th St. (btw. NW 82nd and 87th aves.), Doral ✆ **305/591-1220**); 6254 S. Dixie Hwy. (btw. SW 76th and 78th sts.).

Island Water Sports ★★   You'll find everything from booties and gloves to baggies and tanks. Check in here before you rent that WaveRunner or windsurfer. 16231 Biscayne Blvd. (at NE 163rd St.), North Miami Beach. www.IWSMiami.com. ✆ **305/944-0104.**

South Beach Dive and Surf Center ★★　Prices are slightly higher than many competitors at this beach location, but you'll find the hottest styles and equipment. It also rents surfboards and puts out a free by-phone surf report. 850 Washington Ave., South Beach. www.SouthBeachDivers.com. ✆ **305/531-6110.**

Thrift Stores/Resale Shops

C. Madeleine's ★★　The best, most couture-istic vintage store in town, brands from Gucci, Pucci, Fiorucci, and even Chanel and Balenciaga are usually snatched up by the likes of Jessica Simpson, Lenny Kravitz, or their stylists, who make this fashion emporium a favored haunt. 13702 Biscayne Blvd. (btw. NE 135th St. and Highlands Dr.), North Miami. www.CMadeleines.com. ✆ **305/945-7770.**

The Children's Exchange ★★　Selling everything from layettes to overalls, this nice little shop is chock-full of good Florida-style stuff for kids to wear to the beach and in the heat, and brands include Ralph Lauren and True Religion. 1415 Sunset Dr. (at SW 54th Ave.), Coral Gables. www.TheChildrenExchange.com. ✆ **305/666-6235.**

Out of the Closet ★★　The chain of thrift stores from Northern and Southern California owned and operated by AIDS Healthcare Foundation has a fabulous Miami location on lower Biscayne Boulevard. 2900 Biscayne Blvd. (at NE 29th St.), Edgewater. www. OutoftheCloset.org. ✆ **305/764-3773.**

MIAMI ENTERTAINMENT & NIGHTLIFE

With all the hype it's gotten over the years, you'd expect Miami to have long outlived its 15 minutes of fame by now. But Miami's nightlife, in South Beach (and, slowly but surely, downtown and elsewhere) is hotter than ever before—and also cooler with the opening of each funky, fabulous watering hole, lounge, and club. Not always cool, however, is the presence of ubiquitous, closely guarded velvet ropes used to misleadingly create an air of exclusivity. Don't be fooled or too intimidated; anyone can go clubbing in the Magic City, and throughout this section I've provided tips to ensure that you gain entry to your desired venue.

South Beach is still Miami's premier nocturnal nucleus, but more and more other areas, such as the Design District, Midtown/Wynwood, Brickell, South Miami, and even Little Havana, are increasingly providing fun alternatives without the ludicrous cover charges, "fashionably late" hours (things don't typically get rolling on South Beach until after 11pm), shortage of affordable parking, and outrageous drink prices that are SoBe standard.

And while South Beach dances to a more electronic beat, other parts of Miami boogie more to Latin rhythms—from salsa and merengue to tango and cha-cha. And if you're looking for a less frenetic good time, Miami's bar scene has something for everyone, from haute hotel bars to sleek, lounge-y watering holes.

Parts of downtown, including the Biscayne Corridor, the Miami River, Midtown, Wynwood, and the Design District, are undergoing a trendy makeover a la New York City's Meatpacking District. Lounges, bars, and clubs are popping up and providing the "in" crowds with more urban-chic nocturnal stomping grounds. To get a feel for Wynwood's growing hipster vibe, check out the **Wynwood Art Walk** the second Saturday of every month, when local galleries, artists, bars, and restaurants are packed and these usually quiet blocks brim with pedestrians (info at www.Wynwood ArtWalk.com).

If the possibility of a celebrity sighting in one of the city's lounges, bars, or clubs doesn't fulfill your cultural needs, Miami also provides a variety of first-rate diversions in theater, music, and dance, including a world-class ballet (under the aegis of Edward Villella), a recognized symphony, and a talented opera company. The **Adrienne Arsht Center for the Performing Arts** (p. 127) and the **New World Center** (p. 126), a stunning, sonically stellar, $154-million Frank Gehry–designed training facility, performance space, and outdoor park, are the focal points for the arts. Some 15% of the music events at the New World Center are free to the public.

For up-to-date listing information, and to make sure the club of the moment hasn't expired, check the *Miami Herald*'s "Weekend" section, which runs on Friday; the more comprehensive listings in *New Times,* Miami's free alternative weekly, available each Wednesday; or visit www.Miami.com.

THE PERFORMING ARTS

9

Highbrows and culture vultures complain that there is a dearth of decent cultural offerings in Miami. What do locals tell them? Go back to New York. However, in recent years, Miami's performing arts scene has improved greatly. The city's Broadway Series features Tony Award–winning shows (the touring versions, of course), which aren't always Broadway caliber, but are usually pretty good and not nearly as pricey. Local arts groups such as the Miami Light Project, a not-for-profit cultural organization that presents performances by innovative dance, music, and theater artists, have had huge success in attracting big-name artists such as Nina Simone and Philip Glass to Miami. Also, a burgeoning bohemian movement in Little Havana has given way to performance spaces that are nightclubs in their own right.

Theater

The **Actors' Playhouse** ★★ is based at the restored Miracle Theatre at 280 Miracle Mile, Coral Gables (www.ActorsPlayhouse.org; ✆ **305/444-9293**), a 1948 Art Deco movie palace with a 600-seat main theater, a smaller hall that hosts a number of excellent musicals for kids throughout the year, and a 300-seat children's balcony theater. Tickets run from $15 to $50.

The **GableStage** ★★ at the Biltmore Hotel (p. 56), Anastasia Avenue, Coral Gables (www.GableStage.org; ✆ **305/445-1119**) is well regarded and award winning, usually secures the rights to Broadway and off-Broadway plays, and is known for its occasionally edgy productions. Tickets cost $40 to $55.

The **Jerry Herman Ring Theatre** ★★ is on the University of Miami campus in Coral Gables (www.AS.Miami.edu/RingTheatre; ✆ **305/284-3355**). The theater department uses this stage for student productions of comedies, dramas, and musicals. Faculty and guest actors are regularly featured, as are local playwrights. Performances are usually scheduled Tuesday through Saturday during the academic year. In summer, don't miss "Summer Shorts," superb one-act plays. Tickets sell for $8 to $25.

The **New Theatre** ★★ in Cutler Bay at the South Miami-Dade Cultural Arts Center, 10950 SW 211 St. (www.New-Theatre.org; ✆ **305/443-5909,** tickets 786/573-5300), prides itself on showing renowned works from America and Europe. As the name implies, the focus is contemporary, with occasional classics thrown in.

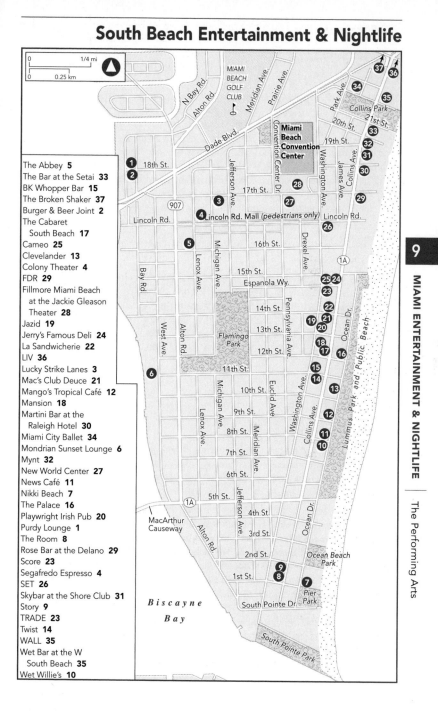

South Beach Entertainment & Nightlife

Performances are staged Fridays through Sundays November through June. Tickets are $26 in advance, $32 the day of the show; student half-price discounts available with adult ticket purchase.

Classical Music

New World Symphony ★★★   Led by artistic director and co-founder Michael Tilson Thomas, this stepping stone for gifted young musicians seeking professional careers specializes in innovative, energetic performances and often features renowned guest soloists and conductors. The season lasts from September to May and includes quite a few free concerts. Since 2010, NWS has occupied a spectacular Frank Gehry–designed campus at the **New World Center** (see below), one of whose features is "wallcasts," projections of live concerts on a 7,000-foot exterior wall, which can be enjoyed by the public for free in a park-like plaza outside. Tours are offered twice a week for $5 (reservations required). 500 17th St. (at Washington Ave.), South Beach. www. NWS.edu. ⓒ **800/597-3331** or 305/673-3330. Tickets free–$150. Fifty percent student discount on select performances.

Opera

Florida Grand Opera ★★   A fixture since 1941, this company regularly features singers from top houses in America and Europe (including world-famous names). Performing at the **Arsht Center for the Performing Arts,** it stages productions in their original language with projected English supertitles. The season runs November to May, with varying numbers of performances each week. Box office: 1300 Biscayne Blvd., Miami. www.FGO.org. ⓒ **305/854-1643,** tickets 800/741-1010. Tickets $19–$175. Student discounts available.

Dance

Several local dance companies train and perform in the Greater Miami area. In addition, top traveling troupes regularly stop at the venues listed below. Keep your eyes open for special events and guest artists.

Ballet Flamenco La Rosa ★★   For a taste of local Latin *sabor,* see this lively troupe perform impressive flamenco and other styles of Latin dance on Miami stages. (They also teach Latin dancing here—see the "You're Gonna Get the Rhythm" box, p. 137.) 13124 W. Dixie Hwy., North Miami. www.BalletFlamencoLaRosa.com. ⓒ **305/899-7729.** Tickets $25 at door; $20 in advance; $10 for students/seniors.

Miami City Ballet ★★   This innovative, artistically acclaimed company, directed by Lourdes Lopez, features a repertoire of nearly 100 ballets, many by George Balanchine, and has had more than 20 world premieres. Its three-story center features eight rehearsal rooms, a ballet school, and a boutique. The season runs from October to April, with performances at the Arsht Center. 2200 Liberty Ave., South Beach. www.Miami CityBallet.org. ⓒ **877/929-7010** or 305/929-7010 for box office. Tickets $20–$169.

Major Venues

Architecturally and aurally groundbreaking, the **New World Center,** 500 17th St., South Beach (ⓒ **305/673-3330**), the Frank Gehry–designed campus of the New World Symphony (above), features practice rooms, rehearsal rooms, technology suites, and a grand performance space. Even if you're not into the music, this is something to see.

Don't miss the $2.50 mini-concerts or the free outdoor "wallcast" concerts, featuring incredible audio effects and visuals projected onto a 7,000-square-foot wall. During these events, most people spread out on the lawn with a blanket and a picnic basket.

A more vintage South Beach showpiece, the 1935 **Colony Theater,** 1040 Lincoln Rd. (www.ColonyTheatreMiamiBeach.com; ✆ **305/434-7091**), reopened in 2006 after a $4.3-million renovation that added wing and fly space, improved access for those with disabilities, and restored the lobby to its original Art Deco look.

At the 1,700-seat **Gusman Center for the Performing Arts,** 174 E. Flagler St., downtown Miami (www.GusmanCenter.org; ✆ **305/374-2444** or 305/434-7091 for tickets), seats are a little tight but the sound is superb. Besides the Miami Film Festival, the elegant former Olympia Theater features pop concerts, plays, film screenings, and special events. Built in 1926, its interior is crammed with ornate Mediterranean-Deco columns, chandeliers, balconies, turrets, twinkling "stars" on the ceiling, and other flights of decorative fancy.

The **Fillmore Miami Beach at the Jackie Gleason Theater,** located in South Beach at Washington Avenue and 17th Street (www.FillmoreMB.com; ✆ **305/673-7300**), may be a mouthful, but when it comes to live music, it truly rocks. The venue's decor is Miami Beach–meets–Hard Rock, complete with requisite bars, chandeliers, and an homage to the original legendary Fillmore in San Francisco. Managed by House of Blues/Live Nation, it brings major talent to the beach, from Lenny Kravitz, Caetano Veloso, and Snow Patrol to comedians Lewis Black, Bill Maher, and Lisa Lampanelli. Fillmore also hosts various awards shows, from the Food Network Awards to the Fox Sports Awards.

Downtown's $446-million **Adrienne Arsht Center for the Performing Arts,** 1300 Biscayne Blvd. (www.ArshtCenter.org; ✆ **877/949-6722** or 305/949-6722), opened in 2006 and includes the 2,400-seat **Sanford and Dolores Ziff Ballet Opera House** and the 2,200-seat **Knight Concert Hall,** venues for the **Concert Association of Florida, Florida Grand Opera, Miami City Ballet,** and **New World Symphony,** as well as premier venues for a wide array of local, national, and international performances, ranging from Broadway musicals and visiting classical artists to world and urban music, Latin concerts, and popular entertainment from many cultures. The **Studio Theater,** a black-box space designed for up to 200 seats, hosts intimate performances of contemporary theater, dance, music, and cabaret. Finally, the **Plaza for the Arts** is a magnificent setting for outdoor entertainment, celebrations, and community gatherings.

Point of interest: Wrapped in limestone, slate, decorative stone, stainless steel, glass-curtain walls, and tropical landscaping, this enormous complex was designed by world-renowned architect Cesar Pelli and is the second-largest in the U.S. If you look closely, near street level you'll notice a small, elegant white tower—it's a 1929 Art Deco remnant from a Sears Roebuck store that couldn't be demolished because it was landmarked.

BARS & LOUNGES

There are countless bars and lounges in and around Miami (most require proof that you are 21 or older), with the biggest concentration of course on trendy South Beach. The selection below is just a sampling. Keep in mind that many of the popular bars—and the easiest to get into—are in hotels (with several notable exceptions; see below). For a clubbier scene, if you don't mind making your way through hordes of trashed club kids, a stroll on Washington Avenue will provide insight into what's hot and what's not. Just hold on to your bags. It's not dangerous, but occasionally a few shady types manage to slip into the crowd. Another very important tip when in a club: Never put your drink down out of your sight—there have been incidents in which drinks have been spiked with chemical substances. For a less hardcore, more collegiate nightlife, head to Coconut Grove, Coral Gables, and downtown's Mary Brickell Village. Oh, yes, and when going out in South Beach, do take a so-called disco nap, as things don't get going until at least 11pm. Otherwise expect to face an empty bar or club. Outside South Beach and in hotel bars, the hours are generally fashionably earlier, with the action starting as early as 7pm.

Keep in mind that the following were in business at press time, but places open or close all the time, so call ahead—and also check for new spots in the free weekly *New Times,* www.Miami.CitySearch.com, or the "Weekend" section of the *Miami Herald.*

The Abbey ★★   Dark and off the beaten path, this microbrewery is a favorite for locals looking to escape the $20-candy-flavored-martini scene. There's never a cover and it's always open until 5am, perfect for those pesky hops cravings that pop up at 3 or 4am. 1115 16th St., South Beach. www.AbbeyBrewingInc.com. 🕿 **305/538-8110.**

Bardot ★★   Modeled after the basement of a 1970s rock star, Bardot is one of mainland Miami's hotter scenes, with a hipster accent. Young and old, gay and straight, and everything in between is what you'll find at this off-the-beaten-path lounge-cum-speakeasy at the back of a Wynwood furniture store. Shag carpeting, comfy couches, and decor straight out of *That '70s Show* make for a comfy backdrop for cocktailing, taking in cool live music, and ogling what may be Miami's most colorful crowd. 3456 N. Miami Ave., Wynwood. www.BardotMiami.com. 🕿 **305/576-5570.**

Blackbird Ordinary ★★   It's slightly tricky to find this quirkily christened indoor/outdoor spot, but you'll be happy you did. Described by locals as "a real big-city lounge," this bird's a biggie, featuring a huge bar with a very creative cocktail list (including the best martini in town, say *Miami New Times* readers), tons of cozy couches and tables, board games, a funky crowd, and live music. Plus it's open until 5am every night. 729 SW 1st Ave., downtown Miami. www.BlackbirdOrdinary.com. 🕿 **305/671-3307.**

The Broken Shaker ★★   Slightly off the SoBeaten path, since late 2012 a mix of hipsters, locals, and young international guests of host hotel/hostel Freehand Miami (p. 55) have been creating a swell, mellow scene at this cozy cubbyhole up on 28th Street with gourmet tipples creative enough to make the joint a James Beard Award finalist. Open 'til 2am. 2727 Indian Creek River Dr., Miami Beach. www.TheFreehand.com. 🕿 **786/325-8974.**

Burger & Beer Joint ★★   Although downstairs at this bustling burger and beer joint is more about food, in back is a sports bar with flatscreen TVs to catch the game. Not in the mood for jockery? The upstairs lounge's chilled-out scene attracts everyone from barflies to models. 1766 Bay Rd., South Beach. www.BurgernBeerJoint.com. 🕿 **305/672-3287.** Also 900 S. Miami Ave. 🕿 **305/523-2244.**

Cafeina ★★   Open Thursday through Saturday, Wynwood's buzzy, kicky hotspot prides itself on its tapas and creative caffeine-infused cocktails. An outdoor garden lounge area is amazing in the cooler months, and the warehouse art gallery–cum–bar and indoor lounge serves as a sleek space to strike a pose. 297 NW 23rd St., Wynwood. www.CafeinaMiami.com. 🕿 **305/438-0792.**

Clevelander ★ If wet-T-shirt contests and a frat-party vibe are your thing, then this Ocean Drive mainstay is your kinda joint. Popular with tourists and locals playing tourist, the "front yard" of the Clevelander hotel (p. 51) attracts an amped-up crowd (by the way, bouncers *will* confiscate fake IDs) who don't care about being part of a "scene" but just wanna party. Check it out on a weekend afternoon, when beach bunnies line the bars for a beer or frozen cocktail. 1020 Ocean Dr., South Beach. www. Clevelander.com. ✆ **305/531-3485.**

DRB Miami ★★ Across from the Arsht Center, DRB—Democratic Republic of Beer—is where Miami meets Williamsburg, Brooklyn, with an epic list of brews from more than 60 countries (Bulgaria! Ethiopia! Sri Lanka!), a pretty decent bar menu, and a crowd of hops-loving hipsters sporting ironic facial hair and quoting Kafka. Fridays are "$20 bottomless craft drafts." 501 NE 1st Ave., downtown. www.DRBMiami.com. 501 NE 1st Ave., ✆ **305/372-4161.**

Electric Pickle Company ★★ This tiny bar with an upstairs lounge and a back parking lot that doubles as its outdoor area is the unofficial clubhouse of Miami's indie music scene—including a live stage—heavy on house and electronica. I totally recommend it; just keep in mind that the nabe can still be a tad iffy. Open Wednesday through Friday. 2826 N. Miami Ave., Wynwood. www.ElectricPickleMiami.com. ✆ **305/456-5613.**

FDR ★★ Named for the 32nd U.S. pres., like the Delano hotel under which it's tucked (p. 46), this amber-lit two-roomer features a retro-mod vibe, a chocolate-and-gold color scheme, and an eclectic clutch of clubbers from young hipsters and swank sophistos to the Betty White crowd (watch out!). It's run by the innovative Light Group (out of Vegas), with SoBe nightlife legend Chris Paciello consulting. 1685 Collins Ave. (in the Delano Hotel), South Beach. www.Delano-Hotel.com. ✆ **305/924-4071.**

Fifty Miami ★★ If you're spooked by heights, you may want to pass on this stunning lounge at the Viceroy 50 stories above Brickell Avenue. But if you're up for a sophisticated swilling spot that caters to Miami's elite, here's where you head. Inside it's reminiscent of a lounge in a classic first-class ocean liner, while outdoors is more L.A., with lap pool, bar, and panoramic views of the downtown skyline. Open Friday to Sunday. 485 Brickell Ave., downtown. www.ViceroyMiami.com. ✆ **305/503-4417.**

Finnegan's River ★★ Finnegan's has five locations (including two in SoBe), but this one, stashed under I-95 in an out-of-the-way corner of downtown, is special: an enormous indoor-outdoor space on the Miami River with a pool, several bars, and a reggae vibe. It's open weekdays from noon 'til the wee hours, on weekends from 11am. Pool parties, live shows, sports watch parties, or just hanging out with a killer skyline view—it's all good. 401 SW 3rd Ave., downtown. www.FinnegansBars.com. ✆ **305/285-3030.**

Mac's Club Deuce ★ A holdout in a sea of trendiness, it's a quintessential dive bar with cheap drinks, zero attitude, and a cast of characters ranging from your typical barfly to your atypical drag queen. It's also got a well-stocked jukebox, friendly bartenders, and a pool table. Plus it's an insomniac's dream, open daily from 8am to 5am. 222 14th St., South Beach. ✆ **305/531-6200.**

Mondrian Sunset Lounge ★★   If you could only hit one South Beach bar, maybe it should be this, thanks to jaw-dropping views of Biscayne Bay and an equally impressive surrealist decor (even more so after a few)—think Alice in Wonderland on spring break. Drinks are delish if pricey (caipirinhas are a specialty). Set aside some green if you can for either bottle service, mezze, or for the automated vending machines hawking little luxuries such as Urban Ears headphones and Miansai jewelry for both women and men. 1100 West Ave., at the Mondrian Hotel, South Beach. www.Mondrian-Miami.com. ✆ **305/514-1941.**

Mynt ★   With a $30 cover charge, Mynt is a 6,000-square-foot living room in which models, D-list celebs, locals, and assorted hangers-on bask in the green glow to the beat of very loud lounge and dance music. But if you want to actually dance—or move, for that matter—this isn't the spot; here it's all about striking a pose. Unless you know the doorman, be prepared to be forced to wait outside for an hour or more—and if so, my advice is: skip it. 1921 Collins Ave., South Beach. www.MyntLounge.com. ✆ **305/532-0727.**

> ### Stargazing
>
> The most popular places for celeb sightings include Mansion, LIV, SET, WALL, Mondrian, FDR, Skybar at the Shore Club, and, when it comes to stars gazing at other stars, Miami Heat basketball games. Edgier, under-the-radar celebs can be spotted at Mac's Club Deuce toward 5 in the morning.

Playwright Irish Pub ★★   Bono came here once when U2 was in town, not because it's so authentic, but because the TV sets over the bar were showing some European soccer (sorry, "football") match and it serves pints of Guinness. A great pre- or post-club spot, it's also one of the few SoBe bars that features live music from time to time. 1265 Washington Ave., South Beach. www.PlaywrightIrishPub.com. ✆ **305/534-0667.**

Purdy Lounge ★★   Over in the mostly locals neighborhood Sunset Harbor, no-nonsense Purdy is not unlike your best friend's basement, featuring a pool table and a slew of board games such as Operation to keep the attention-deficit-disordered from tuning out. The cocktails are relatively cheap, there's no cover, no DJ, and no attitude. On weekends, though, there can be a line, so be prepared. Saturday night has become the preferred night for locals, and weekday happy hour draws a young professional crowd on the prowl. 1811 Purdy Ave., South Beach. www.PurdyLounge.com. ✆ **305/531-4622.**

The Room ★★   It's beer and wine only at this South of Fifth hideaway, where locals come to get away from the insanity just a few blocks up. The beer selection is comprehensive, with brews from across the planet. The wine maybe not so much, but there's no whining here at this tiny, industrial-style, candlelit spot. 100 Collins Ave., South Beach. www.TheOtheRoom.com. ✆ **305/531-6061.**

Rose Bar at the Delano ★★   If every rose has its thorns, the ones at this painfully chic lobby bar are the painfully high cocktail prices ($17). The crowd's dominated by poseurs and self-styled glitterati who view life through rose-colored glasses (Italian-made, of course). 1685 Collins Ave., South Beach. www.Delano-Hotel.com. ✆ **305/674-5752.**

Segafredo Espresso ★★★   Although actually a cafe, Segafredo's become an integral part of SoBe nightlife especially as command central for Euros who miss their cafe society. Euro lounge music, tons of outdoor tables on a prime corner of Lincoln Road, and an always-hopping scene make 'Fredo one of my favorite nocturnal haunts

SWANKEST hotel bars

Long gone are the days of the old-school Holiday Inn lounges. In fact, some hotels seem to spend more money on their bars than they do on their bedding. That aside, hotel bar-hopping is pretty popular in Miami. The fabulous **W South Beach** has several watering holes, from the Living Room lobby bar and poolside Wet Bar to the bar in the star-studded Mr Chow restaurant. Here's our list of the rest of the best:

Rose Bar at the Delano (above): For seeing and being seen.

Skybar at the Shore Club (below): Also for seeing and being seen.

Mondrian (above): Picture Alice in Wonderland going through the wrong mouse hole and ending up in South Beach. Trippy.

Martini Bar at the Raleigh Hotel (© **305/534-6300**): A true throwback to

the days of Deco set to the tunes of Edith Piaf, Tony Bennett, Sinatra, and more. On Tuesdays there are guest mixologists and "curated" martini showcases.

Fifty Miami at the Viceroy (p. 129): There are lofty spots in Miami and then there's this, located high above the city on the 50th floor with some of the best views—and people-watching—in Miami.

The Bar at the Setai (2001 Collins Ave., South Beach; www.thesetaihotel.com; © **305/520-6400**): This simply named spot, along with this blindingly pricey hotel's pool and beach bar, pours correspondingly pricey drinks in stunning settings. Here, though, the cocktails look like drinks but might taste like eats (try the one with the bacon-infused bourbon and see what I mean).

(and not too shabby daytimes, either). Although South Beach has *l'originale*, there's another location in downtown's Brickell area at 1421 S. Miami Ave. 1040 Lincoln Rd., South Beach. www.SZE-Originale.com. © **305/673-0047.**

Skybar at the Shore Club ★★   This is basically the entire backyard of the Shore Club hotel, consisting of areas including a Moroccan-themed garden, the hip-hop–themed indoor Redroom, the Sandbar by the beach, and the Rumbar by the pool, it was once popular on any given night—yet another brilliant example of how hotelier Ian Schrager managed to manipulate the hipsters in a Pavlovian way. They dropped the snootiness when the A-list dropped them; now the vibe is sensuous but more casual. Drinks are pricey, though. 1901 Collins Ave., South Beach. www.ShoreClub.com. © **305/695-3100.**

The Stage ★★   Just like the name says, a premiere venue for local and national talent (including regular open-mic nights). On days when that stage is dark, it's a great spot for lounging to the tune of DJs spinning everything from lounge and down-tempo to rock. 170 NE 38th St., Design District. www.TheStageMiami.com. © **305/576-9577.**

Wet Bar at the W South Beach ★★   The poolside Wet Bar, along with the W's secret-garden Grove and lobby-level Living Room, are among the city's most stylish, creative, and buzz-worthy nightspots, thanks to a combo of master mixologists who shake and stir up some of the most creative—and pricey—cocktails you'll ever quaff; the celebs and locals who swill them; and resplendent settings with Instagram-worthy photo-op backdrops. 2201 Collins Ave., South Beach. www.WSouthBeach.com/Wet-Bar-Grille. © **305/938-3000.**

Wet Willie's ★★   With such telling tipples as "Call a Cab," this beachfront hangout is clearly not the spot if you have any kind of drive ahead of you. Popular with the Harley-Davidson set, tourists, and beach bunnies, Willie's is known for its rooftop patio (get there early if you want to nab a seat) and its half-nekkid bikini beauties. 760 Ocean Dr., South Beach. www.WetWillies.com/Locations/South_Beach.html. 📞 **305/532-5650.**

THE CLUB & MUSIC SCENE
Dance Clubs

Clubs are as much a cottage industry in Miami as is, say, cheese in Wisconsin. Clubland, as it's dubbed, is a way of life for some. There's something going on any given night in Miami—no excuses needed to throw a party here. The Miami party set celebrates everything from the debut of a new DJ or a promoter's birthday to the fact that it's Tuesday. Within this often bizarre after-dark demimonde, a colorful cast of characters emerges, from seemingly typical 9-to-5ers to shady types who have reinvented themselves as hotshots on the club circuit. Although this see-and-be-seen scene may not be your cup of Cîroc, it's certainly never boring.

The music played on Miami's ever-evolving club circuit is good enough to get even the most rhythmically challenged wallflowers busting moves. For aspiring DJs, the local branch of the renowned **Scratch DJ Academy,** 450 NW 28th St., Wynwood (www.Scratch.com; 📞 **305/576-3868**), can turn you into a turntable ninja for $110 per 1-hour session or $450 for a 5-hour package.

---

late-nite BITES

Although some dining spots in Miami stop serving at 10pm, various others are open very late or even 24/7—especially on weekends. So if it's 4am and you need a post-clubbing nosh, no worries. In South Beach there are plenty of pizza and pita places along Washington Avenue open 'til dawn. Especially good are **La Sandwicherie,** 229 14th St. (📞 **305/532-8934**), which serves up great late-night baguette until 5am. Nearby is the **BK Whopper Bar,** 1101 Washington Ave. (📞 **305/673-4560**), Burger King's spin on a hip burger joint, open 24/7, serving beer and as gourmet a burger as BK can muster. Another night-owl perch is the popular, affordable **News Café,** 800 Ocean Dr. (📞 **305/538-6397**), with outdoor seating and an enormous menu offering great all-day breakfasts, Middle Eastern platters, fruit bowls, or steak and potatoes—also round the clock. Craving a corned beef on rye at 5am? **Jerry's Famous Deli,** 1450 Collins Ave. (📞 **305/532-8030**), never closes, either.

If your night out is at one of the Latin clubs over in mainland Miami, stop in at **Versailles,** 3555 SW 8th St. (📞 **305/444-0240;** see p. 77), in Little Havana. What else but a Cuban *medianoche* ("midnight" sandwich) will do? Its hours extend well past midnight—usually until 2:30 or 3:30am on weekends—to cater to posses of partiers young and old. And over near Midtown, **Gigi,** 3470 N. Miami Ave. (📞 **305/573-1520**), is a noodle bar open until 3am Tuesday through Thursday and 5am Friday and Saturday. For detailed restaurant listings, see chapter 6.

GROUND RULES: stepping out IN MIAMI

- Nightlife on South Beach doesn't really get going until after 11pm. So you may want to consider taking a "disco nap" so that you'll be fully charged until the wee hours.

- Unsure of what to wear out on South Beach? Your safest bet is anything black.

- Do *not* try to tip the gents manning the velvet ropes. That will only make you look desperate, and you'll find yourself standing outside for what will seem like an ungodly amount of time. Instead, try to land your name on the ever-present guest list by calling the club early in the day—or better yet, have your hotel concierge do it for you. If you don't have connections or a concierge, then act assertive (not surly!) at the velvet rope, and your patience will usually be rewarded with admittance. If all else fails—for guys, especially—surround yourself with a few leggy model types and you'll be noticed quicker.

- If you're a guy going out with a posse of dudes, unless you're going to a gay bar, you'll most likely not get into any South Beach hotspot without women in your group.

- Finally, have fun. It may look like serious business when you're on the outside, but once you're in, it's another story. Attacking Clubland with a sense of humor is the best approach to a successful, memorable evening out.

To keep things fresh in Clubland, promoters throw one-nighters, essentially parties with various themes or motifs from funk to fashion. Because these change daily, I can't even begin to list them here. Word of mouth, local advertising, and listings in the free weekly *New Times,* www.Miami.CitySearch.com, or the "Weekend" section of the *Miami Herald* are the best ways to find out about these ever-changing events.

Before you get all dolled up to hit the town as soon as the sun sets, remember that Miami is a late town; clubs generally don't rev up before 11pm. Of course, if you're drive in from outside South Beach too late, you may find yourself circling endlessly for parking, because especially on weekends it can be very limited outside of $20+ valet charges. So consider getting over here by early evening and killing time by strolling around and/or grabbing a bite or cocktail somewhere. Also, some clubs don't charge cover before 11pm or midnight, so showing up early can save you big-time.

Most clubs are open every night of the week, though some are open only Thursday to Sunday and others just Monday through Saturday. Call ahead to get the most up-to-date info possible: Things change very quickly around here, and a call in advance can help you make sure that the club you're planning to hit hasn't become a video arcade. Cover charges are haphazard, too. If you're not on the ubiquitous guest list (ask your

Impressions

Working the door teaches you a lot about human nature.
—A former South Beach doorman

WINTER music CONFERENCE

Every March, Miami is besieged by the most unconventional conventioneers the city ever sees. These fiercely dedicated souls descend upon the city in a very audible way, with dark circles under their eyes and bleeps, blips, and scratches that can wake the dead. No, I'm not talking about a *Star Trek* convention, but rather the **Winter Music Conference** (WMC), the world's biggest and most major gathering of DJs, remixers, agents, artists, and pretty much anyone who makes a dime off the booming electronic music industry, from more than 60 countries. But unlike most conventions, this one is completely interactive and open to the paying public, as South Beach and Miami's hottest clubs become showcases for the sundry sonic wares. For a week or more, DJs, artists, and software producers play for audiences of A&R reps, talent scouts, and locals just along for the ride. Parties take place everywhere from hotel pools to street corners. There's always something going on, and most people who really get into the throes of WMC get little or no sleep. Energy drinks become more vital than water, and, for the most part, if you see people popping pills, they're probably not vitamins.

At any rate, the festival's worth checking out if you're sent into (ahem) ecstasy by names like David Guetta, Swedish House Mafia, Peter Rauhofer, Roger Sanchez, Frankie Knuckles, Hex Hector, Paul Oakenfold, Deep Dish, and Armand Van Helden, among many others. For details, go to **www.WMCon.com**.

concierge to get you on the list—he or she can usually do it, which won't help you with the wait to get in, but can knock off the cover charge), you may have to fork over a $20 bill or much more to get past the ropes. On the other hand, there are quite a few clubs and bars that have no cover—they just make up for it by charging $12, $15, or $20 for a cocktail. Many bars/clubs also announce deals and special admissions via social media.

Cameo ★★ In 2007 the renovated white 1936 theater most recently known as crobar first made its Cameo appearance under the management of the Opium nightlife group, and with a supersonic sound system, star DJs, and plenty of VIP seating, it's once again a must on clubber itineraries. It's open Tuesday, Friday, and Saturday from 11pm to 5am. 1445 Washington Ave., South Beach. www.CameoMiami.com. ✆ **305/522-5353.** Cover $20–$50.

Club Space ★★ In this cavernous downtown warehouse of a club (more than 30,000 sq. ft.), you can spin around to a techno beat without worrying about smacking into somebody. It's a Saturday-night spot that's actually more like a Sunday-morning spot, where things don't really get cooking until around 3am and then blast through until 2pm. Known as a venue of choice for world-renowned DJs. 34 NE 11th St., downtown. www.ClubSpace.com. ✆ **305/375-0001.** Sat 11pm–Sun. 2pm. Cover $20–$50; free promotions available.

LIV ★★ Still a big effin' deal in Miami's celeb-saturated nightlife, LIV (as in, "celebrities live for LIV") is the flashy, cavernous dance palace of the Fontainebleau Hotel (p. 48). Go early even if it means lining up in the lobby, and expect to see boldface names ensconced in visible VIP areas. Cover depends on events, with the dudes sometimes paying way more than the ladies. 4441 Collins Ave., Miami Beach. www. LIVNightclub.com. ✆ **305/674-4680.** Wed–Sun 11pm–5am. Cover $40–$90.

Mansion ★★ This massive, multilevel club is, say owners and promoters, entirely "VIP." (Or hey, just buy a ticket online.) And DJs, models, and celebs (Rihanna, Beyoncé, Jay-Z, etc.), plus soaring ceilings, wood floors, brick walls, and a stellar light-and-sound system, do keep Mansion in favor with see-and-be-scenesters. It's so exciting, the personal chef to Miami Heat players was shot dead in the VIP section in 2014. Good times. Anyway, it's open Monday, Wednesday, Friday, and Saturday 11pm to 5am. 1235 Washington Ave., South Beach. www.MansionMiami.com. ✆ **305/735-3344.** Cover $30–$125.

Nikki Beach ★★ Undeniably atmospheric, in an Ibiza sort of way, but these days mostly for tourists who've come to gawk at half-naked ladies and gents venturing into the daylight to see and be scene (Sunday brunch is a big draw). There's an upstairs lounge with restaurant and dance floor, a downstairs lounge, and an outdoor section of beach. Sundays are the big late club night. 101 Ocean Dr., South Beach. www.NikkiBeach Miami.com. ✆ **305/538-1111.** Cover $20 (no cover for diners). Mon–Thurs noon–6pm; Fri–Sat noon–11pm, Sun noon–5am.

SET ★★ One of Opium Group's smaller clubs, SET still has a significant following amongst jet set and Euro types. A luxurious lounge with chandeliers, a dance floor, and design mag–worthy decor is always full of trendsetters, celebs (Justin Bieber was partying here with his father the night he was busted for drag racing), and wannabes. Where you really want to be, though, is upstairs in the VIP areas. The door is notoriously tough; ask your hotel concierge to get you in. 320 Lincoln Rd., South Beach. www. SETMiami.com. ✆ **786/735-1900.** Cover $20–$30; free before midnight some nights. Tues, Thurs–Sun 11pm–5am.

Story ★★ The latest megaclub to hit SoBe, by 2014 Story had rocketed into America's top ten. It was where the Heat chose to celebrate their 2013 championship, and Story attracts names like Fatboy Slim, Pete Tong, David Guetta, and Nicki Minaj. In the former Amnesia space in SoFi (south of Fifth St.), it was voted Miami's best dance spot by *New Times* readers—and I have to say, the frenzied boom-boom between those big twisty columns and epilepsy-inducing light shows is indeed about as pure a distillation of techno-disco inferno as I've ever witnessed. 136 Collins Ave., South Beach. www.StoryMiami.com. ✆ **305/538-2424.** Cover $30 women, $40 men. Thurs–Sun 11pm–5am.

TRADE ★★ SoBe's newest club came on the scene in 2014 aiming to be an antidote to commercial clubland. An edgy-feeling, camo-netting-hung second-floor dance space and lounge holding 700, its thing is underground EDM, with a roster of live artists and DJs, vintage movies and trippy videos projected onto walls, open bar 11pm to midnight, and juice bar for non-alkies. There's no front-door attitude; events are announced on its Facebook page; and the Thursday-night entrance is through the artistically-graffittoed alley out back. All very East Village-y, I must say. 1439 Washington Ave., South Beach. www.TRADEMIA.com. ✆ **305/531-6666.** Cover $20; discounted tickets via www.ResidentAdvisor.net. Thurs–Sun 11pm–5am.

WALL ★★ The W South Beach's requisite velvet roped–off hip nightspot, WALL has a VIP scene complete with sofas reserved for only those dropping megabucks on booze. With its mirrored walls and flashy ambience, a night here feels a little like spinning around inside a disco ball (or so I imagine). 2201 Collins Ave., South Beach. www.WALLMiami.com. ℭ **305/938-3130.** Cover $40 women, $50 men. Tues, Thurs–Sat 11pm–5am.

Live Music

Sad to say, Miami's live music scene isn't exactly thriving. Instead of local bands garnering devoted fans, it's DJs who are more admired, skyrocketing much more easily to fame—thanks to the city's hot dance-club scene. But there are still several places that strive to bring Miami up to speed as far as live music is concerned. You just have to look—and listen—for it a bit more carefully. Here are several spots where you can catch live acts (also check several of the bar listings on p. 127).

The Cabaret South Beach ★★ Paging Liza Minnelli . . . Here's a welcome recent addition to scarce SoBe live music spots, all the more so because it's an intimate, old-fashioned piano-bar style experience in the middle of sometimes overwhelming Clubland. And besides crooners and musicians, they throw in a little old-school burlesque, even circus acts. 233 12th St., South Beach. www.TheCabaretSouthBeach.com. ℭ **305/763-8799.** Daily 7pm–2am. No cover.

Churchill's Pub ★★ Expat Brit Dave Daniels couldn't survive in Miami without a true English-style pub, so in 1979 he opened this, the city's premier space for live rock and other music. Grimy and located in a gritty neighborhood off Biscayne Boulevard, Churchill's is committed to promoting the lagging local music scene, even after Daniels finally sold it in 2014. A fun, fairly no-frills crowd hangs out here, and once the music starts it can get deafening. Monday is open-mic night. 5501 NE 2nd Ave., Little Haiti. www.ChurchillsPub.com. ℭ **305/757-1807.** Daily 11am–3am. Cover free–$15.

Grand Central ★★ The most recent addition to Miami's growing yet still somewhat underground indie music scene, Grand Central is, well, the Grand Central of live indie acts, which parade through here from around the world to perform for adoring hipster fans. 697 N. Miami Ave., downtown. www.GrandCentralMiami.com. ℭ **305/377-2277.** Cover $15–$100.

Jazid ★★ Smoky, sultry, and lit by flickering candelabras, Jazid's a place where you'd expect to hear Sade's "Smooth Operator" on constant rotation. Instead you'll find live jazz (sometimes acid jazz), soul, reggae, and funk, usually starting around 11pm. An eclectic mix of mellow peeps convenes here for a much-needed respite from the Washington Avenue hubbub. And Tuesday's karaoke night! 1342 Washington Ave., South Beach. www.Jazid.net. Ages 21 and over only. Daily 9pm–5am. ℭ **305/673-9372.** Cover $10 Fri and Sat.

Tobacco Road ★★ Al Capone used to hang out here when it was a speakeasy (it celebrated 100 years in 2012). Now locals flock a couple of blocks west of Brickell Avenue (right near Mary Brickell Village) to catch local and national acts such as George Clinton and the P-Funk All-Stars, Koko Taylor, and the Radiators. Tobacco Road (proud holder of Miami's very first liquor license) is small and gritty, and meant to be that way. Escape the smoke and sweat in the backyard patio. The downright cheap nightly specials, such as the $10 prime rib on Monday and $13 lobster on Tuesday, are quite good and served until midnight; the bar's open until 5am. *Note:* Plans were afoot to move around the corner to 69 SW 7 St. in 2015. 626 S. Miami Ave., downtown. www.Tobacco-Road.com. ℭ **305/374-1198.** Cover Fri–Sat $5–$10; free before 9:30pm. Mon–Sun 11:30am–5am.

YOU'RE GONNA GET THE rhythm

Feeling shy about hitting a Latin club because you think your gringo moves will trip you up? Take a few lessons from one of the following dance companies or teachers. They offer individual and group lessons to dancers of any origin who are willing to learn. These folks have made it their mission to teach merengue and flamenco to non-Latinos and Latino left foots, and are among the most reliable, consistent, and popular ones in Miami.

Thursday and Friday nights at **Bongo's Cuban Café,** American Airlines Arena, 601 Biscayne Blvd., downtown (www.BongosCubanCafe.com; ℭ **786/777-2100**), are amazing showcases for some of the area's best salsa dancers, but amateurs need not be intimidated, thanks to instructors who are on hand to help you with your two left feet. Lessons are free.

At **Ballet Flamenco La Rosa** in the Performing Arts Network (PAN) building, 13146 W. Dixie Hwy., North Miami (www.PANMiami.org; ℭ **305/899-7730**), you can learn to salsa or merengue as well as dance flamenco. This is the only professional flamenco company in the area. It charges $15 per class ($48 for four lessons).

Nobody teaches salsa like **Luz Pinto** (www.Latin-Heat.com; ℭ **786/281-9747**). She teaches 7 days a week and, trust me, you'll learn cool turns with ease. Luz charges $60 per private lesson and she's the only instructor who doesn't charge extra if you want to share the lesson with a partner. She teaches everything from classic and hip wedding dances to ballroom, disco, and merengue, as well as L.A.–style and Casino-style salsa (popularized in 1950s Cuba). You'll be impressed with how well and quickly Luz can teach you to have fun and feel great dancing.

Latin Clubs

Given that Hispanics make up a majority of Miami's population and that there's a huge influx of Spanish-speaking visitors, it's no shocker that there's some awesome *ambiente nocturno* hereabouts. Plus with the rise of the Miami-based international music scene, lots of talent traipses through the offices of MTV Latino, Sony International, and various locally-based Latin TV studios—and they're all looking for a good club scene. Many of the Anglo clubs also set aside at least one night a week for Latin rhythms.

Bongos Cuban Café ★★ Paying homage to the sights, sounds, and tastes of pre-Castro Cuba, Gloria Estefan's hit in the restaurant business is a mammoth space attached to the American Airlines Arena in downtown Miami. On Friday after 11pm and Saturday after 11:30pm, Bongo's transforms from a friendly-family eatery into the city's hottest 21-and-over salsa nightclub. Cover charges can be hefty, but consider it your ticket to an astounding display of some of the best salsa dancers in the city. Prepare yourself for standing room only. Salsa lessons are available for those with two left feet. *Note:* At press time, a move was in the works but the new location unannounced; check the website. 601 Biscayne Blvd., downtown. www.BongosCubanCafe.com. ℭ **786/777-2100.** Fri–Sat 11:15pm–5am. Fri women free, men $10; Sat women free until midnight ($20 afterward), men $20 all night.

Hoy Como Ayer ★★ This compact Little Havana hangout showcases plenty of *Buena Vista Social Club*–style nostalgia (its name means "Today Like Yesterday"), but it's also developed a younger hipster following with more contemporary regular acts like Los 3 de la Habana (a luminous vocal trio I first heard years ago at Havana's Café Cantante). It's open Wednesday to Sunday from 9pm to 3am. 2212 SW 8th St., Little Havana. www.HoyComoAyer.us. ℂ **305/541-2631.** Cover $15–$40.

La Covacha ★★ What some consider the hottest Latin joint in South Florida is located waaay out west in an area called Sweetwater. La Covacha books the best in Spanish-language pop and rock, with local and international acts that have included Calle 13, Orishas, and La Oreja de Van Gogh, and it has popular open-bar specials. The club is open Thursday through Sunday from 9pm to 4am, and there's also a restaurant open daily 7am to 7pm. 10730 NW 25th St., Sweetwater. www.LaCovacha.com. ℂ **305/594-3717.** Cover up to $35.

Mango's Tropical Café ★★ Claustrophobes will probably not want to peel this mango—one of Ocean Drive's most popular spots, this enclave of *la vida loca* shakes with the intensity of a Richter-busting earthquake. Mango's is *Cabaret,* Latin-style. Nightly live Brazilian samba and other Latin sounds, not to mention scantily clad male and female dancers, draw gawking crowds in from the sidewalk. But pay attention to the music, if you can: Incognito international musicians often lose their anonymity and jam with the house band on stage. There's a full menu, too. 900 Ocean Dr., South Beach. www.MangosTropicalCafe.com. ℂ **305/673-4422.** Daily 11:45am–5am. Cover varies; usually $10–$15.

THE GAY & LESBIAN SCENE

Miami and the beaches have long been home to what's known as a "first-tier" LGBT community, similar to the Big Apple, the Bay Area, or L.A., at least since the days when Anita Bryant used her rancid citrus power to counter the rise in political activism in the early '70s. Well, things have sure changed since then; Miami-Dade now has a gay-rights ordinance, and by the time you read this, Florida may even have joined the growing ranks of U.S. states compelled to recognize same-sex marriage.

Newcomers intending to party in any nightspot, whether downtown or certainly on the beach, will want to check ahead for the schedule, as many mainstream clubs also have a boys' or girls' night to pay the rent. Get updates on many of those nights, plus other LGBT events/venues, at www.SoBeSocialClub.com, www.SoBeGayInfo.com, and www.JumpOnMarksList.com. By the way, to make your vacation even queerer, give a thought to the **Hôtel Gaythering** ★★, on the bay side of South Beach at 1409 Lincoln Rd. (www.HotelGaythering.com; ℂ **786/284-1176**). And dudes into bath houses might be interested in **Club Aqua,** a few blocks east of Coral Gables at 2991 Coral Way (www.ClubAquaMiami.com; ℂ **305/448-2214**).

Miami is also a capital of the "circuit party" scene, rivaling San Francisco, New York City, Palm Springs, and Sydney for tourist booty (in all senses), and hosting high-profile blowouts like Winter Party and White Party Week (p. 20). The local Pride celebration (www.MiamiBeachGayPride.com; ℂ **863/272-9859**) is held in April.

Now, especially since South Beach got bit by the hip-hop bug, it's also true that more of Miami's gays have been heading up to Fort Lauderdale, where there are many more and varied LGBT establishments than down here. But there's still plenty of *vida loca* in Greater Miami, and here are several of the top venues:

Azúcar ★★ Just east of downtown Coral Gables, South Florida's down-home gay Latin club truly feels like it could be in Honduras or Nicaragua, filled with the full gamut of local LGBT Latinos and Latinas, sprinkled with their admirers. The music's hot and the shows are a hoot, heavy on drag queens like Teresita la Caliente (Horny Little Terry) and Mariloly "The Queen of Comedy." Admittedly for the shtick you'll be lost if you don't *habla español,* but they're still fun to watch. Azúcar (Spanish for "sugar") is open Thursday through Sunday 10:30pm to 5am. 2301 SW 32nd Ave., Miami. www.AzucarMiami.com. ✆ **305/443-7657.** Cover free–$10.

Club Boi ★★ Off Biscayne Boulevard north of downtown, this black-owned club is South Florida's top spot for the brothas (and on Friday nights, the sistahs), with two dance floors, open 10pm to 3am. Saturday and Sunday are gay, Fridays lesbian, and Thursdays straight. 1060 NE 79th St., Miami. www.ClubBoi.com. ✆ **786/395-2272.** Cover free–$20.

The Palace ★★ Steps away from the boys doing their thing on the heavily gay 12th Street Beach, this bar/restaurant and drag-show venue loudly/proudly plants its rainbow flag on Ocean Drive, much to the bemusement of the guests lounging at the Tides hotel next door. If you really want Tiffany Fantasia or Poizon Ivy to get all up in your Cobb salad, snag a sidewalk table before a show (usually Tues–Wed at 8pm and Thurs–Fri at 6pm; on weekends the fun goes on most of the day, with tea dance at 4pm). 1200 Ocean Dr., South Beach. www.PalaceSouthBeach.com. ✆ **305/531-7234.** No cover. Daily 11am–midnight.

Score ★★ There's a reason this Washington Avenue dance spot is called Score. Besides a pickup scene, this exposed-brick space has three bars, a dance floor with a big ol' disco ball right in the middle of it, and a zippily-lit upstairs lounge, all ensconced in a portion of the space once filled by Liquid, the legendary club of the 1990s. There are usually promoter events Thursday through Sunday (often with open bar the first half hour), plus a "Planeta Macho" Latin night on Tuesday. 1437 Washington Ave., South Beach. www.ScoreBar.net. ✆ **305/535-1111.** Cover free–$10; depending on night, may be free before 11pm to 12:30am. Sun–Thurs 9pm–5am, Fri–Sat 6pm–5am.

Twist ★★ One of the most popular bars on South Beach since 1993, this recently expanded two-story club (right across the street from the city police HQ) has a casual, usually hopping atmosphere, along with a stripper bar in the back and an upstairs dance floor that can get hot and heavy in the wee hours. 1057 Washington Ave., South Beach. www.TwistSoBe.com. ✆ **305/538-9478.** No cover. Daily 1pm–5am.

OTHER ENTERTAINMENT

Bowling Alleys

Think of it as the Big Lebowski meets Studio 54, because in Miami, this is not your Sunday-afternoon ESPN bowling tournament. As much a fun rainy-day activity as it is with the kids, bowling in Miami gives new meaning to partying in the gutter.

Lucky Strike Lanes ★★ South Beach's only bowling alley is a pricey blast for adults and kids alike, with 14 lanes, a pair of pool tables, a pulsating nightclub-esque soundtrack, a full bar, TVs, a restaurant, and even free Wi-Fi. Kids are welcome until 9pm, after which the scene turns 21-and-over. 1691 Michigan Ave., South Beach. www.Bowl LuckyStrike.com. ✆**305/532-0307.** $45–$65 per hr., plus $4 shoe rental, except for Mon $15 unlimited bowling. Mon–Thurs 11:30am–1am; Fri 11:30am–2am; Sat 11am–2am; Sun 11am–1am.

Splitsville Luxury Lanes & Dinner Lounge ★★ At Sunset Place mall, Splitsville is South Miami's Lucky Strike, with a dozen lanes, a half-dozen pool tables, a full-service restaurant, TVs, and multiple bars. And here too, it's age 21 and over after 8pm on weekends (after 10pm Sunday through Thursday), when the place turns into a thumping club scene. But Splitsville is much more affordable, and because of that there's often a wait for lanes. Luckily, there are plenty of other distractions while you wait. Sunset Place, 5701 Sunset Dr., South Miami. www.SplitsvilleLanes.com. ✆ **305/665-5263.** $2–$7 per person per game, shoe rental $2–$4. Mon–Thurs 4pm–midnight, Fri 4pm–2am, Sat 11am–2am, Sun 11am–midnight.

Strike Miami ★★ At the Dolphin Mall, Miami's biggest bowling alley boasts 34 lanes and a nightclub vibe, complete with glow-in-the-dark bowling, bars, vid screens—the works. It's 18 and over after 9pm Thursday through Saturday. Dolphin Mall, 11401 NW 12th St., Sweetwater. www.Bowlmor.com. ✆**305/594-0200.** $5–7 per person per game, plus shoe rental $5. Mon 4pm–1am, Tues–Thurs 4pm–midnight, Fri midnight–3am, Sat 11am–3am, Sun 11am–midnight

Gambling

Although gambling is technically illegal in Miami, there are loads of loopholes that allow wads of wagering, at offshore casinos or on shore at bingo, jai alai, card rooms, horse and dog tracks, and Indian reservations. Revived in 2013, the historic **Hialeah Park,** 220 E. 4th Ave. (www.HialeahParkCasino.com; ✆ 305/885-8000) has poker, slots, and big future plans. You can also try **Magic City Casino,** with a dog track 5 minutes from the airport and downtown Miami at 450 NW 37th Ave. (www.Magic-CityCasino.com; ✆ 305/649-3000), and **Calder Casino & Race Course** at 21001 NW 27th Ave. in Miami Gardens (www.CalderRaceCourse.com; ✆ 305/625-1311), featuring 1,200 slot machines, poker, and horse racing. Some folks prefer the less flashy **Miccosukee Indian Gaming,** 500 SW 177th Ave. (off S.R. 41 in West Miami; www.Miccosukee.com/Gaming, ✆ 305/222-4600), where Reno meets the Everglades. This somewhat tacky casino has tab slots, high-speed bingo, and even poker in more than 85,000 square feet of playing space (there's a hotel out here, too).

You can also drive up to Broward County, where Hollywood's **Seminole Hard Rock Hotel and Casino** (www.SeminoleHardRock.com), **Seminole Casino Coconut Creek** (www.SeminoleCoconutCreekCasino.com), **Mardi Gras Casino** (www.Mardi GrasCasinoFL.com), and still-expanding **Gulfstream Park Casino and Racing** (www.GulfstreamPark.com) offer slots, poker—and in the cases of Hard Rock and Gulfstream, blackjack too.

SPECTATOR SPORTS

Check the *Miami Herald*'s sports section for a daily listing of local events and the Friday "Weekend" section for comprehensive coverage and in-depth reports. For last-minute tickets, call the venue directly, as many season ticket holders sell singles and return unused tickets. Expensive tickets are available from brokers or individuals listed in the classified sections of the local papers. Some tickets are also available through **Ticketmaster** (www.Ticketmaster.com; ☎ **800/745-3000**).

BASEBALL The **Florida Marlins** shocked the sports world in 1997 when they became the youngest expansion team to win a World Series, but then floundered as its star players were sold off by then-owner Wayne Huizenga. The team made waves again in 2003 by winning another World Series, and managed to turn many of Miami's apathetic sports fans into major-league ball fans; since trading their best players, though, they're not doing so hot. In 2012 the Marlins moved to their new home (501 NW 16th Ave.), the onetime Orange Bowl, refurbed to the tune of $525 million, including sleazy maneuvering that stuck taxpayers with a huge boondoggle, and they've bled much of their popularity, with game attendance down. If you'd like to catch a game, be warned: Miami's summer heat can be a beast, even in the evening; at least the ballpark features a retractable roof to make it more bearable. Tickets can be bought at http://Miami.Marlins.mlb.com and ☎ **877/627-5467,** and cost from $7.50 to thousands for luxury suites. Box-office hours are weekdays from 9am to 6pm and Saturday from 10am to 4pm.

BASKETBALL The **Miami Heat** (www.NBA.com/Heat; ☎ **786/777-1000**) is one of Miami's hottest tickets, especially since they've won back-to-back NBA championships in 2012 and 2013 thanks to the powerhouse trio of Dwayne Wade, LeBron James, and Chris Bosh. The season runs October to April, and the team plays in the waterfront **American Airlines Arena,** on Biscayne Boulevard downtown. Get ready to pay through the nose; tickets can easily run from the low hundreds to over $7,500. The box-office is open weekdays from 10am to 5pm (until the end of halftime on game nights); tickets are also sold through the NBA (**800/462-2849**) and Ticketmaster (☎ **800/745-3000**).

CAR RACING **Homestead Miami Speedway,** SW 137th Ave. at SW 336th St., Homestead (www.HomesteadMiamiSpeedway.com; ☎ **305/230-5000**), made history in 2009 when it became the first venue ever to host all of North America's premier motor sports championships: the IndyCar, Grand-Am, and Firestone Indy Lights Series; and NASCAR's Sprint Cup, Nationwide, and Camping World Truck Series. Even when races aren't going on, you can channel your inner speed demon via events that allow regular folks to put the pedal to the metal, including Hooked on Driving (www.HookedonDriving.com) and Florida Track Days (www.FloridaTrackDays. com). The track also features private club–level seating. Tickets prices to all events vary.

FOOTBALL Followed by thousands of "Dol-fans," the **Miami Dolphins** play at least eight home games between September and December, at **Sun Life Stadium,** 2269 NW 199th St., Miami Gardens (www.MiamiDolphins.com; ☎ **305/943-8000**). Jimmy Buffett has often been at games, as have celebrity "co-owners" including Gloria and Emilio Estefan, Jennifer Lopez, Marc Anthony, and Fergie from the Black Eyed Peas. In fact, home games now feature an "orange carpet" on which owners and their famous pals preen before fans, and these connections have brought big names in to perform free concerts before games. In 2012, HBO spotlighted the 'Fins on its reality show *Hard Knocks.* In the past couple of years, a flurry of changes and acquisitions left them with a heavily retooled roster, with top players including Mike Pouncey and Mike Wallace. Tickets run from $40 to thousands for executive suites and club seating.

MIAMI ENTERTAINMENT & NIGHTLIFE

Spectator Sports

What the Heck Is Jai Alai?

Although it has roots in ancient Egypt, *jai alai* (pronounced *HI*-a-lie) as it's now played was invented in north Spain's Pyrenees mountains in the 17th century by Basque peasants, using church walls as their courts. Players use *cestas*, curved wicker baskets strapped to their wrists, to hurl balls called *pelotas* at speeds that can exceed 200 mph, and spectators, who are protected behind a Plexiglas wall, place bets on the players. The game looks something like lacrosse, with rules similar to handball or tennis, and is played on a court with numbered lines. What makes it unique is the requirement that the ball must be returned in one continuous motion. The server must bounce it behind the serving line and, with the basket, must hurl it to the front wall, with the aim being that, upon rebound, the ball will bounce between lines four and seven. If it doesn't, it's an under- or overserve and the other team gets a point

The box office is open weekdays 8:30am to 5:30pm; tickets can also be bought via ✆ **888/346-7849** or Ticketmaster (www.Ticketmaster.com; ✆ **800/745-3000**).

HORSE RACING   Located on the Dade–Broward County border in Hallandale (just north of Aventura), **Gulfstream Park,** U.S. 1 north of NE 213 St. (www.Gulfstream Park.com; ✆ **800/771-8873** or 954/454-7000), is like a trailer-park version of Churchill Downs, a sprawling haven for serious gamblers and voyeurs alike. Large purses and important races are commonplace, and the track is typically crowded, especially since a multimillion-dollar facelift that has added a flashy casino, nightspots, shops, and eateries. Races run January through June. Admission and parking are free.

Hialeah Park, 2200 E. 4th Ave. (www.HialeahParkRacing.com; ✆ **305/885-8000**), is a 1925 landmark that closed in 2001 and reopened in 2009. Though currently limited to shorter, less glamorous quarter horse races from late November through February, along with simulcasts from other tracks, Hialeah Park aims to re-introduce thoroughbred events as soon as possible. Racing fans will keep the faith; after all, this is the racetrack where champions like Seattle Slew and Seabiscuit (who made his racing debut here in 1935), made history. Then there's **Calder Race Course,** near Sun Life Stadium at 21001 NW 27th Ave. in Miami Gardens (www.CalderRaceCourse.com; ✆ **305/625-1311**). Owned by the venerable Churchill Downs, Calder first opened as a racetrack in 1971 and has become one of the most successful pari-mutuel franchises in Florida history. Both of the above also have casinos with electronic slots and poker.

And although it's not exactly racing, the **Miami Beach Polo Cup** (www.Miami Polo.com) is a newish event on the South Beach strand each April, featuring sand-kicking polo matches, a parade of the ponies down the beach, and chic parties. Admission to matches throughout the weekend is free to the public, while VIP tickets are available for those seeking more than a view from the sidelines and for coveted events outside the arena.

JAI ALAI   Sort of a Basque indoor lacrosse (see box above), jai alai was introduced to Miami in 1924 and is regularly played in two area frontons (arenas). The Florida Gaming Corporation owns jai alai operations throughout the state, making betting on this sport as legal as buying a lottery ticket. The **Casino Miami Jai Alai,** 3500 NW

37th Ave. (www.CasinoMiamiJaiAlai.com; © **305/633-6400**), is America's oldest fronton, dating from 1926. It schedules 13 nightly games year-round, typically lasting 10 to 20 minutes, occasionally much longer. Admission is free. On Wednesday, Thursday, and Sunday, there are games from noon to 5:30pm. Friday, Saturday, and Monday, there are matinees as well as games from 7pm to midnight. In 2012 it added more than a thousand slot machines as well as poker, dominoes tables, fancy drinking/dining options, and shows (seen as necessary to help make up for the longstanding decline of jai alai as a spectator sport here as elsewhere in America).

THE EVERGLADES & BISCAYNE NATIONAL PARKS

10

The vast ecosystem of Everglades National Park—and most of South Florida, really—is a shallow, 40-mile-wide, slow-moving river. Its current 1½ million acres (less than 20% of its mass when preserved in 1947) remain one of few places to see endangered American crocodiles, leatherback turtles, and West Indian manatees. Take your time: The rustling of a bush might be a tiny, red-throated anole lizard; that splash of purple might be a mule-ear orchid.

Active Pursuits Popular day hikes like the **Coastal Prairie** and **Gumbo Limbo** trails wind through canopies of cypress and gumbo-limbo trees and past waterways with alligators and pink-hued roseate spoonbills. Shark Valley is South Florida's most scenic biking trail, a flat, paved route frequented by sunbathing alligators and turtles. Canoeing through the Everglades allows serene, close-up views of this jungle-like ecosystem.

Flora & Fauna A river of saw grass marks Everglades National Park, punctuated with islands of gumbo-limbo hammocks, royal palms, and pale, delicate orchids. The **Anhinga Trail** teems with native wildlife: the swallowtail butterfly, American crocodile, leatherback turtle, West Indian manatee, and, rarely, the Florida panther.

Tours Shallow-draft, fan-powered airboats career through bayous, rising ever so slightly above swaying saw grass and alongside flocks of snowy egrets. The high-speed runabouts operate just outside park boundaries, including **Gator Park** and **Coopertown Airboat Tours.** At the Shark Valley entrance, **Shark Valley Tram Tours** transport visitors on 2-hour, naturalist-led explorations through the heart of the Everglades. A highlight is the 45-foot observation tower for a bird's-eye view of the "river of grass."

THE best EVERGLADES & BISCAYNE NATIONAL PARK EXPERIENCES

o **Biking Shark Valley:** Anyone who's ever been on a bicycle knows all about bumps in the road. But when biking in this Everglades natural treasure, a 15-mile paved road full of sights, smells, and sounds, those bumps could very well be alligators.

o **Cooling Off with Some Cold War History, 'Glades-Style:** History buffs will love the **Nike Hercules Missile Base HM-69** (p. 154), a military base that arose out of very real Cold War fears. The base was turned back over to the park in 1979 but wasn't open to the public until 2004.

o **Canoeing Through the Everglades:** The **Noble Hammock Canoe Trail** (p. 155) is a 2-mile loop perfect for beginners. Hardier canoers will want to try **Hell's Bay Canoe Trail** (p. 155), a 3- to 6-mile course, depending on how far you go. It got its name for a reason: Fans of the trail like to say, "It's hell to get in and hell to get out."

o **Stuffing Your Face at the Everglades Seafood Festival:** Every February, Everglades City, the tiny town at the edge of the Ten Thousand Islands, is a seafood lover's dream come true, complete with live country music, crafts, and characters.

o **Sleeping in the Everglades:** Spending the night in the Everglades is truly an experience. Some prefer camping, but we prefer the **Ivey House B&B** (p. 151), where you'll feel at home and, best of all, like a local.

EVERGLADES NATIONAL PARK ★★

Although many people think of the Everglades as one big swamp swarming with ominous creatures, the Everglades isn't really a swamp at all, but one of the country's most fascinating natural resources.

For first-timers or the less athletically inclined, the best way to see the 'Glades is probably via airboats, which aren't allowed in the park proper but cut through the saw grass on the park's outskirts, taking you past the amazing flora and fauna. A walk on one of the park's many trails will provide you with a different vantage point: up-close interaction with an assortment of tame wildlife. But the absolute best way to see the 'Glades is via canoe, which allows you to get incredibly close to nature. Whatever you choose, you will marvel at the sheer beauty of the Everglades.

This vast, unusual ecosystem is actually a 40-mile-wide, slow-moving river. Rarely more than knee-deep, the water is the lifeblood of this wilderness, and the subtle shifts in water level dictate the life cycles of its plants and animals. In 1947, 1½ million acres—less than 20% of the Everglades' wilderness—were established as Everglades National Park. At that time, few lawmakers understood how neighboring ecosystems relate to each other. Consequently, the park is heavily affected by surrounding territories and is at the butt end of every environmental insult that occurs upstream in Miami.

Lazy River

It takes a month for 1 gallon of water to move through Everglades National Park.

Although there has been a marked decrease in the indigenous wildlife, Everglades National Park remains one of the few places where you can see dozens of endangered species in their natural habitat, including the swallowtail butterfly, American crocodile, leatherback turtle, Southern bald eagle, West Indian manatee, and Florida panther.

The Everglades

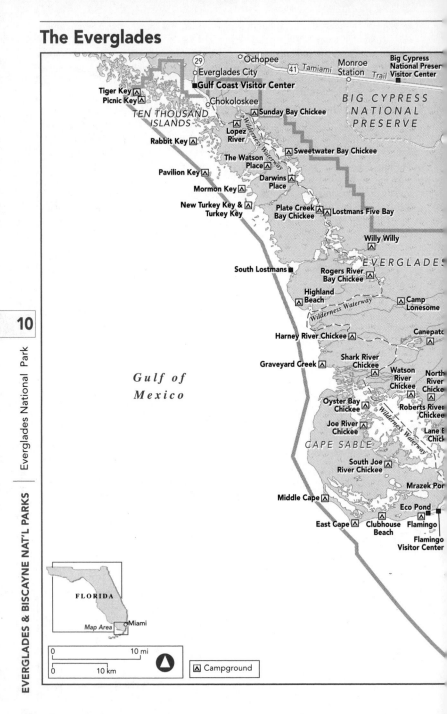

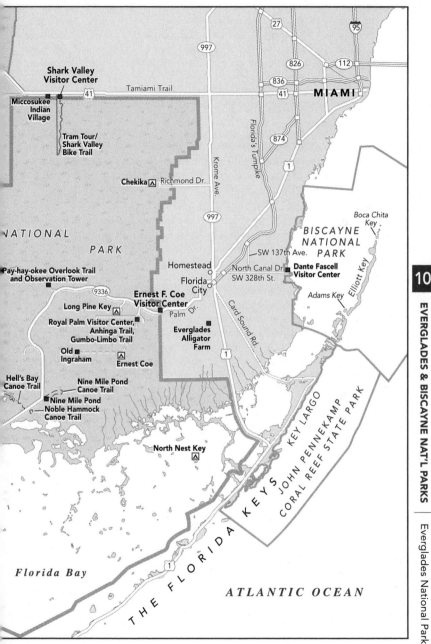

Take your time on the trails, and a hypnotic beauty begins to unfold. Follow the rustling of a bush, and you might see a small green tree frog or tiny brown anole lizard, with its bright-red spotted throat. Crane your neck to see around a bend, and discover a delicate, brightly painted mule-ear orchid.

The slow and subtle splendor of this exotic land may not be immediately appealing to kids raised on video games, but they'll certainly remember the experience and thank you later. There's enough dramatic fun around the park, such as airboat rides, hiking, and biking, to keep them satisfied for at least a day.

Beware of the multitude of mosquitoes that live in the Everglades (the bugs seem to be immune to repellent); wear long pants and cover your arms.

Essentials

GETTING THERE & ACCESS POINTS   Although the Everglades may seem overwhelmingly large, it's easy to get to the park's two main areas: the northern section, accessible via Shark Valley and Everglades City, and the southern section, accessible through the Ernest F. Coe Visitor Center, near Homestead and Florida City.

NORTHERN ENTRANCES   A popular day trip for Miamians, **Shark Valley,** a 15-mile paved loop road (with an observation tower in the middle) overlooking the pulsating heart of the Everglades, is the easiest and most scenic way to explore the park. Just 25 miles west of the Florida Turnpike, Shark Valley is best reached via the Tamiami Trail, South Florida's pre-turnpike two-lane road, which cuts across the southern part of the state along the park's northern border. Roadside attractions (boat rides and alligator farms, for example) along the Tamiami Trail are operated by the Miccosukee Indian Village and are worth a quick, fun stop. An excellent tram tour (leaving from the Shark Valley Visitor Center) goes deep into the park along a trail that's also terrific for biking. Shark Valley is about an hour's drive from Miami.

A little less than 10 miles west along the Tamiami Trail from Shark Valley, you'll discover **Big Cypress National Preserve,** in which stretches of vibrant green cypress and pine trees make for a fabulous Kodak moment. If you pick up S.R. 29 and head south from the Tamiami Trail, you'll hit a modified version of civilization in the form of Everglades City (where the Everglades meet the Gulf of Mexico), where there's another entrance to the park and the **Gulf Coast Visitor Center.** From Miami to Shark Valley, go west on I-395 to S.R. 821 South (Florida Tpk.). Take the U.S. 41/Southwest 8th Street (Tamiami Trail) exit. The Shark Valley entrance is just 25 miles west. To get to Everglades City, continue west on the Tamiami Trail and head south on S.R. 29. Everglades City is approximately a 2½-hour drive from Miami, but because it is scenic, it may take longer if you stop or slow down to view your surroundings.

SOUTHERN ENTRANCE (VIA HOMESTEAD & FLORIDA CITY)   If you're in a rush to hit the 'Glades and don't care about the scenic route, this is your best bet. Just southeast of Homestead and Florida City, off S.R. 9336, the southern access to the park will bring you to the **Ernest F. Coe Visitor Center.** Inside the park, 4 miles beyond the Ernest F. Coe Visitor Center, is the **Royal Palm Visitor Center,** the starting point for the two most popular walking trails, Gumbo Limbo and Anhinga, where you'll witness a plethora of birds and wildlife roaming freely. Thirteen miles west of the Ernest F. Coe Visitor Center, you'll hit Pa-hay-okee Overlook Trail, which is worth a trek across the boardwalk to reach the observation tower, over which vultures and hawks hover protectively amid a resplendent, picturesque, bird's-eye view of the

Everglades. From Miami to the southern entrance, go west on I-395 to S.R. 821 South (Florida Tpk.), which will end in Florida City. Take the first right through the center of town (you can't miss it) and follow signs to the park entrance on S.R. 9336. The Ernest F. Coe Visitor Center is about 1½ hours from Miami.

VISITOR CENTERS & INFORMATION Contact the **Everglades National Park Headquarters,** 40001 S.R. 9336, Homestead (*C* **305/242-7700**) for information. Ask for a copy of *Parks and Preserves,* a free newspaper that's filled with up-to-date info about goings-on in the Everglades. Headquarters is staffed by helpful phone operators daily from 8:30am to 4:30pm. You can also try **www.NPS.gov/ever**.

Note that all hours listed are for the high season, generally November through May. During the slow summer months, many offices and outfitters keep abbreviated hours. Always call ahead to confirm hours of operation.

The **Ernest F. Coe Visitor Center,** at the park headquarters entrance, west of Homestead and Florida City, is the best place to gather information. In addition to details on tours and boat rentals, and free brochures outlining trails, wildlife, and activities, you will find state-of-the-art educational displays, films, and interactive exhibits. A gift shop sells postcards, an impressive selection of books about the Everglades, unusual gift items, and a supply of your most important gear: insect repellent. The center is open daily from 9am to 5pm (from 8am in winter).

The **Royal Palm Visitor Center,** a small nature museum located 3 miles past the main entrance, is a smaller information center. The museum is not great (though displays are equipped with recordings about the park's ecosystem), but this is the departure point for the popular Anhinga and Gumbo Limbo trails. It's open daily from 8am to 4pm.

Knowledgeable rangers, who provide brochures and personal insight into the park's activities, also staff the **Flamingo Visitor Center,** 38 miles from the main entrance at the park's southern access, with natural-history exhibits and information on visitor services, and the **Shark Valley Visitor Center,** at the northern entrance. Flamingo is open daily from 8am to 4:30pm, while Shark Valley is open daily from 9am to 5pm.

ENTRANCE FEES, PERMITS & REGULATIONS Permits and passes can be purchased only at the main park or the Shark Valley entrance station. Even if you're just visiting for an afternoon, you'll need to buy a 7-day permit, which costs $10 per vehicle ($5 for pedestrians and cyclists). An **Everglades Park Pass,** valid for a year's unlimited admission, is available for $25. You may also purchase a 12-month America the Beautiful National Parks and Federal Recreation Lands Pass–Annual Pass for $80, valid for entrance into any U.S. national park. U.S. citizens ages 62 and older pay only $20 for the America the Beautiful National Parks and Federal Recreation Lands Pass–Senior Pass that's valid for life. An Access Pass version is free to U.S. citizens with disabilities. For details, go to www.NPS.gov/fees_passes.htm or call *C* **888/275-8747.**

Permits are required for campers to stay overnight either in the backcountry or at the primitive campsites. See "Camping in the Everglades" on p. 151.

Those who want to fish without a charter captain must obtain a State of Florida saltwater fishing license. These are available in the park, or at any tackle shop or sporting-goods store nearby. Nonresidents pay $30 for a 7-day license or $17 for a 3-day license. Florida residents pay $17 for an annual fishing license. A snook license must be purchased separately at a cost of $10; a lobster permit is $5. For more information on fishing licenses, go to **MyFWC.com/license/saltwater**.

Charter captains carry vessel licenses that cover all paying passengers, but ask to be sure. Freshwater fishing licenses are available at bait-and-tackle stores outside the park at the same rates as those inside the park. A good one is **Don's Bait & Tackle,** 90 N. Homestead Blvd. (www.DonsBaitandTackle.com; ✆ **305/247-6616**). *Note:* Most freshwater fishing hereabouts, limited to murky canals and artificial lakes near housing developments, is hardly worth the trouble with so much good saltwater fishing at hand.

SEASONS   There are two distinct seasons in the Everglades: high season and mosquito season. High season, from late November to May, is also dry season. Most winters are warm, sunny, and breezy—a good mix for keeping bugs away. It's the best time to visit because low water levels attract the largest variety of wading birds and their predators. As the dry season wanes, wildlife follows the receding water; by the end of May, the only living things you're sure to spot will make you itch. The worst, called no-see-ums, are not even swattable. If you choose to visit during the buggy season, be vigilant in applying bug spray. Also be aware that many establishments and operators close or curtail offerings in summer, so always call ahead to check.

RANGER PROGRAMS   More than two dozen ranger programs, free with entry, are offered each month during high season and give visitors an opportunity to gain an expert's perspective. Ranger-led walks and talks are offered year-round from the Royal Palm, Flamingo, and Gulf Coast visitor centers, as well as Shark Valley Visitor Center during winter months. Park rangers tend to be helpful, well informed, and good humored. Some programs run regularly, such as Royal Palm Visitor Center's "Glade Glimpses," a walking tour on which rangers point out flora and fauna and discuss issues affecting the Everglades' survival, scheduled at 1:30pm daily. The Anhinga Amble, a similar program that takes place on the Anhinga Trail, starts at 10:30am daily and lasts about 50 minutes. Because times, programs, and locations can change from month to month, check the schedule, available at any of the visitor centers.

SAFETY   There are many dangers inherent in this vast wilderness area. *Always* let someone know your itinerary before you set out on an extended hike. It's mandatory that you file an itinerary when camping overnight in the backcountry (which you can do when you apply for an overnight permit at either the Flamingo Visitor Center or the Gulf Coast Visitor Center). When you're on the water, watch for weather changes; thunderstorms and high winds often develop rapidly. Swimming is not recommended due to alligators, sharks, and barracudas. Watch out for the region's four poisonous snakes: diamondback and pygmy rattlesnakes, coral snakes (identifiable by their colorful rings), and water moccasins (which swim on the surface of the water). Bring insect repellent to ward off mosquitoes and biting flies. First aid is available from park rangers. The nearest hospital is in Homestead, 10 miles from the park's main entrance.

Where to Stay

There is no lodging within Everglades National Park proper (unless you count your tent). But there are a few options just outside the park that are clean and reasonably priced. A $45-million casino hotel, the **Miccosukee Resort** (www.Miccosukee.com/resort; ✆ **877/242-6464**), is adjacent to the Miccosukee bingo and gaming hall on the northern edge of the park. It's equipped with various resort amenities such as a spa, gym, indoor pool, various bars and clubs, even live entertainment; doubles start at $150. Although bugs can be a major nuisance, especially in the warm months, camping is the best way to fully experience South Florida's wilderness.

CAMPING IN THE EVERGLADES

Campgrounds are open year-round in Flamingo and Long Pine Key. Both have drinking water, picnic tables, charcoal grills, restrooms, and tent and trailer pads, and welcome RVs (Flamingo allows up to 40-ft. vehicles, while Long Pine Key accepts up to 60-footers), though there are no electrical hookups. Flamingo has cold-water showers; Long Pine Key has no showers or hookups. Private ground fires aren't permitted, but supervised campfire programs are conducted during winter. Flamingo accepts and strongly recommends advance reservations, while Long Pine Key accepts reservations only for groups of 10 or more; all reservations can be made through the National Park Reservations Service (www.NPS.gov/ever/planyourvisit/feesandreservations.htm; ✆ 800/444-6677). Campsites are $16 per night; during the winter season (Nov–Apr), there's a 14-day consecutive-stay limit, and a maximum of 30 days a year.

Camping is also available year-round in the **backcountry** (those remote areas accessible only by boat, foot, or canoe—basically, most of the park), on a first-come, first-served basis. Campers must register with park rangers and get a permit in person or by phone no less than 24 hours before the start of their visit; the costs is $10 plus $2 per camper per night. For details, contact the **Gulf Coast Visitor Center** (✆ **239/695-3311**) or the **Flamingo Visitor Center** (✆ **239/695-2945**), which are the only two places that sell the permits. Once you have one, camping sites cost $16 (with a maximum of 8 people per site) or $30 for a group site (maximum of 15 people). In 2011, Flamingo added 41 new sites with electrical hookup at $30 per site. Campers can use only designated campsites, which are plentiful and well marked on maps.

Many backcountry sites are *chickee huts*—covered wooden platforms (with toilets) on stilts. They're accessible only by canoe and can accommodate free-standing tents (without stakes). Ground sites are located along interior bays and rivers, and beach camping is also popular. In summer especially, mosquito repellent is necessary.

LODGING IN EVERGLADES CITY

As Everglades City is 35 miles southeast of Naples and 83 miles west of Miami, many visitors choose to explore this western entrance to Everglades National Park, located off the Tamiami Trail, on S.R. 29. An annual seafood festival held the first weekend in February is a major event that draws hordes of people. Everglades City (the gateway to the Ten Thousand Islands), where the Everglades meet the Gulf of Mexico, is the closest thing you'll get to civilization in South Florida's swampy frontier, with a few touristy shops, a restaurant, and one bed-and-breakfast.

The Ivey House ★★ The first "Certified Green Lodging" in Collier County offers a variety of digs: the Inn, whose spacious rooms arranged around a courtyard pool and waterfall have private bathrooms, TVs, phones, and small fridges; the Lodge, once a social center for the men who built the Tamiami Trail in the 1920s, with 11 small rooms (no TVs, phone, or heat, though) with a communal living area and bathrooms (one female, one male); and the Cottage, with living room, two bedrooms, full kitchen, bathroom, and screened-in porch (sleeps up to four). Owners Sandee and David Harraden are very knowledgeable about the Everglades and assist guests, running a variety of daily excursions. A full hot breakfast is provided during peak season; box lunches available year-round for $13. *Note:* There is no smoking in any of the buildings.

107 Camellia St. (btw. Copeland and Buckner aves.), Everglades City. www.IveyHouse.com. ✆ **877/567-0679** or 239/695-3299. 30 units. Winter $99–$269; off-season $89–$179. 2-night

minimum in cottage. Rates include continental breakfast. **Amenities:** Restaurant (breakfast only); pool; free Wi-Fi.

Rod & Gun Lodge ★★ Set on the banks of the sleepy Baron River, this rustic old white-clapboard house has plenty of history and all kinds of activities, including a pool, bike rentals, a tennis center, and nearby boat rentals and private fishing guides. Hoover vacationed here after his 1928 election victory, and Truman stayed when he flew in to sign Everglades National Park into existence in 1947. Other guests have included Richard Nixon, Burt Reynolds, and Mick Jagger. The public rooms are beautifully paneled and hung with tarpon, wild boar, deer antlers, and other trophies. Guest rooms, meanwhile, are unfussy but plenty comfortable; all have porches looking out on the river. Out by the pool, a screened veranda with ceiling fans is a pleasant place for a libation. An excellent seafood **restaurant** serves breakfast, lunch, and dinner.

Riverside Dr. and Broadway, Everglades City. www.EvergladesRodandGun.com. ✆ **239/695-2101.** 17 units. Winter $110–$140 double; off-season $95. No credit cards. **Amenities:** Restaurant; bike rental; pool; tennis courts; no Wi-Fi.

LODGING IN HOMESTEAD & FLORIDA CITY

Homestead and Florida City, two adjacent towns that were almost blown off the map by Hurricane Andrew in 1992, have come back better than before. About 10 miles from the park's main entrance, along U.S. 1, 35 miles south of Miami, these somewhat rural towns offer several budget options, including chain hotels. There's a **Days Inn** (www.DaysInn.com; ✆ 305/245-1260) in Homestead at 51 S. Homestead Blvd., and a **Ramada Inn** (www.Ramada.com; ✆ 800/272-6232 or 305/247-8833) in Florida City at 124 E. Palm Dr., right off the turnpike. The best options are in Florida City: The **Best Western Gateway to the Keys,** 411 Krome Ave. (U.S. 1; www.BestWestern.com; ✆ 800/528-1234 or 305/246-5100), **Florida City Travelodge,** 409 SE 1st Ave. (www. TLFLCity.com; ✆ 305/248-9777); and **Everglades International Hostel,** 20 SW 2nd Ave. (www.EvergladesHostel.com; ✆ 800/372-3874 or 305/248-1122).

Where to Eat in & Around the Park

Here for nearly a quarter of a century, **El Toro Taco,** 1 S. Krome Ave., at E. Mowry Dr., Homestead (✆ 305/245-8182), opens daily at 10am and stays crowded until at least 9pm most days. The fresh grilled meats, tacos, burritos, salsas, guacamole, and stews are all mild and delicious. No matter how big your appetite, it's hard to spend more than $15 per person at this Mexican outpost. Bring your own beer or wine.

Housed in a one-story building that looks vaguely like a medieval fort, the **Capri Restaurant,** 935 N. Krome Ave., Florida City (www.DineCapri.com; ✆ 305/247-1544), has been serving hearty Italian-American fare since 1958. Great pastas and salads complement meat and fish; portions are big. It's open for lunch and dinner Monday through Thursday until 9:30pm, Friday until 10:30pm (weekends dinner only). **White Lion Café,** 146 NW 7th St., Homestead (www.WhiteLionCafe.com; ✆ 305/248-1076), is a quaint home-and-gardens-cum-cafe with live blues, jazz, and swing music at night, and blue-plate specials and cheekily named appetizers and entrees such as "Garlic Romanian," skirt steak served with mushrooms, spinach, and garlic over mashed potatoes and gravy. Entrees run $10 to $22. Lunch is served Monday through Saturday 11am to 3pm, dinner Tuesday through Saturday from 5pm until "the fat lady sings."

The **Miccosukee Restaurant,** just west of the Shark Valley entrance on the Tamiami Trail/U.S. 41 (𝄐 **305/223-8380**), serves authentic pumpkin bread, fry bread, fish, and not-so-authentic Native American interpretations of tacos and fried chicken. It's worth a stop for brunch, lunch, or dinner.

Near the Miccosukee reservation, the **Pit Bar-B-Q,** 16400 SW 8th St. (𝄐 **305/226-2272**), is rustic, palapa-roofed, more than a half-century old, and known for some of the best smoked ribs, barbecued chicken, and corn bread (not to mention gator ribs, sausage, and burgers) this side of the Deep South. Meal prices run $10 to $20 (sandwiches from $7); it's open weekdays 11am to 9pm, Saturday 11am to 11pm, Sunday 9am to midnight.

In Everglades City, the **Oyster House** at 875 S. Copeland Ave. (www.Oyster-HouseRestaurant.com; 𝄐 **239/695-2073**) is a large, homey seafood restaurant with modest prices (sandwiches from $8, seafood baskets from $12), excellent service, and a fantastic view of the Ten Thousand Islands. Try the hush puppies. For more authentic local flavor, try the **Camellia Street Grill,** 202 Camellia St. (𝄐 **239/695-2003**), an off-the-beaten-path, rusty waterfront fish joint fusing Southern hospitality with outstanding seafood served with a gourmet twist. An onsite herb and veggie garden provides the freshest ingredients and stellar salads. Everything is homemade, including the Key lime pie, and there's live music on Fridays and Saturdays. It generally closes for the summer.

Seeing the Highlights

Shark Valley, a 15-mile paved road (ideal for biking) through the Everglades, provides a fine introduction to the wonders of the park, but don't plan on spending more than a few hours here. Bicycling (p. 154) and taking a guided tram tour (p. 154) are fantastic ways to cover the highlights.

If you want to see a greater array of plant and animal life, make sure that you venture into the park through the main entrance, pick up a trail map, and dedicate at least a day to exploring from there.

Stop first along the Anhinga and Gumbo Limbo trails, which start right next to each other, 3 miles from the park's main entrance. These trails provide a thorough introduction to the Everglades' flora and fauna and are highly recommended to first-time visitors. Each is a half-mile round-trip. **Gumbo Limbo Trail** (my pick for best walking trail in the Everglades) meanders through a gorgeous, shaded, jungle-like hammock of gumbo-limbo trees, royal palms, ferns, orchids, air plants, and a general blanket of vegetation, though it doesn't put you in close contact with much wildlife. **Anhinga Trail** is one of the most popular trails in the park because of its abundance of wildlife. There's more water and wildlife in this area than in most parts of the Everglades, especially during dry season, and alligators, lizards, turtles, river otters, herons, egrets, and other animals abound. Arrive early to spot the widest selection of exotic birds, such as the trail's namesake anhinga bird, a large black fishing bird so used to humans that many build their nests in plain view. Take your time (at least an hour is recommended for each trail). Both trails are wheelchair accessible. If you treat the trails and modern boardwalk as pathways to get through quickly, rather than destinations to experience and savor, you'll miss out on the still beauty and hidden treasures that await you.

To get closer to nature, a few hours in a canoe along any of the trails allows paddlers the chance to sense the park's fluid motion and to become a part of the ecosphere. Visitors who choose this option end up feeling more like explorers than observers. (See "Outdoor Activities," below.)

No matter which option you choose, I strongly recommend staying for the 7pm program, available during high season at the Long Pine Key Amphitheater. This ranger-led talk and slide show will give you a detailed overview of the park's history, natural resources, wildlife, and threats to its survival.

And while the nature tours and talks are fascinating, so are the tours of **Nike Hercules Missile Base HM-69 ★**, conceived by President John F. Kennedy and his advisors based on very real Cold-War fears. The base was turned back over to the park in 1979 but wasn't open to the public until 2004. From December to April, daily ranger-led tours take visitors on a 90-minute driving and walking tour of the missile assembly building, three barns where 12 missiles were stored, the guardhouse, and the underground control room. Tours depart from the Dan Beard Research Center, near Ernest Coe Visitor Center, and are first-come, first-served; they're also free of charge, but the $10 park admission still applies. For details, call ✆ **305/242-7700.**

Outdoor Activities

BIKING   The relatively flat, 38-mile paved **Main Park Road** is great for biking because of the multitude of hardwood hammocks (treelike islands or dense stands of hardwood trees that grow only a few inches above land) and a dwarf cypress forest (stunted and thinly distributed cypress trees, which grow in poor soil on drier land).

Shark Valley, though, is the best trail by far. If the park isn't flooded from too much rain (which it often is, especially in spring), this is South Florida's most scenic bicycle trail. Many locals haul their bikes out to the 'Glades for a relaxing day of wilderness-trail riding. You'll share the flat, paved road only with other bikers, trams, and a menagerie of wildlife. (Don't be surprised to see a gator lounging in the sun or a deer munching on grass.) There are no shortcuts, so if you get tired or can't finish the 15-mile trip, turn around and return on the same road. Allow 2 to 3 hours to bike the entire loop.

Those who love to mountain-bike and who prefer solitude might check out the **Southern Glades Trail,** a 14-mile unpaved trail lined with native trees and teeming with wildlife such as deer, alligators, and the occasional snake. The trail runs along the C-111 canal, off S.R. 9336 and Southwest 217th Street.

Bicycles are available from **Shark Valley Tram Tours,** at the park's Shark Valley entrance (www.SharkValleyTramTours.com; ✆ **305/221-8455**), for $8.50 per hour; rentals can be picked up between 8:30am and 4pm and must be returned by 5pm.

BIRDWATCHING   More than 350 species of birds make their home in the Everglades. Tropical birds from the Caribbean and temperate species from North America can be found, along with exotics that have flown in from more distant regions. Eco and Mrazek ponds, located near Flamingo, are two of the best places for birding, especially in early morning or late afternoon in the dry winter months. Pick up a free birding checklist from one of the visitor centers (p. 149) and inquire about what's been spotted in recent days. One recent survey revealed that there were more than 77,000 nests in the Everglades (including a massive increase in nesting by the endangered woo stork). For expert guiding, consider **Everglades Area Tours** (www.EvergladesAreaTours. com; ✆ **800/860-1472** or 239/695-3633) and its **"National Park and Grand Heritage**

Birding Tour," a 6- to 7-hour naturalist-led tour via powerboat, kayak, and a beach walk, so you don't miss any of the spectacular feathered (among others) species who call the park home. The cost is a steep $300 per person ($160 for ages 11 and younger) and limited to six per tour.

CANOEING Canoeing through the Everglades may be one of the most serene adventures you'll ever have. From a canoe (where you're incredibly close to the water level), your vantage point is priceless. Canoers in the 'Glades can coexist with the gators and birds in a way no one else can; the animals treat you more like part of the ecosystem—which doesn't happen on an airboat. A ranger-guided boat tour is your best bet, and often they're either free or very inexpensive, around $7 to $12 per person. As always, a ranger will help you understand the surroundings and what you're seeing. They don't take reservations, but for details on the various boat tours, call ✆ **239/695-3311.**

Everglades National Park's longest "trails" are designed for boat and canoe travel, and many are marked as clearly as walking trails. The **Noble Hammock Canoe Trail,** a 2-mile loop, takes 1 to 2 hours and is recommended for beginners. The **Hell's Bay Canoe Trail,** a 3- to 6-mile course for hardier paddlers, takes 2 to 6 hours, depending on how far you choose to go. Park rangers can recommend other trails that suit your abilities, time limitations, and interests.

You can rent a canoe at the **Ivey House B&B** (www.EvergladesAdventures.com; ✆ **877/567-0679**) for $35 per full day (any 8-hr. period), or for $25 per half-day (1–5pm). Kayaks and tandem kayaks are also available. The rental agent will shuttle your party to the trail head of your choice and pick you up afterward. Rental facilities are open daily from 7:30am to 5pm.

During ideal weather conditions (stay away during bug season), you can paddle right out to the Gulf and camp on the beach. However, Gulf waters at beach sites can be very rough, and people in small watercraft such as a canoe should exercise caution.

Everglades Area Tours (www.EvergladesAreaTours.com; ✆ **239/695-3633**) offers not just guided fishing charters, but also guided kayak eco-tours, customized bird-watching and photo expeditions, and full-moon/sunset paddling, as well as bicycle and aerial tours of the Everglades. Its signature "Boat Assisted Kayak Eco Tour" puts six kayaks and six passengers into a dedicated motorboat for a trip out to the Wilderness Waterway deep within Everglades National Park, where you'll paddle in absolute wilderness, spotting birds, dolphins, manatees, sea turtles, alligators, and perhaps even the elusive American crocodile. The shuttle then brings you back to Everglades City/Chokoloskee. The trip costs $150 (half-price for ages 12 and under) and includes transportation, guide, kayaks, and all safety equipment.

FISHING About a third of Everglades National Park is open water. Freshwater fishing is popular in brackish **Nine-Mile Pond** (25 miles from the main entrance) and other spots along the Main Park Road, but because of the high mercury levels found in the Everglades, freshwater fishers are warned not to eat their catch. Before casting, check in at a visitor center, as many of the park's lakes are preserved for observation only. Fishing licenses are required; see p. 149 for more information.

Saltwater anglers will find snapper and sea trout plentiful. For an expertly guided fishing trip through the backcountry, **Adventures in Backwater Fishing** (www.Fishing-Florida.com/adventures; ✆ **239/774-6765**) will send you out with Captain George LeClair, who promises unique fishing—fly-fishing and spin casting, among other things—without breaking the bank. Six-hour trips start at $385.

MOTORBOATING   Motorboating around the Everglades seems like a great way to see plants and animals in remote habitats, and, indeed, it's a fascinating, fulfilling experience. But environmentalists have been noting the damage inflicted by motor-boats (especially airboats) on the delicate ecosystem. If you choose to motor, remem-ber that most of the areas near land are "no wake" zones and that, for the protection of nesting birds, landing is prohibited on most of the little mangrove islands. Motorboat-ing is allowed in certain areas, such as Florida Bay, the backcountry toward Everglades City, and the Ten Thousand Islands area. In all the freshwater lakes, however, motor-boats are prohibited if they're above 5 horsepower. There's a long list of restrictions and restricted areas, so get a copy of the boating rules from park headquarters.

The Everglades' only marina—accommodating about 50 boats with electric and water hookups—is **Flamingo Marina,** 815 Copeland Ave., S.R. 29, Everglades City (www.EvergladesNationalParkBoatToursFlamingo.com; ✆ **239/695-3101**). The marina is the only remnant of the now-demolished Flamingo Lodge, which suffered terrible damage from hurricanes Katrina and Wilma in 2005. Word is that if funding can be rounded up, it'll be replaced with a hurricane-resistant complex featuring a small hotel, cottages, and eco-tents. The well-marked channel to the Flamingo is accessible to boats with a maximum 4-foot draft and is open year-round. Reservations can be made through the marina store (it can take 24 hours for a phone or e-mail response). You can rent 17-foot skiffs with 40-horsepower motors at $80 for 2 hours, $150 for 4 hours, $195 for 8 hours, and $390 for 24 hours. A $100 deposit is required.

10 Organized Tours

AIRBOAT TOURS   Shallow-draft, fan-powered airboats were invented in the Ever-glades by frog hunters tired of poling through the brushes. Airboats cut through the saw grass sort of like hydraulic boats; at high enough speeds, they actually rise into the air. Even though airboats are the most efficient (not to mention fast and fun) way to get around, they aren't permitted in the park—the shallow-bottom runabouts tend to inflict severe damage on animals and plants. Just outside the boundaries of the Everglades, however, you'll find a number of outfitters offering rides. *Tip:* These high-speed boats are *loud,* and while sometimes operators provide plugs, bring a pair just in case.

One of the best outfitters is **Gator Park,** 12 miles west of the Florida Turnpike at 24050 SW Eighth St. (www.GatorPark.com; ✆ **800/559-2205** or 305/559-2255; daily 9am–5pm), one of the most informative and entertaining airboat-tour operators around, and the only one to give out free earplugs. Some of the guides deserve medals for hop-ping into the water and poking around a massive alligator, even though they're not really supposed to. After the boat ride there's an interactive show featuring alligator wrestling and other startling acts involving scorpions. And check out the peacocks that live in the trees! Admission for the boat ride (departures every 20 minutes until 5pm) and show is $23 for adults, $12 for ages 6 to 11 ($18/$10 if bought online, $45 includ-ing shuttle to/from hotels on Miami Beach, Bal Harbour, Surfside, and Sunny Isles).

Another outfitter worth recommending is **Coopertown Airboat Tours** (www. CoopertownAirboats.com; ✆ **305/226-6048**), about 11 miles west of the Florida Turn-pike on the Tamiami Trail (U.S. 41). The super-friendly staff has helped the company garner the title of "Florida's Best" by the *Miami Herald* for 40 years. You never know what you're going to see, but with great guides, you're sure to see *something* of interest on the 40-minute, 8-mile round-trip tours. A restaurant and a small gator farm are also on the premises. Airboat rides cost $23 for adults, $11 for children 6 to 11; private airboat tours are $50 per hour per person (discounts can be found on the website). Opening hours are daily 8am to 6pm; tours leave frequently.

The **Everglades Alligator Farm,** 4 miles south of Palm Drive at 40351 SW 192nd Avenue, Homestead (www.Everglades.com; ✆ **305/247-2628**), offers half-hour guided airboat tours daily from 9am to 6pm. The price, which includes admission to the park, is $23 for adults and $16 for ages 4 to 11.

CANOE TOURS   Slink through the mangroves, slide across saw grass prairies, and walk the sands of the Ten Thousand Islands—a canoe tour is a great way to explore the Everglades backcountry. Contact **Everglades Adventures** (www.Everglades Adventures.com; ✆ **877/567-0679**) at Ivey House B&B (p. 151) for an expert guide.

ECO-TOURS   Although it's fascinating to explore on your own, it would be a shame to only see the Everglades without a clue about what you're seeing. **Everglades Adventures** (see "Canoe Tours," above) can guide and entertain you, as well as explain key issues like the differences between alligators and crocodiles, or between swamps and the Everglades.

MOTORBOAT TOURS   Both Florida Bay and backcountry tours are offered Thursday to Monday at the **Flamingo Marina** (see "Motorboating," above). Florida Bay tours cruise nearby estuaries and sandbars, while six-passenger backcountry boats visit smaller sloughs. Passengers can expect to see birds and a variety of other animals (I once saw a raccoon and some wild pigs). Both cost $33 for adults, $16 for children 5 to 12. Tours depart throughout the day; reservations are recommended. Charter-fishing and sightseeing boats can also be booked through the resort's main reservation number (✆ **239/695-3101**). If you're on the Gulf Coast side of things, there's a naturalist-guided Gulf Coast boat tour of the Ten Thousand Islands out of the **Gulf Coast Marina** (located in the **Gulf Coast Visitor Center,** 5 miles south of Hwy. 41/Tamiami Trail on S.R. 29, in the Everglades City area; ✆ **239/695-2591**) lasting about an hour and a half. There's also a mangrove wilderness tour through the swampier part of the park. Tour prices are the same as the tours at the Flamingo Marina.

TRAM TOURS   At the park's Shark Valley entrance, open-air tram buses take visitors on 2-hour naturalist-led tours that delve 7½ miles into the wilderness and are the best quick introduction you can get to the Everglades. At the trail's midpoint, passengers can disembark and climb a 45-foot-high observation deck with good views of the 'Glades (though the tower on the Pa-hay-okee Trail is better). Visitors will see plenty of wildlife and endless acres of saw grass. Tours run mid-December through April, daily on the hour between 9am and 4pm (reservations recommended), and May through mid-December at 9am, 11am, 2pm, and 4pm. The tours are sometimes stalled by flooding or particularly heavy mosquito infestation. The cost is $22 for adults, $19 over age 61, and $13 for ages 3 to 12. For further information, contact **Shark Valley Tram Tours** (www.SharkValleyTramTours.com; ✆ **305/221-8455**).

BISCAYNE NATIONAL PARK ★

With only about 500,000 visitors each year (mostly boaters and divers), the unusual Biscayne National Park is one of the least crowded parks in the country. Perhaps that's because the park is a little more difficult than most to access—more than 95% of its 181,500 acres is underwater.

The park's significance was first formally acknowledged in 1968 when, in an unprecedented move (and despite intense pressure from developers), President Lyndon B. Johnson signed a bill to conserve the barrier islands off South Florida's east coast as a national monument—a protected status just a rung below national park. After being twice enlarged, once in 1974 and again in 1980, the waters and land surrounding the northernmost coral reef in North America became a full-fledged national park—the largest of its kind in the country.

To be fully appreciated, Biscayne National Park should be thought of as more preserve than destination. Use your time here to explore underwater life, but also to relax. The park's small mainland mangrove shoreline and keys are best explored by boat. Its extensive reef system is great for diving and snorkeling.

The park consists of 44 islands, but only a few are open to visitors. The most popular is **Elliott Key,** which has campsites and a visitor center, plus freshwater showers (cold water only), restrooms, trails, and a buoyed swim area. It's about 9 miles from **Convoy Point,** the park's official headquarters on land. During Columbus Day weekend there's a very popular regatta for which a lively crowd of party people gathers— sometimes in the nude—to celebrate. If you'd prefer to rough it a little more, the 29-acre island known as **Boca Chita Key,** once an exclusive haven for yachters, has now become a popular spot for all manner of boaters. Visitors can camp and tour the island's restored historic buildings, including the county's second-largest lighthouse and a tiny chapel.

Essentials

GETTING THERE & ACCESS POINTS   Convoy Point, the park's mainland entrance, is 9 miles east of Homestead. To reach the park from Miami, take the Florida Turnpike to the Tallahassee Road (SW 137th Ave.) exit. Turn left, then left again at North Canal Drive (SW 328th St.), and follow signs to the park. Another option is to rent a speedboat in Miami and cruise south for about 1½ hours. From U.S. 1, whether you're heading north or south, turn east at North Canal Drive (SW 328th St.). The entrance is about 9 miles away. The rest of the park is accessible only by boat.

Because most of Biscayne National Park is accessible only to boaters, mooring buoys abound, as it is illegal to anchor on coral. When no buoys are available, boaters must anchor on sand or on the docks surrounding the small harbor off Boca Chita. Boats can also dock here overnight for $20. Even the most experienced boaters should carry updated nautical charts of the area, which are available at Convoy Point's Dante Fascell Visitor Center. The waters are often murky, making the abundant reefs and sandbars difficult to detect—and there are more interesting ways to spend a day than waiting for the tide to rise. There's a boat launch at adjacent Homestead Bayfront Park and 66 slips on Elliott Key, available free on a first-come, first-served basis.

Once it's open again, transportation to and from the visitor center to Elliott Key costs $50 (plus tax) round-trip per person and takes about an hour. This is a convenient option, *available only if you have six people to fill a boat,* ensuring that you don't get lost on some deserted island by boating there yourself. If you don't have six people, you can charter the boat to and from the key for $300. Round-trip transportation to and from Boca Chita Key, however, is $50 per person regardless of how many people are going out. Call ⓒ **305/230-1100** for the seasonal schedule.

VISITOR CENTERS & INFORMATION   Open daily from 9am to 5pm, the **Dante Fascell Visitor Center** (often referred to by its older name, Convoy Point Visitor

Center), 9700 SW 328th St., Homestead, at the park's main entrance (www.NPS.gov/bisc; *©* **305/230-1100**), is the natural starting point for any venture into the park without a boat. It provides comprehensive information about the park, and (on request), rangers will show you a short video.

For information on transportation, glass-bottom boat tours, and snorkeling and scuba-diving expeditions, contact the park concessionaire, **Biscayne National Underwater Park, Inc.,** Homestead (www.BiscayneUnderwater.com; *©* **800/979-3370** [ticketing] or 305/230-1100). It's open daily from 9am to 5pm.

ENTRANCE FEES & PERMITS Park entrance is free, but from October through April there's a $20 overnight docking fee at both Boca Chita Key Harbor and Elliott Key Harbor, which includes a campsite. Campsites are $15 for those staying without a boat. Group camping costs $30 a day and covers up to five tents and 30 people. (Fees are waived May through Sept.) See p. 149 for information on fishing permits. Backcountry camping permits are free and can be picked up from the Dante Fascell Visitor Center. For more information on fees/permits, call *©* **305/230-1144, ext. 052.**

Where to Stay

Besides campsites, there are no facilities for overnight guests to this watery park. Most non-camping visitors come for an afternoon, on their way to the Keys, and stay overnight in nearby Homestead (see p. 152 for listings). The good news is that Biscayne National Park boasts some of the state's most pristine **campsites.** Because they're inaccessible by motor vehicle, you'll be sure to avoid the mass of RVs prevalent in many of Florida's other campgrounds. The Elliott Key and Boca Chita sites can be reached only by boat. If you don't have your own, call *©* 305/230-1100 to arrange a drop-off. Transport to Elliott Key from the visitor center costs $50 (plus tax). They don't provide rides to Boca Chita, so you'll have to rent a boat. Boca Chita has only saltwater toilets (no showers or sinks); Elliott Key has freshwater, cold-water showers and toilets, but is otherwise no less primitive. If you didn't pay for the overnight docking fee, campsites are $15.

With a backcountry permit (free at the visitor center) you can pitch your tent somewhere even more private. Ask for a map and bring plenty of bug spray. Sites cost $15 a night for up to six people staying in one or two tents. Backcountry camping is allowed only on Elliott Key, a very popular spot (accessible only by water) for boaters and campers. About 9 miles from the visitor center, it has hiking trails, fresh water, boat slips, showers, and toilets. Don't miss the Old Road, a 7-mile tropical hammock trail running the key's length. It's one of the few places left in the world to see the highly endangered Schaus swallowtail butterfly, recognizable by its black wings with diagonal yellow bands, and usually out from late April to July.

Seeing the Highlights

Because the park is primarily underwater, the only way to truly experience it is with snorkel or scuba gear. Beneath the surface of Biscayne National Park, the aquatic universe pulses with multicolored life: abounding bright parrotfish and angelfish, gently rocking sea fans, and coral labyrinths. (See the "Snorkeling & Scuba Diving" section, below, for more information.) Afterward, take a picnic out to Elliott Key and taste the crisp salt air blowing off the Atlantic. Or head to Boca Chita, an intriguing island that was once the private playground of wealthy yachters.

EVERGLADES & BISCAYNE NAT'L PARKS

Biscayne National Park

Sports & Outdoor Activities

CANOEING & KAYAKING   Biscayne National Park affords excellent canoeing, both along the coast and across the open water to nearby mangroves and artificial islands dotting Florida's longest uninterrupted shoreline. Because tides can be strong, only experienced canoeists should attempt to paddle far from shore. If you do plan to go far, first obtain a tide table from the visitor center and paddle with the current. Free ranger-led canoe tours are scheduled 9am to noon on the second and fourth Saturdays of the month between mid-January and late April; phone for information. You can rent a canoe at the park's concession stand for $16 to $25 for the 90 minutes, and 50% of the initial cost per additional hour. Paddleboats are also available for $30 to $40 for the 90 minutes, and 50% of the initial cost per additional hour. Call © **305/230-1100** for reservations, information, ranger tours, and boat rentals. You can also visit the website of the park's concession at www.BiscayneUnderwater.com.

FISHING   Ocean fishing is excellent year-round at Biscayne National Park; many anglers cast from the breakwater jetty at Convoy Point. A fishing license is required (p. 149). Bait isn't available in the park but is sold in adjacent Homestead Bayfront Park. Stone crabs and Florida lobsters can be found here, but you're allowed to catch these only on the ocean side in season. There are strict limits on size, season, number, and method of take (including spearfishing) for both fresh- and saltwater fishing. The regulations are available at marinas, bait-and-tackle shops, and park's visitor centers; or contact the **Florida Fish and Wildlife Conservation Commission,** Bryant Building, 620 S. Meridian St., Tallahassee, FL 32399-1600 (www.MyFWC.com; © **850/488-4676**). Biscayne National Park offers free "fisheries awareness classes" at Miami's Suniland Park, 12855 S. Dixie Hwy. (www.NPS.gov/bisc/planyourvisit/fisheries-awareness-class.htm; © **305/230-1144, ext. 036**).

HIKING & EXPLORING   As most of this park is underwater, hiking is not the main attraction here, but there are some interesting sights and trails nonetheless. At Convoy Point, you can walk along the 370-foot boardwalk and along the half-mile jetty that serves as a breakwater for the park's harbor. From here, you can usually see brown pelicans, little blue herons, snowy egrets, and a few exotic fish.

Elliott Key is accessible only by boat, but once you're there, you have two good trail options. True to its name, the Loop Trail makes a 1.5-mile circle from the bayside visitor center, through a hardwood hammock and mangroves, to an elevated oceanside boardwalk. You'll likely see land crabs scurrying around the mangrove roots.

Boca Chita Key was once a playground for wealthy tycoons, and still has the peaceful beauty that attracted elite anglers from cold climates. Many of the historic buildings are still intact, including an ornamental lighthouse never put to use. Take advantage of the 3-hour tours, including a boat trip, usually led by a park ranger, every Sunday in winter at 1:30pm. The price is $35 for adults, $25 for seniors, $20 for children 11 and under. But call in advance to see if the sea is calm enough for the trip—the boats won't run in rough waters. See "Snorkeling & Scuba Diving," below, for information about daily trips.

SNORKELING & SCUBA DIVING   The clear, warm waters of Biscayne National Park are packed with colorful tropical fish that swim in the reefs. If you didn't bring your own gear, you can rent or buy snorkeling and scuba gear at the full-service dive shop at Convoy Point. Rates are in line with those at mainland dive shops.

The best way to see the park underwater is via a snorkeling or diving tour operated by **Biscayne National Underwater Park** (www.BiscayneUnderwater.com; (C) **800/979-3370** or 212/209-3370). Snorkeling tours 3 to 4 hours long cost $40 to $55 per person. There are also private two-tank dives for certified divers; the price is $99, including two tanks and weights. Reserve in advance. The shop is open daily 9am to 5pm.

Before entering the water, be sure to apply waterproof sunblock; once you begin to explore, it's easy to lose track of time, and the Florida sun is brutal, even during winter.

SWIMMING   You can swim off the protected beaches of Elliott Key, Boca Chita Key, and adjacent Homestead Bayfront Park, but none matches the width or softness of other South Florida beaches. Check water conditions before heading in: The strong currents that make this a popular destination for windsurfers and sailors can be dangerous even for strong swimmers. Homestead Bayfront Park is really just a marina next to Biscayne National Park, but it does have a beach and picnic facilities, as well as fishing areas and playground. It's located at 9698 N. Canal Dr., Homestead ((C) **305/230-3033**).

THE KEYS & THE DRY TORTUGAS

The drive from Miami to the Keys is a slow descent into an unusual, often breathtaking American ecosystem, some stretches with nothing but emerald waters on either side. (On weekends, however, you'll also see plenty of traffic in front of and behind you.) Strung out across the Atlantic like loose strands of cultured pearls, more than 400 islands make up this 150-mile-long necklace.

Despite the usually calm landscape, these rocky isles can be treacherous, as tropical storms, hurricanes, and tornadoes are always possibilities. The exposed coast poses dangers to those on land as well as at sea.

When Spanish explorers Juan Ponce de León and Antonio de Herrera sailed amid these craggy rocks in 1513, they and their men dubbed the islands "Los Mártires" (The Martyrs) because they thought the rocks looked like men suffering in the surf. It wasn't until the early 1800s that rugged and ambitious pioneers, who amassed fortunes by salvaging cargo from ships sunk nearby, settled the larger islands. (Legend has it that the shipwrecks were sometimes caused by these "wreckers," who removed navigational markers from the shallows to lure unwitting captains aground.) At the height of the salvaging mania in the 1830s, Key West boasted the U.S.'s highest per-capita income.

But wars, fires, hurricanes, mosquitoes, and the Depression took their toll on these resilient islands in the early part of the 20th century, causing wild swings between boom and bust. In 1938, the Overseas Highway (U.S. 1) was finally completed atop the ruins of Henry Flagler's railroad (destroyed by a hurricane in 1935, leaving only bits and pieces still visible today), opening the region to tourists, who had never before been able to drive to this sea-bound destination. These days, the highway connects more than 30 of the populated islands. The hundreds of small, undeveloped ones that surround these "mainline" Keys are known locally as the "backcountry" and are home to dozens of exotic animals and plants. That's where some of the best outdoor sporting opportunities lie, from bonefishing to spearfishing and—at certain times of the year—diving for lobsters and stone crabs. To get to the backcountry, you must take to the water—a must for any visit down here. Whether you fish, snorkel, dive, or cruise, include time on a boat in your itinerary; otherwise you haven't truly experienced the Keys.

While people come down here for the peaceful waters and year-round warmth, the sea and the teeming life beneath and around it are the main attractions. Countless species of brilliantly colored fish can be found swimming above the ocean floor, and you'll also discover a stunning abundance of tropical and exotic plants, birds, and reptiles.

The warm, shallow waters (deeper and rougher on the eastern/Atlantic side) nurture living coral that supports a complex, delicate ecosystem of plants and animals—sponges, anemones, jellyfish, crabs, rays, sharks, turtles, snails, lobsters, and thousands of types of fish. This vibrant underwater habitat thrives on one of the few living tropical reefs on the entire North American continent. As a result, anglers, divers, snorkelers, and water sports enthusiasts of all kinds come to explore.

Heavy traffic has taken its toll on this fragile eco-scape, but conservation efforts are underway (traffic laws are strictly enforced on Deer Key, for example, due to deer crossings that have been contained, thanks to newly installed fences). In fact, environmental efforts in the Keys exceed those in many other high-traffic destinations.

Although the atmosphere all over is that of a laid-back beach town, don't expect many impressive beaches. Nice beaches are mostly found in a few private resorts, though there are some small, sandy strips in John Pennekamp Coral Reef State Park, Bahia Honda State Park, and Key West. One great exception is Sombrero Beach in Marathon (p. 177), well maintained by the county and larger and considerably nicer than other local beaches.

The Keys are divided into three sections. The Upper and Middle Keys are closest to the Florida mainland, so are popular with weekenders who come by boat or car to fish or relax in places like Key Largo, Islamorada, and Marathon. Farther on, just beyond the impressive Seven-Mile Bridge (which actually measures 6½ miles), are the Lower Keys, a small, unspoiled swath of islands teeming with wildlife. It's here in these more protected regions where you're most likely to catch sight of the area's many endangered animals—with patience, you may spot the rare eagle, egret, or Key deer. You should also keep an eye out for alligators, turtles, rabbits, and a huge variety of birds.

Key West, the most renowned—and last—island in the Lower Keys, is the southernmost point in the continental United States (made famous by Ernest Hemingway). Its historic Old Town is the most popular destination in the Keys, overrun with cruise-ship passengers and day-trippers, as well as franchises and T-shirt shops. More than 1.6 million visitors pass through it each year. Still, the self-styled "Conch Republic" has a tightly knit community of permanent residents who cling fiercely to their live-and-let-live attitude—an atmosphere that has made Key West famously popular with painters, writers, and free spirits, despite the influx of money-hungry developers who want to turn Key West into Palm Beach South.

The last section in this chapter is devoted to the Dry Tortugas, a national park located 68 nautical miles from Key West.

THE best KEYS & THE DRY TORTUGAS EXPERIENCES

o **Starting (or Capping) Off Your Keys Trip at Alabama Jack's:** This venerable road house way off the beaten path is a ritual for pre-and post-Keys visitors. With just mediocre food but great water views (keep an eye out for manatees) and a uniquely local atmosphere to a country music soundtrack, Alabama Jack's is a Zac Brown or Jimmy Buffett song come to life, truly of another place and time.

o **Swimming with Dolphins:** The eco-culture and consciousness of the Florida Keys are unparalleled, which is why if you're going to swim with dolphins (everyone should do it at least once in their lives), you'll want to do it here, with trained professionals who respect the animals.

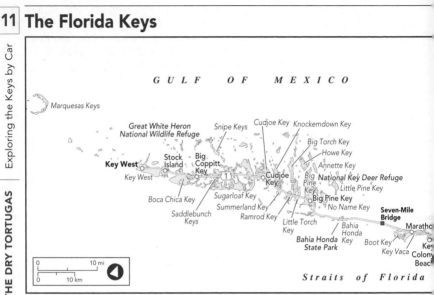

o **Snorkeling in the Looe Key National Marine Sanctuary:** What Key West's Duval Street is to wacky people-watching, Looe Key is to coral-watching. Here you'll see 150 varieties of hard and soft coral—some centuries old—and scores of tropical fish including gold and blue parrotfish, moray eels, barracudas, and French angels.

o **Hiring a Captain at Old Charter Boat Row, Key West:** The kind of captains reality shows are made about are found right here at historic Charter Boat Row, home to more than 30 charter-fishing and party boats. Not only will you get the cruise of a lifetime, but you may end up with a friend for life, too.

o **Happy Hour Anywhere, Anytime:** The song "It's Five O'Clock Somewhere" definitely describes the Keys, where when it comes to boozing, it's 5 o'clock just about all day, any day. Belly up to a bar and order a cocktail or cold one.

EXPLORING THE KEYS BY CAR

After you've left the Florida Turnpike and hit U.S. 1, aka Overseas Highway (see "Getting There" under "Essentials," below), you'll have no trouble negotiating these narrow islands, as only one main road connects the Keys. The scenic, lazy drive from Miami can be even more enjoyable if you have the patience to linger and explore the diverse towns and islands along the way. If you have the time, I recommend allowing at least 2 days to work your way down to Key West, and 3 or more days once there.

Encouraging you to slow down is the 106-mile **Florida Keys Overseas Heritage Trail,** a work in progress that's creating a scenic paved trail for bikers, hikers, runners, fishermen, and sightseers running parallel to the Overseas Highway from Key Largo all the way down to Key West. With more than 70 of the 106 miles completed and 12 miles of trail and five bridges under construction, the rest of the trail is scheduled for completion in 2015 (updated information at www.FloridaStateParks.org/FloridaKeys).

Most of U.S. 1 is a two-lane highway with occasional wider passing zones. The speed limit is usually 55 mph (35–45 mph on Big Pine Key and in some commercial

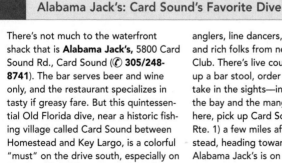

areas). There's been talk of expanding the road, but plans have not been finalized. Even so, you can usually get from downtown Miami to Key Largo in a bit more than an hour. If you're determined to drive straight through to Key West, allow at least 3½ hours. Weekends are another matter: When the roads are jammed with travelers from the mainland, the trip can take up to 5 or 6 hours (when there's an accident, traffic stops cold). Try to avoid driving anywhere in the Keys on Friday afternoon or Sunday evening.

Most addresses in the Keys (except in Key West and parts of Marathon) are delineated by **mile markers** (MM), small green roadside signs that show the distance from Key West. The markers start at no. 127, just south of the Florida mainland. The zero marker is in Key West, at the corner of Whitehead and Fleming streets. Addresses in this chapter are accompanied by a mile marker (MM) designation when appropriate.

Alabama Jack's: Card Sound's Favorite Dive

There's not much to the waterfront shack that is **Alabama Jack's,** 5800 Card Sound Rd., Card Sound (✆ **305/248-8741**). The bar serves beer and wine only, and the restaurant specializes in tasty if greasy fare. But this quintessential Old Florida dive, near a historic fishing village called Card Sound between Homestead and Key Largo, is a colorful "must" on the drive south, especially on Sunday, when bikers mix with barflies,

anglers, line dancers, Southern belles, and rich folks from nearby Ocean Reef Club. There's live country music, so pull up a bar stool, order a cold one, and take in the sights—in the bar and out in the bay and the mangroves. To get here, pick up Card Sound Road (the old Rte. 1) a few miles after you pass Homestead, heading toward Key Largo. Alabama Jack's is on the right side—can't miss it.

THE UPPER & MIDDLE KEYS

58 miles SW of Miami

The Upper Keys are a popular year-round refuge for South Floridians, who take advantage of the islands' proximity to the mainland. This is the fishing and diving capital of America, and the swarms of outfitters and billboards never let you forget it.

Key Largo, once called Rock Harbor but renamed to capitalize on the success of the 1948 Humphrey Bogart film (which wasn't shot here), is the largest Key and is more developed than its neighbors. Dozens of chain hotels, restaurants, and tourist information centers service the water enthusiasts who come to explore the nation's first underwater state park, **John Pennekamp Coral Reef State Park,** and its adjacent marine sanctuary. **Islamorada,** the unofficial capital of the Upper Keys, has the area's best atmosphere, food, fishing, entertainment, and lodging. It's an unofficial "party capital" for mainlanders seeking a quick tropical getaway; on its four islands, nature lovers can enjoy walking trails and historic exploration, while a quieter, less party-hearty experience can be found on other Keys. **Marathon,** smack in the middle, is known as the heart of the Keys and is one of the most populated. But don't judge it by its main drag; to appreciate Marathon you need to go beyond U.S. 1. It's part fishing village, part tourist center, part nature preserve. This area's well developed infrastructure includes resort hotels, a commercial airport, and a highway that expands to four lanes.

Essentials

GETTING THERE From Miami International Airport (there's also an airport in Marathon), take Le Jeune Road (NW 42nd Ave.) to Route 836 West. Follow signs to the Florida Turnpike South about 7 miles. The turnpike extension connects with U.S. 1 in Florida City. Continue south on U.S. 1. For a scenic option, take Card Sound Road, south of Florida City, a backcountry drive that reconnects with U.S. 1 in upper Key Largo. The view from Card Sound Bridge is spectacular and well worth the $1 toll.

If you're coming from Florida's west coast, take Alligator Alley to the Miami exit, then turn south onto the turnpike extension. The turnpike ends in Florida City, at which time you will be dumped directly onto the two-lane U.S. 1, which leads to the Keys. Have around $15 for the tolls. If you take U.S. 1 straight down and bypass the turnpike, it's free, but a lot longer.

Greyhound (www.Greyhound.com; © **800/231-2222** or 305/871-1810) has two buses leaving Miami for Key West daily, with stops in Key Largo, Tavernier, Islamorada, Marathon, Big Pine Key, Cudjoe Key, Sugarloaf, and Big Coppitt on the way south. Prices range from $49 to $54 one-way and $98 to $108 round-trip; the trip takes from 1 hour and 40 minutes to 4 hours and 30 minutes, depending on how far south you're going. Seats fill quickly in season, so come early, as it's first-come, first-served.

VISITOR INFORMATION Make sure you get your information from an official not-for-profit center. The **Key Largo Chamber of Commerce,** U.S. 1 at MM 106, Key Largo (www.KeyLargo.org; © **800/822-1088** or 305/451-1414), runs an excellent facility with plenty of brochures. Headquartered in a handsome clapboard house, it's also an information clearinghouse for all of the Keys and is open daily from 9am to 6pm.

The **Islamorada Chamber of Commerce,** U.S. 1 at MM 87, Islamorada (www. IslamoradaChamber.com; ✆ **800/322-5397** or 305/664-4503), is housed in a little red caboose and offers maps and literature on the Upper Keys.

The rather more modest **Greater Marathon Chamber of Commerce** visitor center (12222 Overseas Hwy.; www.FloridaKeysMarathon.com; ✆ **800/262-7284** or 305/ 743-5417) nonetheless comes through with a good selection of free information on local events, festivals, attractions, dining, and lodging.

Check out the free **Florida Keys app** available for the iPhone, iPod touch, iPad, and Android. It allows access to information on weather, events, venues, and maps, as well as GPS and audio driving tours. Details: www.FloridaKeysApps.com.

Where to Stay

U.S. 1 is lined with chain hotels in all price ranges. In the Upper Keys, the best moderately priced option is the **Courtyard Key Largo,** off U.S. 1 at MM 100, Key Largo (www.marriott.com; ✆ **305/451-3939**), which has a waterfront heated pool, marina with tour boats, boat rentals, and a restaurant and tiki bar, and is just 3 miles from John Pennekamp Coral Reef State Park. Another good Upper Keys option is the actively pet-friendly **Days Inn Islamorada Oceanfront Resort,** U.S. 1 at MM 82.5 (www. DaysInnFlaKeys.com; ✆ **305/664-3681**). In the Middle Keys, Marathon's **Siesta Motel,** U.S. 1 at MM 51 (www.SiestaMotel.net; ✆ **305/743-5671**), offers clean, reasonably priced oceanside rooms. The **Holiday Inn Express & Suites,** 13201 Overseas Hwy., Marathon (www.HolidayInnExpressMarathon.com; ✆ **888/465-4329** or 305/289-0222) is a smoke-free and also pet-friendly hotel featuring free hot breakfast, marina, tiki bar, large outdoor pool, and free Wi-Fi.

EXPENSIVE

Casa Morada ★★★   The closest thing to a boutique hotel in the Florida Keys is the brainchild of a trio of New York women who used to work for hip hotelier Ian Schrager. The 16-suite Casa Morada is tucked off a sleepy lane, radiating serenity and style in an area where serenity abounds, but style not so much (decor is decidedly island, but think Cabo cool rather than Gilligan's). Sitting on 1¾ acres of prime bayfront, it features a limestone grotto, freshwater pool, and poolside drinks service. Each of the cool rooms has either a private garden or a terrace; request the one with the open-air Jacuzzi facing the bay. There's no restaurant, though a breakfast is included daily. Enjoy free use of bikes, paddleboards, snorkel equipment, bocce pitch, and morning yoga.

136 Madeira Rd., Islamorada. www.CasaMorada.com. ✆ **888/881-3030** or 305/664-0044. 16 units. Winter $299–$659; off-season $289–$489. Rates include continental breakfast. From U.S. 1 S., at MM 82.2, turn right onto Madeira Rd., continue to the end of the street. Ages 16 and older only. Pets welcome. **Amenities:** Concierge; complimentary bikes, paddleboards, snorkel equipment; outdoor pool; massage services; free Wi-Fi.

Cheeca Lodge & Spa ★★★   Extensively overhauled in 2009 following a fire, this sprawling, historic resort on 27 lush acres of beachfront offers world-class amenities in a laid-back setting. The standard rooms have West Indies–style decor and marble bathrooms, and 840-square-foot "premier suites" feature floor-to-ceiling windows opening to ocean or island views, as well as open-air tubs for two on roomy balconies. Dining includes **Limoncello** (rustic Mediterranean), **Nikai** (sushi), and the signature restaurant, **Atlantic's Edge,** featuring top-notch seafood, steaks, and organic local produce. **The Spa at Cheeca** features fair-trade products and a raft of treatments (including signature clamshell massage), a fitness room, and butler-serviced poolside cabanas. Besides hanging out at that 1,200-foot beachfront or 2 pools, activities include tennis, bikes, a 9-hole Jack Nicklaus–designed golf course, and pier fishing (included in the resort fee), plus eco-tours, sunset cruises, snorkel excursions, boats with seasoned guides for backcountry fishing, the Camp Cheeca kids' program, and plenty more.

U.S. 1 at MM 82, Islamorada. www.Cheeca.com. ✆ **800/327-2888.** 214 units. In season $429–$929 double, $549–$1,389 suite; off-season $199–$499 double, $249–$1,099 suite. Resort fee $39 per day. **Amenities:** 3 restaurants; 2 lounges (1 poolside); 2 outdoor heated pools; saltwater lagoon; concierge; babysitting; bike rental; kids' nature programs; golf course; tennis; 2 Jacuzzis; room service; full-service spa; fitness center; watersports equipment/rentals; local shuttle service; Wi-Fi (included).

Hawks Cay Resort ★★★

Taking up most of an island in the Middle Keys, this 60-acre spread specializes in families and in activities up the wazoo and down the reef. Besides sailing, fishing, snorkeling, diving, Snuba, waterskiing, kiteboarding, parasailing, and stand-up paddleboarding, guests can interact directly with dolphins in the Dolphin Connection program (reserve well in advance). Rooms have spacious bathrooms, Tommy Bahama–style furniture, and balconies with ocean or garden views; there are also 225 waterfront villas with full kitchens. The 7,000-square-foot spa provides stellar treatments, and kids' activities include marine- and eco-inspired programs. Dining includes the nuevo-Latino **Alma,** with a bar featuring hard-to-find rums; the **Beach Grill,** featuring light fare; **Ocean,** the open-kitchen main restaurant; and **Island Time,** a shop including a Starbucks menu. Just as popular as the pools is a good-size lagoon where families can splash, kayak, and paddleboard.

61 Hawks Cay Blvd., at MM 61, Duck Key. www.HawksCay.com. ✆ **888/395-5539** or 305/743-7000. 432 units, including 242 2- and 3-bedroom villas. Winter $329–$659 double, $549–$1,300 suite, $519–$1,400 villa; off-season $199–$559 double, $479–$900 suite, $449–$1,000 villa (packages available). Daily resort fee $29. **Amenities:** 4 restaurants; lounge; bike rental; children's programs ($40–$75 per child); concierge; exercise room; Jacuzzi; 5 outdoor pools (4 heated); room service; full-service spa; 8 tennis courts (6 hard, 2 clay, 2 lighted); watersports equipment/rentals; Wi-Fi (included).

Jules' Undersea Lodge ★★

Staying here is an experience of a lifetime—if you're up to taking the plunge. Built as a research lab, this underwater habitat, which rests on pillars on the seabed, now operates as a pricey two-room hotel most popular with diving honeymooners. To get inside, guests swim 21 feet under the structure and pop up into the unit through a 4×6-foot "moon pool" that gurgles soothingly day and night. The 30-foot-deep submarine suite consists of two separate bedrooms that share a common living area. Room service will deliver your meals, newspapers, even a late-night pizza in waterproof containers, at no extra charge. If you don't have the time, desire, or budget to overnight, you can hang out in the lodge for 3 hours for $150 per person.

51 Shoreland Dr., Key Largo. www.JUL.com. ✆ **305/451-2353.** 2 units. From $675 per person, depending on package/number of guests. Rates include breakfast and dinner, as well as all equipment and unlimited scuba diving in the lagoon for certified divers. From U.S. 1 S., at MM 103.2, turn left onto Transylvania Ave., across from the Central Plaza shopping mall. **Amenities:** Kitchenette; room service; stereo; DVD player.

Kona Kai Resort, Gallery & Botanic Garden ★★★

This little haven is an exquisite, adults-only property right on Florida Bay, offering stunning sunset views overlooking Everglades National Park. Colorful, comfortable, and modern rooms and suites are nestled in a lush 2-acre botanic garden brimming with tropical vegetation; there's also an orchid house and small tropical fruit garden. Guests are encouraged to take a free 90-minute grounds tour with a staff ethnobotanist. A beachfront pool (heated in winter and cooled in summer), complimentary bottled water and fresh fruit poolside, a Jacuzzi, and one of the largest private beaches on the island make Kona Kai the perfect place for escape and relaxation. A complimentary concierge services organizes eco tours; fishing trips; snorkeling/diving excursions; and parasail, kayak, paddleboard, bicycle, and kiteboard outings. Tennis, beach ping-pong, kayaks, paddleboats, Wi-Fi, CD/DVD libraries, and parking are all included, and there's no resort fee.

U.S. 1 at MM 97.8, Key Largo. www.KonaKaiResort.com. ✆ **800/365-7829** or 305/852-7200. 13 units. Winter $299–$439 double and $369–$1,078 suites; off-season $219–$325 double and $279–$820 suites. Free parking. Ages 16 and older only. **Amenities:** Concierge; Jacuzzi; heated/cooled pool; beach; in-room and on-beach spa treatments; lighted tennis court; shuffleboard; watersports equipment; full kitchen in suites only; no phones in rooms; free Wi-Fi.

The Moorings Village & Spa ★★★ You may never see another soul at this pricey 18-acre resort, a former coconut plantation, if you choose not to (there isn't even maid service unless you ask for it). The whitewashed units, from cozy cottages to three-bedroom houses, come with fully equipped kitchens and rustic-contemporary decor. Most have washers and dryers, and all have CD and DVD players; ask when you book. The real reason to come here is to relax on a beaut of a thousand-foot beach (one of the only real beaches hereabouts). You'll also find a great pool, a hard tennis court, and a few kayaks and sailboards, but no motorized water vehicles. There's also no room service or restaurant, but Morada Bay and Pierre's across the street are excellent. This is a place for people who like each other a lot. And best leave the kids at home unless they're really well behaved and not easily bored.

123 Beach Rd., off U.S. 1 MM 81.5, Islamorada. www.TheMooringsVillage.com. ✆ **305/664-4708.** 18 units. Winter $649–$2,469; off-season $359–$1,725. Resort fee $20 per day. **Amenities:** Concierge; outdoor heated pool; spa; yoga; tennis court; watersports equipment; bikes; Wi-Fi (included).

MODERATE

Conch Key Cottages ★★ Occupying their own private micro-island just off U.S. 1, these romantic, brightly painted cottages just steps from the ocean are a place to get away from it all, exuding what management touts as "bohemian luxury," including Old Florida–style architecture with tin roofs and Dade County pine. The two-bedroom oceanview stilt cottages, the garden-view cottage, and the marina/sunset cottage are the most spacious and well designed, and ideal for families. There are several other cottages, apartments, and villas situated around the pool and property. All units feature full-size kitchens and outdoor grills with all the pots, pans, and utensils you'd need (and the luxe villas, sleeping 10–12, each come with their own pool and spa). There's also free use of kayaks and an unlimited supply of fresh Florida oranges that you can juice right in your own kitchen.

U.S. 1 at MM 62.3, Marathon. www.ConchKeyCottages.com. ✆ **800/330-1577** or 305/289-1377. 15 units. $132–$184 room, $225–$410 cottage. Villas from $4,000 weekly. Minimum stay 2 nights for cottages, 1 week for villas. Rates include continental breakfast. AAA/AARP discount 10%. **Amenities:** Concierge; heated pool; beach; sea kayak; spa services; full kitchen; no phone; free Wi-Fi.

Hilton Key Largo Resort ★★ A great escape for a weekend or longer, ensconced on 13 acres of forest and Gulf shore, and most rooms have water views. There are two pools, one for kids, one for grownups, but I'd recommend you spend most of your time on the private, white-sand beach, where you can do a variety of watersports, stroll nature trails, lounge on chaise-longues, or hang out at the tiki bar. It's all very peaceful and beautiful, which you'd never guess from the somewhat standard-issue facade. There's a restaurant and it's pretty good—but stick to area restaurants or, better yet, bring some snacks and stick them in the in-room fridge; once you lay eyes on the beach here, you may not want to leave for mere food.

97000 Overseas Hwy., Key Largo. www.KeyLargoResort.com. *(C)* **888/871-3437** or 305/852-5553. 200 units. Winter $159–$289 double, $319–$449 suite; off-season $149–$259 double, $249–$379 suite. Dogs welcome up to 60 lbs. ($50 one-time fee). **Amenities:** 3 restaurants; 3 bars; children's activities; Jacuzzi; 2 outdoor heated pools; 2 tennis courts; watersports equipment/rentals; fitness center; marina; massage services; room service; free Wi-Fi.

Lime Tree Bay Resort ★★   Just one of two spots to stay in the tiny town of Layton (pop. as of 2012: 186) sits on a pretty piece of waterfront, midway between Islamorada and Marathon, graced with hundreds of palm trees and tropical foliage. It prides itself on its promise of no hustle, no valets, and no bartenders in Hawaiian shirts. Rooms and efficiencies have smallish bathrooms, but are pleasant and well maintained. The best deal is the two-bedroom bay-view suite, with a spacious living area, a large private deck overlooking the Gulf, full kitchen, and two full baths. Fifteen efficiencies and suites have kitchenettes. Pretty cool in their own right, the new 2-bedroom Hemingway suites have balconies, fantastic views, and luxury appointments, and several units are pet friendly. At press time the restaurant was slated to be closed until late spring 2015.

U.S. 1 at MM 68.5, Long Key. www.LimeTreeBayResort.com. *(C)* **800/723-4519** or 305/664-4740. 56 units. Winter $119–$429; off-season $109–$309. Several pet-friendly units. **Amenities:** Restaurant; Jacuzzi; 2 outdoor pools (1 heated); complimentary sea kayaks; BBQ grills; kitchenette or kitchen in most units; Wi-Fi.

Pines and Palms of Islamorada Resort ★★   Looking for a beachfront cottage or, better yet, oceanfront villa, without blowing half your kid's college fund? Here's the spot, with cheery, cozy one- to three-bedroom cottages, Atlantic views, and a private beachfront with hammocks and a pool, all in a relaxed tropical paradise with friendly, accommodating service. All units have full kitchens and balconies, ideal for extended stays. Although there's no restaurant, the staff will be happy to bring a barbecue to your patio so you can grill out by the beach. There's usually a 2-night weekend minimum.

U.S. 1 at MM 80.4 (ocean side), Islamorada. www.PinesandPalms.com. *(C)* **800/624-0964** or 305/664-4343. 25 units. Year-round $89–$159 1-bedroom; $129–$289 suite; $119–$489 cottage; $399–$589 villa. **Amenities:** Bike/kayak rental; bar; outdoor heated pool; watersports equipment/rentals; kitchen; wine/beer room service; free Wi-Fi.

Postcard Inn Beach Resort & Marina at Holiday Isle ★★★   The famously rough-and-tumble, rum-soaked Holiday Isle got a much-needed major makeover, and today it's mostly whimsical surfer-chic with waterfront rooms awash in white woods and sand-colored stripes, with cute quotes from ocean lovers hand-stenciled on the walls. Around a half-dozen units were left untouched (to satisfy the nostalgia of some guests), along with the "World Famous Tiki Bar," which has an improved sound system but the same funky vibe of yore—and still mixing up hyper-potent Rumrunners that will make you need a room if you don't have one already. There's also an eatery called Shula 2, inspired by legendary Miami Dolphins coach Don, as well as sundry other eating (and of course drinking) venues. The beachfront has been cleaned up and now features lounges and a lawn with Adirondack chairs. The staff? Friendly and helpful as ever.

U.S. 1 at MM 84.5, Islamorada. www.HolidayIsle.com. © **800/327-7070** or 305/664-2321. 143 units. Year-round $199–$899. Daily resort fee $15. Pets welcome up to 45 lbs. (one-time fee $50). **Amenities:** 2 restaurants; 3 bars; 2 outdoor pools; dive shop; watersports equipment/rentals; massage services; charter fishing boats; marina; *Wi-Fi (included)*.

Tranquility Bay Beachfront Hotel & Resort ★★★
On a tropically landscaped dozen Gulfside acres and worlds away from the busy, not-so-lovely Marathon stretch of U.S. 1, you'll feel like you're in your own beach house—literally, because besides the standard guestrooms the stars here are gorgeous two- and three-bedroom conch-style cottages. They also come with everything a tech-savvy beach bum requires, plus spacious porches with French doors, wooden deck chairs, and wide-open water views. The **Butterfly Café** (p. 172) has seasonal seafood menus. There's an onsite watersports center featuring WaveRunner, kayak, paddleboard, and boat rentals, as well as gazebos, a great lawn with putting green, a beachfront tiki bar, and a trio of swimming pools. Activities from adventure fishing to snorkeling and spa services can be arranged through the front desk.

2600 Overseas Hwy., Marathon. www.TranquilityBay.com. © **888/755-7486** or 305/289-0888. 103 units. Winter $199–$399 double, $399–$699 beach house; off-season $149–$249 double, $229–$399 beach house. Resort fee $25 per day. **Amenities:** Restaurant; tiki bar; fitness room; 3 outdoor heated pools; private beach; watersports equipment rentals; putting green; kitchen (in beach house), Wi-Fi (included).

INEXPENSIVE

Ragged Edge Resort ★★
Honestly, I'm not sure where the "ragged" thing comes in, because this oceanfront property's Tahitian-style units are spread along more than a half-dozen gorgeous, grassy waterfront acres. All are immaculately clean and comfy, and most are outfitted with full kitchens and pleasant if not fancy furnishings. There's no bar, restaurant, or even staff, per se, but the retreat's affable owner is happy to lend bicycles and give advice on area offerings. A large dock attracts boaters and a variety of local and migratory birds. An outdoor heated freshwater pool is a bonus for those months when temperatures get a bit cooler.

243 Treasure Harbor Rd., at U.S. 1 MM 86.5, Islamorada. www.Ragged-Edge.com. © **800/436-2023** or 305/852-5389. 11 units. Year-round $69–$159 double; $119–$259 suite/apartment. **Amenities:** Free use of bikes; heated outdoor pool; marina; kitchen (in some); free Wi-Fi.

CAMPING

John Pennekamp Coral Reef State Park ★★
One of Florida's best parks (p. 178), Pennekamp has 47 well-separated campsites, half of which are available by advance reservation. Tent and RV sites are small but equipped with restrooms, hot water, and showers. Note that it can get buggy, especially in late summer, so bring repellent. Two man-made beaches and a small lagoon attract many large wading birds. Reservations are held until 5pm; the park must be notified of late arrival on the check-in date. Pennekamp opens at 8am and closes around sundown.

U.S. 1 at MM 102.5, Key Largo. www.PennekampPark.com. © **305/451-1202.** Camping reservations through Reserve America © **800/326-3521.** 47 campsites. $36 (with electricity) per site, 8 people maximum. Park entry $8 per vehicle with driver (plus 50¢ per person Monroe County surcharge). Annual permits and passes available.

Long Key State Park ★★
The Upper Keys' other main state park is more secluded than its northern neighbor—and more popular. All sites are located ocean-side

and surrounded by narrow rows of trees and nearby restroom facilities. Reserve well in advance, especially in winter.

U.S. 1 at MM 67.5, Long Key. www.FloridaStateParks.org/LongKey. ℰ **305/664-4815** or reservations through Reserve America ℰ **800/326-3521.** 52 sites. $36 per RV or tent site for 1–8 people; $5 per vehicle (plus 50¢ per person Monroe County surcharge).

Where to Eat

Not exactly known as a culinary hot spot (though it's improving), the Upper and Middle Keys do have some very good restaurants, most of which specialize in seafood. Oftentimes visitors (especially those who fish) take advantage of accommodations that have kitchen facilities and cook their own meals. Some restaurants will also clean and cook your catch for a fee.

EXPENSIVE

Butterfly Café ★★ SEAFOOD   The restaurant at the Tranquility Bay resort is one of the Middle Keys' newer gourmet dinner spots, with water views and a marvelous menu of fresh local seafood. Among dishes not to miss: panko-encrusted grouper and grilled pork chops with garlic, lime, and cumin, served with black beans and rice. Service is very friendly and knowledgeable, and desserts are to die for (save room for the sticky toffee pudding or nutty-crust Key lime pie with white-chocolate mousse).

2600 Overseas Hwy., in the Tranquility Bay Resort, Marathon. www.TranquilityBay.com. ℰ **305/289-7177.** Main courses $15–$42. Daily 6–9pm. Reservations recommended.

Green Turtle Inn ★★★ SEAFOOD   This landmark Keys eatery serves cuisine crafted with locally farmed vegetables and micro greens for a fabulous dining experience. Along with a recent expansion and revamp has come a new menu, yet key favorites remain, such as turtle chowder with pepper sherry and luscious conch chowder. But the new eats are also a treat (like the seared tuna with shrimp, sweet-pepper hash, wilted spinach, sweet soy glaze, and wasabi). And don't pass up the bread pudding. There's also a tasty breakfast (coconut French toast!) and lunch (yellowtail po'boy!). After eating, check out the art gallery and gourmet shop. For those craving Asian, the menu at Green Turtle's sister restaurant, **Kaiyo Grill & Sushi,** MM 81.7 (www.KaiyoKeys.com; ℰ **305/664-5556**), is excellent.

81219 Overseas Hwy., at MM 81.2, Islamorada. www.GreenTurtleKeys.com. ℰ **305/664-2006.** Main courses $20–$36. Tue–Wed, Sun 7am–9pm; Thu 7am–1am; Fri–Sat 7am–10pm.

Marker 88 ★★ SEAFOOD   Upper Keys institution Marker 88 has been pleasing locals and visitors since 1967. New chefs and owners recently infused a new life into the premises and the menu, making use of fresh produce, local ingredients, and fish caught in local waters. Among the menu highlights are the crispy yellowtail meunière, sautéed and finished with a Key lime butter; and onion-crusted mahi-mahi in a sauce of butter, white wine, and Key lime juice. The waitresses are pleasant enough but can require a bit of patience. The food, though—not to mention the spectacular Gulf views—is worth it.

88000 Overseas Hwy., at MM 88 (bay side), Islamorada. www.Marker88.info. ℰ **305/852-9315.** Reservations suggested. Main courses $24–$38; burgers and sandwiches $11–$17. Daily 11am–10pm.

Ziggie and Mad Dog's ★★ STEAKHOUSE   When the late onetime Miami Dolphins player and sportscaster Jim Mandich, aka Mad Dog, bought Ziggie's Crab Shack in 2005, he decided to keep the ex-owner's name up there with his own.

Nowadays, people are mad for this casually elegant steak and chop house. It's quite the Upper Keys scene, attracting locals, tourists, and day-trippers looking for something more than a ramshackle fish shack. If you're starving, we dare you to order the 28-ounce Csonka Porterhouse named after Mandich's fellow 'Fins teammate Larry Csonka. Folks also rave about the bone-in rib-eye and the mac and cheese. Service is friendly and the vibe is fun. Sports fans love it here not just because of the games on in the bar, but because many of Mandich's famous jock pals still come here.

83000 Overseas Hwy., MM 83, Islamorada. www.ZiggieandMadDogs.com. © **305/664-3391.** Reservations suggested. Main courses $20–$40. Sun–Thu 5:30–10pm; Fri–Sat 5:30–11pm.

MODERATE

Island Grill ★★ SEAFOOD   If you zip too fast over Snake Creek Bridge, you may miss one of the coolest Keys dining experiences around. On the bay just below the bridge, Island Grill is a local favorite, with an good-size outdoor deck and bar and cozy waterfront dining room serving some fresh fare, including guava barbecued shrimp, graham cracker–crusted calamari, and famous tuna nachos. There are also salads, sandwiches—OMG, that lobster roll—and entrees, including a whole yellowtail snapper with Thai sweet chili sauce that's out of this world. Bring your own catch and they'll cook and prepare it for you—served family-style with veggies and rice for only $12. Live entertainment almost every day brings in a colorful Keys crowd.

MM 85.5 (at Snake Creek Bridge), Islamorada. www.KeysIslandGrill.com. © **305/664-8400.** Main courses $16–$40; sandwiches $7–$14. Sun–Thurs 7am–10pm; Fri–Sat 7am–11pm.

Key Largo Conch House ★★ AMERICAN   A funky, cozy, off-the-beaten-path hot spot for breakfast, lunch, and dinner, Key Largo Conch House is a gingerbread Victorian set amid lush foliage, complete with resident dog, parrot, wraparound veranda for outdoor dining, and a warm and inviting indoor dining room reminiscent of your grandma's. Food is fresh and fabulously priced—from the heaping $15 plate of Mom's Andouille Alfredo to $8 to $14 twists on the usual eggs Benedict, including my favorite, the crab cakes Benedict. Featured on the Food Network, Conch House should be a stop on everyone's trip down to the Keys, if only for a cup of excellent coffee and a slice of homemade Key lime pie. It's also one of the few pet-friendly restaurants in the area.

U.S. 1 at MM 100.2, Key Largo. www.KeyLargoConchHouse.com. © **305/453-4844.** Reservations recommended. Main courses $13–$31; wraps/sandwiches $9–$14; breakfast $7–$15. Daily 8am–10pm.

Lazy Days ★★ SEAFOOD   True to its name, this laid-back oceanfront eatery is the quintessence of the Keys lifestyle; get a table out on the upstairs verandah overlooking the Atlantic or down on the sand right at water's edge. Chef/owner Lupe Ledesma is anything but lazy, though, serving excellent fresh seafood, seafood pastas, vegetarian pastas, sandwiches, steaks, and chicken. He'll even cook your own catch. A popular 4 to 6pm happy hour features three-for-$1 appetizers (at the bar only). Lazy Days is so popular that Lupe and wife Michelle have opened **Lazy Days South,** featuring waterfront seating and the same menu at Marathon Marina (© **305/289-0839**).

79867 Overseas Hwy., MM 80, Islamorada. www.LazyDaysRestaurant.com. © **305/664-5256.** Reservations recommended. Free Wi-Fi. Main courses $15–$28; lighter fare/appetizers $7–$14; sandwiches $10–$15. Sun–Thurs 11am–9:30pm; Fri–Sat 11am–10pm.

Lorelei Restaurant and Cabana Bar ★★ SEAFOOD   Follow the siren call of the enormous roadside mermaid—you won't be dashed onto the rocks. This big ol' fish house and bar with great bay views is a fine spot for a snack, a beer, or breakfast/lunch/dinner. A good-value menu focuses mainly on seafood; in season, lobster is the way to go. Other fare includes the standard clam chowder, fried shrimp, and doughy conch fritters. For those tired of fish, the menu offers a few beef options, but I say the simpler the better. Food is definitely trumped by ambience. The outside bar has live music every evening and a limited menu of snacks and light fare.

U.S. 1 at MM 82, Islamorada. www.LoreleiCabanaBar.com. ☎ **305/664-2692.** Reservations not necessary. Main courses $15–$23; sandwiches $9–$15. Free Wi-Fi. Daily 7am–midnight.

INEXPENSIVE

Islamorada Fish Company ★★ SEAFOOD   Pick up a cooler of stone crab claws in season (mid-Oct to Apr), or try the great fried-fish sandwiches. A few hundred yards up the road (at MM 81.6) is Islamorada Fish Company Restaurant & Market, the newer establishment, which looks like an average diner but has fantastic seafood, pastas, and breakfasts. Locals gather here for politics and gossip as well as grits, oatmeal, omelets, and pastries. Keep your eyes open while dining outside—the last time I was here, baby manatees were floating around, waiting for their close-ups.

81532 Overseas Hwy, MM 81.5, Islamorada. www.IslamoradaFishCo.com. ☎ **305/664-9271.** Reservations not accepted. Main courses $13–$24; sandwiches $10–$16. Daily 11am–10pm.

Snapper's ★★ SEAFOOD   This locals' waterfront favorite serves fresh seafood caught by local fishermen—or by you. The blackened mahi-mahi is exceptional and a bargain, complete with salad, vegetable, and choice of starch. There's also live music nightly and a lively, colorful—and deliciously casual—crowd. A popular Sunday brunch features live jazz from the barge out back and a make-your-own Bloody Mary bar. Kids love feeding the tarpon off the docks, and for those who just can't stay away from work, there's free Wi-Fi, indoors and out. If you caught a big one, clean it and they'll cook it for you at $14 for 8 ounces a person. For an even more casual dining experience, check out the Turtle Club, the entirely outdoor, waterfront bar and grill located out back and featuring live music and a more casual menu of sandwiches, snacks, and pub grub.

U.S. 1 at MM 94.5, Key Largo. www.SnappersKeyLargo.com. ☎ **305/852-5956.** Main courses $22–$29 or market price; sandwiches $9–$16. Mon–Sat 11am–10pm; Sun 10am–10pm.

Exploring the Upper & Middle Keys

Crane Point Museum and Nature Center ★★ NATURE RESERVE   A little-known but worthwhile stop, especially for those interested in the Keys' rich botanical and archaeological history, this private 64-acre nature reserve is considered one of the area's most important historic sites, with probably the last virgin thatch-palm hammock in North America, as well as a rainforest exhibit, an archaeological site with prehistoric Indian and Bahamian artifacts, and the Keys' oldest house outside Key West.

Also headquarters for the Florida Keys Land Trust, the hammock's impressive nature museum has simple, informative displays of local wildlife, including a walk-through replica of a coral-reef cave and life-size dioramas with tropical birds and Key deer. Kids can make art projects, see 6-foot-long iguanas, climb through a scaled-down pirate ship, and touch a variety of indigenous aquatic and land animals.

5550 Overseas Hwy. (MM 50), Marathon. www.CranePoint.net. ☎ **305/743-9100.** Admission $13 adults, $11 ages 66 and over, $8.50 ages 5–13, free ages 4/under. Mon–Sat 9am–5pm; Sun noon–5pm.

Dolphin Research Center ★★ NATURE RESERVE   Of the several such centers in the continental United States, this nonprofit, founded in 1984, is one of the most organized and informative. Although some people argue that training dolphins is cruel and selfish, this is one of the most respected of the institutions that study and protect them. Trainers here will also tell you that the dolphins need stimulation and enjoy human contact. They certainly seem to, nuzzling and kissing the people who get to interact with them in daily programs. The "family" of more than 20 dolphins and sea lions swims in 90,000 square feet of natural saltwater pools set up along the shoreline. If you can't get into an interactive program, you can watch the sessions, which cover topics including fun facts about dolphins, their therapeutic qualities, and research projects in progress. Because the Dolphin Encounter swimming program is the most popular, reservations are required (they can be made months in advance); the cost is $199 per person. If you're not brave enough to swim with them, try the Dolphin Dip program, in which participants stand on a submerged platform from which they can "meet and greet" the critters ($119 per person); the cost to include kids younger than 5 in both programs is $50.

Note: Swimming with dolphins has both its critics and its supporters. For details, visit the Whale and Dolphin Conservation Society's site at **www.WDCS.org**.

58901 Overseas Hwy. (U.S. 1 at MM 59), bay side, Marathon. www.dolphins.org. ✆ **305/289-1121.** Admission $23 adults, $20 U.S. military/veterans, $18 ages 4–12. Daily 9am–4:30pm. Narrated sessions with bottlenose dolphins and sea lions and educational presentations approximately every half-hour.

Florida Keys Wild Bird Center ★★ NATURE RESERVE   Wander through lush stands of mangroves on wooden walkways to get up close and personal with some of the Keys' most famous residents—the large variety of native birds, including broadwing hawks, great blue and white herons, roseate spoonbills, cattle egrets, and lots and lots of pelicans. This nonprofit functions as a hospital for the many birds that have been injured by accident or disease. In 2002 the World Parrot Mission was established here, focusing on caring for parrots and educating the public about them. Visit at feeding time, usually about 3:30pm, when you can watch the dedicated staff feed the hundreds of hungry birds.

U.S. 1 at MM 93.6 (bay side), Tavernier. www.FKWBC.org. ✆ **305/852-4486.** Donations suggested. Daily sunrise–sunset.

Pigeon Key ★★★ HISTORIC SITE   At the curve of the old bridge on Pigeon Key is an intriguing historic site that's been under renovation since 1993. This 5-acre island was the camp for the crew that built the old railway in the early 20th century, then served as housing for the bridge builders. From here the vista includes the vestiges of Henry Flagler's old Seven-Mile Bridge and the one on which traffic presently soars, as well as many old wooden cottages and a tranquil stretch of lush foliage and sea. If you miss the shuttle boat from the Pigeon Key visitor center or would rather walk or bike to the site, it's about 2½ miles. Either way, you might like to bring a picnic to enjoy after a guided tour and a museum visit to what's become an homage to Flagler's railroad, featuring artifacts and photos of the old bridge. An informative 28-minute video of the island's history runs every hour starting at 10am. Parking is available at the Knight's Key end of the bridge, at MM 48, or at the visitor center at MM 47, on the ocean side.

East end of the Seven-Mile Bridge near MM 47, Marathon. www.PigeonKey.net. ✆ **305/743-5999.** Admission $12 adults, $9 ages 5–12. Prices include shuttle boat from the visitor center. Daily 10am–4pm; shuttle tours depart Marathon every 2 hours 10am–2pm; return trips 10:20am–3:45pm.

Robbie's of Islamorada ★★ ATTRACTION   The main attraction at this funky marina on the Lignumvitae Channel is out at the end of one of the piers, where the steely tarpons, a prized catch for backcountry anglers, have been gathering for the past 20 years (you may recognize these prehistoric-looking giants growing up to 200 pounds; many are displayed as trophies on local restaurant walls). Dozens circle the shallow waters waiting for you to feed them. Robbie's also offers ranger-led boat tours and guided kayak tours to Indian Key, where you can go snorkeling or just bask in the natural surroundings. On land, there's a dockside restaurant/bar and some cool local artists/artisans to browse.

U.S. 1 at MM 77.5, Islamorada. www.Robbies.com. (C) **800/979-3370.** Complex entrance free; admission to tarpon dock $1, bucket of fish to feed them $3. Daily 8am–5pm. Make a right U-turn off highway, then it's a short drive before HUNGRY TARPON restaurant. Robbie's entrance is just before the restaurant.

Seven-Mile Bridge ★★ ICON   A stop at this wide, arching span, completed in 1985 at a cost of more than $45 million, is a rewarding and relaxing break on the drive south. Built alongside the ruins of oil magnate Henry Flagler's incredible Overseas Railroad, the "new" bridge (btw. MMs 40 and 47) is considered an architectural feat, its apex the highest point in the Keys. Both it and its now-defunct neighbor provide excellent vantage points from which to view the stunning waters. In the daytime you may want to walk, jog, or bike along the 4-mile stretch of old bridge. Or you may join local anglers, who catch barracuda, yellowtail, and dolphin (the fish, not the mammal) on what is known as "the longest fishing pier in the world." Parking is available on both sides of the bridge.

Btw. MMs 40 and 47 on U.S. 1.

Theater of the Sea ★★ AQUARIUM   Established in 1946, the family-owned Theater of the Sea is one of the world's oldest, continually operated marine mammal parks. The park's dolphin and sea lion shows are entertaining and informative, especially for kids. If you want to swim with dolphins and haven't booked well in advance, you may be able to get in here with just a few hours' notice, as opposed to Marathon's Dolphin Research Center (above). This feels more like a theme park than the DRC; that's not to say the dolphins aren't well cared for, but it's not as professionalized. Still, it's more diverse, and the shows and walking tours to visit various species of reptiles, birds, and fish are both entertaining and educational for all ages. If you want to swim with dolphins, sea lions, nurse sharks, sea turtles, or southern rays, or do one of the other interactive programs, you need to reserve ahead. Except for the dolphin wade, all swimmers must be at least 5 years old to participate (other restrictions apply). There are also twice-daily 4-hour cruises to nearby keys and to snorkel the reef ($69, $45 for ages 3–10), during which you can learn about local history and ecology.

U.S. 1 at MM 84.5, Islamorada. www.TheateroftheSea.com. (C) **305/664-2431.** Admission $32 adults, $22 ages 3–10. Military/senior/AAA online discounts. Animal encounters $65–$185; reservations a must. Daily 10am–5pm (ticket office closes at 3:30pm). Dogs welcome.

The Turtle Hospital ★★ ATTRACTION   Adapted from a former bar and motel on Boot Key, this nonprofit is the world's only state-certified hospital for marine turtles, rescuing and rehabilitating animals that are sick or injured, especially by traumatic contact with humans, such as run-ins with motorboats or monofilament fishing lines. Visitors can take 90-minute tours of the surgical facilities and tanks, including a multimedia presentation on sea turtle conservation. I find it truly a unique, sometimes moving, experience.

2396 Overseas Hwy. (bay side), Marathon. www.TurtleHospital.org. *℃* **305/481-7669.** Reservations recommended. Admission $18, $9 ages 4–12. Daily 9am–6pm. Tours hourly 10am–4pm.

OUTDOOR SIGHTS & ACTIVITIES

Anne's Beach, MM 73.5 (on Lower Matecumbe Key, at the southwest end of Islamorada), is more picnic spot than full-fledged beach, but die-hard tanners congregate on this lovely, tiny strip of coarse sand, heavily damaged by storms in 1998. The place has been spruced up a bit, even the restrooms, which are (for now) clean and usable.

A better choice for real beaching is **Sombrero Beach ★★** in Marathon, at the end of Sombrero Beach Road (near MM 50). This wide swath of uncluttered beachfront actually benefited from Hurricane George in 1998, getting generous deposits of extra sand and a face-lift courtesy of the Monroe County Tourist Development Council. More than 90 feet of sand is dotted with palms, Australian pines, and royal poincianas, as well as grills, clean restrooms, and tiki huts for relaxing in the shade. It's also a popular nesting spot for turtles that lay their eggs at night.

Want to see the Keys in their natural, pre-modern state? You need to leave the highway and take to the water. Two backcountry islands offering a glimpse of the "real" Keys are **Indian Key** and **Lignumvitae Key ★★★**, where folks come to relax and enjoy colorful birds and lush hammocks (elevated pieces of land above a marsh).

Named for the *lignum vitae* ("wood of life") trees found there, Lignumvitae Key supports a virgin tropical forest, the kind that once thrived on most of the Upper Keys. Human settlers imported "exotic" plants and animals, changing the botanical makeup of many backcountry islands and threatening much of the indigenous wildlife. Over the past 25 years, however, the Florida Department of Natural Resources has successfully removed most of this foreign vegetation, leaving the 280-acre site much as it existed in the 18th century. The island also holds the Matheson House, a coral-rock structure built in 1919 which has survived numerous hurricanes. Inside is a museum of the area's history, nature, and topography, but even more interesting are the **Botanical Gardens** which surround the house and are a state preserve. Lignumvitae Key has a visitor center at MM 78.5 (www.FloridaStateParks.org/LignumVitaeKey; *℃* **305/664-2540**).

Indian Key, a much smaller island on the Atlantic side of Islamorada, was occupied for thousands of years before Europeans got here. Amazingly, this 10-acre site was also the original seat of then Dade County before the Civil War. You can see the ruins of the settlement and tour the lush grounds on well-marked trails (off Indian Key Fill, Overseas Hwy., MM 79). Details: www.FloridaStateParks.org/IndianKey; *℃* **305/664-2540.**

If you want to see both islands, plan to spend at least half a day. If you have a boater safety card (you can take a free course online), you can rent your own powerboat from **Robbie's Boat Rentals,** U.S. 1 at MM 77.5 (on the bay side), on Islamorada. It's then a $2.50 admission fee to each island (the guided ranger tour is another $2 per person). I also recommend Robbie's tours to Lignumvitae and Indian keys, costing $47 for adults and $31 for ages 12 and under, including park admission. They leave at 8:30am Friday through Sunday, but only operate November through February or March. Robbie's also does eco-tours, 2-hour trips through passages among the sea-grass beds that rim the many protected shallow bays and among the hundreds of small, uninhabited mangrove and hardwood hammock islands, which host an amazing variety of wildlife. For details, call *℃* **305/664-9814** or visit Robbie's.

TWO EXCEPTIONAL STATE PARKS

One of the best places to discover the diverse ecosystem of the Upper Keys is its most famous park, **John Pennekamp Coral Reef State Park ★★★**, located on U.S. 1 at MM 102.5, in Key Largo (www.PennekampPark.com; ✆ **305/451-6300**). Founded in 1960 and named for a former *Miami Herald* editor and conservationist, the 188-square-mile park was the nation's first undersea preserve, sanctuary for part of the only living coral reef in the continental United States.

Because the water is extremely shallow, the 40 species of coral and more than 650 species of fish here are accessible to divers, snorkelers, and glass-bottom-boat passengers. To experience this park, visitors must get in the water—you can't see the reef from the shore. Your first stop should be the visitor center, which has a mammoth 30,000-gallon saltwater aquarium recreating a reef ecosystem. At the adjacent dive shop, you can rent snorkeling and diving equipment and join one of the boat trips that depart for the reef throughout the day. Visitors can also rent motorboats, sailboats, sailboards, and canoes. The 2½-hour glass-bottom-boat tour is the best way to see the coral reefs if you don't want to get wet. Watch for the lobsters and other sea life residing in the fairly shallow ridge walls beneath the coastal waters. *Remember:* These are protected waters, so you may not remove anything from them.

Canoeing around the park's narrow mangrove channels and tidal creeks is also popular. You can go on your own in a rented canoe or, in winter, sign up for a tour led by a local naturalist. Hikers have two short trails from which to choose: a boardwalk through the mangroves, or a dirt trail through a tropical hardwood hammock. Ranger-led walks are usually scheduled daily from the end of November to April. Call ✆ **305/451-6300** for schedules and reservations.

Park admission is $8 per vehicle of two to eight passengers, $4 for a single driver, and $2 for pedestrians and bicyclists, plus a 50¢ Monroe County surcharge per person. On busy weekends there's often a line of cars waiting to get in. On your way in, ask the ranger for a map. Glass-bottom-boat tours cost $24 for adults and $17 for ages 11 and younger; they depart three times daily, at 9:15am, 12:15pm, and 3:15pm. Snorkeling tours are $30 for adults and $25 for ages 17 and younger ($39 for an extended tour). Canoes rent for $20 per hour; kayaks are $12 per hour for a single, $17 per hour for a double. For experienced boaters only, four different sizes of powerboats rent for $160 to $259 for 4 hours and $210 to $359 for a full day (deposit required, depending on boat size); the boat-rental office is open daily 8am to 5pm (last rental at 3pm). Phone for tour and dive times. Reservations are recommended. Also see below for more options on diving, fishing, and snorkeling off these reefs.

Long Key State Recreation Area ★★★, U.S. 1 at MM 67.5, Long Key (www. FloridaStateParks.org/LongKey; ✆ **305/664-4815**), is one of the best places in the Middle Keys for hiking, camping, snorkeling, and canoeing. This 965-acre site is situated atop the remains of an ancient coral reef. At the entrance gate, ask for a free flyer describing the local trails and wildlife.

Three nature trails can be explored on foot or by canoe. Golden Orb Trail is a 40-minute walk through mostly plants; Layton Trail is a 15-minute walk along the bay; and Long Key Canoe Trail glides along a shallow-water lagoon. The excellent 1½-mile canoe trail is short and sweet, allowing visitors to loop around the mangroves in about an hour. Long Key is also a great spot to stop for a picnic en route to Key West. Campsites are available along the Atlantic. The swimming and saltwater fishing (license required) are top-notch, as is the snorkeling, which is shallow and also on the Atlantic shoreline. For novices, educational programs on the aforementioned are available, too.

Railroad builder Henry Flagler created the Long Key Fishing Club here in 1906, and the waters surrounding the park are still popular with game fishers. In summer, sea turtles lumber onto the protected coast to lay their eggs. Educational programs are available to view this amazing phenomenon.

Hours are daily 8am to sunset, and admission is $4 to $5 per car, $2 per pedestrian or bicyclist, plus a 50¢ per-person county surcharge. You can rent canoes at the trail head for about $5 per hour, $10 each additional hour. The nearest place to rent snorkel equipment is the **Postcard Inn at Holiday Isle,** 84001 Overseas Hwy., Islamorada (www.HolidayIsle.com; *©* **305/664-2321**). Camping is popular, and a project completed in July 2012 upgraded the park's campsites; the cost is $36 per night.

WATERSPORTS

There are hundreds of outfitters in the Keys who will arrange all kinds of water activities, from cave dives to parasailing. If those recommended below are booked up or unreachable, ask the local chamber of commerce for a list of qualified members.

BOATING   Besides the state parks' rental shops, you'll find dozens of outfitters along U.S. 1 renting runabouts and skiffs to boaters of any experience level. **Captain Pip's,** 1410 Overseas Hwy., Marathon (www.captainpips.com; *©* **800/707-1692** or 305/743-4403), charges $195 to $330 per day. Lodging is available and includes discounted boat rental: $190 to $430 in season, $120 to $325 off-season; weekly rates 20% off. Rooms are Key West–comfortable and charming, with ceiling fans, tile floors, and pine paneling. **Robbie's Boat Rentals,** U.S. 1 at MM 77.5, Islamorada (www.Robbies.com; *©* **305/664-9814**), rents 18- to 21-foot motorboats with engines of 90 to 130 horsepower. Rentals cost $135 to $185 for a half-day and $185 to $235 for a full day.

CANOEING & KAYAKING   I can think of no better way to explore the uninhabited backcountry on the Gulf side of the Keys than by kayak or canoe, because you can reach places that bigger boats can't get to. Manatees will sometimes cuddle up to the boats, thinking them to be another friendly species.

Many area hotels rent kayaks and canoes to guests, and so do companies such as **Florida Bay Outfitters,** U.S. 1 at MM 104, Key Largo (www.KayakFloridaKeys.com; *©* **305/451-3018**), whose canoes and sea kayaks for use in and around John Pennekamp Coral Reef State Park run $40 to $55 for a half-day, $50 to $75 for a full day. **The Kayak Shack,** U.S. 1 at MM 77, Islamorada (www.KayaktheFloridaKeys.com; *©* **305/664-4878**), at Robbie's, offers backcountry tours, historic-site tours of Indian Key, and sunset tours through the mangrove tunnels and saltwater flats. Tours are $45; kayak rentals range from $20 to $28 per hour to $50 to $55 per day.

Big Pine Key's **Reflections Nature Tours** (www.FloridaKeysKayakTours.com; *©* **305/872-7474**) specializes in kayak tours through the Lower Keys. Per-person rates for guided excursions are $50 for 3 hours, for a 2-hour full-moon tour; $125 for a 4-hour custom tour with mother ship transport of kayaks and paddlers (all by appointment only). Rental of a single kayak costs $25 for 2 hours, $45 for a day, and $60 for a tandem.

Nature lovers can slip through the silent backcountry waters off Key West and the Lower Keys in a kayak, exploring flora and fauna that make up the unique Keys ecosystem, on **Blue Planet Kayak Tours'** (www.Blue-Planet-Kayak.com; *©* **305/294-8087**) tours led by environmental scientists lasting 2½ to 3 hours. No previous kayaking experience is necessary, and the cost is $50 per person.

FISHING **Robbie's Party Boats & Charters,** U.S. 1 at MM 77.5, Islamorada (www.Robbies.com; ✆ **305/664-8070**), located at Robbie's marina on Lower Matecumbe Key, operates day and night deep-sea and reef-fishing trips aboard a 65-foot party boat. Big-game fishing charters are also available, and "splits" are arranged for solo anglers. Party-boat fishing costs about $40 for a 4-hour tour ($5 for rod-and-reel rental). A full-day charter runs around $1,100 (usually split among a group, of course).

Bud n' Mary's Marina, U.S. 1 at MM 79.8, Islamorada (www.BudnMarys.com; ✆ **800/742-7945** or 305/664-2461), one of the biggest marinas between Miami and Key West, is packed with sailors offering backcountry charters—just the place if you want to stalk tarpon, bonefish, and snapper. If the seas aren't too rough, deep-sea and coral fishing trips can also be arranged. Backcountry charters start at $450 for a half-day, $650 for a full day; reef and offshore from $650 for a half-day, $850 for a full day.

JET-SKIING Based at a timeshare complex called The Hammocks, **Jerry's Watersports and Rentals,** U.S. 1 at MM 48, Marathon (www.JerrysWatersports.com; ✆ **800/775-2646** or 305/289-7298) offers WaveRunner rentals at $95 an hour and 2-hour guided tours for $190 (in both cases, for one or two riders).

SCUBA DIVING & SNORKELING Just 6 miles off Key Largo, a U.S. Navy Landing Ship Dock is the latest artificial wreck site to hit the Keys—or, better put, to be submerged 130 feet below them.

Florida Keys Dive Center, U.S. 1 at MM 90.5, Tavernier (www.FloridaKeys DiveCtr.com; ✆ **800/433-8946** or 305/852-4599), takes snorkelers and divers to the reefs of John Pennekamp Coral Reef State Park and environs every day. PADI (Professional Association of Diving Instructors) training courses are available for the uninitiated. Tours leave at 8am and 12:30pm; the per-person cost is $38 to snorkel (plus $10 for mask, snorkel, and fin rental), and $65 to dive (plus an extra $19 if you need to rent all the gear. Add $10 to that $19 if you're going on a major "heavy metal" dive to sites such as *Spiegel Grove,* a landing ship dock that was sunk to create an artificial reef).

At **Hall's Dive Center & Career Institute,** U.S. 1 at MM 48, Marathon (www. HallsDiving.com; ✆ **800/331-4255** or 305/743-5929), snorkelers and divers can dive at Looe Key, Sombrero Reef, Delta Shoal, Content Key, or Coffins Patch. Tours are scheduled daily at 9am and 1pm. You'll spend an hour at each of two sites per tour. It costs $40 per person to snorkel, $35 for children, and $55 to $65 per person (weights included) to dive; tanks rent for $8.50 to $12 each, masks $5, snorkels $4, fins $5.

ORGANIZED TOURS

Key Largo Bike and Adventure Tours (www.KeyLargoBike.com; ✆ **305/395-1551**) provides guided tours like the Islamorada Historical Tour, a 2-hour ride with 10 stops ($45 with bike rental, $35 without). It also runs one- and two-night excursions to Key West ($200/$400) for cyclists used to riding along the road, starting in Key Largo and ending at the southernmost point in the continental United States. Participants can choose to explore Key West for the afternoon or spend the night for an additional charge.

Entertainment & Nightlife

Nightlife in the Upper Keys tends to start before the sun goes down, often at noon, as most people—visitors and locals alike—are on vacation. Not to mention the fact that many anglers and sports-minded folk go to bed on the early side.

Hog Heaven, 85361 Overseas Hwy., just off the main road on the ocean side south of Snake Creek Bridge in Islamorada (www.HogHeavenSportsBar.com; ✆ **305/664-9669**), opened in the early 1990s, a joint venture of young locals tired of tourist traps. This whitewashed indoor/outdoor biker bar is a welcome respite from the neon-colored cocktail circuit, with a waterside view and diversions such as big-screen TVs and video games. The food isn't bad, either. The atmosphere can be cliquish because it's mostly locals, so start up a game of pool to break the ice. It's open daily from 11am to 4am.

No trip to the Keys is complete without a stop at the **Tiki Bar at the Postcard Inn Beach Resort & Marina at Holiday Isle,** U.S. 1 at MM 84, Islamorada (www. HolidayIsle.com/TikiBar; ✆ **305/664-2321**). This palapa-roofed classic starts pulling in the thirsty daily from noon onward (11am on weekends), but the live rock starts at 8pm and goes until around 1am. In the afternoon and early evening (when everyone is either sunburned, drunk, or just happy to be grooving to reggae), head for the 21-and-over version of Swiss Family Robinson meets the Florida Keys at **Rum Runner's,** also at Holiday Isle and open daily until midnight.

Locals and visitors mingle at the outdoor cabana bar at **Lorelei** (see "Where to Eat," p. 173). Most evenings after 5pm you'll find local bands playing on a thatched-roof stage—mainly rock or reggae, sometimes blues.

Or try the stained-glass and mahogany-wood bar and club at **Zane Grey Long Key Lounge,** on the second floor of World Wide Sportsman, MM 81.5 (✆ **305/664-9271**). Outside, enjoy a view of the calm waters of the bay; inside, soak up the history of real longtime anglers. It's open daily from 11am to 10pm. Call to find out who's playing on Friday and Saturday nights, when there's live entertainment and no cover.

THE LOWER KEYS

128 miles SW of Miami

Unlike their neighbors to the north and south, the Lower Keys (including **Big Pine, Sugarloaf,** and **Summerland**) are devoid of rowdy spring-break crowds, have few T-shirt and trinket shops, and almost no late-night bars. What they do offer are the best opportunities to enjoy the vast natural resources on land and water that make this region so rich and unique. Stay overnight in the Lower Keys, rent a boat, and explore the reefs—it might be the most memorable part of your trip.

Essentials

GETTING THERE See "Essentials" for the Upper and Middle Keys (p. 166) and continue south on U.S. 1. The Lower Keys start at the end of the Seven-Mile Bridge. There are also airports in Marathon and Key West.

VISITOR INFORMATION The **Big Pine and Lower Keys Chamber of Commerce,** ocean side of U.S. 1 at MM 31, Big Pine Key (www.LowerKeysChamber.com; ✆ **800/872-3722** or 305/872-2411), is open Monday through Friday from 9am to 5pm, and Saturday from 9am to 3pm. The pleasant staff will help with anything a traveler may need. Call, write, or stop in for a comprehensive, detailed information packet.

Where to Stay

There are a number of cheap, fairly unappealing fishing shacks along the highway for those who want bare-bones accommodations. So far there are no national hotel chains in the Lower Keys. For information on lodging in cabins or trailers at local campgrounds, see "Camping," below.

EXPENSIVE

Little Palm Island Resort & Spa ★★★   This exclusive offshore escape—host to presidents and royalty—is a destination unto itself. On a private 5½-acre island accessible only by boat or seaplane, guests stay in thatched-roof bungalows amid lush foliage and flowering tropical plants—and Key deer, which are to this island what cats are to Key West (on my last visit, while having dinner I watched them swim right onto the beach). Many bungalows have ocean views and private decks with hammocks. Inside, the romantic suites sport all the comforts of a swank beach cottage, but without phones, TVs, or alarm clocks. Mosquitoes can be a nuisance, even in winter. (Bring spray and lightweight, long-sleeve clothing.) Known for a stellar spa and innovative (and of course pricey) cuisine, Little Palm also hosts visitors just for meals. If you're a guest, opt for the full American plan, which includes three squares a day.

U.S. 1 at MM 28.5, Little Torch Key. www.LittlePalmIsland.com. ℂ **800/343-8567** or 305/872-2524. 30 units. Winter $990–$2,590 double; off season $790–$1,390 double. Rates include transportation to and from the island and unlimited watersports (non-motorized). Meal plans 3 meals daily for $195 per person per day. Ages 16 and older only. **Amenities:** Restaurant; pool; bar; concierge; fitness center; limited room service; spa; watersports equipment; fitness center; no phone; free Wi-Fi.

INEXPENSIVE

Parmer's Resort ★★   A fixture for more than a quarter century and member of Florida's Green Lodging program, Parmer's is known for its charming hospitality, helpful staff, and modest but comfortable cottages, each of them unique. Some are waterfront, many have kitchenettes, and others are just a bedroom. The "Wahoo" room, a one-bedroom efficiency, is especially nice, with a small sitting area facing the water. All units have been updated, are very clean, and many can be combined to accommodate families. The waterfront location, not to mention the fact that it's only a half-hour from Key West, almost makes up for the fact that you have to pay extra for maid service.

565 Barry Ave, off U.S. 1 MM 28.5, Little Torch Key. www.ParmersResort.com. ℂ **305/872-2157.** 45 units. From $139 double; from $184 efficiency; from $333 cottage. Rates include continental break-fast. From U.S. 1, turn right onto Barry Ave. Resort is ½ mile down on the right. **Amenities:** Out-door heated pool; mini golf; bocce pitch; barbecue grills; boat slips; kitchenettes/kitchens in some; free Wi-Fi.

CAMPING

Bahia Honda State Park ★★ (www.FloridaStateParks.org/BahiaHonda/default.cfm; ℂ **305/872-2353**) offers some of the best camping in the Keys, and it's as loaded with facilities and activities as it is with campers. But don't be discouraged by its popular-ity—this park encompasses more than 500 acres of land, 78 campsites spread across three areas, and six spacious, comfortable cabins. Cabins hold four to six guests and come complete with linens, kitchenettes, wraparound terraces, barbecue pits, and rock-ing chairs. For up to four people, camping costs about $36 per site. Cabin rates are $120 in low season and $160 in high season.

Another great value can be found at the **KOA Sugarloaf Key Resort ★★**, near U.S. 1, MM 20 (www.KeyWestKoa.com; ℂ **800/562-7731** or 305/745-3549). This 5-acre ocean-side spread has some 200 fully equipped sites with water, electricity, and sewer, renting for $89 to $103 a night in season, $80 to $98 in summer (no-hookup sites cost $64–$69 year round). You can also stay in one of five shiny Airstream trailers sleeping up to four for $154 a night. This place is especially nice because of its private beaches and access to diving, snorkeling, and boating; its grounds are well maintained, and it offers amenities including a pool and bike rentals. It's also quite pet-friendly, with a dog park and everything.

Where to Eat

For upscale dining, there's little in the Lower Keys except for the pricy **Dining Room at Little Palm Island ★★★**, MM 28.5, Little Torch Key (www.LittlePalmIsland.com/The-Dining-Room.aspx; ✆ **305/872-2551**), which will wow you with gourmet French Caribbean fare that looks like a meal but tastes like a vacation. You need to take a ferry to this chichi private island, where you can eat at the ocean-side restaurant (and right on the beach) even if you're not staying (last time I was here I saw Key deer swimming right up onto the beach). Let me stress again that dining here is not for the faint of wallet; dinner will easily run $150 per person. Reservations are, of course, required.

MODERATE

Mangrove Mama's Restaurant ★★ SEAFOOD/CARIBBEAN   As the locals who come daily for happy hour will tell you, this is a Lower Keys institution and a dive in the best sense of the word (it's a converted gas station). Diners (outside, anyway) share the joint with stray cats and some miniature horses out back. It's run-down, but in a charming Keys sort of way (hey, they serve beer in jelly glasses), and a handful of tables, inside and out, are shaded by banana palm trees. Fish is a mainstay, though soups, salads, sandwiches (try the lobster Reuben), and omelets are also good, as are meatless chef's salads and spicy barbecued baby back ribs. Sunday brunch especially rocks, with amazing Benedicts, and there's great live music every night.

U.S. 1 at MM 20, Sugarloaf Key. www.MangroveMamasRestaurant.com. ✆ **305/745-3030.** Sandwiches $10–$15; main courses $13–$30; lunch $10–$14; brunch $5–$15. Daily 8am–10pm.

INEXPENSIVE

Coco's Kitchen ★★ CUBAN   This storefront has been dishing out black beans, rice, and shredded beef since 1969, specializing in rib-sticking Cuban and Keys fare, with stars including fried shrimp, whole fried yellowtail, and Cuban-style roast pork (special on Saturday only). Top off the hearty meal with a rich, caramel-soaked *flan* and a cup of Cuban coffee strong enough to grow hair on your chest (and maybe even a few places you wouldn't have thought possible).

283 Key Deer Blvd., Big Pine Shopping Center, near MM 30.5, Big Pine Key. www.CocosKitchen.com. ✆ **305/872-4495.** Sandwiches $4–$7; main courses $10–$18; breakfast $3–$9; lunch $4–$7. Daily 7am–2pm & 4:30–7pm.

No Name Pub ★ PUB FARE/PIZZA   Founded as a general store and bait-and-tackle shop in 1931, this funky, hard-to-find honky tonk out in the boondocks (tagline: "You Found It") is affable indeed, but not up late (it closes at 10pm). Pizzas are tasty— try one topped with local shrimp—or consider a bowl of chili with all the fixings. One of the Keys' oldest bars, blanketed with thousands of signed dollar bills, this rustic dive remains very much a locals' hangout for drinking beer and listening to a jukebox heavy with 1980s tunes.

¼ mile south of No Name Bridge at 30813 Watson Blvd., Big Pine Key. www.NoNamePub.com. ✆ **305/872-9115.** Pizzas $6–$18; subs $5–$9. Daily 11am–10pm. Turn right at Big Pine's only traffic light (near MM 30.5) onto Key Deer Blvd. Turn right on Watson Blvd. At the stop sign, turn left. Look for a small wooden sign on the left marking the spot.

Exploring the Lower Keys

Once the centerpiece (these days, it's Big Pine Key) of the Lower Keys and still one of its gems, **Bahia Honda State Park** ★★★, U.S. 1 at MM 37, Big Pine Key (www. BahiaHondaPark.com or www.FloridaStateParks.org/BahiaHonda/default.cfm; ℂ **305/ 872-3210**), can boast one of South Florida's loveliest coastlines. The 524-acre park (whose name is pronounced "*bay*-ya" and Honda like the car) covers a wide variety of ecosystems, including coastal mangroves, beach dunes, and tropical hammocks, and is splendid for hiking, birding, swimming, snorkeling, and fishing. There are miles of trails packed with unusual plants and animals, plus several white-sand beaches, among the Lower Keys' best. Shaded seaside picnic areas are equipped with tables and grills.

True to its name (Spanish for "deep bay"), the park has relatively deep waters close to shore—perfect for diving and for easy snorkeling that gives even novices a chance to hang suspended in warm water and simply observe all sorts of marine life swim by. Or else head to the stunning reefs at Looe Key, where the coral and fish are more vibrant than anywhere else in the U.S. Snorkeling trips leave from the Bahia Honda concessions to Looe Key National Marine Sanctuary (4 miles offshore), departing twice daily (9:30am and 1:30pm; $30 adults, $25 ages 6–17, $8 for equipment rental); reserve online or at ℂ **305/872-3210.** Other activities include biking, fishing, kayaking, hiking trails, scuba diving, geocaching, and guided tours.

Entry to the park is $8 per vehicle of two to eight passengers, $4 for a single driver, $2 per pedestrian or bicyclist, and free for children 5 and under, with a 50¢-per-person Monroe County surcharge. It's open daily from 8am to sunset.

The most famous residents of the Lower Keys are the tiny, federally protected Key deer. Of the estimated 300 in the world, two-thirds live in Big Pine Key's 84,000-acre **National Key Deer Refuge** ★, 28950 Watson Blvd. (www.FWS.gov/NationalKey Deer; ℂ **305/872-2239**). To get your bearings, stop by the rangers' office at the Big Pine Key Plaza, near MM 30.5 off U.S. 1, for an informative brochure and map of the area. Visitors can come into the refuge at any time, but the visitor center is open Monday through Friday from 8am to 4pm (depending on staffing, though, it can stay open later as well as on weekends, so it's worth calling ahead to find out).

You can also check out the **Blue Hole,** a former quarry now filled with the fresh water vital to the deer's survival. To get there, turn right at Big Pine Key's only traffic light at Key Deer Boulevard (take the left fork immediately after the turn) and continue 1½ miles to the observation-site parking lot, on your left. The half-mile **Watson Hammock Trail,** about ⅓ mile past the Blue Hole, is the refuge's only marked footpath. The deer are more active in cool hours, so try coming out in early morning or late evening to catch a glimpse of these gentle dog-size creatures; there's an observation deck from which you can watch and photograph them. Refuge lands are open daily from a half-hour before sunrise to a half-hour after sunset. Don't be surprised to see a lazy alligator warming itself in the sun, particularly in outlying areas around the Blue Hole. If you do see a gator, do not touch it or even go near it; if you must get a photo, use a zoom lens. Also, whatever you do, do not feed the deer—it will threaten their survival. Call the **park office** to find out about the infrequent free tours scheduled throughout the year.

OUTDOOR ACTIVITIES

BIKING   The Lower Keys are a great place to get off busy U.S. 1 to explore the beautiful back roads. On Big Pine Key, cruise along Key Deer Boulevard (at MM 30).

Those with fat tires can ride into the National Key Deer Refuge. Many lodgings offer bike rentals.

BIRDWATCHING A stopping point for migratory birds on the Eastern Flyway, the Lower Keys are populated with many West Indian species, especially in spring and fall. The small, vegetated islands of the Keys are the only nesting sites in the U.S. for the white-crowned pigeon. They're also some of the few breeding places for the reddish egret, roseate spoonbill, mangrove cuckoo, and black-whiskered vireo. Look for them on Bahia Honda Key and the many uninhabited islands nearby.

BOATING Dozens of shops rent powerboats for fishing and reef exploring. Most also rent tackle, sell bait, and have charter captains available. **Florida Keys Boat Rental** (www.KeysBoat.com; © **305/664-2203**) offers an impressive selection from $125 to $450 for a half-day and $105 to $650 for a full day. It also offers kayaks and paddleboats.

CANOEING & KAYAKING Overseas Highway (U.S. 1) touches on just a few dozen of the many hundreds of islands that make up the Keys. To really see the Lower Keys, rent a kayak or canoe—perfect for these shallow waters. **Reflections Kayak Nature Tours,** operating out of the Old Wooden Bridge Fishing Camp, 1791 Bogie Dr., MM 30, Big Pine Key (www.FloridaKeysKayakTours.com; © **305/872-7474**), offers fully outfitted backcountry wildlife tours, either on your own or with the expert, Coast-Guard–licensed Captain Bill Keogh, who wrote the book on the subject, *The Florida Keys Paddling Guide* (Countryman Press), covering all the unique ecosystems and inhabitants, as well as favorite routes from Key Biscayne to the Dry Tortugas. Three-hour tours cost $50 per person; a 4-hour backcountry tour for two to six people costs $125 per person and uses a mother ship to ferry kayaks and paddlers to the remote reaches of the refuge. Reservations are required.

FISHING A day spent fishing, in the shallow backcountry or in the deep sea, is a fine way to ensure a fresh-fish dinner, or you can release your catch and just relish the challenge. Whatever your pleasure, **Strike Zone Charters,** U.S. 1 at MM 29.5, Big Pine Key (www.StrikeZoneCharter.com; © **305/872-9863**), is the charter service to call. Prices for fishing boats start at $575 for a half-day; $700 for 6 hours; $850 for a full day; a $50 fuel surcharge may be added. If you have enough anglers to split the cost (up to 6 people), it isn't too steep; the outfitter may also be able to match you with other interested visitors. Strike Zone also offers daily trips to Looe Key National Marine Sanctuary on a glass-bottom boat. The half-day trip costs $28 for viewing, $38 for snorkeling, and $48 for scuba diving, all with a $3-per-person fuel charge. Strike Zone's 5-hour **Eco Island** excursion offers a vivid history of the Keys from the glass-bottom boat. The tour stops for snorkeling and light tackle fishing, and docks at an island for an island fish cookout. The cost is $59 per person plus an additional $3 fuel surcharge, including mask, snorkel, fins, vests, rods, reel, bait, fishing licenses, food, and soft drinks.

HIKING You can hike throughout the flat, marshy Keys on both marked trails and meandering coastlines. The best places to trek through nature are **Bahia Honda State Park,** at MM 29.5, and **National Key Deer Refuge,** at MM 30. Bahia Honda has a free brochure describing an excellent self-guided tour along the Silver Palm Nature Trail. You'll traverse hammocks, mangroves, and sand dunes, and cross a lagoon. The walk (less than a mile) explores a great cross section of the natural habitat in the Lower Keys and can be done in less than half an hour.

SNORKELING & SCUBA DIVING Snorkelers and divers should not miss the Keys' most dramatic reefs at the **Looe Key National Marine Sanctuary.** Here you'll see more than 150 varieties of hard and soft coral—some centuries old—as well as every type of tropical fish, including gold and blue parrotfish, moray eels, barracudas, French angels, and tarpon. **Looe Key Dive Center** (Looe Key Reef Resort & Center), U.S. 1 at MM 27.5, Ramrod Key (www.DiveFlaKeys.com; ✆ 305/872-2215), offers an awesome 5-hour tour aboard a 45-foot catamaran with two shallow 1-hour dives for snorkelers and scuba divers. Snorkeling costs $44; divers pay $69, equipment included. You can also do a fascinating dive at the *Adolphus Busch,* a shipwreck off Looe Key in 100 feet of water, for $50 ($80 for 2 divers, $20 per additional diver up 'til 6).

Entertainment & Nightlife

Although the mellow Lower Keys aren't exactly known for rootin'-tootin' nightlife, there are some friendly bars and restaurants where both locals and visitors head for a night out. **No Name Pub** (p. 183) is of course one of the best, but there are also the bar scene at **Looe Key Marina** (see above) and **Springer's Bar & Grill,** MM 31, Big Pine Key (www.SpringersBar.com; ✆ 305/872-3022). Then of course there's **Hogfish Bar & Grill,** 6810, Stock Island (www.HogfishBar.com; ✆ 305/293-4041), at a marina on the last key before Key West. It features a thatched roof; good, seafood-heavy menu; and quite the collection of local characters.

KEY WEST ★★★

159 miles SW of Miami

Key West is the land of the eternal vacation. It seems the sun is always shining here, making the island a perfect destination for sunbathers, fishermen, divers, and motorcyclists. Munch on fresh seafood, watch the jugglers in Mallory Square, and have another margarita.

Things to Do The preferred activity in Key West is relaxing. Visitors inclined toward more active pursuits head to the docks, where divers explore submarine reefs, and anglers head off from **Garrison Bight Marina** in hopes of landing sailfish and tarpon in the azure waters of the Gulf of Mexico.

Shopping You might start to think the main island souvenir is a tacky T-shirt. But if you can make it past the crude, occasionally lewd stuff, you'll discover a nice supply of swimsuits, strappy sandals, sunglasses, and hand-rolled cigars along Duval Street.

Nightlife & Entertainment When the sun begins to sink, sunset celebration goes into full swing in **Mallory Square.** Magicians, jugglers, and one-man bands do their thing for the crowds each evening as the sun tints the sky and waves with orange and purple. After dark, do the **Duval Street** bar crawl. Favorite spots include Sloppy Joe's, an old Hemingway haunt, the Green Parrot, and Hog's Breath Saloon ("Better than no breath at all," they quip).

Restaurants & Dining "New Town," through which you pass when arriving on the island, has all the fast-food chains and many budget options, while Old Town ranges from budget to fine dining on a par with any in the world. And of course it goes without saying that this is the place to sample anything involving pink shrimp (aka "pinks" and Key lime).

Essentials

GETTING THERE For directions by car, see "Essentials" (p. 166) for the Upper and Middle keys, and continue south on U.S. 1. When entering Key West, stay in the far-right lane onto North Roosevelt Boulevard, which becomes Truman Avenue in Old Town. Continue for a few blocks and you'll find yourself on **Duval Street ★★**, in the heart of the city. If you stay to the left, you'll also reach the city center after passing the airport and the remnants of historic houseboat row, where a motley collection of boats once made up one of Key West's most interesting neighborhoods.

Several regional airlines fly nonstop (about 55 min.) from Miami to Key West. **American Eagle** (✆ 800/433-7300), **Delta/Express Jet** (✆ 800/221-1212), Silver Airways (✆ 800/229-9990), and **US Airways Express** (✆ 800/428-4322) land at **Key West International Airport,** 3491 S. Roosevelt Blvd. (www.KeyWestInternational Airport.com; ✆ 305/296-5439), on the island's southeast corner.

Greyhound (www.Greyhound.com; ✆ 800/231-2222) has buses leaving Miami for Key West every day. Prices range from $49 to $54 one-way and $98 to $108 round-trip. Seats fill up in season, so come early. The ride takes about 4½ hours.

You can also get to Key West from Ft. Myers or Marco Island via the **Key West Express** (www.SeaKeyWest.com; ✆ 888/539-2628 or 239/463-5733), catamarans 140 to 170 feet long that get you there in about 3½ hours with air-conditioned cabins, sun decks, observation decks, satellite TV, and full galley and bar. Prices range from $20 to $86 one-way and $40 to $147 round-trip per person.

GETTING AROUND Old Town Key West has limited parking, narrow streets, and sometimes congested traffic, so driving can be more of a pain than a convenience. Unless you're staying in one of the more remote accommodations, consider trading in your car for a bicycle. The island is small and flat as a board, which makes it easy to negotiate, especially away from the crowded downtown. Many tourists choose to cruise by moped, but this can be risky, especially because there are no helmet laws in Key West. Hundreds are injured each year, so be careful and spend the extra few bucks to rent a helmet.

Rates for simple one-speed cruisers start at about $10 per day. Scooters start at about $20 for 2 hours, $35 per day, and $109 per week. Top choices include **A&M Scooter and Bicycle Center,** 523 Truman Ave. and 513 South St. (www.AMScootersKeyWest. com; ✆ 305/896-1921); the **Moped Hospital,** 601 Truman Ave. (www.MopedHospital.com; ✆ 866/296-1625); and **Tropical Bicycles & Scooter Rentals,** 1300 Duval St. (www.TropicalRentaCar.com; ✆ 305/294-8136). **The Bike Shop,** 1110 Truman Ave. (www.TheBikeShopKeyWest.com; ✆ 305/294-1073), rents cruisers for $12 per day, $60 weekly.

PARKING Parking in Key West's Old Town is limited, but there's a **municipal lot** at Grinnell and Caroline Streets ($2 per hour, $13 daily maximum). If you've brought a car, you may want to stash it here while you enjoy the very walkable downtown part of Key West.

VISITOR INFORMATION The **Key West Chamber of Commerce,** 510 Greene St. (www.KeyWestChamber.org; ✆ 800/527-8539 or 305/294-2587), provides both general and specialized information. Walk-ins and phone enquiries are attended to weekdays from 8am to 6pm and weekend 9am to 6pm. Gay travelers may want to contact the **Key West Business Guild** (www.KWBGOnline.org; ✆ 305/294-4603),

Key West

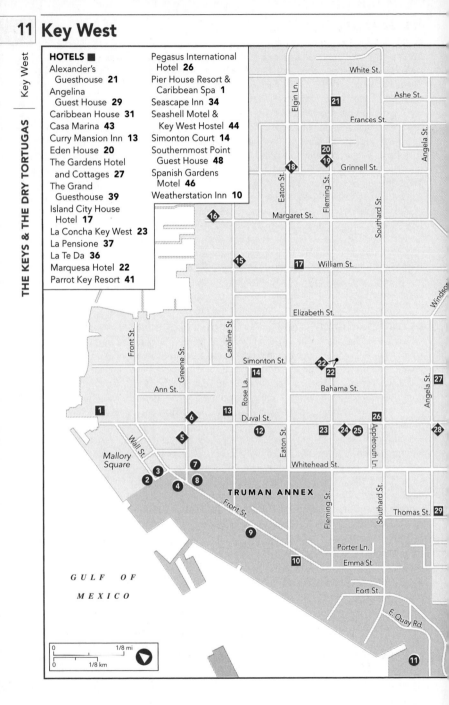

HOTELS ■

Alexander's
  Guesthouse **21**
Angelina
  Guest House **29**
Caribbean House **31**
Casa Marina **43**
Curry Mansion Inn **13**
Eden House **20**
The Gardens Hotel
  and Cottages **27**
The Grand
  Guesthouse **39**
Island City House
  Hotel **17**
La Concha Key West **23**
La Pensione **37**
La Te Da **36**
Marquesa Hotel **22**
Parrot Key Resort **41**

Pegasus International
  Hotel **26**
Pier House Resort &
  Caribbean Spa **1**
Seascape Inn **34**
Seashell Motel &
  Key West Hostel **44**
Simonton Court **14**
Southernmost Point
  Guest House **48**
Spanish Gardens
  Motel **46**
Weatherstation Inn **10**

RESTAURANTS ◆

Amigos Tortilla Bar **5**
Azur **19**
Blue Heaven **30**
Café Marquesa **22**
El Siboney **38**
Louie's Backyard **45**
Mangoes **28**
Margaritaville **24**
Paseo Caribbean Restaurant **18**
Pepe's **15**
Sloppy Joe's **6**
Square One **35**
Turtle Kraals Restaurant and Bar **16**

Key West Cemetery **40**

Truman Ave.

Virginia St.

Grinnell St.

Olivia St.

Packer St.

Margaret St.

Royal St.

William St.

Amelia St.

Catherine St.

United St.

South St.

Washington St.

Von Phister St.

Flagler Ave.

Johnson St.

Reynolds St.

William St.

Flagler Ave.

Alberta St.

Vernon St.

Simonton St.

Louisa St.

United St.

South St.

Truman Ave.

Duval St.

Virginia St.

Whitehead St.

Petronia St.

Olivia St.

Julia St.

Thomas St.

ATLANTIC

OCEAN

BAHAMA VILLAGE

Howe St.

Amelia St.

Emma St.

Fort St.

DeKalb Ave.

**HARRY S. TRUMAN
U.S. NAVAL RESERVATION**

ATTRACTIONS ●

Audubon House & Tropical Gardens **7**
Custom House Museum **4**
East Martello Museum and Gallery **42**
Ernest Hemingway Home & Museum **32**
Florida Keys Eco-Discovery Center **11**
Harry S. Truman Little White House **9**
Key West Aquarium **2**

Key West Butterfly & Nature Conservatory **47**
Key West Cemetery **40**
Key West Lighthouse & Keeper's Quarters Museum **33**
Key West's Shipwreck Treasure Museum **3**
Mel Fisher Maritime Heritage Museum **8**
Oldest House Museum & Garden **12**
San Carlos Institute **25**

with a visitor center at 513 Truman Avenue, which represents more than 50 gay-owned or gay-friendly guesthouses and other businesses.

Check out the **Key West Map and Walks** app from the iTunes and Google store, with a great overview and more than 40 sites, including some art galleries and nightlife; the "light" version is free, full version $5. Or try the **Key West Historic Marker Tour** (© **305/393-9777**), free at www.KeyWestHistoricMarkerTour.org, with more than 50 sites, from former cigar factories and the home of philosopher John Dewey to Key West's oldest house and the southernmost house in the continental U.S.

ORIENTATION A mere 2×4-mile island, Key West is easy to navigate, even though there's no real order to the arrangement of streets and avenues. As you enter town on U.S. 1 (Roosevelt Blvd.), you'll find yourself driving past most of the moderate chain hotels and fast-food restaurants. Many of the better restaurants and shops are crammed onto Duval Street, the main thoroughfare of Key West's Old Town. On surrounding streets, various inns are set in picturesque Victorian/Bahamian homes. On the southern side of the island are the coral-beach area and some of the larger resort hotels.

The part of town called Bahama Village is very much not a tourist trap; it's a hippie-ish neighborhood, complete with street-roaming chickens and cats. It's also what passes for "rough" and "urban" hereabouts, and can seem slightly dicey at night if you aren't familiar with the area. But though you might see a few drug deals on street corners, they're nothing to get your knickers in a twist about: Business owners keep an eye out, but honestly, the area feels a little worse than it is. I actually find it kind of funky (in a good way) and a welcome diversion from the sometimes crazy, sometimes cheesy vibe over on much of Duval. And in fact, Bahama Village now even sports some trendy restaurants, shops, and guesthouses, so that's a very good sign indeed.

Where to Stay

You'll find a wide variety of places to stay in Key West, from resorts with all the amenities and quaint bed-and-breakfasts to clothing-optional guesthouses and plain motels. You can usually find a place to stay at the last minute, except during the most popular holidays: Fantasy Fest (around Halloween), when Mardi Gras meets South Florida for the NC-17 set and most hotels have outrageous rates and 5-night minimums; Hemingway Days (in July), when Papa is seemingly and eerily alive and well; and Christmas and New Year's—or for a big fishing tournament (many are held Oct–Dec) or a boat-racing tourney. However, you may want to book early, especially in winter, when prime properties fill up, many require 2- or 3-night minimum stays, and prices skyrocket, with a decent room for less than $200 a night all but impossible.

I'd recommend trying **Vacation Key West** (www.VacationKW.com; © **800/595-5397** or 305/295-9500), a wholesaler that offers discounts of 20% to 30% and is skilled at finding last-minute deals. It represents mostly larger hotels and motels, but can also place visitors in guesthouses. Phones are answered weekdays 9am to 6pm or 7pm and Saturdays 11am to 4pm. The **Key West Innkeepers Association** (www.KeyWestInns.com; © **800/492-1911**) can also help you find lodging in any price range from among its more than 60 members and affiliates.

For LGBT travelers, a couple of properties are mentioned below, as well as lodging at **Island House** and attached to **Bourbon Street Pub** (p. 212), but you may also want to check with the **Key West Business Guild** (www.GayKeyWestFL.com; © **305/294-4603**), which represents more than 50 guesthouses and B&Bs in town, as well as many other gay-owned businesses.

EXPENSIVE

Casa Marina ★★★ This pedigreed grande dame resort was conceived by Henry Flagler, the magnate whose railroad first opened up the island (and much else in Florida) to unprecedented commerce and well-heeled tourism, but finished only after his death. Its fortunes have waxed and waned since the doors first opened in 1920, but in 2007 the property underwent an overhaul that, beyond the cosmetic, also put in place many eco-friendly improvements such as recycling systems and more efficient energy use. These days, as an AAA Four-Diamond property under Hilton's Waldorf Astoria flag, it's a great choice for couples and especially families looking for a touch of class along with plenty of activities, upscale amenities, and extras (such as an on-staff sand sculptor). Its unique crowning glory is its 1,100 feet of sandy beachfront. Rooms, meanwhile, are cool, earth-toned and contemporary in feel, with tropical touches such as rattan couches.

1500 Reynolds St. (at Johnson St.). www.CasaMarinaResort.com. ✆ **866/397-6342** or 305/296-3535. 311 units. Winter $249–$499 double, $349–$899 suite; off-season $179–$359 double, $309–$699 suite. Resort fee $25/day. **Amenities:** Restaurant; bar; bike/scooter rental; concierge; fitness center; 2 pools; room service; spa services; watersports equipment/rentals; valet parking ($30/night); pets accepted ($75/day); Wi-Fi (included).

Curry Mansion Inn ★★★ Back in the day, Bahamian immigrant William Curry became Key West's first millionaire via the shady business of shipwreck salvaging, and used some of the boodle to start this big white pile just a half-block from Duval Street in 1869 (his son finally finished it 30 years later). Besides rich maple and Tiffany glass, the woody interior is crammed with museum-quality antiques and curios, and the architecture and furnishings are documented in a fascinating brochure meant for guests and random sightseers alike (if you want to check out the widow's walk way up top, just keep in mind that those widows must've been both skinny and spry). Upstairs, out back, and in a separate house across the street, the guest rooms have all the expected mod-cons but are of course much less "busy," with hardwood or tiled floors, canopy beds, white wicker, or combinations thereof. There's a sweet little pool and patio out back that hosts regular cocktail hours and music. The roster of interesting repeat guests skews a bit mature but of varying ages. Noise sensitive? Ask for a room facing away from Duval.

511 Caroline St. (btw. Duval and Simonton sts.). www.CurryMansion.com. ✆ **800/253-3466** or 305/294-5349. 28 units. Winter $240–$315 double, $330–$345 suite; off-season $205–$270 double, $285–$295 suite. Rates include breakfast buffet. Small pets at no charge. Free onsite parking. **Amenities:** Dining room; bike rental; concierge; pool; Jacuzzi; laundry facilities; free Wi-Fi.

The Gardens Hotel and Cottages ★★★ "Oasis of tranquility just steps away from the Duval Street hubbub" describes any number of small hostelries in Old Town, but truly a star among them is this lush spread, once Key West's largest private estate–cum–botanical garden, created in the 1930s from an 1880s manse, opened to the public in 1968, and an inn since the 1990s. Surrounding two pools and poolside bar in the center of it all are not only a clutch of Bahamian-style buildings housing 21 tropically elegant rooms, suites, and cottages with hardwood floors and handsome four-poster beds, but those eponymous lush, mazelike gardens with brick walkways; bubbling fountains; funky sculptures; a gazebo; a big fancy birdcage; and several huge, antique clay jars from Cuba called *tinajones*. Since 2004, innkeeper Kate Miano has polished this gem to a high gloss with friendly, personalized service and a handful of imaginative innovations such as Sunday afternoon jazz concerts and the "d'vine Wine

Gallery," a fancy automat allowing folks to sample a variety of interesting international vintages by the partial and full glass (both, by the way, are also open to the general public). Great expanded breakfast service, too (sticky thumbs-up to that luscious Key lime French toast).

526 Angela St. (at Simonton St.). www.GardensHotel.com. ✆ **800/526-2664** or 305/294-2661. 21 units. Winter $305–$450 double, $445–$675 suite/cottage; off-season $165–$275 double, $275–$370 suite/cottage. Rates include expanded continental breakfast. Ages 16 and older only. Onsite parking ($20/night). **Amenities:** Bar; 2 pools, self-serve wine bar; free Wi-Fi.

Island City House Hotel ★★ Another charmer of a variation on the Key West theme of historic architecture and a fetching heated pool set amid palmy verdant gardens. Behind a striking, balustraded, triple-decker facade, Island City House also brings a particular distinction to the table: It's the island's oldest still-operating guesthouse, established in 1912 from a merchant's home built in 1880 (if you're looking for period decor, the original building is the place, with hardwood floors, lace curtains, wainscoting, four-posters, and antiques). Two adjacent, also historic buildings were added and now house half of the units, which lean toward a more contemporary flavor; some, for example, with white pickled-wood paneling, others with a more Tommy Bahama/rattan vibe. It's also great for folks who want to do a little cooking, as all have full kitchens. Here kitties are part of the scenery, and currently four of them, with names like Blackie and Mr. Toes, get fed through a cute cat-shaped hole next to reception.

411 William St. (btw. Eaton and Fleming Sts). www.IslandCityHouse.com. ✆ **800/634-8230** or 305/294-5702. 24 units. Winter $230–$420 double; off-season $150–$300 double. **Amenities:** Bike rental; concierge; access to nearby health club; outdoor heated pool; kitchen; coffee/tea and light snacks daily; free Wi-Fi.

La Concha Key West ★★ Key West's tallest building (a whopping 6 stories) and one of its original hotel classics from way back (1926), this pale yellow-stucco landmark astride upper Duval Street has long depended on the kindness of both a loyal clientele and history made by the likes of Ernest Hemingway (who wrote it into *To Have and Have Not*) and Tennessee Williams (who penned *A Streetcar Named Desire* here). Now part of the Crowne Plaza brand, the La Concha has managed to keep up with the times fairly nicely while both preserving key elements of its historic flair. Room decor is updated retro with louvered shutters; there's a new rooftop spa whose treatment rooms have the best view in town; and a good restaurant called Jack's Seafood Shack (Florida snapper meunière a top catch), but in a location like this, of course all of Duval Street dining—both highbrow and low—is at your feet. If you want to sleep better at night, ask for a room in back.

430 Duval St. (at Fleming St.). www.LaConchaKeyWest.com. ✆ **305/296-2991.** 160 units. Winter $249–$299 double, suites $349–$399; off-season $239–$289 double, $339–$389 suite. Valet parking ($20/day). **Amenities:** Restaurant; bar; coffee shop; pool; concierge; gift shop; spa; meeting space; room service; weekday local newspaper; free Wi-Fi.

Marquesa Hotel ★★★ Back in 1986, Carol Whiteman transformed a lovely pair of 1880s clapboards into a four-building complex that today houses a pair of Key West's most cozy, fetching, and pricey small hotels and restaurants (see **Café Marquesa**, p. 199) that are close to, yet apart from, Duval Street's bustle. Rooms are good-sized, appointed with a tasteful mix of the antique and the contemporary, and more often than not have porches for enjoying room-service breakfast, a glass of wine, or just some veg-out time. They're arranged around a pair of pools (one heated) and lovely landscaping (love the hanging orchids), but apart from the elegance and blessed tranquility, what takes the experience to the next level is the low-key but friendly and attentive service from staff. One caveat: Those with mobility issues should mention that when booking, because there are no ramps or elevators.

600 Fleming St. (at Simonton St.). www.Marquesa.com. © **800/869-4631** or 305/292-1919. 27 units. Winter $345–$395 double, $495–$510 suite; off-season $210–$290 double, $300–$400 suite. Ages 14 and older only. **Amenities:** Restaurant; bike rental; concierge; access to nearby health club; 2 outdoor pools (1 heated); computer room; room service breakfast; free Wi-Fi.

Pier House Resort & Caribbean Spa ★★ It's fair to say that no hostelry is more "front and center" hereabouts than this former pineapple factory, which helped put Key West on the map as a vacation destination upon opening in 1968, provided a hangout for the likes of Truman Capote, and helped launch careers like those of treasure hunter Mel Fisher, chef Norman van Aken, Bob Marley, and Parrothead-in-Chief Jimmy Buffett. Besides location, it offers good service and 6 acres' worth of bells and whistles including a sweet little beach and the island's largest, most comprehensive spa. Last refurbed in 2008, rooms come in various flavors, but tend toward a low-key, traditional style (for more contemporary and opulent, go for the spa rooms); most also sport balconies or patios. All that plus the fairly friendly, social vibe seems to engender a good degree of loyalty both among repeat visitors and management; one recent general manager, for example, was on the job for 20 years. New ownership and management, already big local players, thankfully haven't messed with the formula that's made Pier House a veteran favorite.

1 Duval St. (near Mallory Sq.). www.PierHouse.com. © **800/723-2791** or 305/296-4600. 142 units. Winter $309–$569 double, $509–$3,000 suite; off-season $249–$449 double, $409–$2,000 suite. Onsite parking ($20/day). **Amenities:** 2 restaurants; 2 bars; babysitting; bike rental; concierge; fitness center; Jacuzzi; heated pool; room service; steam room; spa; watersports equipment/rentals; free Wi-Fi.

Simonton Court ★★ Behind the unassuming, palm-hidden facade of a onetime cigar factory is a lushly landscaped little world unto itself: 11 converted Bahamian-style houses and cottages dating from the 1880s. Though all have the usual modern amenities, units vary quite a bit, from the rustic-feeling cigar-factory rooms, paneled in Dade County pine, to suites with a more contemporary, Asian-inflected flavor. Most also sport travel mementos of and artwork by Simonton Court's owner since the 1980s, Kentucky-born Sue Clay Moloney (Like that watercolor? Have they got a deal for you). A handful of narrow "shotgun" cottages, near the entrance, were once occupied by cigar-factory workers that have been converted to luxe loft duplexes complete with rockers and swings on front porches. The two corners of the main pool are fragments of the brick walls of the water cistern that once stood on the very spot. Atmosphere like this, plus the friendly, helpful staff, keep regulars coming back, and also mean it can be tough to score a reservation—especially in season.

320 Simonton St. (btw. Eaton and Caroline sts.). www.SimontonCourt.com. © **800/944-2687** or 305/294-6386. 30 units. Winter $275–$375 double in mansion, $500–$620 cottage, $275–$425 inn, $330–$475 manor house, $330–$425 town house; off-season $175–$240 double in mansion, $395–$435 cottage, $175–$295 inn, $240–$350 manor house, $210–$295 town house. Rates include continental breakfast. Ages 18 and older only. Onsite parking ($25/night). **Amenities:** Concierge; 4 outdoor pools; Friday wine tasting; some units have kitchens and Jacuzzi tubs; free Wi-Fi.

Weatherstation Inn ★★ Weather can be a big deal in the Gulf of Mexico, which is why the U.S. Navy built this two-story, neoclassical-style storm-tracking station in

1912. By the 1990s, it had been transformed into a bed-and-breakfast of just eight genteel rooms (though weather balloons are occasionally still launched from the roof). I'd have to say that because of its unusual history and small size, as well as unique location—on a very peaceful residential block of the former Navy base, yet a short, no-sweat stroll to Mallory Square and Duval Street—this is one inn that's definitely for a very particular type of vacationer. There are no gregarious cocktail hours by the pool or extensive gardens; here the allure is intimacy and tranquility, and innkeeper Barbara Church plays hostess outstandingly. One nifty little twist on the "breakfast" part: instead of being served in a common area, it's delivered to your door in a cute little basket, so you can take it poolside or anywhere else you want. The inn is trickier to find than the address might indicate, but Barbara will send you detailed directions.

57 Front St. (in Truman Annex). www.WeatherStationInn.com. © **800/815-2707** or 305/294-7277. 8 units. Winter $235–$355 double; off-season $180–$245 double. Rates include continental breakfast. Ages 15 and older only. Free onsite parking. **Amenities:** Concierge; outdoor pool; free Wi-Fi.

MODERATE

Alexander's Guesthouse ★★
Key West has long ranked among the world's top destinations for gay and lesbian vacationers. It's still up there, but changing times, demographics, and trends have taken their toll, and while you'll still see prominent gay nightspots, celebrations, and drag queens on Duval Street, LGBT guesthouses have shrunk from dozens to a small handful, of which the premier example is Alexander's. A stalwart for more than 30 years, it's housed in a pair of old clapboard houses on a quiet stretch of Fleming Street, a 15-minute stroll from Duval. And now, under owners Raul Diaz and Orlando Torres, it's snazzier than ever in looks (bright, clean, and contemporary) and service (friendly and attentive from attractive staffers). There's a pool and hot tub out back, plus a couple of clothing-optional decks. Another factor in Alexander's perseverance has no doubt been that it also welcomes open-minded straight folks—many, one manager told me, from Europe, booking here because "they want to meet 'the new Americans, the progressive thinkers.'" For anyone with cat allergies, Hercules and Junior are sweethearts but they also are, indeed, kitties.

1118 Fleming St. (btw. Frances and White sts.). www.AlexandersKeyWest.com. © **800/654-9919** or 305/294-9919. 17 units. Winter $220–$415 double, $495–$515 apartment; off-season $200–$310 double, $395–$415 apartment; $30 per additional person. Rates include expanded continental breakfast. LGBT mixed; non-gay also welcome. **Amenities:** Outdoor pool; Jacuzzi; complimentary daily happy hour; clothing-optional sundecks; computer terminal; free Wi-Fi.

Eden House ★★
Owner and quirky Key West character Mike Eden bought the half-century-old Gibson Hotel in 1975 and turned it into Eden House. Today it's one of those places that engender such loyalty and repeat business that on my last visit a front-desk staffer, once a frequent guest, had just 4 months earlier left her life in Illinois to come work here. While it's a great example of a typical KW tropical hideaway—pool, hot tub, hammocks, and sundecks amid lush landscaping—the secret sauce has to be the alchemy from a mix of guests from twentysomethings to seniors, plus friendly, helpful staff such as Ryan and Randy, who more often than not reflect the owner's no-nonsense, often irreverent sensibility; it's on full display during the daily afternoon happy hour. Another plus is an impressive variety of quarters—from shared-bath "budget" doubles to an entire floor of a house, sleeping up to five—all with low-key island touches such as wood paneling, slate floors, plus a glass-brick wall here and a stained-glass window there. At attached restaurant **Azur,** guests get a 20% discount off breakfast and lunch.

1015 Fleming St. (btw. Grinnell and Frances Sts). www.EdenHouse.com. ✆ **800/533-5397** or 305/296-6868. 40 units. Winter $235–$400 double, $400–$425 apartment, $475–$495 conch house single floor; off-season $150–$290 double, $295–$330 apartment, $310–$340 conch house single floor. Limited free onsite parking. **Amenities:** Restaurant; heated outdoor pool; Jacuzzi; shop; passes to local gym; afternoon happy hour; massage services; fridge in some rooms; free Wi-Fi in common areas.

The Grand Guesthouse ★★   Built in the 1880s as a boarding house for workers at a nearby cigar factory, this guesthouse is tucked away on a quiet residential street a half-dozen blocks away from Duval. It's also an easy several-block stroll from Higgs Beach—especially helpful because there's no pool. Apart from some nice landscaping and a hammock out back, on-premises bells and whistles are at a minimum, but the ten rooms are clean, comfy, and tasteful and come with all the expected mod-cons. A definite plus is the friendliness and attentiveness of manager Derek Karevicius and his staff, not to mention Jim Brown and Jeffrey Daubman, owners since 1998. The hominess quotient is further enhanced by Snuggles the 4-pound Chihuahua (aka "Snuggles the Mighty").

1116 Grinnell St. (btw. Virginia and Catherine sts.). www.GrandKeyWest.com. ✆ **888/947-2630** or 305/294-0590. 10 units. Winter $198–$238 double, $238–$278 suite; off-season $128–$158 double, $158–$198 suite. Rates include expanded continental breakfast. Limited free parking. **Amenities:** Bike rental; concierge; kitchenette (in suites), free Wi-Fi.

La Pensione ★★   Four blocks from Duval Street along Truman Avenue (which also happens to be the last stretch of 2,369-mile interstate U.S. 1), this quaint, low-key bed-and-breakfast occupies a handsome yellow-and-white Classic Revival manse built in 1891 by a bigwig in Key West's once powerful cigar-making industry. Restored in the early 1990s, it's been owned for the past 18 years by Monica Wiemer and Jamie Rodriguez. It's unpretentious and casual, with friendly, attentive staff and a mix of period-style furnishings, rattan, florals, and "Tommy-Bahama tropical." The rectangular pool out back is great—and clothing-optional. A couple of caveats: You won't find some in-room amenities many of us have come to expect, such as a TV. Truman is Old Town's other main street, and while not hustling and bustling like Duval, traffic's certainly heavier than on side streets, so if noise is an issue, request a non-front-facing room. Even given all that, if you're looking for affordability, La Pensione is a pleasant pick indeed.

809 Truman Ave. (btw. Windsor and Margaret sts.). www.LaPensione.com. ✆ **800/893-1193** or 305/292-9923. 9 units. Winter $168–$278 double; off-season $168–$188 double. Rates include breakfast. Discount 10% for AARP, AAA. Ages 21 and older only. **Amenities:** Bike rental; outdoor pool; free Wi-Fi.

La Te Da ★★   The name of this Duval Street institution isn't high-falutin' insouciance. It's sort of short for La Terraza de Martí ("Martí's Terrace"), named after the upper front porch, from which Cuba's most revered independence hero speechified to drum up support from local Cubans—cigar makers, workers, and others—in 1891 to 1892. I wonder what Martí would make of the fact that today that floor houses a cabaret (p. 136) specializing in drag shows? The hotel has 15 rooms in either wicker/rattan or a British colonial motif split among three buildings, along with a creative open-air restaurant and popular bar located between the recently renovated pool and the street; an engaging staff; and a sometimes entertaining cast of Key West characters. There's also live music in the lobby bar nightly during high and shoulder seasons and on weekends in low season. If noise is an issue, ask for a room back behind the pool.

1125 Duval St. (btw. Amelia and Catherine sts.). www.LaTeDa.com. ✆ **877/528-3320** or 305/296-6706. 15 units. High season $195–$245; off-season $135–$175; includes full breakfast. Age 21 or older only; **Amenities:** Restaurant; 3 bars; outdoor pool; cabaret; clothing-optional roof deck; free Wi-Fi.

Parrot Key Resort ★★★   White-picket-fence-lined lanes lead through 5 acres of lush tropical landscaping with a secret-garden feel, at its core a quartet of tucked-away pools accented with funky modern sculptures and antique doorways; sandy sunbathing areas canal-side; and the poolside **Café Blue** and tiki bar, serving breakfast and lunch. The beachy, Conch-clapboard-style villas, suites, and rooms, meanwhile, are class acts all the way, and the largest in Key West, including deluxe king or double queen rooms, deluxe one- and two-bedroom suites, and luxury two- and three-bedroom villas (these last feature gourmet kitchens; private porches and balconies; flatscreen TVs; premium cable; and DVD/stereos). The only real drawback is a location in strip-mallish New Town, minutes from the Duval Street/Old Town action but not easy walking distance.

2801 N. Roosevelt Blvd. (btw. Kennedy Dr. and Key Plaza). www.ParrotKeyResort.com. ℂ **888/211-0348** or 305/809-2200. 148 units. Winter $199–$399 double, suites/villas $299–$399; off-season $149–$249 double, $199–$299 suites/villas. Resort fee $25 per day. **Amenities:** 4 outdoor pools; poolside cafe and tiki bar; bike rental; concierge; fitness room; spa services; watersports equipment/rentals; beach shuttle; Wi-Fi (included).

Pegasus International Hotel ★★   After the best possible deal right on Duval Street? Here's your home base, in the thick of it all. With a vaguely nautical, blue-and-white Deco-style facade, this latest incarnation of a hotel that's occupied the corner since the 1940s was recently given an inside/out refresh by owner Sandeep Singh, whose family has owned the Pegasus for 3 decades. The rooms have a motel-ish feel but are comfortable and well equipped, and the main common area is a nice little roof deck with a pool, a Jacuzzi, and a bar serving light fare (Indian fare, even, just to spice things up a bit). Let me stress that given its front-and-center location, it's probably not the place to drop your bags unless you're okay with some late-night ruckus from the streets below. Remarks Sandeep ruefully, "Ninety percent of guests say they want a room overlooking Duval, but then there's always a few who complain about noise."

501 Southard Street (at Duval St.). www.PegasusKeyWest.com. ℂ **800/397-8148.** 26 units. Winter from $179 double, $400 suite; off-season from $119 double, $159 suite; rates include continental breakfast. Off-street parking $10/night. **Amenities:** Bar; outdoor heated pool; Jacuzzi; roof deck; lobby computer terminal; wine/beer/soda/coffee available in lobby 24/7; shuttle to/from airport ($10) and ferry (free); microwave; free Wi-Fi.

Seascape Inn ★★   For a low-key, intimate, and comfy bargain just a half-block from Duval Street, this 1840 clapboard (under new owners since December 2012 but with the same welcoming feel) makes for a sweet little oasis, with a small backyard pool and Jacuzzi, sundecks, shaded breakfast area, and a handful of pastel rooms with floral prints and wicker. It seems to be particularly popular with Europeans. You should know (whether you're allergic or a cat-lover) that there's a house kitty (named Mario), and that the local roosters like to start crowing early. The upper back deck has a view into the Hemingway House complex; there's a panel with details about the site, and on Friday evenings some guests come up to gawk at the weddings that are often held in that backyard.

420 Olivia St. (btw. Duval and Whitehead sts.). www.SeascapeTropicalInn.com. ℂ **800/765-6438** or 305/296-7776. 6 units. Winter $199–$229 double, $204–$239 suite; off-season $109–$149 double, $169–$199 suite. Rates include champagne breakfast/wine hour. Multi-day specials available.

Off-street parking $10/night. **Amenities:** Outdoor pool; Jacuzzi; shuttle to/from airport ($10) and ferry (free); free Wi-Fi

Southernmost Point Guest House ★★   Why at the lower end of Duval Street is there a cluster of hostelries labeled "Southernmost"? Well, right down the block on South Street is that famous, garish, buoy-looking thingy marking the southernmost point in the continental U.S. (though actually, this is still true only if you're counting natural landmass—the manmade Truman Annex reaches farther south). This gracious white Queen Anne clapboard, now owned by Cuban-American Mona Santiago, is especially significant to Key West history because it was built by a businessman who helped define it in the late 1880s: Eduardo Hidalgo Gato, who came from Cuba to become a honcho in one of the signature local industries of the day, cigar-making (his descendants lived here until 1951). The interior today isn't as elaborate, but as a bed-and-breakfast it offers a nice respite with its outdoor patios, hammocks, a small pool (guests can also use the bigger, busier pool at the Southernmost Hotel across the street), and a half-dozen appealing rooms with contemporary decor, watercolors, wicker furniture, and mosquito-netting-draped beds. If you're interested in the action near the Mallory Square end of Duval, that'll be a bit of a stroll away (about 20 min.).

1327 Duval St. (at South St.). www.SouthernmostPoint.com. ℂ **305/294-0715.** 6 units. Winter $175–$245 double, $265 efficiency; $335–$345 suite; off-season $125–$170 double, $180 efficiency; $215–$230 suite. Rates include expanded continental breakfast. Free parking. **Amenities:** Outdoor pool; full kitchen in efficiency/suite; free Wi-Fi.

INEXPENSIVE

Angelina Guest House ★★   The gambling and whoring of the Roaring '20s are long gone at this distinctive two-story, double-gable yellow clapboard from the 1890s, located 2 blocks down from Duval. What's left these days is a little charmer of a B&B that's one of Key West's best bedding-down bargains given its convenient location and little heated lagoon pool in a very cozy, nicely landscaped backyard. The tradeoff: minimal in-room amenities (no TV, for example), and, for the best rates, shared bathrooms (4 rooms). But the rooms are cute, clean, and homey, and the owners friendly and service-oriented.

302 Angela St. (at Thomas St.). www.AngelinaGuesthouse.com. ℂ **888/303-4480** or 305/294-4480. 13 units. Ages 18 and over. Winter $119–$199 double, $219 suite; off-season $84–$134 double, $144 suite. Rates include continental breakfast. **Amenities:** Concierge; outdoor heated pool; biker rentals; fridge in some rooms, no phone; free Wi-Fi.

Caribbean House ★★   A bargain guesthouse in another 19th-century clapboard, just two blocks from Duval Street, Caribbean House has been cheerily run for the past half-dozen years by the well-liked, Paris-born Marie Barrabes and her husband Michel. Its 10 spotless (though admittedly petite) rooms are mood-lifters, too, with their bright colors and cool modern art. It's otherwise short on the bells and whistles, such as a pool, but you're within walking distance of several beaches, the closest being our favorite, in Fort Zachary Taylor State Park, just a 10-minute stroll away. And if you love to travel with your dog(s), these may be the best digs on the island at any price, because Marie and Michel are dog people, too (they have three Yorkies), and welcome visiting canines at no charge, just a credit-card deposit.

226 Petronia St. (btw. Thomas and Emma sts.). www.CaribbeanHouseKW.com. ℂ **877/296-0999** or 305/296-0999. 10 units. Winter $119–$139 double; off-season $89 double. Ages 12 and older only. Free parking. Pets allowed at no charge. **Amenities:** Backyard patio; complimentary coffee/tea service; free Wi-Fi.

Seashell Motel & Key West Hostel ★   At the island's only hostel, a bare-bones set-up three blocks from Higgs Beach and four blocks from the Atlantic end of Duval Street, the private rooms in particular are an okay option for those looking to economize, with some attempts to spiff them up in terms of amenities and decor such as white IKEA-style furniture. The three hostel rooms (one male, one female, one mixed; 10 beds each), on the other hand, rank among the least appealing of the dorm digs I've come across in my travels, at least in the U.S. Service can also be tricky, because while the front office is supposedly open 9:30am to 9pm, I don't think I've ever found it staffed before 2:30pm, nor does it always return messages. Although it's useful to have this option available, it wouldn't be my first budget choice.

718 South St. (at William St.). www.KeyWestHostel.com. ✆ **305/296-5719.** 60 dorm beds, 14 motel rooms. Year-round $39–$49 dorm bed; winter $129–$169, off-season $74–$119 double. Free parking. **Amenities:** Bike rental; free Wi-Fi.

Spanish Gardens Motel ★★   On an island not exactly bursting with low-cost options, this modest family-owned motel, just a block from the Atlantic end of Duval Street, can offer a lifeline with 26 rooms that are small (and that goes for bathrooms and storage space, too), but clean and even with a touch of style, sporting beige-tiled floors and wood wainscoting. The pool out in a corner of the parking lot provides a nice enough dip, but also keep in mind that Higgs Beach is an easy stroll away and Smathers Beach a little up from that. Rates can vary quite a bit depending on your dates, spiking as high as $300 a night during any one of Key West's many special events.

1325 South St. (at Simonton St.). www.SpanishGardensMotel.com. ✆ **888/898-1051** or 305/294-1051. 26 units. Winter from $139 double; off-season from $89 double. Free parking. **Amenities:** Outdoor pool; free Wi-Fi.

Where to Eat

Despite its share of the inevitable fast-food franchises—mostly up on New Town's Roosevelt Boulevard—and Duval Street succumbing to Hard Rock Cafe and Starbucks, an upscale and high-quality dining scene has also been thriving in Key West. Just wander Old Town or the newly spruced-up Bahama Village, and browse menus after you've exhausted my list of picks below.

If you're staying in a condominium or an efficiency, you may want to stock your fridge from the area's oldest grocer, **Fausto's Food Palace.** Open since 1926, Fausto's has two locations: 1105 White St. and 522 Fleming St. The Fleming Street location will deliver with a $25 minimum order (www.Faustos.com; ✆ **305/296-5663**). Hours are Monday through Saturday 7:30am to 8pm and Sunday 7:30am to 7pm.

EXPENSIVE

Blue Heaven ★★ CARIBBEAN/SEAFOOD/NATURAL   A one-of-a-kind local institution founded by artist-and-writer couple Richard and Suanne in 1992, this, more than any other eatery I can think of, captures the barefoot quirkiness of the island at its best. Interior dining rooms are cute, with funky painted tables and mismatched chairs, but what defines the place is the rustic courtyard with its hippie-commune vibe and roaming cats and chickens (ambulatory poultry aren't an uncommon sight anywhere here in the Bahama Village section). Back in the day, this space hosted gambling, whoring, cockfighting, even boxing (some matches refereed by Ernest Hemingway himself). These days the menu is actually more sophisticated than the surroundings, including great seafood specials such as sautéed yellowtail snapper in citrus beurre blanc, as well as some tasty treats for vegetarians. My favorite meal here is breakfast/brunch, thanks to the selection of pancakes in flavors including banana, pecan, and pineapple, and a variety of eggs Benedict dishes. Or just come and soak up the vibe at the bar (open all day) or take in the live music staged (usually daily) 11am to 1pm and 7 to 9pm

305 Petronia St. www.BlueHeavenKW.com. ✆ **305/296-8666.** Main courses $25–$35; lunch $8–$19; breakfast $6–$20. Reservations recommended for dinner. Daily 8am–10:30pm; closed for 5 weeks following Labor Day.

Café Marquesa ★★★ CONTEMPORARY AMERICAN

One of Key West's best boutique hotels also houses one of its finest restaurants, a single-room, yellow-sponge-painted 50-seater with large mahogany mirrors on one side, and on the other, large windows out onto the tranquil surrounding streets (oh, and at the far end, check out that whimsical trompe-l'oeil painted kitchen surrounding the actual kitchen pass-through window). Chef Susan Ferry lightens her menu with plenty of international influences and ingredients, and as you might expect, she's also big on both local sourcing and seasonality. A recent menu included the classic local pink shrimp grilled and paired with Florida lobster tail and baby bok choy in a Thai butter sauce; other specialties include filet of black Angus beef wrapped in savory prosciutto and macadamia-crusted yellowtail snapper. Nice veggie platter, too.

In the Marquesa Hotel, 600 Fleming St. (at Simonton St.). www.Marquesa.com/Cafe-Marquesa. htm. ✆ **305/292-1244.** Reservations recommended in season/on weekends. Main courses $23–$43. Daily 6–10:30pm.

Louie's Backyard ★★★ CARIBBEAN

Still going strong after more than 40 years, both the setting and the creative island menu help make Louie's one of Key West's most cherished, romantic, and quintessential—not to mention pricey—upper-end restaurants. Set in a big ol' 19th-century clapboard house right on the Atlantic, the restaurant's interior features dark wood floors and pale violet walls, which manages to be both elegant and casual. Ambience-wise, though, it's all about the great outdoors, with three levels and a beachside bar. For the full-blown fine-dining experience, long-time chef Doug Shook's creative menu (Florida meets the Caribbean, then they tour the world together) includes highlights such as a silky splendid conch chowder with a spot of the spicy, Florida lobster braised in truffle butter with spinach and prosciutto, and grilled pork chop with tamarind glaze. To keep your tab down, come for lunch, weekend brunch, or world-cuisine tapas on the "Upper Deck," with the likes of flaming ouzo shrimp, Moroccan-spiced grilled quail, and duck confit pizza.

700 Waddell Ave. www.LouiesBackyard.com. ✆ **305/294-1061.** Reservations recommended. Main courses $30–$42; lunch $14–$20; tapas $6–$17. Daily 11:30am–3pm & 6–10:30pm; Afterdeck Bar 11:30am–1am; Upperdeck/Wine Bar Tues–Sat 5–10pm.

Square One ★★★ NEW AMERICAN/FUSION

This local favorite for a quarter century might have a fairly new owner, restaurant veteran Dominique Falkner, but the quality and service are as good as or better than I've ever experienced here. Paris-born Falkner is also a chef, and his kitchen team now turns out a creative world fusion tour de force. The Korean-influenced beef short rib "pot-au-feu" is a signature, but I recently loved the seafood lasagna, featuring lobster, shrimp, and crab, and a flavorful Moroccan-spiced veggie tagine. Some folks might appreciate that a number of the menu offerings are marked as vegetarian, vegan, or gluten-free. Service is impeccable, and although I love the interior makeover, starring the whimsical art of local Marky Pierson, there's nothing quite like savoring it all while seated out on the plaza.

1075 Duval St. (in Duval Square btw. Truman Ave. and Virginia St.). www.SquareOneKeyWest.com. ℭ **305/296-4300.** Small plates $12–$16; large plates $15–$30. Reservations preferred but not required. Oct–May daily 11:30am–3pm & 5:30–10pm, June-Sept daily 4–10pm.

MODERATE

Azur ★★ MEDITERRANEAN   Owners Michael Mosi and Drew Wenzel are Key West fine-dining-scene veterans, and here on a quiet stretch several blocks off Duval Street they take their cues not just from Mosi's Italian heritage but mix and match from across the Mediterranean—especially Spain, Greece, France (whence of course comes the restaurant's name)—and North Africa. Flavors are bright and the touch is light on specialties such as several tasty varieties of gnocchi; braised lamb ribs over Moroccan-spiced chickpeas with feta and tzatziki; and lavender crème brûlée. And if you can get over here for weekday breakfast ('til 11am) or Sunday brunch, you've gotta try the French toast layered with Key lime pie and topped with berry compote (fair warning: This sugar baby is yummy but super-sweet, so bring your glucometer). I recommend sitting out on the shrubbery-screened sidewalk patio out front.

425 Grinnell St. (at Fleming St.). www.AzurKeyWest.com. ℭ **305/292-2987.** Reservations recommended. Appetizers $5–$15; main courses $14–$29; breakfast items $9–$18. Mon–Fri 8am–3pm & 6–10pm; Sat 9–11am & 6–10pm; Sun 9am–3pm & 6–10pm; closed in Sept.

Mangoes ★★ AMERICAN/FLORIBBEAN   A longtime favorite thanks to its prime perch midway along Duval Street, Mangoes' red-brick patio under the banyan tree is mellow, yet affords great people watching. The ambience plus tasty fare—sourced in Florida but often with a Caribbean inflection (hence "Floribbean")—has earned it a following even among locals. Case in point: the "Caribbean seafood sopito," a tasty mix of local "pinks" (pink shrimp) with the catch of the day, scallops, and mussels in coconut milk and fish stock, plus lime, shallots, cilantro, and bell peppers. Carnivores may want to check out the pork chop rubbed with Cuban coffee, served with roast apples and blue-cheese sauce. At lunch, I love the snapper sandwich with Key lime mayo (speaking of which, if you're in for dinner but want to keep it lighter and/or cheaper, ask to order from the lunch menu).

700 Duval St. (at Angela St.). www.MangoesKW.com. ℭ **305/292-4606.** Lunch $3–$16; dinner main courses $17–$29. Reservations recommended at dinner, especially in season. Daily noon–midnight.

Margaritaville ★★ AMERICAN/CARIBBEAN   If you're searchin' for your lost shaker of salt, head for the mother ship of Jimmy Buffet's 25-member hospitality empire, which first set sail right here back in 1985. Yeah, it's touristy, but so is much of Duval Street, and "wasted away again in Margaritaville" being firmly part of local lore, it's worth a stop whether you're a parrot head or not. Food ranges from workmanlike to good—I like the obligatory "Cheeseburger in Paradise" even if I've had better—and the menu is unshockingly Florida- and Caribbean-flavored, with the likes of jerk chicken, coconut shrimp, smoked fish spread, and conch fritters (there's even a gluten-free version of the menu, and vegans make out okay). Of course much of the fun comes from the noisy, music-filled atmosphere and pastiche of Key West architecture and memorabilia (get a load of that mural of The Man Himself sporting that painfully '70s look from the cover of *Havana Daydreamin'*). When videos of Buffett and others aren't up on the big screen, there's usually a live act on the stage right below.

500 Duval St. (btw. Fleming and Southard sts.). www.MargaritavilleKeyWest.com. ℭ **305/292-1435.** Burgers/sandwiches $9–$14; appetizers $9–$14; main dishes $16–$27. Reservations recommended for dinner in season and when cruise ships are in port. Daily 11am–midnight.

Pepe's ★★ AMERICAN   The island's oldest still-operating eatery was founded by Pepe Peláez back in 1909, and it's definitely got that old-timey look and feel, with rustic wooden booths, tables, and all manner of Key Westiana crowding the walls and hanging from the ceiling. Another good option is the brick patio alongside, which besides its big ol' spreading mahogany in the middle is also cooled by canvas shades overhead and an enormous fan at back. Whether it's French toast or a hearty omelet for breakfast/brunch (which some consider Pepe's best meals), a fresh fish sandwich at lunchtime, or a nice juicy dinner steak, both quality and portions are satisfying. There may occasionally be a wait for a table, especially on weekends, but fortunately the menu is also an interesting read, including tidbits about life and times in the founding year 1909 as well as a primer on Apalachicola oysters from Florida's panhandle, a house specialty.

806 Caroline St. (btw. Margaret and Williams sts.). www.PepesCafe.net. © **305/294-7192.** Main courses $10–$33; breakfast $5–$18; lunch $6–$20. Daily 7:30am–10pm.

Turtle Kraals Restaurant and Bar ★★ SEAFOOD/SOUTHWESTERN   Named in homage to the turtle cannery that once stood here, this funky dockside icon is popular with plenty of locals, especially (need I say) at daily happy hour with its appealing food specials and half-off drinks. Grab a chunky green table on the covered deck below, or a seat on the upper Tower Bar deck overlooking the boats bobbing in the marina alongside. Try one of the seafood specialties, including ceviche, the grouper with coconut rice, and especially the oysters (for non-pescavores, steaks and sandwiches are also available). For some less-than-fast but still fun action, try to stop by for one of the turtle races on Mondays and Fridays at 6pm. Live bands regularly do their thing in the evenings, too. If you're here during the day, be sure to take a peek in the nearby one-room museum about the turtles and their conservation.

231 Margaret St. (at Caroline St.). www.TurtleKraals.com. © **305/294-2640.** Appetizers $7–$12; main courses $18–$30; sandwiches $11–$13. Mon–Sat 11am–10pm; Sun noon–10pm; bar closes at midnight.

INEXPENSIVE

Amigos Tortilla Bar ★★ MEXICAN   On the scene near Mallory Square since 2011, the brainchild of another longtime Key West character—tattooed, slightly scruffy, kite-boarding chef Paul Menta—is a boon for the budget conscious and fans of Mexican food (up until now I hadn't been much impressed with the island's offerings on this score). The central "gimmick" is a soft, fresh-made taco that's square, which actually makes it easier to handle than many round tacos. Fillings are all delish—such as angus brisket with mole sauce, achiote-marinated pork, fish, or conch with mango chili sauce—and Menta makes a point to go the extra mile on quality by buying local and antibiotic/hormone-free, as well as keeping the menu as gluten-free as possible. If you're feeling a little adventurous, try the nopal cactus gumbo. The wood-paneled joint itself has indoor/outdoor seating and a fun, cheery atmosphere very much in keeping with the lower Duval Street vibe.

425 Greene St. (btw. Duval St. and Telegraph La.). www.AmigosKeyWest.com. © **305/292-2009.** Tacos/combination platters $3–$22. Sun–Thurs 7:30am–midnight; Fri–Sat 24 hours.

El Siboney ★★ CUBAN   Key West and Cubans go way, way back, of course, and since 1993 this unassuming eatery, tucked into a slightly out-of-the-way residential neighborhood, has been a prominent part of the Cuban community that's still very much a part of the local fabric. It's not much to look at, but behind the cheesy looking fake-brick facade, you'll find Latinos and gringos alike chowing down on generous portions of authentic favorites such as roast pork with onions and lemon-garlic *mojo* sauce, *vaca frita* (grilled shredded beef), and shrimp *enchilados* (in a light and slightly sweet tomato-based sauce); they also do a yeoman's job with sangria, the classic *sandwich cubano* (ham, pork, Swiss cheese, pickles, and mustard on pressed Cuban baguette), and paella.

900 Catherine St. (at Margaret St.). www.ElSiboneyRestaurant.com. © **305/296-4184.** Sandwiches $3–$8; main dishes $10–$18. Daily 11am–9:30pm.

Paseo Caribbean Restaurant ★★ CARIBBEAN/CUBAN   Several blocks from the Duval Street scene, this tiny spot is worth going out of your way for its very tasty Caribbean-inspired artisan sandwiches on baguettes, the most popular a variation on the classic Cuban sandwich, the "Paseo Press" (roast pork, smoked ham, and Swiss cheese with caramelized onions, banana peppers, and aioli). Its dressings, from the aioli and savory garlic tapenade to other house-secret marinades, give the goods their luscious edge. It's not just about sandwiches; filling platters include fish, pork, chicken scallops, prawns, and tofu. As sides, I recommend the black beans (a little sweeter than Cuban standard but still *muy* tasty) and especially the fire-roasted corn slathered with aioli, grated cheese, and paprika. Owner Lorenzo Lorenzo (no, not a typo) actually has two of these in Seattle, where he was settled as a child refugee from the Castro dictatorship, but in 2011 decided to open this one in the city where he spent time as a young man. And more than a few Conchs are grateful. One drawback: Seating could be better—it's just a kind of picnic table outside.

1000 Eaton St. (at Grinnell St). © **305/517-6740.** Sandwiches $6–$9; main dishes $12–$13. Wed–Sun 11am–7pm.

Sloppy Joe's ★★ AMERICAN   Yes, the island's most famous saloon/eatery is touristy, but you haven't fully experienced Key West without setting foot in this icon, founded by Ernest Hemingway wingman Joe Russell the day Prohibition was repealed in 1933, and made legendary by Papa and his cronies. Even gussied up for the masses, the joint exudes character up the wazoo, with its distinctive Cuban-tile floor; hanging flags; walls crammed with photos, memorabilia, and stuffed trophy fish; seemingly nonstop live music; and moments very much in keeping with the, er, quirky local sensibility (case in point last time I was in: a dude with a tattooed potbelly, wearing only a backwards ball cap and a tiny stars-and-bars Speedo, ambling around offering photo ops). Beyond the atmosphere, the light fare can be surprisingly good, including the slightly sweet/tangy eponymous sloppy joe sandwich, the fish tacos, and one of the better local takes on conch fritters.

201 Duval St. (at Greene St.). www.SloppyJoes.com. © **305/294-5717.** Small plates $5–$17; sandwiches $5–$15; pizzas $9–$12. Mon–Sat 9am–4am; Sun noon–4am.

Exploring Key West

Key West's greenest attraction, the **Florida Keys Eco-Discovery Center,** 35 E. Quay Rd. (FloridaKeys.noaa.gov/eco_discovery.html; © 305/809-4750), overlooks the waterfront at the Truman Annex and features 6,000 square feet of interactive exhibits depicting Keys underwater and upland habitats—with emphasis on the ecosystem of North America's only living contiguous barrier coral reef, which parallels the Keys. Kids dig the interactive yellow submarine, while adults seem to get into the cinematic depiction of an underwater abyss. Admission is free, and the center is open 9am to 4pm Tuesday through Saturday.

Before shelling out for any of the dozens of worthwhile attractions in Key West, I recommend getting an overview on either of the two comprehensive island tour companies, the **Conch Tour Train** or the **Old Town Trolley** (p. 209). There are simply too many attractions and historic houses to list. I've noted the highlights below, but I encourage you to check out others.

Audubon House & Tropical Gardens ★★★ HISTORIC SITE   A manse built by one of the many rich shipwreck salvagers on the island, it's a kind of museum of that period, named after iconic painter and naturalist John James Audubon, who paid a visit to the house and included its flora in his work during an 1832 research trip. A number of first-edition Audubons are on display, along with furnishings reflecting the lives of well-heeled locals circa the mid-19th century (such is the proprietors' devotion to accuracy that at one point they swapped out a flashy Biedermeier credenza for a plainer one more in keeping with the time and place). A newer addition out back in the lovely 1-acre garden is an antique-furnished re-creation of an outdoor kitchen. The nature-focused gift shop/art gallery makes for a charming browse as well. *Note:* This is a popular spot for weddings, so it may occasionally close early (especially on weekends).

205 Whitehead St. (btw. Greene and Caroline sts.). www.AudubonHouse.com. ✆ **305/294-2116.** Admission $12 adults; $11 seniors; $7.50 students; $5 ages 6–12; free ages 5 and under; $9 per person for groups of 5 of more. Daily 9:30am–5pm.

Custom House Museum ★★ MUSEUM   Built in 1891 to house both the government's customs office and postal service and courts, this imposing four-story red-brick landmark alongside Mallory Square made an early mark as the site of inquiry into the sinking of the USS *Maine* in Havana harbor, which led the United States into the Spanish-American War. Since 1999 it's been home to a bright, appealing museum showcasing local artists—especially Mario Sanchez, Key West's answer to Grandma Moses—and exhibitions focusing on historical periods and events that defined and changed the island, including the arrival of the railroad, the hurricane of 1935, cigar making, the impact of Ernest Hemingway, and more.

281 Front St. (at Greene St.). www.KWAHS.org/visit/Custom-House. ✆ **305/295-6616.** Admission $9 adults; $8 ages 62 and over/AAA members; $5 ages 6–12/students with ID; free ages 5 and under. Daily 9:30am–4:30pm.

East Martello Museum and Gallery ★★ MUSEUM   Key West was controlled by the Union during the Civil War, which built this small brick fortress on the Atlantic coast, but it never saw action—or indeed, was even finished. In 1950 the island historical society restored and opened it as a museum curating an overview of local history, including cigar-making, wreck-salvaging, sponge-diving, and Cuban heritage. This being Key West, the weird and wacky are also well-represented, including the story of a doctor who spent years sleeping with the corpse of his wife and a creepy larger-than-life doll named Robert, who even today some believe to be possessed (it's on display right across from an antique horse-drawn hearse, to play up the spookiness). Other galleries display island folk artists such as Stanley "Barefoot" Papio and Mario Sanchez, the much ballyhooed local counterpart to Grandma Moses. Before leaving, head up to the roof for the sweeping view out over the ocean.

3501 S. Roosevelt Blvd., next to airport. www.KWAHS.org/visit/Fort-East-Martello. ✆ **305/296-3913.** Admission $9 adults; $8 ages 62 and over/AAA members; $5 ages 6–12 and students with ID; free under 6. Daily 9:30am–4:30pm.

Ernest Hemingway Home & Museum ★★★ HISTORIC HOME   Papa may have been a rolling stone, but this genteel, two-story limestone manse and grounds built in 1851 was as close as it got to home. He spent most of the 1930s here, the decade in which most of his best-known works were written; he also stayed here in the '50s during stopovers in Key West between his newer home bases in Cuba and Idaho. A museum since 1964, it remains the centerpiece of the Hemingway legend and lore that's so much a part of this island's history. You can hop on a half-hour guided tour or just show yourself around the eight rooms—which, by the way, reflect the taste of wife number two, Pauline, as much or more than the writer himself (I find more of Papa's own personality in his spread outside Havana). It makes for a fascinating visit, both inside and on the rest of the grounds (get a load of that impressive pool out back, built in the late '30s on the spot where Hemingway used to have a boxing ring). You'll likely spot some of the dozens of famous six-toed cats—and see if you can spot the fountain adapted from a *pissoir* taken from Sloppy Joe's saloon.

907 Whitehead St. (btw. Truman Ave. and Olivia St.). www.HemingwayHome.com. ℂ **305/294-1136.** Admission $13 adults; $6 ages 6 and over. Includes 30-minute tour. Daily 9am–5pm.

Harry S. Truman Little White House ★★ HISTORIC SITE   It may not jump to mind as readily as other Key West associations, but the U.S. Navy has been a big presence here for nearly 2 centuries. The naval station, now known as the Truman Annex, was thrust into the public eye when U.S. President Truman made the former commandant's quarters his winter White House from 1946 to 1952. It was later used for both business and pleasure by Eisenhower, JFK (including during the Cuban Missile Crisis), and other presidents and government officials to this day—symposia, receptions, and negotiations occasionally close the house to visitors, but at other times you never know when you might bump into a U.S. Senator or Cabinet member in town on a fishing trip. Historic decisions were made here (including dropping the atom bomb on Japan), and the docents do a nice job of bringing it all alive as they walk visitors through the '40s vintage interior (which is the only way you can see the place).

111 Front St., Truman Annex. www.TrumanLittleWhiteHouse.com. ℂ **305/294-9911.** Admission $16 adults; $14 seniors/students/military; $5 ages 5–12; free under 5 (all around $1 cheaper when bought online). Daily 9am–4:30pm.

Key West Aquarium ★★ AQUARIUM   There's something I find endearing about this very old-fashioned little aquarium at water's edge, founded in 1934. Although it's not big, high-tech, or flashy, with shark tunnels and killer whale shows, it just may end up charming you with its well-designed, informative exhibits showcasing Florida and Caribbean marine and shore environments and their denizens, with highlights including alligators, huge marine turtles, plenty of sharks, and a recently added stingray touch tank. Speaking of sharks, it's very much worth timing your visit to take one of the four-times-daily tours, because not only do the guides put a lot in context, but it's always instructive (and dare I say slightly queasy fun?) to watch the sharks being fed.

1 Whitehead St. (at Mallory Sq.). www.KeyWestAquarium.com. ℂ **888/544-5927** or 305/296-2051. Admission $15 adults; $13 ages 62 and over; $9 ages 4–12. Discounts via website, as well as coupons at local hotels, at Duval St. kiosks, and from trolley and train tours. Daily 10am–6pm.

Key West Butterfly & Nature Conservatory ★★ NATURE RESERVE   This 13,000-square-foot pavilion will get nature lovers flitting with excitement, thanks to the 5,000-square-foot, glass-enclosed butterfly aviary as well as a gallery, learning center (with exhibits and a film), and gift shop exploring all aspects of the butterfly world. In the conservatory's controlled climate, a winding path lets you wander freely among the more than 1,500 butterflies, 3,500 plants (including rare orchids), and other fauna including fish, turtles, and small birds. Expect to spend about an hour here.

1316 Duval St. (btw. South and United sts.). www.KeyWestButterfly.com. ✆ **305/296-2988.** Admission $12 adults; $9 seniors/U.S. military; $8.50 ages 4–12; children under 4 free. Daily 9am–5pm; last ticket sold at 4:30pm.

Key West Cemetery ★★ CEMETERY   This groovy graveyard is the epitome of quirky Key West: irreverent and sometimes downright rib-tickling. Take note of the stacked tombs made as such because digging 6 feet under through rocky soil back in the early settler days was nearly impossible. Best of all, however, is the gallows humor, with epitaphs such as AT LEAST I KNOW WHERE HE'S SLEEPING TONIGHT. Some of the inscriptions are tricky to find even with the free walking-tour guide, but this place is fun to explore. Plan to spend 30 minutes to an hour or more, depending on how morbid your curiosity is.

Entrance at the corner of Margaret and Angela sts. Free admission. Daily dawn–dusk.

Key West Lighthouse & Keeper's Quarters Museum ★★ MUSEUM   Ships and shipping were the lifeblood of Key West for most of its history, so for more than a century after it was built in 1848 (replacing one built in 1825 but swept away by a hurricane), this 86-foot-tall white tower was one of the island's more important buildings, guiding military, commercial, and pleasure vessels through shallow waters and treacherous reefs; sonar and radar rendered it obsolete by the 1960s. Climb the 88 steps to the narrow platform encircling it at the top and you'll be treated to the best 360-degree view on the island (safety wires are strung over the railing, but the gaps are wide enough that you'll want to take special care with babies and small children). The keeper's quarters, with their wood-plank interior, are also pretty interesting, and include a great video summing up the whole thing.

938 Whitehead St. (at Truman Ave.). www.KWAHS.org/visit/Lighthouse-Keepers-Quarters. ✆ **305/294-0012.** Admission $10 adults; $9 seniors/AAA members; $5 ages 7–12/students. Daily 9:30am–4:30pm.

Key West's Shipwreck Treasure Museum ★★ MUSEUM   Shipwreck salvaging was the source of Key West's first great boom in the early to mid-19th century, so although this slick multimedia bit of business has a certain theme-park feel to it, if you're curious about the phenomenon, and that era in general, this is probably the single most comprehensive collection there is. The two-story re-creation of an 1850s warehouse mixes film, actors playing period roles, and artifacts from salvaged cargo

A Smokin' Park

The recently inaugurated **Gato Village Pocket Park,** 616 Louisa St., honors the island's once-flourishing cigar-making industry. Located on the site of a former cigar maker's cottage in what was once called Gatoville—a community built by cigar baron Eduardo Gato for his factory workers—the park features a re-creation of the cottage's front porch and facade, a 13-foot-tall metal cigar and signage recounting the community's ashy history.

items. As a bonus, you can climb the 65-foot lookout tower atop the museum for a great view over this corner of the island and out to sea.

1 Whitehead St. (at Mallory Sq.). www.KeyWestShipwreck.com. ℂ **305/292-8990.** Admission $15 adults; $13 ages 62 and up; $8.50 ages 4–12. Tickets cheaper on website. Daily 9:40am–5pm; shows every half-hour 9:45am–4:40pm.

Mel Fisher Maritime Heritage Museum ★★ MUSEUM   The name Mel Fisher ring any bells? In 1985, after 16 years of trying, a team led by this chicken-farmer-turned-dive-operator-turned-treasure hunter bagged one of the biggest prizes in treasure-hunting history: the wreck of the Spanish galleon *Our Lady of Atocha,* which sank off the Keys in a 1622 hurricane. Fisher's crew brought up a batch of the boodle that went down with the ship—nearly half a billion dollars' worth of silver and gold bars, coins, jewels, and artifacts. Though he died in 1998, the for-profit salvage operation continues. An interesting part of this museum, established in 1992 in a historic firehouse, is a shop; here you'll find replicas, but can also drop anywhere from a few hundred bucks to six figures on various items of treasure from the *Atocha.* Displays do a nice job of telling the story of both ship and salvage operation, including a good representative cross-section of the loot and historic artifacts. The second floor hosts eclectic temporary exhibitions such as the recent "Harry Potter's World: Renaissance Science, Magic, and Medicine," from the U.S. National Institutes of Health. There's also a behind-the-scenes tour of the conservation lab where artifacts are cleaned, conserved, and analyzed.

200 Greene St. (at Front St). www.MelFisher.org. ℂ **305/294-2633.** Admission $13 adults; $11 students; $6.25 ages 6–12. Lab tour $13 ($23 in combination with museum admission). Mon–Fri 8:30am–5pm; Sat–Sun & holidays 9:30am–5pm.

Oldest House Museum & Garden ★★ HISTORIC HOME   Built in 1829 by a merchant from the Bahamas, this compact, two-story cedarwood clapboard spent most of its history in the family of sea captain Francis Watlington. The last descendant died in 1972, and shortly afterward the house was restored and opened to the public. Today just the first floor is open, but it provides an interesting look at some original family furnishings and paintings, supplemented by other artifacts to show what life was like back in 19th-century Key West. Be sure to have a look at the gardens and buildings out back, too, including an outdoor kitchen.

322 Duval St. (btw. Caroline and Eaton sts.). www.OIRF.org. ℂ **305/294-9501.** Free admission. Mon–Tues & Thurs–Sat 10am–4pm.

San Carlos Institute ★★ HISTORIC SITE   As the closest bit of the United States to Cuba, 90 miles south, this island has had a history intertwined with that of the Latin island since at least the 1870s, when Cubans arrived after fleeing fallout from uprisings against colonial ruler Spain. Founded in 1871 as a center of Cuban culture and education, the San Carlos moved once, burned down once, and was destroyed by a hurricane once, so the gracious building with columns, arches, and stained glass we see now actually dates from 1924. Have a peek inside at the lovely tile work, too. There are also exhibitions, but relatively modest and few—and most often devoted not to Cubans and their history in Key West, but rather to various aspects of the home country, such as the life of its foremost independence hero José Martí, and an interesting collection of photos I saw on my last visit depicting Havana's monumental Colón cemetery.

516 Duval St. (btw. Fleming and Southard sts.). www.InstitutoSanCarlos.org. ⓒ **305/294-3887.** Free admission. Sun–Wed 11am–5pm, Thurs–Sat 11am–9pm.

11

THE KEYS & THE DRY TORTUGAS

Key West

OUTDOOR ACTIVITIES

BEACHES   Key West actually has a few small strands, although they don't compare with the wide natural wonders on the Florida mainland; down here they're typically narrow and rocky. Your options are Smathers Beach, off South Roosevelt Boulevard, west of the airport; Higgs Beach, along Atlantic Boulevard, between White Street and Reynolds Road; and Fort Zachary Beach, off the western end of Southard Boulevard.

A magnet for partying teens, manmade **Smathers Beach** is Key West's largest and most crowded. Despite this, the beach is actually fairly clean. If you go early enough in the morning, you may notice people sleeping on the beach from the night before. The water, though, can be a mixed bag, and sometimes has had bacteria alerts (you may want to check before going).

Down from Smathers, **Higgs Beach** is a favorite of locals (and of mine), especially among Key West's gay crowd. It also has a playground and tennis courts, and is near the minute Rest Beach, which is actually hidden by the White Street pier. The sand here is coarse and rocky, but Higgs is known as a great snorkeling beach. If it's sunbathing you want, skip Higgs and go to Smathers. (Interesting historical note: Off to one side there's a burial ground of African refugees from slave ships who died here in 1860 before they could be repatriated to Africa.)

Although there is an entrance fee ($6 per car of 2–8, $4 single-occupant vehicle, $2 pedestrians and bicyclists; plus 50¢ per person for Monroe County surcharge), we recommend the beach at **Fort Zachary Taylor State Park ★,** as it has clearer water and a more scenic setting—not to mention a great historic fort; a Civil War museum; and a large picnic area with tables, barbecue grills, restrooms, and showers. Large trees scattered across 87 acres provide shade for those who are reluctant to bake in the sun.

BIKING & MOPEDING   A popular mode of transport for locals and visitors, bikes and mopeds are available at many rental outlets in the city. Escape the hectic downtown scene and explore the island's scenic side streets by heading away from Duval Street toward South Roosevelt Boulevard and the beachside enclaves en route.

FISHING   As any angler will tell you, there's no fishing like Keys fishing. Key West has it all: bonefish, tarpon, dolphin, tuna, grouper, cobia, and more—sharks, too.

Historic Charter Boat Row's a Great Catch

Historic Charter Boat Row (www.Key WestFishingBoats.com), located in the City Marina at 1801 N. Roosevelt Blvd., has more than 30 charter fishing boats to choose from. Choosing is actually an intriguing process as you can stroll through and hear stories of award-winning captains and record-breaking catches. If you're here at the right time (generally noon, 2, and 4pm) you'll find proud crews, happy fishermen (and women), and prized catches. Boats range from 18 to 65 feet and can accommodate all styles of fishing: flats, fly, offshore, inshore, bottom fishing, wreck/reef, trophy, shark, and more. Prices vary based on type of boat and type of fishing. Party boats are as low as $50 per person. A typical private quarter-day trip starts at $650.

Step aboard a small exposed skiff for an incredibly diverse day of fishing. In the morning, you can head offshore for sailfish or dolphin (the fish, not the mammal), and then by afternoon get closer to land for a shot at tarpon, permit, grouper, or snapper. Here in Key West, you can probably pick up more cobia—one of the best fighting and eating fish around—than anywhere else in the world. For a real fight, ask your skipper to go for the tarpon—the greatest fighting fish there is, famous for its dramatic "tail walk" on the water after it's hooked. Shark fishing is also popular.

There's plenty of competition among the charter-fishing boats in and around Mallory Square. You can negotiate a good deal at **Charter Boat Row,** 1801 N. Roosevelt Ave. (across from the Shell station), home to more than 30 charter-fishing and party boats. You can either make your arrangements in person or contact **Garrison Bight Marina** (www.GarrisonBightMarina.com; © 305/294-3093) for details.

The advantage of the smaller, pricier charter boats is that you can call the shots. They'll take you where you want to go, to fish for what you want to catch. These "light tackles" are also easier to maneuver, which means you can go to backcountry spots for tarpon and bonefish, as well as out to the open ocean for tuna and dolphin fish. You'll really be able to feel the fish, and you'll get some good fights, too. Larger boats, for up to six or seven people, are cheaper and are best for kingfish, billfish, and sailfish. For every kind of charter, from flats and offshore to backcountry and wreck fishing, call **Almost There Sportfishing Charters** (www.AlmostThere.net; © 800/795-9448).

The huge commercial party boats are more for sightseeing than serious angling, though you can be lucky enough to get a few bites at one of the fishing holes. Some party boats, however, offer the best of both worlds, with all the required gear, bait, and license. Party boats target snappers, groupers, sharks, and a variety of other bottom fish. One especially good deal is the *Gulfstream IV* (www.GulfstreamKeyWest.com; © 305/296-8494), a 6-hour charter departing daily at 10am ($65 for adults, $60 for seniors, $40 for ages 6–12, under 6 free). This 58-foot party boat carries up to 60 anglers. You can bring your own lunch (and beer/wine) or buy onboard.

Serious anglers should consider the light-tackle boats out of **Oceanside Marina** on Stock Island at 5950 Peninsula Ave., 1½ miles off U.S. 1 (www.OceansideKeyWest.com, © 305/294-4676). It's a 20-minute drive from Old Town on the Atlantic side. There are more than 30 light-tackle guides, which range from flatbed, backcountry skiffs to 28-foot open boats. There are also a few larger charters and a party boat that goes to the Dry Tortugas.

For a light-tackle outing with a very colorful Key West flair, call **Captain Bruce Cronin** (www.FishBruce.com; © 305/294-4929) one of the more renowned (and pricey) captains, working these docks for more than 20 years. You'll pay from $800 for a full day (usually 8am–4pm) and from $500 for a half-day. You'll find a comprehensive list of Keys fishing guides at www.CCAFlorida.org/florida-fishing-guides/florid-keys-guides.

GOLF The area's only public golf club, **Key West Golf Club** (www.KeyWestGolf.com; © 305/294-5232), is an 18-hole course at the entrance to the island of Key West at MM 4.5 (turn onto College Rd. to the entrance). Designed by Rees Jones, the course has plenty of mangroves and water hazards on its 6,500 yards. It's open to the public and has a pro shop. Call ahead for tee-time reservations. Greens fees run $42 to $72 per player in summer and $52 to $97 in winter, including cart.

KAYAKING **Lazy Dog Adventure,** 5114 Overseas Hwy. (www.LazyDog.com; © 305/295-9898), operates a first-rate, 2-hour daily kayaking tour through the Key

West backcountry for $40 per person. For the really adventurous, there's also a 4-hour kayak-and-snorkel tour through the mangroves and backcountry for $60 per person.

SCUBA DIVING   One of the area's largest scuba schools, **Dive Key West, Inc.,** 3128 N. Roosevelt Blvd. (www.DiveKeyWest.com; ✆ **800/426-0707** or 305/296-3823), offers instruction at all levels; its dive boats take participants to scuba and snorkel sites on nearby reefs.

Key West Marine Park (www.ReefRelief.org/Key-West-Marine-Park, ✆ **305/294-3100**), established in 2001, incorporates no-motor "swim-only" lanes marked by buoys, providing swimmers and snorkelers with a safe way to explore the waters. The park's boundaries stretch from the foot of Duval Street to Higgs Beach.

Wreck dives and night dives are two of the special offerings of **Lost Reef Adventures,** 261 Margaret St. (www.LostReefAdventures.com; ✆ **800/952-2749** or 305/296-9737). Phone for regularly scheduled runs and private charters.

In 2009, the *General Hoyt S. Vandenberg,* a 524-foot former U.S. Air Force missile tracking ship, was sunk 6 miles south of Key West to create an artificial reef. You can find a map of the **Florida Keys Shipwreck Heritage Trail,** a network of wrecks from Key Largo to Key West, at www.FloridaKeys.NOAA.gov/shipwrecktrail.

ORGANIZED TOURS

BY TRAM & TROLLEY-BUS   Yes, you might feel a little sheepish riding this 60-foot tram of yellow cars, but it's worth it to get the island's whole story in a neat, 90-minute package on the **Conch Tour Train,** which covers all its rich, raunchy history. In operation since 1958, the "train" is pulled by a propane-powered jeep disguised as a locomotive, and the cars are open-air, which can make the ride uncomfortable in bad weather. Tours depart from both Mallory Square and the Welcome Center, near where U.S. 1 becomes North Roosevelt Boulevard. For information, call ✆ **888/916-8687,** or go to www.ConchTourTrain.com. The cost is $30 for adults, $27 for seniors/U.S. military, free for ages 12 and under ($3 cheaper on the website). Daily departures are every half-hour from 9am to 4:30pm.

The **Old Town Trolley** is the choice in lousy weather or if you're staying at one of the hotels on its route. Humorous drivers maintain a running commentary as the enclosed trolley loops around the island's streets past the major sights. Trolleys depart from Mallory Square and various other points, including many hotels. For details, visit www.TrolleyTours.com or call ✆ **888/910-8687.** Tours cost $30 for adults, $25 for seniors, and free for ages 12 and under (about $3 less on the website), and departures run daily every half-hour (though not always on the half-hour) from 9am to 4:30pm. One recent addition: **"Ghosts & Gravestones Frightseeing Tour,"** a 90-minute look at Key West's scariest sites and stories, with departures from 501 Front St. at 6:30 and 8pm. Tickets are $34 per person, and while it's not recommended for kids younger than 13, if they do come, it's $26; again, all prices are cheaper online. Whichever you choose, both of these entertaining, trivia-packed tours are well worth the price.

BY AIR   **Conch Republic Air Force,** at Key West Airport, 3469 S. Roosevelt Blvd. (www.KeyWestBiplanes.com; ✆ **305/851-8359**), offers open-cockpit biplane flights over Key West and the coral reef in a 1942 Waco. The rides accommodate two passengers in the forward cockpit, but real adrenaline junkies will also thrill to a spin in a Pitts Special S-2C, which does loops, rolls, and sideways figure eights. For photographers, a 1941 J-3 Cub does a super slow flight over Key West and the reef; dual instruction, tail-wheel checkouts, and banner towing in the Cub are also available. For war bird enthusiasts, there's the 1944 North American T-6 Texan, originally used for advanced fighter training in World War II. The company founder, the late Fred Cabanas, was decorated in 1991 after he spotted a Cuban airman defecting to the United States in a Russian-built MIG fighter. Flights cost $174 to $400 depending on type and duration.

BY BIKE   One of the best ways to explore Key West is by bike. Top tour outfits include **Key Lime Bike Tours** (www.KeyLimeBikeTours.com; ✆ **305/340-7834**), $39 for 2½ hours each morning, and **Southernmost Bike Tours** (www.KeyWestByBike. com; ✆ **305/849-2706**), running 2 hours on weekend mornings at prices of $40 for adults, $25 for kids.

BY BOAT   The catamarans and the glass-bottom boat of **Fury Water Adventures,** 617 Front St. (www.FuryCat.com; ✆ **888/976-0899**), depart on daytime coral-reef tours and evening sunset cruises. Reef trips cost $41 per adult, $21 for ages 6 to 12; sunset cruises start at $38/$19 (cheaper when bought on the website).

Built in 1939, the schooner *Western Union* (www.SchoonerWesternUnion.org; ✆ **305/290-2045**) served as a cable-repair vessel until it was designated the flagship of the city of Key West and began day, sunset, and charter sailings. Sunset sailings are especially memorable and include entertainment and cocktails. Prices vary but start at $49 for adults and $29 for ages 4 to 12.

Classic Harbor Line Key West (www.Sail-KeyWest.com; ✆ **888/224-2794**) operates sightseeing and sunset tours aboard the stunning schooners *America 2.0,* a 105-foot tribute ship that just happens to be the winner of the 2011 Great Chesapeake Bay Schooner Race, which actually will compete in races with you on it for $75. It's an awesome experience for speed freaks. Other tours start at $35; 20% discounts for 10-day advance purchases.

Sunset Culinaire Tours (www.SunsetCulinaire.com; ✆ **305/296-0982**) offers a cruise aboard the vessel *RB's Lady* that includes a Key West harbor tour and a three-course gourmet dinner (with beer or wine) prepared by chef Brian Kirkpatrick. The vessel departs from Stock Island's Sunset Marina, off U.S. 1 at 5555 College Rd.; the cost is $85 per person (call for times).

OTHER TOURS   For both lively and well lubricated, try the **"Key West Pub Crawl"** (www.KeyWestWalkingTours.com; ✆ **305/294-7170**), a 2½-hour stumble through the island's most famous bars, given on Tuesday and Friday at 8pm and costing $30, including five(!) drinks. Another fun option is the 90-minute **ghost tour** (www.HauntedTours.com; ✆ **305/294-9255**), leaving nightly (call for times) from the kiosk at 430 Greene St. ($15 for adults, $10 for ages 12 and under when bought online). This spooky and pretty interesting tour provides insight into lots of island legends.

Since the early 1940s, Key West has been a haven for gay luminaries such as Tennessee Williams, Truman Capote, and Broadway legend Jerry Herman. The **"Gay and Lesbian Historic Trolley Tour,"** created by the Key West Business Guild, showcases the history, contributions, and landmarks associated with the island's flourishing LGBT culture. Highlights include Williams's house, the art gallery of Key West's first gay mayor, and a variety of guesthouses whose owners fueled the island's architectural-restoration movement. The 70-minute, $25 tour takes place Saturday at 4pm, departing from the HTA Depot at Duval and Angela streets. Look for the trolley with the rainbow flags, of course. Details/reservations at ✆ **800/535-7797** or www.GayKey WestFL.com/featureevent.cfm?id=16.

Shopping

You'll find all kinds of unique gifts and souvenirs in Key West, from coconut postcards to Key lime pies. On Duval Street, T-shirt shops outnumber almost any other business. If you must get a wearable memento, be careful of unscrupulous salespeople. Despite efforts to crack down on ripoffs, it still pays to check prices before signing any sales slips. You are entitled to a written estimate of any T-shirt work before you pay for it.

At Mallory Square you'll find the **Clinton Street Market,** an overly air-conditioned mall of kiosks and stalls designed for the many cruise-ship passengers who never venture beyond this hyper-commercial zone. There are some coffee and candy shops, and some high-priced hats and shoes. There's also a free and clean restroom.

Once the main industry of Key West, cigar making is enjoying a modest comeback at the remaining handful of factories, including several started or reinvigorated by Cuban immigrants. At several around town, you'll find *viejitos* (little old-timers) seated at benches rolling fat stogies just as they used to do in their homeland across the Florida Straits. One of the best shops at the moment is **Cigar City USA,** near Mallory Square at 410 Wall St. (www.CigarCityUSA.com; ℂ **305/295-2622**), with a full line of Arturo Fuente and other stogies both imported and locally rolled. Remember that buying or selling cigars made in Cuba is still illegal in the U.S., and so shops advertising "Cuban cigars" are referring to smokes made of tobacco grown from seeds that originated in Cuba decades ago. To be fair, though, many premium cigars today grown from Cuban seed tobacco in places like the Dominican Republic, Honduras, and Nicaragua, are considered by aficionados as good or sometimes better than today's cigars from Cuba.

If you're interested in local or Caribbean art, you'll find nearly a dozen galleries and shops on Duval Street between Catherine and Fleming streets; there are also some excellent shops on the side streets. One worth seeking out is the **Haitian Art Co.,** 605 Simonton St. (www.Haitian-Art-Co.com; ℂ **305/296-8932**), where you can browse roomfuls of originals from Haitian artists well known and obscure, at prices from a few dollars to a few thousand.

From sweet to spicy, **Peppers of Key West,** 602 Greene St. (www.PeppersofKey West.com; ℂ **305/295-9333**), is a hot-sauce lover's fiery heaven, with hundreds of variations from fairly mild to brutally searing. Grab a seat at the tasting bar and be prepared to let your taste buds sizzle. *Tip:* Bring beer, and they'll let you sit there as long as you want, tasting some of their secret sauces.

Literature and music buffs will appreciate the local book and record stores. **Key West Island Bookstore,** 513 Fleming St. (www.KeyWestIslandBooks.com; ℂ **305/ 294-2904;** Mon–Sat 10am–9pm, Sun 10am–6pm), carries new, used, and rare books specializing in fiction by Keys residents including Ernest Hemingway, Tennessee Williams, Shel Silverstein, Judy Blume, Barbara Ehrenreich, Ann Beattie, Richard Wilbur, and John Hersey.

Entertainment & Nightlife

Duval Street is the Bourbon Street of Florida. Amid the T-shirt shops and clothing boutiques you'll find bar after bar serving neon-colored frozen drinks to revelers drinking and partying from noon to dawn. Bands and crowds vary from night to night and season to season. Your best bet is to start at Truman Avenue and head up Duval to check them out for yourself. Cover charges are rare, except in gay clubs (see "The Gay

& Lesbian Scene," below), so stop into a dozen and see which you like. Key West is a late-night town, and most bars and clubs don't close until around 3 or 4am.

Captain Tony's Saloon ★★   Just around the corner from Duval's beaten path, this smoky old bar is about as authentic as you'll find. It comes complete with old-time regulars who remember the island before cruise ships; they say Hemingway drank, caroused, and even wrote here. The late owner, Capt. Tony Tarracino, was a former controversial Key West mayor—immortalized in Jimmy Buffett's "Last Mango in Paris." 428 Greene St. www.CaptTonysSaloon.com. ✆ **305/294-1838.**

Cowboy Bill's Honky Tonk Saloon ★★   "The southernmost honkytonk in the USA" features indoor and outdoor bars, pool, darts, video games, 12 TVs, line dancing, tricycle races, live music, and the Keys' only mechanical bull (kicking Tues–Sat 10pm–2am, plus a special "sexy" bull-riding competition Wed at 11pm). Watch or hop on, but keep in mind that there are webcams catching all the action. 610 Duval St. www.CowboyBillsKW.com. ✆ **305/440-2605.**

The Green Parrot Bar ★★   A landmark since 1890, the Green Parrot is a locals' favorite, featuring stiff drinks, salty drinkers, and topnotch live music, from bluegrass and country to Afro-punk. 601 Whitehead St. www.GreenParrot.com. ✆ **305/294-6133.**

Sloppy Joe's ★★   You'll have to stop in here just to say you did. Scholars and drunks debate whether this is the same Sloppy Joe's that Hemingway wrote about, but there's no argument that this classic bar's early-20th-century wooden ceiling and cracked-tile floors are Key West originals. There's live music nightly, as well as a cigar room and martini bar (read more about Sloppy's on p. 202). 201 Duval St. www.Sloppy Joes.com. ✆ **305/294-5717.**

QUEER REPUBLIC: KEY WEST'S GAY/LESBIAN SCENE

Key West's live-and-let-live atmosphere extends to its thriving and quirky LGBT community. Before and after Tennessee Williams, Key West has provided the perfect backdrop to a gay scene unlike that of most other U.S. cities; seamlessly blending with the larger culture, there is no "gay ghetto"—all of Key West is *fabulous.*

Here the best music and dancing in town can be found at the mostly gay clubs, whereas many other local hotspots are geared toward tourists mostly out to get trashed. Covers vary, but rarely top $10.

Bourbon Street Pub, 714 Duval St. (www.BourbonStPub.com; ✆ **305/293-9800**) is a popular spot open 'til 4am, with strippers and a dudes-only, clothing-optional tiki bar and pool out back (there are also rooms for rent). Across the street, **801 Bourbon Bar** at 801 Duval St. (www.801Bourbon.com; ✆ **305/294-4737**), features a downhome bar out front, a somewhat sleazier back bar, and a popular upstairs drag cabaret that also hosts karaoke and drag bingo. Just up the street, **Aqua,** 711 Duval St. (www. AquaKeyWest.com; ✆ **305/294-0555**), has a good dance floor. You might also find drag queens belting out torch songs or judging "best package" in a wet-tighty-whities contest, and even spot celebs such as Suzanne Westenhoefer, David Arquette, Martina Navratilova, and Christian Slater.

Sunday nights are fun at **La Te Da,** 1125 Duval St. (www.LaTeDa.com; ✆ **305/296-6706;** see also the hotel review on p. 195), a great spot to gather poolside for the best martinis in town. Plus upstairs is the **Crystal Room** (✆ **305/296-6706**), hosting what some say are Key West's highest-caliber cabaret performances, often featuring popular celebrity impersonators Randy Roberts and Christopher Peterson.

For adult fun that's even more "interactive," the all-male guesthouse **Island House** hotel, 1129 Fleming St. (www.IslandHouseKeyWest.com; ℂ **305/294-6284**), doubles as a bath house; admission is $25 from time of purchase until 8am the following morning.

THE DRY TORTUGAS ★★

70 miles W of Key West

Few people realize that the Florida Keys don't end at Key West, as about 70 miles west is a chain of seven small islands known as the Dry Tortugas. Because you've come this far, you might want to visit them, especially if you're into birding, their primary draw.

Ponce de León, who discovered this far-flung cluster of coral keys in 1513, christened them "Las Tortugas" because of the many sea turtles, which still flock to the area during nesting season in the warm summer months. Oceanic charts later carried the preface "dry" to warn mariners that fresh water was unavailable here. Modern technology has made drinking water available, but little else.

These pristine islands make an interesting day trip both because of nesting grounds and roosting sites for thousands of tropical and subtropical oceanic birds. Visitors will also find a historic fort, good fishing, and terrific snorkeling around shallow reefs.

Getting There

BY BOAT *Yankee Freedom II* (www.YankeeFreedom.com; ℂ **800/634-0939** or 305/294-7009), zips you to and from the Dry Tortugas in 2 hours and 15 minutes. The round-trip fare ($170 for adults, $160 for seniors, $125 for ages 4–16) includes continental breakfast, water, lunch, snorkeling gear, and a 45-minute guided tour of the fort. The boat leaves Key West for Fort Jefferson at 8am and returns by 5:15pm.

BY PLANE **Key West Seaplane Adventures** at the Key West International Airport (www.KeyWestSeaplaneCharters.com; ℂ **305/293-9300**) offers morning, afternoon, and full-day trips to the Dry Tortugas National Park via 10 passenger DHC-3 Turbine Otter seaplanes. Prices run $295 to $515 for adults and $236 to $412 for kids, including soft drinks and snorkeling gear but not the $5-per-person park entry fee.

Exploring the Dry Tortugas

Of the seven islands, Garden Key is the most visited because it is where Fort Jefferson and the visitor center are located. Loggerhead Key, Middle Key, and East Key are open only during the day and are for hiking. Bush Key is for the birds—literally. It's a nesting area for birds only, though it's open from October to January for special excursions. Hospital and Long keys are closed to the public.

Fort Jefferson, a six-sided 19th-century fortress, is almost at the water's edge of Garden Key, so it appears to float in the middle of the sea. The monumental structure is surrounded by 8-foot-thick walls rising from the sand to a height of nearly 50 feet. Impressive archways, stonework, and parapets make this 150-year-old monument a grand sight, even though with the invention of the rifled cannon, the fort's masonry construction became obsolete and it was never completed. But from 1863 to 1873 Fort Jefferson did serve as a prison, a kind of "Alcatraz East." Among its inmates were four of the "Lincoln conspirators," including Samuel A. Mudd, the doctor who set the broken leg of fugitive assassin John Wilkes Booth. In 1935, the fort became a national monument administered by the National Park Service. These days it's beset by erosion

The rustic beauty of **Garden Key** (the only Dry Tortugas island where you can pitch tents) is a camper's dream. There are no RVs or motor homes; they can't get here. The abundance of birds doesn't make it quiet, but the camping—a stone's throw from the water—is as beautiful as it gets. Picnic tables, cooking grills, and toilets are provided, but there are no showers. All supplies must be packed in and out. Sites are $3 per person per night and available on a first-come, first-served basis. The 10 sites book up fast. For details, check with the **National Park Service** at www.nps.gov/drto or ☏ **305/242-7700**.

from the salt air and sea. Iron used in the gun openings and the shutters in the walls has accelerated deterioration, and the structure's openings need to be rebricked, so the NPS has slated it for a $15-million facelift, a project that may take up to a decade to complete.

For more information, visit www.FortJefferson.com, www.NPS.gov/drto, or call the **Everglades and Dry Tortugas National Park** (☏ **305/242-7700**). Fort Jefferson is open during daylight hours. A self-guided tour describes the history of the human presence in the Dry Tortugas while leading visitors through the fort.

OUTDOOR ACTIVITIES

BIRDING   Bring your binoculars and your bird books: Birdwatching is a key reason to visit this island cluster, in the middle of the migration flyway between North and South America, thus serving as an important rest stop for the more than 200 feathered varieties that pass through annually. The season peaks from mid-March to mid-May when thousands of birds show up, but many West Indies species can be found here year-round.

FISHING   In 2001, a federal law banned all fishing in a 90-square-mile tract of ocean called the Tortugas North and the 61-square-mile Tortugas South in order to conserve dwindling fish populations (a result of commercial overfishing and environmental factors). But rules have been relaxed to allow some sport fishing in the Dry Tortugas. I recommend a charter such as **Two Fish Charters** (www.TortugasFishing.com; ☏ **305/797-6396**), which will get you on a 50-foot catamaran into deep water where you can reel in dolphin (fish, not mammals), tuna, wahoo, king mackerel, sailfish, and an occasional marlin. Trips are two nights and cost $4,000 (plus $1,200 per extra day) for up to 6 anglers. Don't have the time or money? **Captain Andy Griffiths** (www.FishAndy.com; ☏ **305/296-2639**) does overnighters as well, but will also take you out on the proverbial 3-hour tour to fish the Tortugas at $99 per passenger (4-person minimum) out of Stock Island.

SCUBA DIVING & SNORKELING   The warm, clear, shallow waters of the Dry Tortugas produce optimum conditions for snorkeling and scuba diving. Four endangered species of sea turtles—green, leatherback, Atlantic Ridley, and hawksbill—can be found here, along with myriad marine species. The region just outside the seawall of Fort Jefferson is excellent for underwater touring; an abundant variety of fish and coral live in 3 to 4 feet of water.

A SIDE TRIP TO FORT LAUDERDALE

I f you're visiting Miami for a week or more (or are flying into/out of Fort Lauderdale-Hollywood International Airport, or are including in your trip a cruise out of Port Everglades), you might want to consider popping up across the county line into Broward County, whose largest city, Fort Lauderdale, is also the one most popular with visitors. It's got the beach and the water in common with Miami and the Keys, but not much else.

With some 169,000 inhabitants, Fort Lauderdale dates back to settlements in the early 19th century but most famously showed up on America's radar in a major way in the 1960 film (and Connie Francis song) *Where the Boys Are*. For generations, spring break was both its blessing and its curse. That's never gone away completely, but development in the past few years has made the area more attractive and multidimensional for families and for visitors interested in culture, dining, shopping, and various other pursuits, with something for every budget. It's very boaty, too, with 165 miles of Intracoastal Waterway and canals.

Visiting Fort Lauderdale in the summer has its pluses and minuses. On the downside, it can get hot and buggy. The good news is that more bargains are available May through October, when many locals take advantage of package deals and uncrowded resorts.

EXPLORING BY CAR

Like most of South Florida, Fort Lauderdale consists of a mainland and adjacent barrier islands. Interstate 95, which runs north-south, is the area's main highway, and the fastest and best way to get up here from Miami. Also on the mainland, U.S. 1 generally runs parallel to I-95 (to the east) and is a narrower thoroughfare that for the most part is lined with strip malls and seedy hotels, except for its stretch in Fort Lauderdale itself, where it becomes Atlantic Boulevard and runs directly along the beach. The main east-to-west expressway (that you would use to get out to the megamall Sawgrass Mills and to the Everglades, for example) is I-595, aka the Fort Everglades Expressway.

FORT LAUDERDALE

23 miles N of Miami

Once famous (or infamous) for the annual mayhem it hosted during college spring break, these days **Fort Lauderdale** attracts a more affluent, better-behaved crowd overall, though there are still a good number of spring breakers. The lifestyle here is outdoors-oriented, with miles of navigable waterways and innumerable canals permitting thousands of residents to anchor boats in their backyards. On land, institutions such as the Museum of Art Fort Lauderdale and Museum of Discovery and Science give the city cultural resonance, and recent additions to local dining and hospitality offerings have greatly broadened, deepened, and upgraded its image (and reality) since those hazy, crazy days of spring break.

About Broward County

Fort Lauderdale's home county of Broward is more laid-back (and certainly less Latin in flavor) than Miami-Dade County; some would say it's friendlier, too. In fact, there's a friendly rivalry of sorts; some Miamians consider themselves more sophisticated and cosmopolitan than their northern neighbors, who, in turn, dismiss this alleged sophistication as overblown snobbery and prefer their own county's gentler pace.

With more than 23 miles of beachfront and 300 miles of navigable waterways, Broward County is also a great outdoor destination. Scattered amid the shopping malls, condos, and tourist traps is a beautiful landscape lined with hundreds of parks, golf courses, tennis courts, and, of course, beaches. Key Broward cities you'll pass on the way up to Fort Lauderdale include Hallandale Beach, a peaceful oceanfront town just north of Dade County's Aventura that's still pretty much a retirement community, although enterprises such as the huge, revamped **Westin Diplomat Resort & Spa** and the expanding **Gulfstream Park** are trying to revitalize and liven up the area.

Just north of Hallandale, the burgeoning city of Hollywood was once sleepy and is now bustling with 1.5 million people from a rainbow of ethnicities, from white and African American to Jamaican, Chinese, and Dominican. Hollywood Beach has its own busy boardwalk, and for some reason has long been especially popular with French Canadian vacationers and snowbirds. Above Hollywood is Dania Beach, just below Fort Lauderdale-Hollywood International Airport, best known for a sport called jai alai (p. 142), its antiques row (p. 227), and John U. Lloyd Beach State Park.

Finally, just northeast of the airport is Florida's deepest harbor, Port Everglades, which, after a $75-million cruise terminal expansion, is on its way to being the busiest cruise port in the world.

Essentials

GETTING THERE If you're driving from Miami, it's a straight shot north to Fort Lauderdale; the main exit to look for is 27, then take a right onto Broward Boulevard east toward downtown and Las Olas Boulevard. Exit 29 takes you to Sunrise Boulevard toward Wilton Manors (p. 219), popular with the gay community, and the northerly reaches of Fort Lauderdale Beach.

GETTING AROUND If you're staying out at the beach or the downtown/Las Olas area, you can get around both reasonably well on foot. But to best take advantage of all Fort Lauderdale has to offer, you'll want a rental car, which presumably you've driven up here from Miami. Other local options include taxis (top companies include **Broward Taxi** (✆ **954/456-1111**) and **Yellow Cab** (✆ **954/777-7777**), and water taxis (see box p. 227). **Broward B-Cycle** (www.Broward.bcycle.com; ✆ **754/200-5672**) runs 17 automated stations that rent bikes from $5 for a half-hour to $50 for an entire day.

VISITOR INFORMATION The **Greater Fort Lauderdale Convention & Visitors Bureau,** 100 E. Broward Blvd. (www.Sunny.org; ✆ **800/227-8669** or 954/765-4466), is an excellent resource for area information. Call in advance to request a free

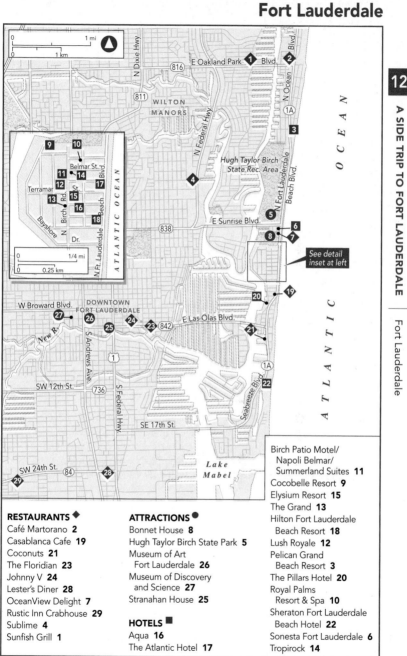

RESTAURANTS ◆
Café Martorano **2**
Casablanca Cafe **19**
Coconuts **21**
The Floridian **23**
Johnny V **24**
Lester's Diner **28**
OceanView Delight **7**
Rustic Inn Crabhouse **29**
Sublime **4**
Sunfish Grill **1**

ATTRACTIONS ●
Bonnet House **8**
Hugh Taylor Birch State Park **5**
Museum of Art
Fort Lauderdale **26**
Museum of Discovery
and Science **27**
Stranahan House **25**

HOTELS ■
Aqua **16**
The Atlantic Hotel **17**

Birch Patio Motel/
Napoli Belmar/
Summerland Suites **11**
Cocobelle Resort **9**
Elysium Resort **15**
The Grand **13**
Hilton Fort Lauderdale
Beach Resort **18**
Lush Royale **12**
Pelican Grand
Beach Resort **3**
The Pillars Hotel **20**
Royal Palms
Resort & Spa **10**
Sheraton Fort Lauderdale
Beach Hotel **22**
Sonesta Fort Lauderdale **6**
Tropirock **14**

guide covering Broward County events, accommodations, and sightseeing. The CVB also offers a free iPhone and Android dining guide app called "Fork Lauderdale."

Where to Stay

There are plenty of lodgings spread across the city, but if you're making an overnight side-trip up here, you may as well stay near the beach. Out here there's a hotel or motel on nearly every block, ranging from shabby to chichi; some of the more affordably priced options can be found in the North Beach neighborhood. Check also the list of small lodgings compiled by the **Greater Fort Lauderdale Convention & Visitors Bureau** (www.Sunny.org/Hotels/ssl); it's especially helpful if you're looking for charming, affordable mom-and-pops. Following is a list of our favorites.

EXPENSIVE

The Atlantic Hotel ★★★   Front and center on the beachfront, one of the pioneers of the local luxe lodging renaissance, the Atlantic is a class act, rearing back in 16 tiered stories. Meant to suggest an Italianate palazzo, it does have a Mediterranean flair, paired with a stylish retro-mod interior decor in soft yellows, beiges, creams, and touches of blue. The 124 rooms and suites naturally boast all the mod cons you'd expect in century 21/decade two, and each has a balcony and kitchenette or full kitchen with snazzy granite counters, refrigerator, microwave, and stovetop (if you really want to live it up, there are two- and three-bedroom suites on the top floors, some of which have private elevators). There's a fetching, 10,000-square-foot-spa; the Ocean Market Grille, which serves up a farm fresh nouvel-eclectic menu (it has a local foodie following); and a fifth-floor terrace with a heated pool and bar overlooking the ocean—very nice indeed.

601 N. Fort Lauderdale Beach Blvd. (btw. Auramar and Terramar sts.). www.AtlanticHotelFL.com. ✆ **866/318-1101** or 954/567-8020. 124 units. Winter $299–$619 double, $399–$999 suite; off season $199–$329 double, $499 suite. Valet parking $28. **Amenities:** 2 restaurants; bar; bike rentals; concierge; outdoor heated pool; room service; spa; watersports equipment/rentals; free Wi-Fi in lobby.

Pelican Grand Beach Resort ★★   There's quite a bit to like about this family-friendly but luxe hotel. Elegant public spaces, 159 bright, cheery rooms; ocean-facing suites with balconies; a huge veranda out back where you can sit in rocking chairs and gaze out to sea; a zero-entry pool and "lazy river" right alongside it. But if you're coming to Lauderdale for the beach (and really, who on vacation isn't?), one key difference about the Pelican Grand is that it's astride its own 500-foot stretch of sand instead of across the street, as is the case with most every other property hereabouts. Sweet. That, plus a smoke-free environment; a laid-back atmosphere; and other amenities like an old-fashioned ice-cream parlor and location near, yet an arm's length away from "the scene," make it especially suited for families.

2000 N. Ocean Blvd. (btw. NE 20th and 21st sts.). www.PelicanBeach.com. ✆ **800/525-6232** or 954/568-9431. 159 units. Winter $289–$369 double, $389–599 suite; off season $159–$259 double, $199–$399 suite. Parking $28. **Amenities:** 2 restaurants; ice-cream parlor; bar; gym; pool; free Wi-Fi.

The Pillars Hotel ★★   Hidden away several blocks off the beach, the Pillars is a more intimate luxury option, the prime pick of the redeveloping enclave known as North Beach Village, between Atlantic Boulevard and the Intracoastal Waterway. A genteel, island-planation-style vision in yellow and white, it's got just two floors and 22 luxurious rooms with eclectic decor (some plantation chic here, a touch of

WHERE THE gay BOYS (and girls) ARE

Fort Lauderdale is especially worth a look for LGBT visitors to South Florida, as the scene and community up here are more developed in many ways than Miami-Dade's. Much of it is centered north of Sunrise Boulevard in the town of **Wilton Manors,** with several bars, eateries, and shops in the **Shoppes of Wilton Manors,** 2266 Wilton Dr., including popular watering hole/eatery **Georgie's Alibi** (www.AlibiWiltonManors.com; ✆ **954/565-2526**), club **Hunters** (www.Facebook.com/HuntersFL; ✆ **954/630-3556**), and stores like **Pride Factory** (www.PrideFactory.com; ✆ **954/463-6600**). Other Wilton hot spots include **The Manor,** 2345 Wilton Dr. (www.TheManorComplex.com; ✆ **954/626-0082**), with a lounge, dance club, and gastro-pub specializing in craft beers and tapas; the down-'n'-dirty **Ramrod,** 1508 NE 4th Ave. (RamrodBar.com; ✆ **954/763-8219**). Steam queens, meanwhile, will love one of Florida's best bath houses, the **Club Fort Lauderdale** (www.TheClubs.com; ✆ **954/525-3344**), near downtown at 110 NW 5 Ave., while beach bunnies should head to the **gay section of Fort Lauderdale Beach** at Sebastian Street. To interact with locals in a lower-key context, the local **Pride Center,** 2040 N. Dixie Hwy. (www.PrideCenterFlorida.org; ✆ **954/463-9005**), runs activities and events daily.

If an overnight appeals, there are dozens of gay-oriented guesthouses and hotels, some clothing-optional, to choose from (although at last count they were all male-oriented, sorry girls). Many like the 50-room party palace **Royal Palms Resort & Spa,** 717 Breakers Ave. (www.RoyalPalms.com; ✆ **800/237-7256** or 954/564-6444), a bar/grill, gym, and "straight-friendly" reservations policy; high-season rates start at $279 (you can also just visit for free). Also top-notch: **The Grand Resort and Spa,** 539 N. Birch Rd. (www.GrandResort.net; ✆ **800/818-1211;** from $120), and the clothing-optional **Lush Royale,** 2901 Terramar St. (www.LushRoyaleFortLauderdale.com; ✆ **954/564-6442;** from $229) and **Elysium Resort,** 552 N. Birch Rd., (www.ElysiumResort.net; ✆ **800/533-4744;** from $119).

For more info, check sites such as www.GayFtLauderdale.com, www.GuyMag.net, www.HotspotsMagazine.com, www.Sunny.org/lgbt, and www.SouthFloridaGayNews.com.

mid-century-mod there) and of course the up-to-date amenities you'd expect at a Small Luxury Hotels of the World member. Out back is a modest-sized kidney-shape pool, along with a dock where you can dine with sweet views of the water and the yachts gliding by (gourmet multi-culti fare courtesy of Chef Youssef Hammi with exotic touches from his native Morocco). The service is discreet, friendly, and attentive.

111 N. Birch Rd. (at Sebastian St.). www.PillarsHotel.com. ✆ **954/467-9639.** 22 units. Winter $365–$385 double, $449–$599 suite; off season $195–$235 double, $325–$429 suite. Free off-street parking. **Amenities:** Restaurant; concierge; pool; room service; spa services; library; free Wi-Fi.

Sonesta Fort Lauderdale ★★ One of the newer highrises along Fort Lauderdale's beachfront boulevard, this dozen-story bit of business next to the historic Bonnet House estate (p. 225) is a great choice both for value and for fans of full-service resorts. Besides bright contemporary rooms (all with ocean views), highlights include a small outdoor heated pool and two dining options, one of which, **Saia,** boasts a Thai chef who serves up sushi and some exotically exquisite flavors amid mod-elegant surroundings garnering buzz among local and visiting foodies. The other venue boasts one of those cool wine automat thingies. One key thing about the Sonesta is its location at the northerly end of the Lauderdale beachfront. Here you'll find yourself a bit farther from the main action down closer to Las Olas Boulevard—not a plus if you're really into the scene but definitely one if you want the beach without all the craziness (in any case, there's a small cluster of nightlife right around the corner, p. 228).

999 N. Fort Lauderdale Beach Blvd. (at Sunrise Hwy.). www.Sonesta.com/FortLauderdale. © **800/ 662-4683** or 954/564-1000. 240 units. Winter $249–$429 double; off-season $159–$289 double. Valet parking $28 overnight, $12 day visit. **Amenities:** 2 restaurants; 2 bars; virtual concierge; pool; room service; gym; free Wi-Fi.

MODERATE

Aqua ★★   Located like the luxury Pillars in the gentrifying North Beach Village neighborhood, heading in from the beach, this is a great example of a once skanky old motel transformed into a chic boutique property, one of 20 owned by a dynamic company called North Beach Village Resorts. This one has 39 bright units with flatscreen TVs and cool white decor accented in—you guessed it—aqua, and decor referencing beach culture, from gussied-up surfing and waterskiing art to actual surfboards. Linens are crisp and white, as are mod bathrooms, furniture, and kitchenettes.

3016 Windamar St. (at Breakers Ave.). www.AquaFortLauderdale.com. © **800/888-2639**. 39 units. High season $189–$319; low season $119–$189. **Amenities:** 2 heated pools; free on-property parking; gas barbecue grill; gym (across street); shuttle service; kitchenettes; free Wi-Fi.

Hilton Fort Lauderdale Beach Resort ★★   One of the sleeker new breed of Hiltons, this snazzy, 25-story affair on the beachfront is a quick stroll north of the main nightlife/ dining action. Highlights include a palm-studded sixth-floor terrace with a compact but dreamy infinity pool and cabanas (one downside is that it all slips into shadow well before afternoon's end—but hey, the ocean's still a hop and a skip away) and the fine contemporary Mediterranean restaurant **ilios** (on the same floor, giving you an option of dining outdoors). Two other onsite eateries are **S3** for fish, steak, and sushi and a casual sandwich shop/bakery; additional on-premises amenities include a nice little spa, fitness room, and kids' program. The 374 studios and suites are roomy and all have water views; most are outfitted with kitchen or kitchenette as well as (nice touch) both shower and tub. One interesting thing to note is that the property tries to make a point of being green; it was the first to be so certified here on the beachfront, and as of this writing, the latest addition in 2014 was the installation of wind turbines on the roof. Thar she blows!

505 N. Fort Lauderdale Beach Blvd. (at Riomar St.). www.FortLauderdaleBeachResort.Hilton.com. © **800/445-8667** or 954/414-2222. 374 units. Winter $209–$329 double, off-season $169–$209. Valet parking $33 (self-parking not available but street parking nearby). **Amenities:** 3 restaurants; concierge; pool; room service; spa; fitness center; Wi-Fi ($15 per day, per device).

Sheraton Fort Lauderdale Beach Hotel ★★   One of the very few local resorts directly on the sand, and a short hop below the main beachfront bar/restaurant scene, the iconic onetime Yankee Clipper is cruising along better than ever after a $30 million spruce-up in 2010. It still sports an "Ahoy, matey!" silhouette and the famous Wreck Bar, with its wood, ropes, and live "mermaid" show. But otherwise it's taken its nautical motifs in a more contemporary direction, including aquarium-mod touches in the lounge-y lobby and soothing marine hues in the 486 well-equipped rooms. The marquis dining spot is an indoor-outdoor branch of the fancy New York City Mexican Dos Caminos – long, narrow, and a bit on the dimly lit side but *muy* tasty. There's also a beach bar and grill, Internet cafe, fitness center, kids' club, and a pair of great pools (one of which has portholes into the Wreck Bar, so careful!).

1140 Seabreeze Blvd. (just below Harbor Dr.). www.Sheraton.com/FortlauderdaleBeach. ✆ **800/325-3535** or 954/524-5551. 486 units. Winter $199–$329 standard, $399–$529 suite; off season $109–$199 standard, $269–$349 suite. Valet parking $25. **Amenities:** 2 restaurants; bar; fitness center; 2 outdoor heated pools; 24-hour room service; water sports; free Wi-Fi.

INEXPENSIVE

Cocobelle Resort ★

Although "resort" is certainly overstating the case, this sweet little spot is a harbor of tranquility at the north end of the gentrifying so-called North Beach Village section, a hop and a skip in from the waterfront action. Its 15 pleasant beige-stuccoed studios and one-bedrooms are equipped with kitchens, and many can sleep three or four.

2831 Vistamar St. (btw. Antioch and Orton aves.). www.CocobelleResort.com. ✆ **800/888-2639** or 954-565-5790. 15 units. High season $139–$189, low season $89–$129. On-premises parking. **Amenities:** Heated pool; barbecue grill; shuttle service; kitchenettes; free Wi-Fi.

Napoli Belmar ★

This North Beach Village mom-and-pop complex (actually three double-decker properties, including the Birch Patio Motel and Summerland Suites) is a good-value holdout—not fancy, but clean, friendly, and well managed. Mom and pop are Angela and Tony de Santo, who treat guests like family, while their 74 rooms, efficiencies, and suites are on the basic side but cheerful and reasonably well equipped.

617 N. Birch Rd. (btw. Auramar and Belmar sts.). www.NapoliBelmar.com, www.BirchPatio.com, www.SummerlandSuites.com. ✆ **954/564-3205.** 74 units. Standard rooms $65–$80 low season; $90–$110 high season; efficiencies/suites $75–$95 low season, $130–$160 high season; significant discounts for seven-night stays. Free on-premises parking. **Amenities:** 4 pools (3 heated); barbecue area; picnic tables; bocce court; shuffleboard; washer/dryer; efficiencies/suites include full kitchens; free Wi-Fi.

Tropirock ★

A North Beach Village triple-decker deal dating from 1960, with a "funkier" (for want of a better word) renovation than most—with stylish if slightly dated decor that might include the state of Florida over your bed in one room, a mod four-poster in another. It's got nice poolside landscaping, great staff, and a loyal following, plus a nice little shop at reception.

2900 Belmar St. (at N. Birch Rd.). www.Tropirock.com. ✆ **800/888-2639** or 954/565-5790. 33 units. Rates low season $59–$119, high season $109–$179. On-premises parking. Pet-friendly. **Amenities:** Heated pool; gas barbecue grill; shuttle service; bicycle rentals; shop; kitchenettes; free Wi-Fi.

Where to Eat

Las Olas Boulevard has so many eateries that the city put a moratorium on the opening of new ones on the 2-mile street. Beyond that, there's been something of a trend of some big-name, high-end restaurants bypassing Miami for Fort Lauderdale for a change. Check hotel listings above, too, for other great dining options, such as **Ocean Market Grille** at the Atlantic Hotel and **Saia** at B Ocean.

EXPENSIVE

Café Martorano ★★ ITALIAN

Yo, cuz! Steve Martorano is quite the piece of work—a big tattooed lug of a South Philly DJ-turned-restaurant guy who set up shop in a strip mall on a busy thoroughfare in 1993, and went on to become a Lauderdale icon. His café is loud, it's festive, it's glitzy black-and-mirrors, complete with disco ball, and the menu is tasty Italian-American soul food all the way (the meatballs especially have a deserved rep). Honestly, it's turned into a bit of a mozzarella-cheesy shtick by now, and it's not everyone's cup of chianti, but the place remains a crowd pleaser and even something of a celebrity magnet (hey, there's now a CM at Seminole Hard Rock in Hollywood as well as at the Rio in Las Vegas, so they're obviously pushing the right buttons, *goombah*).

3343 E. Oakland Park Blvd. (btw. NE 33 Ave. and N. Ocean Blvd.). www.CafeMartorano.com. *C* **954/561-2554.** Reservations recommended (via website). Main courses $18–$48. Daily 5:45–11pm.

Johnny V ★★★ FLORIBBEAN   Chef Johnny Vinczencz may originally hail from Ohio, but since the 1990s he's been making tropical waves in South Florida at various distinguished venues, collecting snappy nicknames along the way like "Caribbean Cowboy," and "Guava Gaucho." At his contemporary-stylish latest and greatest, smack in the middle of downtown Las Olas Boulevard, the cowboy rustles up some mighty imaginative grub if you've got the budget for it. The Caribbean does indeed wash over the menu (a la jerk-seared local black grouper), but there are hints of Spain, Italy, and Asia in there, too. The 350-label wine list is exceptional, and another unusual touch is the international cheese selection. Mmm, *cheese.*

625 E. Las Olas Blvd. (btw. SE 8th Ave. and S. Federal Hwy.). www.JohnnyVLasOlas.com. *C* **954/761-7920.** Reservations suggested. Main courses $28–$38. Daily 11:30am–3pm; Sun–Thurs 5–11pm; Fri–Sat 5pm–midnight.

MODERATE
Casablanca Cafe ★★ MEDITERRANEAN   There are a ton of swell dining spots along the beachfront, but you must remember this: As time goes by, few have been able to match the ambience and romance of this historic neo-Mediterranean manse turned restaurant and piano bar, tucked rather unexpectedly onto a corner amid the condos and hotels. Chef Dario Marquez comes up with tasty victuals such as walnut chicken, which besides walnut crust also involves goat cheese, saffron risotto, spinach pesto, roasted red peppers, and balsamic reduction. There's also nightly live entertainment. There are no reservations, so (especially on weekends) you might want to show up before 7pm or after 9pm, or expect a wait of an hour (but hey, there's a bar for that).

A rum DEAL

It's not in Fort Lauderdale proper, and on the culinary merits there are much better seafooders out there, but **Cap's Place Island Restaurant ★★** (2765 NE 28 Ct., Lighthouse Point; www.CapsPlace.com; *C* **954/941-0418**), Broward County's oldest, is worth a run 8 miles up north just on the strength of its colorful history and funky location. Back in the day, Broward could be a rough-and-ready kinda place, and "Cap" Theodore Knight was a Prohibition-era rumrunner who opened this joint on a tiny islet in 1928 as a speakeasy and gambling joint. And while it certainly became respectable in the years since—graduating from the likes of Al Capone and Meyer Lansky to Franklin Roosevelt and Errol Flynn, then more recently Joe Namath, Mariah Carey, and Bill Clinton—what remains is the charm of the rustic surroundings and the fact that you have to hop a quick boat ride over. The fare? Fresh, (mostly) local, and old-fashioned—good, solid Old Florida, just like the surroundings. Not cheap, though—be forewarned.

3049 Alhambra St. (at N. Fort Lauderdale Blvd.). www.CasablancaCafeOnline.com. ☏ **954/764-3500.** Reservations not accepted. Main dishes $20–$34. Sun–Thurs 11:30am–10:45pm; Fri–Sat 11:30am–11:30pm.

Coconuts ★★ AMERICAN

A block in from the beach, dockside on the Intracoastal, Coconuts sports a very local-South-Florida feel to it and a loyal local following to match. Choice of dining is indoors, out on a shaded deck, or right down dockside with a front-row seat to the passing boats, paddleboarders, and pelicans. Top choices include the lobster roll, fish tacos, coconut cheesecake, and the blue-crab "scoobies" appetizer, marinated in butter, garlic, and chili. And if you can make it here for Sunday brunch, you'll find the likes of chocolate chip pancakes, a variety of tasty Benedicts, and a weekly changing French toast. The young, fresh-faced waitstaff, meanwhile, does its best to live up to the restaurant's widely displayed tagline, "Be nice." A lovely bunch of coconuts, indeed.

429 Seabreeze Blvd. (btw. E. Las Olas Blvd. and SE 5th St.). www.CoconutsFortLauderdale.com. ☏ **954/525-2421.** Reservations accepted for parties of 5 or more only. Complimentary valet parking. Sandwiches $10–$16; appetizers $8–$14; main courses $14–$27. Mon–Sat 11:30am–10pm; Sun 10am–10pm.

Rustic Inn Crabhouse ★ SEAFOOD

Do I really have to spell it out for you? Alrighty then—the word "rustic" in the name isn't just a marketing ploy—this seafood joint just west of the airport has been kicking around since the year Disneyland opened, and the fact that it has practically zero ambience doesn't bother anybody a whit. Sitting in a noisy, woody dining room with a checkerboard linoleum floor and hanging lobster traps (or outside on the covered deck next to a canal), all they care about is whacking away at crustaceans with wooden mallets. The house specialty is garlic crabs—"world-famous," they aver—but there's plenty else on the menu (lots but not all of it fried, and not all of it fish, shrimp, or mollusks). A word of advice: If you do go for the crabs, don't wear anything you wouldn't want to see ruined.

4331 Ravenswood Rd. (btw. SW 42nd Ct. and SW 45th St.). www.RusticInn.com. ☏ **954/584-1637.** Reservations not accepted. Sandwiches $8–$22; main courses $13–$20; crabs market price. Mon–Sat 11:30am–10:45pm; Sun noon–9pm.

Sublime ★★ VEGETARIAN

Even confirmed carnivores could be won over by the magic wrought here with mushrooms, rice, all manner of veggies, and a kind of textured soy called *gardein* (in sliders, I couldn't tell it wasn't hamburger, and prepared in lemony piccata sauce over mashed potatoes and sautéed spinach, it's a dead ringer for chicken). The stuff's amazingly good, and the kitchen does wonders with it. Cocktails such as the "pomtini" are also inventive and tasty, and I'd go back just for the soy-milk Key lime cheesecake. The ambience is cool and contemporary, with uplighted areas, skylights, and picture windows with water coursing down. Owned by the president of the Animal Rights Foundation of Florida, Sublime contributes all of its profits to animal welfare.

1431 N. Federal Hwy. (btw. NE 14th Ct and NE 15th St.). www.SublimeRestaurant.com. ☏ **954/615-1431.** Reservations suggested on weekends. Main courses $15–$19. Tues–Sun 5:30–10pm.

Sunfish Grill ★★ SEAFOOD

One of the things I especially love about South Florida dining is the swell stuff that comes to us fresh from the ocean, and I'm thankful we've got the likes of the Sunfish, a couple of miles in from the beach, which since the 1990s has maintained a sterling reputation for fresh, creative, yet not overly gimmicky seafood. Owner-chef Erika DiBattista, who founded the place with her ex-husband,

and executive chef Bill Bruening continue to please their loyal following with a seasonal menu including signatures like spaghetti tuna Bolognese, Asian pear and arugula salad, and crab-crusted Scottish salmon. And room for dessert is an especially dandy idea, because that's Erika's thing, and both her "Symphony of Chocolate" and her very pointy "Not the Usual Key Lime Pie" will totally rock your sweet tooth . . . even if you don't have one.

2775 E. Oakland Park Blvd. (at Bayview Dr.). www.SunfishGrill.com. ℭ **954/561-2004.** Reservations recommended. Main courses $18–$32. Mon–Sat 5–10pm.

INEXPENSIVE

The Floridian ★ DINER   Cherish is the word I use to describe "the Flo." It's been holding down the fort on a less than lovely downtown stretch of Las Olas since 1937, but it looks like except for refreshing some of the photos of celebs and pols, time pretty much stopped here in the 70s (I guess 'cause that's the way, aha, aha, they like it, to paraphrase KC and the Sunshine Band on the juke last time I was in). I'm talking mirrors, drop ceiling, and hanging plants—plus waitresses who just might greet you with a "Hiya, hon!" The menu is voluminous, the diner fare hearty and good, the portions generous.

1410 E. Las Olas Blvd. (at SE 15th Ave.). ℭ **954/463-4041.** No reservations. Main courses $9–$17. Daily 24 hours.

Lester's Diner ★ AMERICAN   Down near Port Everglades, the original Lester's (there are two branches) is another Fort Lauderdale institution, slinging hefty portions of good greasy-spoon fare (including breakfast 24/7) since 1967, when it started out as a truck stop. It's got snappy, no-nonsense yet friendly waitresses; a following of office workers, clubbers, bluehairs, families, and other assorted locals; and a copious menu of stick-the-the-ribs American and Greek favorites (highlights include chicken-fried steak, moussaka, a raft of breakfast items all day long, and of course the much-touted 14-ounce cup of coffee). Decor is updated classic diner—black-and-white tile floors, neon trim.

250 S.R. 84 (btw. SW 2nd and 3rd aves.). ℭ **954/525-5641.** No reservations. Main courses $5–$19. Daily 24 hrs.

OceanView Delight ★ MEDITERRANEAN/SANDWICHES   In business since 2010 and owned by a South African–Turkish couple, this tiny beachfront hole-in-the-wall (just four tables inside and another four out on the sidewalk) is part of a mini-neighborhood of bars and shops across from a more northerly stretch of Fort Lauderdale beach. The specialties tend to be light and often on the healthy side, such as wraps, subs, and smoothies (banana nut, yum), and all-day breakfast. They also do a dandy job with shish kebabs and hummus platters. They'll even deliver it all to your spot on the sand. And yes, although the traffic can get a little busy at times, the ocean view is indeed a delight.

845 N. Fort Lauderdale Beach Blvd. (at NE 9th St.). www.OceanviewDelight.com. ℭ **954/630-1351.** No reservations. Sandwiches/burgers/wraps $7–$13; platters $6–$14. Daily 7am–8pm (sometimes later on weekends in season).

Exploring Fort Lauderdale

HITTING THE BEACH

Broward County has the region's most popular and amenities-laden beaches, which stretch for more than 23 miles (7 miles of which are in Fort Lauderdale proper). The **Fort Lauderdale Beach Promenade** underwent a $26-million renovation and looks

RUB-A-DUB grub

Another one of Broward's famously funky eateries worth a foray from Lauderdale proper, **Le Tub Saloon ★★** (1100 N. Ocean Dr.; www.TheLeTub.com; ℰ **954/931-9425**) is a few minutes' cruise south of the airport out near Hollywood Beach (on the Intracoastal Waterway side). A pack rat, the late Russell Kohuth, bought a gas station in 1974, loaded it up with all manner of flotsam and bric-a-brac (including, yes, bathtubs), and it was pretty much a locals' secret until *GQ* magazine touted its burgers in 2006, followed by *Esquire*, Oprah, and yadda yadda yadda. Yes, they are indeed tasty (not to mention large), and so is the chili, seafood salad, and Key lime pie. Sit dockside, chill out, and enjoy the quirky atmosphere.

fantastic. It's especially peaceful in the mornings, when there's just a smattering of joggers and walkers, but even at its most crowded on weekends, the expansive promenade provides room for everyone. Just across the street is a solid stretch of hotels, bars, and shops, including a retail/dining complex, the **Gallery at Beach Place** (which is more than anything a drinking complex) on Atlantic Boulevard midway between Las Olas and Sunrise boulevards.

On the sand just across the road, you'll find hardcore volleyball players who always welcome anyone with a good spike, and an inviting ocean for swimmers of any level. The unusually clear waters are under the careful watch of some of Florida's hottest lifeguards. Freshen up afterward in the clean showers and restrooms conveniently located along the strip. Pets have been banned from most of the beach in order to maintain the impressive cleanliness; a designated area for four-footed pals can be found away from the main sunbathing areas (specifically a 100-yard stretch from Sunrise Blvd. north to the next lifeguard station, and only late afternoons/early evenings Fri–Sun).

Especially on weekends, parking at the oceanside meters is nearly impossible; try biking, skating, or water taxi instead. The strip is located on Fla. A1A (here also called Fort Lauderdale Beach Blvd.), between SE 17th St. and Sunrise Boulevard.

SEEING THE SIGHTS

Bonnet House ★★★ HISTORIC HOME   Little do most beachgoers suspect what lies behind the fence and wall of greenery a few yards away. This 35-acre spread named after the Bonnet lily is a trip back in time to 1921, when artist and collector Frederic Clay Bartlett built a gracious two-story manse in a kind of Caribbean plantation style, filled with art and surrounded by lush tropical gardens, where he wintered with a first, then a second wife (the latter of whom, Evelyn, some of the friendly and talkative volunteer guides even met). Visits are by 90-minute guided tour only, and a fascinating one at that.

900 N. Birch Rd. (off Sunrise Blvd.). www.BonnetHouse.org. ℰ **954/563-5393.** Admission $20 adults, $18 ages 60 and over, $16 ages 6–12, free for ages 5 and under. Tram tour $2 extra. Grounds only $10. Tues–Sun 9am–4pm.

Hugh Taylor Birch State Park ★★ NATURE PARK   A block in from the beach, this rare and worthy spot of greenery is set amid the waterways, the sands, and the sprawl. Its preserves a peaceful patch of hammock (subtropical hardwood forest) in which you're welcome to hike, bike, skate, kayak, canoe, fish, or picnic. There's a visitor center with nature/history exhibits, but it's closed for renovations and not expected to re-open until at least 2016; in the meantime, tours are available on audio as well as in person from park rangers each Friday at 10:30am, lasting 60 to 90 minutes.

3019 E. Sunrise Blvd. (btw. N. Fort Lauderdale Blvd. and Sunrise La.). www.FloridaStateParks.org/HughTaylorBirch. ☏ **954/564-4521.** Admission $6 per vehicle; $4 per motorcycles or single-person vehicles; $2 per pedestrian or bicyclist. Daily 8am–sunset.

Museum of Art Fort Lauderdale ★★ ART MUSEUM An exceptional trove

of modern art downtown, MOAIFL has permanent collections including 50 sculptures; pop art by the likes of Warhol, Lichtenstein, and Rivers; 200 works from Europe's postwar CoBrA (Copenhagen/Brussels/Amsterdam) movement; Pablo Picasso ceramics that'll rock your crockery; and contemporary works from a wide range of exiled Cuban artists from across the planet. There are always great temporary shows cycling through, as well, bringing in not just fine art and ethnography (such as a recent one focusing on pre-Inca cultures of Peru), but photography documenting important history, such as images by Bob Adelman of America's '60s civil rights movement and from Roman Vishniac of Jewish life in Eastern Europe between the world wars. There's also a nice little café here, along with a branch of Miami's excellent Books & Books (p. 115). Each Thursday evening there are lectures, films, and performances; check the website for those and other events.

1 E. Las Olas Blvd. (at S. Andrews Ave.). www.MOAFL.org. ☏ **954/525-5500.** Admission $10 adults, $7 seniors/active U.S. military, $5 ages 13–17, 12 and under free. Tues–Wed and Fri–Sat 11am–5pm, Thurs 11am–8pm; Sun noon–5pm.

Museum of Discovery and Science ★★ MUSEUM A swell example of a

science museum that successfully leverages high tech and interactivity to make science fun for kids—and just as engaging for grownups—starting with a funky, 52-foot "kinetic-energy" sculpture out front called the "Great Gravity Clock." One of the highlights on its two floors is an "EcoDiscovery Center" with simulated hurricane winds and Everglades airboat ride, and a chance to "dig" for fossils. Other cool stuff includes exhibits about space, minerals, and Florida flora and fauna including snakes, alligators, bees, even a living coral reef. Plus there's a great hands-on area especially for tykes ages 6 and under. There are temporary exhibits like 2014's "Goosebumps! The Science of Fear," and the five-story IMAX screen is a big draw for young and old, too, with varied programing from nature films to Hollywood flicks.

401 SW 2nd St. (btw. SW 4th and 5th aves.). www.MODS.org. ☏ **954/467-6637.** Admission $14 adults, $13 seniors, $12 ages 2–12; with IMAX film $19–$20 adults, $18–$20 seniors, $15–$17 ages 2–12. Mon–Sat 10am–5pm; Sun noon–6pm. Movie theater closes later.

Stranahan House ★★ HISTORIC HOME Granted, Fort Lauderdale doesn't

exactly ooze history, but it's here if you look for it. A case in point is the city's oldest remaining edifice, tucked away alongside downtown's New River. It dates back to 1901, when the eponymous Frank Stranahan built it as a trading post when this was still a frontier settlement and Seminole Indians would pull up in dugout canoes. Stranahan built another building for trade, turning this into a home for himself and his wife Ivy. Now it's an interesting little museum of that era, a window into the roots of Fort Lauderdale. It can be visited by guided tour only, be sure to get there on time (1, 2, or 3pm)!

335 SE 6th Ave. (at Las Olas Blvd. at the New River Tunnel). www.StranahanHouse.org. ☏ **954/524-4736.** Admission $12 adults; $11 seniors; $7 students and children. Daily 1–3pm. Tours are on the hour; last tour at 3pm. Accessible by water taxi.

ONE IF BY LAND, taxi IF BY SEA

Try to spend at least an afternoon or evening cruising the many miles of local waterways the only way possible: by boat. The **Water Taxi of Fort Lauderdale** (www.WaterTaxi.com; ✆ **954/467-6677**) is a trusty fleet of older port boats that both transport and entertain visitors as they cruise through the "Venice of America" and down to Hollywood. Because of its popularity, the water taxi fleet now includes several sleek, 70-passenger "water buses" (featuring indoor/outdoor seating with an atrium-like roof).

Taxis operate on demand along a fairly regular route, carrying up to 48 passengers to 20 stops. If you're staying at a hotel en route, you can be picked up there, usually within 15 minutes of calling, and be shuttled to any of dozens of restaurants, bars, and attractions on or near the waterfront. If you aren't sure where you want to go, ask one of the personable captains, who can point out historic and fun spots along the way.

Starting daily at 8am, boats run until midnight 7 days a week, depending on the weather. Check the website for exact pickup times. The cost is $22 for an all-day pass with unlimited stops on and off, $18 for ages 65 and over, $11 for ages 4 to 11, and $15 for adults boarding after 5pm; $60 "family pack" for up to 5 fares. Tickets can be bought onboard, via hotel concierges, or the website.

BOATING

Often called the "yachting capital of the world," Fort Lauderdale provides ample opportunity for visitors to get out on the water, either along the Intracoastal Waterway or on the open ocean. If your hotel doesn't rent boats, **Aloha Watersports** at Marriott's Harbor Beach Resort, 3030 Holiday Dr. (www.AlohaWatersports.com; ✆ **954/462-7245**), can outfit you with a variety of craft. Rates start at $75 per half-hour for Wave-Runners ($15 each additional rider; doubles and triples available), $70 to $125 for catamarans, $25 per half-hour for paddleboards or $100 for an hour including a lesson, and $95 per person for a 15-minute parasail. Aloha also offers a thrilling speedboat ride for $50 for a half-hour or $100 for a 90-minute outing; a surfing school (boards $25 per hour, lessons $50 per hour—though the waves are hardly rippin' hereabouts); and a Coast Guard class (9am daily), through which adults can obtain their Florida boaters license for $3. Treasure hunters can rent a metal detector here for $20 per hour.

Shopping

As in most of Florida, here in Broward County it's mostly about malls, and two of the best are upscale **Galleria,** at Sunrise Boulevard near the Fort Lauderdale Beach, and for bargains, there's no better place than **Sawgrass Mills** (see box below).

However, for unusual boutiques, especially art galleries, head to quaint **Las Olas Boulevard ★★** (www.LasOlasBoulevard.com), located west of A1A and a block east of Federal Highway/U.S. 1, off SE 8th Street, where there are more than 70 shops and galleries with alluring window decorations (say, kitchen utensils posing as modern-art sculptures) and intriguing merch (mural-size oil paintings and larger-than-life statues).

If you're really an antiques hound (and especially if you're a bargain-hunter), consider stopping off en route between Miami and Lauderdale at the modest **Art and Antique District** of **Dania Beach** (www.VisitDaniaBeach.com/antiques.asp).

I CAME, I sawgrass, I SHOPPED

Hardcore shopping devotees will definitely want to consider a pilgrimage to the western Broward County city of Sunrise, where **Sawgrass Mills** is the largest darn outlet mall in the whole U.S. of A. Depending on the type of shopper you are, this experience can either be blissful or overwhelming—either way, it can easily take days to work your way through these more than 350 stores, not all of which offer bargain prices. The recently expanded **Colonnade Outlets** subsection features more than 40 outlet versions purporting savings of up to 70% on brands like Burberry, Coach, Gucci, Prada, and Salvatore Ferragamo. Parking is free, but don't forget where you parked or you could spend hours hunting for your wheels. The address is 12801 W. Sunrise Blvd.; take I-95 north to 595 west to Flamingo Road. Exit and turn right, driving 2 miles to Sunrise Blvd. You can't miss this monster on the left. For details, log on to www.Simon.com/Mall/Sawgrass-Mills (which includes news about sales and specials), or call ☎ **954/846-2300** (office) or 954/846-2350 (shopping line).

Bars & Clubs

Ah, Fort Liquordale. For visitors, much of the local nightlife is naturally concentrated along Fort Lauderdale Beach Boulevard, starting with the tiny but famed **Elbo Room** at the corner of E. Las Olas Boulevard (www.ElboRoom.com; ☎ **954/463-4615**). Starting as a sailors' dive in 1938, it became popular with generations of springbreakers, starred in both the original and remake of *Where the Boys Are,* and continues to pull in a wide variety of comers, with live music at seemingly all hours of day or night. Another party HQ several blocks up the street, **The Gallery at Beach Place,** 17 S. Fort Lauderdale Beach Blvd. (www.GalleryAtBeachPlace.com; ☎ **954/760-9570**), includes spots such as **Lulu's Bait Shack, Fat Tuesday,** and **Hooters.** A few blocks farther north, just before Sunrise Boulevard, there's a little cluster of spots including the likes of **McSorleys Beach Pub** and **Rooftop Lounge,** 837 N. Fort Lauderdale Beach Blvd. (www.McSorleysFtL.com; ☎ **954/565-4446**) and **Sandbar,** 900 Sunrise La. (www.SandbarFortLauderdale.com; ☎ **954/990-7578**). The beach also has developed a somewhat more sophisticated nightlife side, mostly based in hotels, including the lounge/outdoor patio scene at **S3,** in the Hilton at 505 N. Fort Lauderdale Beach Blvd. (www.S3Restaurant.com; ☎ **954/523-7873**), and a pair at the W, **Living Room** and **Whiskey Blue,** 401 N. Fort Lauderdale Beach Blvd. (www.WFortLauderdale Hotel.com/living-room; ☎ **954/414-8200**).

In the Las Olas/downtown area, check out **American Social,** 721 E. Las Olas Blvd. (www.AmericanSocialBar.com; ☎ **954/764-7005**), **Briny Riverfront Irish Bar,** 305 S. Andrews Ave. (☎ **954/376-4742**), **Original Fat Cats,** 320 Himmarshee Blvd. (☎ **954/524-5366**), **YOLO** and **O Lounge,** 333 E. Las Olas Blvd. (www.YOLORestaurant.com; ☎ **954/523-1000**), **Vibe,** 301 E. Las Olas Blvd. (www.VibeLasOlas.com; ☎ **954/713-7313**), **Off the Hookah,** 111 SW 2 Ave. (www.OffTheHookah.com; ☎ **954/761-8686**), and **America's Backyard,** 100 SW 3 Ave. (www.MyAmericasBackyard.com; ☎ **954/449-9569**).

PLANNING YOUR TRIP TO SOUTH FLORIDA

Whether you plan to spend a day, a week, 2 weeks, or longer in the southern end of the Sunshine State, you'll need to make many "where," "when," and "how" choices before leaving home. With myriad affordable flights, a balmy climate year-round, a vibrant cultural scene in Miami, and beautiful beaches all along the coast, there's a good vacation to be had here by everyone, no matter how you choose to answer these questions. What's not a question is whether or not to visit in general. You bought this book, so what are you waiting for?

As South Florida shifts from a seasonal to a more year-round destination, there's always a good time to visit. Really. Even during hurricane season (June–November), when prices are lower and crowds are thinner, hurricanes are—knock on wood—scarce (we haven't had one since Katrina and Wilma in 2005). When temperatures plummet elsewhere, folks flock here to thaw and things get a bit more lively, albeit also more crowded. For those who love heat, humidity, and sweating, summertime is the ideal time to visit and saves you a trip to the sauna.

For additional help planning your trip and for further on-the-ground resources, please turn to "Fast Facts: South Florida," p. 232.

GETTING THERE

Getting to South Florida
BY PLANE
Most major domestic airlines fly to and from various Florida cities, such as **American, Delta, United,** and **US Airways.** Of these, Delta and US Airways have the most extensive network of commuter connections within Florida (see "Getting Around," below).

Several low-fare carriers also fly to Florida, the biggest and best being **Southwest Airlines,** with flights from many U.S. cities to Fort Lauderdale, Jacksonville, Orlando, Tampa, and Panama City. Others flying to South Florida include **Air Tran, JetBlue, Virgin America, Frontier Airlines,** and **Spirit.**

The major airports in the area of Miami and the Keys are **Miami International Airport (MIA)** and **Fort Lauderdale–Hollywood International Airport (FLL).**

Tip: When booking airfare to Miami, consider flying into the Fort Lauderdale–Hollywood International Airport for considerably cheaper fares. The airport is only 30 to 40 minutes from downtown Miami.

Price comparison and booking websites such as **Kayak.com**, **Momondo.com**, and **Hipmunk.com** make it easy to compare prices and purchase tickets.

BY CAR

Although four major roads run to and through Miami—Interstate 95, S.R. 826, S.R. 836, and U.S. 1—chances are you'll reach Miami and the Keys via I-95. This north-south interstate is South Florida's lifeline and an integral part of the region. The highway connects all of Miami's different neighborhoods, the airport, the beaches, and the rest of South Florida to the rest of the country. Miami's road signs are notoriously confusing and notably absent when you most need them. Think twice before you exit the highway if you aren't sure where you're going; some exits lead to unsavory neighborhoods.

Other highways that will get you to Florida include I-10, which originates in Los Angeles and terminates at the tip of Florida in Jacksonville, and I-75, which begins in north Michigan and runs through the center of the state to Florida's west coast.

Florida law allows drivers to make a right turn on a red light after a complete stop, unless otherwise indicated. In addition, all passengers are required to wear seat belts, and children 3 and under must be securely fastened in government-approved car seats.

See "Getting Around" (below) for more information about driving in Florida and the car-rental firms that operate here.

International visitors should note that insurance and taxes are almost never included in quoted rental-car rates in the U.S. Be sure to ask your rental agency about these fees, as they can add a significant cost to your car rental.

Most car-rental companies in Florida require that you be 25, and even when they don't, there's a hefty surcharge applied to renters 21 to 24 years old.

BY TRAIN

Amtrak (www.Amtrak.com; ✆ **800/872-7245**) operates passenger train service to Florida from both the East and West coasts. It takes some 26 hours to reach Miami from New York, and 68 hours from Los Angeles. Amtrak's fares aren't much lower—and are sometimes higher—than many of the airlines' lowest fares.

Amtrak's *Silver Meteor* and *Silver Star* both run daily between New York and Miami (the station in actually in Hialeah, 8303 NW 37th Ave.), with various intermediate stops along the East Coast and in Florida. Amtrak's Thruway Bus Connections are available from the Fort Lauderdale Amtrak station and Miami International Airport to Key West. Sleeping accommodations are available for an extra charge. If you intend to stop along the way, you can save money with Amtrak's **USA Rail Passes.**

Amtrak's **Auto Train** runs daily from Lorton, Virginia (12 miles south of Washington, D.C.), to Sanford, Florida (just northeast of Orlando). You ride in a coach while your car is secured in an enclosed vehicle carrier. Make your train reservations as far in advance as possible.

BY BUS

Greyhound (www.Greyhound.com; ✆ **800/231-2222**) has 47 stops within the state of Florida and more than 3,800 service locations in North America. Although buses aren't the fastest way to get to South Florida, they can be the most economical.

GETTING AROUND

The best and easiest way to see South Florida's sights or to get to and from the beach is by car. Public transportation is available only in the cities and larger towns, and even there, it may provide infrequent or inadequate service. When it comes to getting from one city to another, cars and planes are the ways to go.

BY PLANE

The commuter arms of **Delta** and **US Airways** provide extensive service between Florida's major cities and towns. Fares for these short hops tend to be reasonable.

Cape Air flies between Key West and Fort Myers, which means you can avoid backtracking to Miami from Key West if you're touring the region. (You can also take a 3-hour boat ride between Key West and Fort Myers Beach or Naples.)

Some large airlines offer transatlantic or transpacific passengers special discount tickets under the name **Visit USA,** which allows mostly one-way travel from one U.S. destination to another at very low prices. Unavailable in the U.S., these discount tickets must be purchased abroad in conjunction with your international fare. This system is the easiest, fastest, cheapest way to see the country.

BY CAR

If you're visiting from abroad and plan to rent a car in Florida, keep in mind that foreign driver's licenses are usually recognized in the U.S., but you should get an international one if your home license is not in English.

Jacksonville is about 350 miles north of Miami and 500 miles north of Key West, so if you're traveling to South Florida from a northern city, don't underestimate how long it will take you to drive all the way down the state. The speed limit is 65mph to 70mph on the rural interstate highways, so you can, however, make good time between cities. Not so on U.S. 1, U.S. 17, U.S. 19, U.S. 41, and U.S. 301; although most have four lanes, these older highways tend to be heavily congested, especially in built-up areas.

Every major car-rental company is represented here, including **Alamo, Avis, Budget, Dollar, Enterprise, Hertz, National,** and **Thrifty.**

State and local **taxes** will add as much as 20% to your final bill. You'll pay an additional $2.05 per day in statewide use tax, and local sales taxes will tack on at least 6% to the total, including the statewide use tax. Some airports add another 35¢ per day and as much as 10% in "recovery" fees. You can avoid the recovery fee by picking up your car in town rather than at the airport. Budget and Enterprise both have numerous rental locations away from the airports. But be sure to weigh the cost of transportation to and from your hotel against the amount of the fee.

Competition is so fierce among Florida rental agencies that most have now stopped charging **drop-off fees** if you pick up a car at one place and leave it at another. Be sure to ask in advance if there's a drop-off fee.

To rent a car, you must have a valid **credit card** (not a debit or check card) in your name, and most companies require you to be at least 25 years old. Some also set maximum ages and may deny cars to anyone with a bad driving or credit record. Ask about requirements and restrictions when you book to avoid problems upon arrival.

BY TRAIN

International visitors and U.S. residents alike can buy a **USA Rail Pass,** good for 15, 30, or 45 days of unlimited travel on **Amtrak** (www.Amtrak.com; © **800/872-7245**). The pass is available online or through many overseas travel agents; it can't be applied to Auto Train or Acela Express. See Amtrak's website for the cost of travel within the western, eastern, or northwestern United States. Reservations are generally required and should be made as early as possible. Regional rail passes are also available.

BY BUS
Greyhound (www.Greyhound.com; ✆ **800/231-2222**) is the sole nationwide bus line.

TIPS ON ACCOMMODATIONS

Lodgings in Miami and the Keys are wildly varied in style and amenities, ranging from five-star luxury hotels, beach resorts, cozy one-room cottages, and posh penthouses to B&Bs, beachfront high-rise condominiums, and back-to-nature-style Everglades and Keys cabins and campsites. For sports or nature lovers, there are hotels and motels located on golf courses, marinas, or surrounded by nature preserves and hiking trails. For families, there are theme hotels. For the hip, there's the requisite boutique properties with mandatory celebrity sightings. And for those who just want to get away from it all, there are countless hidden hotels, motels, and cottages—even a few on private islands.

[Fast FACTS] MIAMI & THE KEYS

Area Codes **305:** All of Miami-Dade County and Monroe County: Miami, Coral Gables, and the Keys. **786:** A newer area code for Miami-Dade only.

Business Hours "Normal" business hours are 9am to 5pm, but in these parts, for some "mom-and-pop" businesses it pays to call ahead and double-check.

Customs Every visitor 21 or older may bring in, free of duty, the following: (1) 1 liter of alcohol; (2) 200 cigarettes, 100 cigars (but not from Cuba), or 3 pounds of smoking tobacco; and (3) $100 worth of gifts. These exemptions apply to travelers who spend at least 72 hours in the United States and who have not claimed them within the preceding 6 months. It is forbidden to bring into the U.S. almost any meat products (including canned, fresh, and dried

products such as bouillon, soup mixes, and the like). Generally, condiments such as vinegars, oils, pickled goods, spices, coffee, tea, and some cheeses and baked goods are allowed. Avoid bringing rice products, as rice can harbor insects. Fruits and vegetables are prohibited because these may also harbor pests or disease. International visitors may carry in or out up to $10,000 in U.S. or foreign currency with no formalities; larger sums must be declared on entering or leaving, and visitors must file form CM 4790. For further details, consult your nearest U.S. embassy or consulate, or the **U.S. Customs** website, www.CBP. gov.

Disabled Travelers Florida is exceptionally accommodating to those with special needs. In addition to special parking set

aside at every establishment, out-of-state vehicles with disability parking permits from other states can park in these spots. Florida state law and the Americans with Disabilities Act (ADA) require that service dogs be permitted in all establishments and attractions, although some ride restrictions do apply. Those with hearing impairments can dial ✆ **711** for **TDD service** via the Florida Relay Service. There are several resources for people with disabilities who are traveling within Florida, including special wheelchairs with balloon tires provided free of charge at many Florida beaches. For the best information on traveling with disabilities, go to www.VisitFlorida.com/ Disabilities_Travel.

Drinking Laws The legal age for purchase and consumption of alcoholic beverages is 21, though, strangely and somewhat hypocritically, a person serving or selling alcohol can be 18; proof of age is required and often requested at bars, nightclubs, and restaurants, so it's always a good idea to bring ID when you go out. Do not carry open containers of alcohol in your car or any public area that isn't zoned for alcohol consumption. The police can fine you on the spot. Don't even think about driving while intoxicated. Florida state law prohibits the sale of alcohol between 3am and 7am, unless the county chooses to change the operating hours later. For instance, Miami-Dade County liquor stores may operate 24 hours. Alcohol sales on Sundays vary by county; some, such as Miami-Dade County, can start serving booze as early as 7am, while other counties such as Monroe don't start popping corks until noon. Check with the specific county you're visiting to see what time spirits start being served. Supermarkets and other licensed establishments can sell only beer, low-alcohol liquors, and wine. The hard stuff must be sold in dedicated liquor stores, which may be in a separate part of a grocery or a drugstore. Beer must be sold in quantities of 32 ounces or less or greater than 1 gallon. Forty- and 64-ounce alcoholic beverages are illegal.

As for open container laws: Having open alcoholic containers on public property, including streets, sidewalks, or inside a vehicle, is prohibited, though open bottles of liquor are allowed inside a car trunk. Drivers suspected of being under the influence of alcohol or drugs must agree to breath, blood, or urine testing under "implied consent" laws. Penalties for refusing testing can mean suspension of the driver's license for up to 1 year. In Florida, the first conviction carries a mandatory suspension of the driver's license for 6 months; for the second offense, 1 year; for the third offense, 2 years. Underage drivers (20 or younger) have a maximum legal blood-alcohol content percentage of .02%. Above this amount, they are subject to DUI penalties. At .20% above the legal limit of .08%, a driver faces much harsher repercussions. This also applies to drivers refusing chemical testing for intoxication.

Electricity Like Canada, the United States uses 110 to 120 volts AC (60 cycles), compared to 220 to 240 volts AC (50 cycles) in most of Europe, Australia, and New Zealand. Downward converters that change 220–240 volts to 110–120 volts are difficult to find in the United States, so bring one with you.

Embassies & Consulates All embassies are in the U.S. capital, Washington, D.C. Some consulates are in major cities including Miami, and most countries have a mission to the United Nations in New York. If yours isn't listed below, call D.C. information (📞 202/555-1212) or check **www.Embassy.org**.

The embassy of **Australia:** 1601 Massachusetts Ave. NW (www.usa.embassy.gov.au; 📞 202/797-3000). Consulates in Chicago, Denver, Honolulu, Houston, Los Angeles, New York City, San Francisco.

Canada's embassy: 501 Pennsylvania Ave. NW (www.canadainternational.gc.ca/washington; 📞 202/682-1740). Consulates in Atlanta, Boston, Chicago, Dallas, Denver, Detroit, Houston, Los Angeles, Miami, Minneapolis, New York City, Palo Alto, San Diego, San Francisco, Seattle.

The embassy of **Ireland** is located at 2234 Massachusetts Ave. NW (www.embassyofireland.org; 📞 202/462-3939). Irish consulates are in Boston, Chicago, New York, San Francisco, and other cities. See website for details.

New Zealand's embassy can be found at 37 Observatory Circle NW (www.nzembassy.com/usa-washington; 📞 202/328-4800), there's also a consulate in Los Angeles.

You'll find the embassy of the **United Kingdom** at 3100 Massachusetts Ave. NW (www.gov.uk/government/world/organisations/british-embassy-washington; 📞 202/588-6500). Other British consulates: Atlanta,

Boston, Chicago, Denver, Houston, Los Angeles, Miami, New York City, San Francisco.

Emergencies To reach the police, ambulance, or fire department, dial © **911** from any phone. No coins are needed.

Family Travel Florida is a favorite destination among families, and most hotels and restaurants happily cater to families traveling with children. Many hotels and motels let guests age 17 and younger stay free in a parent or guardian's room (be sure to ask when reserving).

At beach areas, it's the exception rather than the rule for resorts not to have a children's activities program (some will even mind youngsters while parents enjoy time off). Or if they don't specifically have a children's program, most will arrange babysitting.

Recommended family travel websites include **Family Travel Forum** (www. MyFamilyTravels.com), which allows customized trip planning; **Family Travel Network** (www.Family TravelNetwork.com), with travel tips and destination coverage; and **TravelWith YourKids.com** (www.Travel WithYourKids.com), a comprehensive site written by parents for parents, offering sound advice particularly for long-distance and international travel.

Health Florida doesn't present any unusual health hazards for most people.

Those with certain medical conditions such as liver disease, diabetes, and stomach ailments should avoid eating raw **oysters.** Cooking kills the bacteria, so if in doubt, order oysters steamed, broiled, or fried.

Florida does have millions of **mosquitoes** and invisible biting **sand flies** (known as no-see-ums), especially in the coastal and marshy areas. Fortunately, neither insect carries malaria or other diseases. Rare isolated cases of mosquito-borne diseases like dengue or West Nile virus have popped up but are not a problem in Florida. In any case, it's always advisable (and certainly more comfortable) to keep these pests at bay with a good insect repellent.

It's also important to protect yourself against **sunburn.** Do not under-estimate the strength of the sun's rays down here, even in the middle of winter. Use a sunscreen with a high protection factor and apply it liberally.

Insurance During hurricane season (June–Nov), travel insurance may especially come in handy. You can find information on traveler's and trip-cancellation insurance, as well as medical insurance while traveling, at www.Frommers.com/planning.

Internet & Wi-Fi When it comes to Internet and Wi-Fi, South Florida is pretty connected, with a selection of both free and

pay-as-you-go Wi-Fi hot spots. To find Internet cafes in your destination, try checking **www.CyberCafe. com**. Most public libraries throughout also offer free Internet access/Wi-Fi.

Language Miami owes its culture to the diversity of its denizens, more than half of whom were born outside the U.S. This diversity shows above all linguistically: It's the second-largest U.S. city with a Spanish-speaking majority. Although by no means necessary, knowing a bit of Spanish can help you get around and enrich your experience (and in some parts of the county, such as the city of Hialeah, it can help quite a bit).

Legal Aid While driving, if you are pulled over for a minor infraction (such as speeding), never attempt to pay the fine to a police officer; this could be construed as attempted bribery, a much more serious crime. Pay fines by mail, or directly into the hands of the clerk of the court. If you are accused of a more serious offense, say and do nothing before consulting a lawyer. In the U.S., the burden is on the state to prove a person's guilt beyond a reasonable doubt, and everyone has the right to remain silent. Once arrested, a person can make one telephone call to a party of his or her choice. The international visitor should call his or her embassy or consulate.

LGBT Travelers The editors of gay and lesbian

newsletter *Out and About* have described Miami's **South Beach** as the "hippest, hottest, most happening gay travel destination in the world" (for details on the local LGBT scene, see p. 138). **Key West** (p. 212) has long been one of America's most popular gay meccas, and **Fort Lauderdale** (p. 219) has perhaps the most vibrant South Florida LGBT community and scene of all.

The **International Gay and Lesbian Travel Association** (IGLTA; www.IGLTA.org; ✆ **954/ 630-1637**) is the LGBT travel industry trade association, maintaining an online directory of gay- and lesbian (and LGBT-friendly) travel businesses.

The **Miami-Dade Gay and Lesbian Chamber of Commerce** (✆ **305/673-4440**) operates www.GoGayMiami.com, which spotlights gay and gay-friendly hotels, restaurants, and attractions, and also runs a walk-in **LGBT Visitor Center,** with daily hours at 1130 Washington Ave., South Beach (✆ **305/ 397-8914**).

Mail At press time, domestic postage rates were 34¢ for a postcard and 49¢ for a letter. For international mail, a first-class letter of up to 1 ounce costs $1.15; a first-class postcard costs the same as a letter.

For more information, go to **www.USPS.com**.

If you aren't sure what your address will be in the United States, mail can be sent to you, in your name, c/o General Delivery at the main post office of the city or region where you expect to be. (Call ✆ **800/275-8777** for information on the nearest post office.) The addressee must pick up mail in person and must produce proof of identity (driver's license, passport, and so forth). Most post offices will hold mail for up to 1 month, and are open Monday to Friday from 8am to 6pm, and Saturday from 9am to 3pm.

Always include zip codes when mailing items in the U.S. If you don't know your zip code, visit **www.USPS.com/zip4**.

Medical Requirements Unless you're arriving from an area known to be suffering from an epidemic (particularly cholera or yellow fever), inoculations or vaccinations are not required for entry into the United States.

Mobile Phones A Florida resident without a cellphone is as rare as an albino crocodile. But a few do exist. Reception varies from excellent to spotty, depending on where you are. The Everglades used to have abysmal cell phone

reception, but thanks to new telephone towers, reliable service is almost as guaranteed as a gator sighting. Typically, the more remote the area you are visiting, the smaller the chance is that your phone will work—but reception everywhere is constantly improving.

If you need to stay in touch at a destination where you know your phone won't work, **rent** a phone from **InTouch USA** (www.InTouch Global.com; ✆ **800/872-7626**) or a rental-car location. You'll pay 89¢ a minute or more for airtime. Or you can purchase an inexpensive pay-as-you-go mobile phone—they're all but ubiquitous at convenience stores and other retail outlets.

If you're not from the U.S., you'll be appalled at the poor reach of our **GSM (Global System for Mobile Communications) wireless network,** which is used by much of the rest of the world. Your phone will probably work in most major U.S. cities; it definitely won't work in many rural areas. To see where GSM phones work in the U.S., check out www.gsm-auto.com and click on "USA GSM map." And you may or may not be able to send SMS (text messaging) home.

THE VALUE OF THE U.S. DOLLAR VS. OTHER POPULAR CURRENCIES

US$	Aus$	Can$	Euro (€)	NZ$	UK£
1.00	1.06	1.09	0.74	1.15	0.59

WHAT THINGS COST IN SOUTH FLORIDA $

	$
Taxi from the airport to major destination	18.00–25.00
Double room, moderate	189.00
Double room, inexpensive	150.00
Three-course dinner for one without wine, moderate	25.00–50.00
Bottle of beer	3.00–6.00
Cup of coffee	2.00–6.00
1 gallon of gas	3.45–4.95
Admission to most museums	Free–16.00
Admission to most national parks	2.00–8.00

Money & Costs Frommer's lists prices in the local currency. The conversions quoted above were correct at press time. But rates fluctuate, so for up-to-date figures, consult a website such as **www.OANDA. com/currency/converter** (OANDA, XE Currency, and others also have conversion apps you can use on your trip).

Beware of hidden credit card fees while traveling. Check with your credit or debit card issuer to see what fees, if any, will be charged for overseas transactions. Recent reform legislation in the U.S., for example, has curbed some exploitative lending practices. But many banks have responded by increasing fees in other areas, including fees for customers who use credit and debit cards while out of the country—even if those charges were made in U.S. dollars. Check with your bank before departing to avoid any surprise charges on your statement.

For help with currency conversions, tip calculation, and more, download Frommer's convenient Travel Tools app for your mobile device. Go to **www. Frommers.com/go/mobile** and click on the Travel Tools icon.

Newspapers & Magazines The *Miami Herald* is Miami's only English-language daily. It is especially known for its extensive Latin American coverage and has a decent Friday "Weekend" entertainment guide. The most respected alternative weekly is the giveaway tabloid *New Times,* which contains up-to-date listings and reviews of food, films, theater, music, and whatever else is happening in town. Also free, if you can find it, is *Ocean Drive,* an oversize glossy magazine that's limited on text (no literary value) and heavy on ads and society photos. It's worth perusing if you want to know who's who and where to go for fun; it's available at a number of

chic South Beach boutiques and restaurants, as well as some newsstands. In the same vein, *Miami Magazine* has a bit more literary value in addition to the gloss and is free and available throughout the city. In the Florida Keys, check out *The Key West Citizen.*

Packing South Florida is typically a warm-weather destination, but not always. In winter, it can't hurt to pack a jacket, long sleeves, and pants in case the weather cools or, more likely, you go into a place where the A/C plunges to arctic temperatures. Long sleeves and pants also come in handy during pesky mosquito season. For more helpful information on packing for your trip, download our convenient Travel Tools app for your mobile device. Go to **www.Frommers. com/go/mobile** and click on the Travel Tools icon.

Passports All persons, including U.S. citizens, traveling by air between the United States and Canada,

Mexico, Central and South America, the Caribbean, and Bermuda are required to present a valid passport. **Note:** U.S. and Canadian citizens entering the U.S. at land and sea ports of entry from within the Western Hemisphere must now also present a passport or other documents compliant with the Western Hemisphere Travel Initiative (WHTI; see www.GetYouHome.gov for details). Travelers 15 and younger may continue entering with only a U.S. birth certificate or other proof of U.S. citizenship. If you do not have a passport, contact the appropriate agency in your country of citizenship:

Australia Australian Passport Information Service (www.passports.gov.au; ✆ **131-232**).

Canada Passport Canada (www.ppt.gc.ca; ✆ **800/567-6868**).

Ireland Passport Office (www.foreignaffairs.gov.ie/passports-citizenship; ✆ **01/671-1633**).

New Zealand Passports Office, (www.Passports.govt.nz; ✆ **0800/22-50-50** in New Zealand or 04/463-9360).

United Kingdom Visit your nearest passport office, major post office, or travel agency, or contact the Identity and Passport Service (www.IPS.gov.uk; ✆ **0300/222-0000**).

Police To reach the police, dial ✆ **911** from any phone. No coins are needed.

Safety Although crime should not be a matter of undue concern for travelers to South Florida, it pays to use common sense when traveling throughout the region. On the beach, keep close watch on your personal items; when in Miami Beach, the Keys, and pretty much any other Sunshine State hot spot, watch your drinks and never leave them unattended. And although I encourage exploration, there are neighborhoods of Miami you'll want to avoid, such as Liberty City, Overtown, and parts of west Coconut Grove, all of which are plagued by high rates of violent crime, as well as desolate parts of downtown.

Senior Travel With one of the largest retired populations of any state, Florida offers a wide array of activities and benefits for seniors. Don't be shy about asking for discounts, but always carry some kind of identification, such as a driver's license, that shows your date of birth. Mention the fact that you're a senior when you make your travel reservations. In most cities, people 60 and older qualify for reduced admission to theaters, museums, and other attractions, as well as discounted fares on public transportation.

Members of **AARP** (www.AARP.org; ✆ **888/ 687-2277**) get discounts on hotels, airfares, and car rentals. Anyone 50 or older can join.

The U.S. National Park Service offers an **America the Beautiful Senior Pass** (formerly the **Golden Age Passport**), which gives folks 62 years or older lifetime entrance to all properties administered by the NPS—national parks, monuments, historic sites, recreation areas, and national wildlife refuges—for a one-time fee of $20 via mail or $10 in person at any federal recreation area listed on the website below. Besides free entry, the pass also provides a 50% discount on some federal-use fees for camping, swimming, parking, boat launching, and tours. For details, go to www.NPS.gov/fees_passes.htm or call ✆ **888/275-8747**.

Quite a few organizations target the mature market. One of them is **Road Scholar** (www.RoadScholar.org; ✆ **800/454-5768**), which arranges worldwide study programs for those age 40 and older (though their companions can be as young as 21). **ElderTreks** (www.ElderTreks.com; ✆ **800/741-7956** or 416/588-5000 outside North America) runs small-group tours for travelers 50 and older to adventure-travel and off-the-beaten-path destinations.

Smoking Lighting up is prohibited in all enclosed indoor workplaces. A major exception is bars or clubs where little or no food is served. All establishments making more profit from food than from beverages are also smoke-free, though the occasional renegade eateries may defy the law despite the hefty fees and allow smoking indoors.

Taxes The Florida state sales tax is 6%. Many municipalities add 1% or more to that, and most levy a special tax on hotel and restaurant bills. In general, expect at least 9% to be added to your final hotel bill. The United States has no value-added tax (VAT) or other indirect tax at the national level. Every state, county, and city may levy its own local tax on all purchases, including hotel and restaurant checks and airline tickets. These taxes will not appear on price tags.

Telephones Many convenience stores sell **prepaid calling cards** in denominations up to $50, as well as inexpensive cellphones for which you pay as you go. Many public pay phones at airports now accept American Express, MasterCard, and Visa. **Local calls** made from most pay phones (if you can find one) cost either 25¢ or 35¢. Most long-distance and international calls can be dialed directly from any phone. **To make calls within the United States and to Canada,** dial 1 followed by the area code and the seven-digit number. **For other international calls,** dial 011 followed by the country code, the city code, and the number you are calling.

Calls to area codes **800, 888, 877,** and **866** are

toll-free. However, calls to area codes **700** and **900** can be expensive—charges of 95¢ to $3 or more per minute. Some numbers have minimum charges that can run $15 or more.

For **reversed-charge or collect calls,** and for person-to-person calls, dial the number 0 and then the area code and number; an operator will come on the line, and you should specify whether you are calling collect, person-to-person, or both. If your operator-assisted call is international, ask for the overseas operator.

For **directory assistance** ("Information"), dial ✆ **411** for local numbers and national numbers in the U.S. and Canada. For dedicated long-distance information, dial 1, then the appropriate area code plus 555-1212.

Time The area covered in this book—as is the case with most of Florida except for its northern Panhandle west of the Apalachicola River—observes **Eastern Standard Time.**

Daylight saving time is in effect from 1am on the second Sunday in March to 1am on the first Sunday in November, except in Arizona, Hawaii, the U.S. Virgin Islands, and Puerto Rico. Daylight saving time moves the clock 1 hour ahead of standard time.

The continental United States is divided into **four time zones:** Eastern Standard Time (EST), Central Standard Time (CST),

Mountain Standard Time (MST), and Pacific Standard Time (PST). Alaska and Hawaii have their own zones. For example, when it's 9am in Los Angeles (PST), it's 7am in Honolulu (HST), 10am in Denver (MST), 11am in Chicago (CST), noon in New York City (EST), 5pm in London (GMT), and 2am the next day in Sydney.

For help with time translations and more, download our convenient Travel Tools app for your mobile device. Go to **www.Frommers. com/go/mobile** and click on the Travel Tools icon.

Tipping In hotels, tip **bellhops** at least $1 per bag ($2–$3 if you have a lot of luggage), and tip the **chamber staff** $1 to $2 per day (more if you've left a big mess for him or her to clean up). Tip the **doorman** or **concierge** only if he or she has provided you with some specific service (for example, calling a cab for you or obtaining difficult-to-get theater tickets). Tip **valet-parking attendants** every time you get your car (how much depends on the context, but a minimum of $2, generally up to $5).

In restaurants, bars, and nightclubs, tip **service staff** and **bartenders** 15% to 20% of the check, tip **check-room attendants** $1 per garment. *Note:* Keep an eye on your bill in tourist areas such as South Beach, where as much as a 20% gratuity could already be added to the total check.

As for other service personnel, tip **cab drivers** 15% of the fare; tip **skycaps** at airports at least $1 per bag ($2–$3 if you have a lot of luggage); and tip **hairdressers** and **barbers** 15% to 20%.

For help with tip calculations, currency conversions, and more, download our convenient Travel Tools app for your mobile device. Go to **www.Frommers.com/go/mobile** and click on the Travel Tools icon.

Toilets As elsewhere in the U.S. you won't find public toilets or "restrooms" on the streets in Miami and the Keys, but they can be found in hotel lobbies, bars, restaurants, museums, department stores, railway and bus stations, and service stations. Large hotels and fast-food restaurants are often the best bet for clean facilities. Restaurants and bars in resorts or heavily visited areas may reserve their restrooms for patrons.

Visas The U.S. State Department has a **Visa Waiver Program (VWP)** allowing citizens of the following countries to enter the United States without a visa for stays of up to 90 days: Andorra, Australia, Austria, Belgium, Brunei, Czech Republic, Denmark, Estonia, Finland, France, Germany, Greece, Hungary, Iceland, Ireland, Italy, Japan, Latvia, Liechtenstein, Lithuania, Luxembourg, Malta, Monaco, the Netherlands, New Zealand, Norway, Portugal, San Marino,

Singapore, Slovakia, Slovenia, South Korea, Spain, Sweden, Switzerland, Taiwan, and the United Kingdom. (**Note:** This list was accurate at press time; for the most up-to-date list of countries in the VWP, consult www.Travel.State. gov/content/visas/english/visit/visa-waiver-program. html.) Even though a visa isn't necessary, in an effort to help U.S. officials check travelers against terrorist watch lists before they arrive at U.S. borders, visitors from VWP countries must register online through the Electronic System for Travel Authorization (ESTA) before boarding a plane or a boat to the U.S. Travelers must complete an electronic application providing basic personal and travel-eligibility information. The Department of Homeland Security recommends filling out the form at least 3 days before traveling. Authorizations will be valid for up to 2 years or until the traveler's passport expires, whichever comes first. Currently, there is a US$10 fee for the online application. Existing ESTA registrations remain valid through their expiration dates. **Note:** Any passport issued on or after October 26, 2006, by a VWP country must be an **e-Passport** for VWP travelers to be eligible to enter the U.S. without a visa. Citizens of these nations also need to present a round-trip air or cruise ticket upon arrival. E-Passports contain computer

chips storing biometric information such as the required digital photograph of the holder. If your passport doesn't have this feature, you can still travel without a visa if the valid passport was issued before October 26, 2005, and includes a machine-readable zone; or if the valid passport was issued between October 26, 2005, and October 25, 2006, and includes a digital photograph. Canadian citizens may enter the United States without visas, but will need to show passports and proof of residence.

Citizens of all other countries must have (1) a valid passport that expires at least 6 months later than the scheduled end of their visit to the U.S., and (2) a tourist visa. For information about U.S. visas go to **Travel.state.gov** and click on "Visas." Or go to one of the following websites:

Australian citizens can obtain up-to-date visa information from the U.S. consulates in Sydney, Melbourne, and Perth (check the embassy site Canberra.usembassy.gov/visas.html for details).

British subjects can obtain current visa information from the U.S. Embassy, 24 Grosvenor Square, London W1K 6AH, by calling its **Visa Information Line** (✆ **09042-450-100** from within the U.K. at £1.23 per minute; or ✆ **866/382-3589** from within the U.S. at a flat rate of $20; payable by credit card only) or by visiting the Visas section of the embassy website **London.usembassy.gov/ visas.html**.

Irish citizens can obtain up-to-date visa information through the **U.S. Embassy Dublin,** 42 Elgin Rd., Ballsbridge, Dublin 4 (© (01)903-6255 from within Ireland; **Dublin.usembassy.gov**).

Citizens of **New Zealand** can obtain visa information from the **U.S. Consulate General,** Citigroup Centre, 23 Customs St. East, Auckland CBD (**www.USTravel Docs.com/nz;** © **64/9-303-2724**).

Visitor Information

The most comprehensive visitor information in the state is provided by **Visit Florida,** whose website www.VisitFlorida.com, features deals, maps, and all sorts of excellent information on beaten- and off-the-beaten-path spots. For Miami, the local convention and visitors bureau can be consulted at **www.Miami andBeaches.com**; for the Keys it's **www.Fla-Keys. com**. You can also find a list of Frommer's travel apps at **www.Frommers.com/go/ mobile**.

Index

See also Accommodations and Restaurant indexes, below.

General Index

Find Miami Int. Airport Station

Miami Beach Airport Flyer
(150)

41st and Indian Creek
Walk to 41st and Collins
119 North to Collins & 81st